Critical Essays on
WILLIAM FAULKNER: THE SUTPEN FAMILY

CRITICAL ESSAYS
ON
AMERICAN LITERATURE

James Nagel, General Editor
University of Georgia, Athens

Critical Essays on

WILLIAM FAULKNER: THE SUTPEN FAMILY

edited by

ARTHUR F. KINNEY

G. K. Hall & Co.
An Imprint of Simon & Schuster Macmillan
New York

Prentice Hall International
London Mexico City New Delhi Singapore Sydney Toronto

G. K. Hall & Co.
An Imprint of Simon & Schuster Macmillan
1633 Broadway
New York, New York 10019

Library of Congress Cataloging-in-Publication Data

Critical essays on William Faulkner : the Sutpen family / edited by Arthur
    F. Kinney.
        p. cm.—(Critical essays on American literature)
    Includes bibliographical references and index.
    ISBN 0-8161-7314-1 (alk. paper)
        1. Faulkner, William, 1897–1962—Characters—Sutpen family.
    2. Sutpen family (Fictitious characters) 3. Southern States—In
literature. 4. Family in literature.   I. Kinney, Arthur F., 1933–
    II. Series.
    PS3511.A86Z779   1995
    813'.52—dc20   94-44656
                                                                  CIP

The paper used in this publication meets the minimum requirements of
American National Standard for Information Sciences—Permanence of
Paper for Printed Library Materials, ANSI Z39.48–1984. ∞ TM

10   9   8   7   6   5   4   3

Printed in the United States of America

For members of my family:
Megan, Sean, Tabitha, and for
Nancy, Ronald, Mark, Lisa, Joanne, Carol, and June

and for
Alan and Ann Cochet, Sidney and Suzanne Johnson,
and Guy Turnbow

and in memory of
Rebecca Ann Evans Pegues

Maybe nothing ever happens once and is finished. Maybe
happens is never once but like ripples maybe on water
after the pebble sinks, the ripples moving on, spreading

William Faulkner at the time he wrote *Absalom, Absalom!*
Photograph courtesy of Louis Daniel Brodsky.

Sutpen and Sartoris and Compson and Edmonds and McCaslin and Beauchamp and Grenier and Habersham and Holston and Stevens and DeSpain, generals and governors and judges, soldiers . . . and statesmen failed or not, and simple politicians and over-reachers and just simple failures, who snatched and grabbed and passed and vanished, name and face and all. . . . the record and chronicle of your native land . . . this miniature of man's passions and hopes and disasters—ambition and fear and lust and courage and abnegation and pity and honor and sin and pride—all bound, precarious and ramshackle, held together by the web, the iron-thin warp and woof of his rapacity but withal yet dedicated to his dreams.

—William Faulkner, *The Town*
(1957)

Sutpen['s story is the] story of a man who wanted a son and got too many, got so many that they destroyed him. . . . Sutpen, the story of a man who wanted sons.

—William Faulkner at Virginia,
13 April 1957

Q. Do you happen to remember when Charles Bon realizes that Sutpen is his father?

A. I should think that his mother dinned it into him as soon as he was big enough to remember, and that he came deliberately to hunt out his father, not for justice for himself, but for revenge for his abandoned mother. He must have known that, that must have been in his—the background of his childhood, that this abandoned woman never let him forget that.

—William Faulkner and student
at Virginia, 27 April 1957

Sutpen . . . was going to take what he wanted because he was big enough and strong enough, and I think that people like that are destroyed sooner or later, because one has got to belong to the human family, and to take a responsible part in the human family.

—William Faulkner at Virginia,
13 April 1957

Contents

♦

General Editor's Note

◆

This series seeks to anthologize the most important criticism on a wide variety of topics and writers in American literature. Our readers will find in various volumes not only a generous selection of reprinted articles and reviews but original essays, bibliographies, manuscript sections, and other materials brought to public attention for the first time. This volume, *Critical Essays on William Faulkner: The Sutpen Family*, is the most comprehensive collection of essays ever published on this important group in Faulkner's fiction. It contains a sizable gathering of early reviews, a broad selection of modern scholarship, two works of fiction by Faulkner, as well as original essays by distinguished scholars. Among the authors of reprinted articles and reviews are Malcolm Cowley, Bernard DeVoto, Thadious M. Davis, John T. Irwin, Elisabeth Muhlenfeld, Hershel Parker, André Bleikasten, and Linda Wagner-Martin. In addition to a substantial introduction by Arthur F. Kinney, there are also seven essays commissioned specifically for publication in this volume. Andrea Dimino explores the patriarchal nature of the Sutpen family, and Woodrow Stroble offers a defense of Thomas Sutpen. Jun Liu directs attention to the Judith-Henry-Charles triangle while Claire Crabtree examines the use of indirection in the portrayal of Judith Sutpen and Adelaide P. McGinnis discusses the ways in which Charles Bon embodies the myth of New Orleans. In a related essay, Tonya R. Folsom considers the untold story of Eulalia Bon. For his part, Robert Dale Parker gives full attention to the Coldfield family. We are confident that this book will make a permanent and significant contribution to the study of American literature.

JAMES NAGEL
University of Georgia

Publisher's Note

♦

Producing a volume that contains both newly commissioned and reprinted material presents the publisher with the challenge of balancing the desire to achieve stylistic consistency with the need to preserve the integrity of works first published elsewhere. In the Critical Essays series, essays commissioned especially for a particular volume are edited to be consistent with G. K. Hall's house style; reprinted essays appear in the style in which they were first published, with only typographical errors corrected. Consequently, shifts in style from one essay to another are the result of our efforts to be faithful to each text as it was originally published.

Textual Notes

◆

The publication of *Absalom, Absalom!: The Corrected Text* in 1986 expanded the original edition by a total of 30 pages. Critical studies published before 1987 follow the pagination and context of the original text (1936); later works follow the pagination of the corrected text, either in cloth (1986) or, repaginated, in paper (1990).

Citations to journals follow the *MLA Style Manual* and not necessarily the style of the journals themselves.

Introduction

◆

The paternalism of the plantation system was preserved after the Civil War not only in the economic system but also in the concept of family which underlies some of the darkest and most terrible of Faulkner's dramas. Southern pride in family and intense interest in genealogy.

—Elizabeth Kerr[1]

Throughout William Faulkner's powerful creation of Yoknapatawpha County, Mississippi, through the family lines that together constitute it, only once, in tracing ancestors and descendants of Thomas Sutpen, does he study genealogy as dynasty. The formation of the Sutpen-Bon-Coldfield line is marked by crudity, idealism, passion, naïveté, heroism, promise, achievement, grief, sacrifice, and defeat; the family seems haunted by their will to dominate or their will to survive, pursued by anxiety and shame that seem endemic to the Southern culture they themselves help to construct. The events that signal the stages of Thomas Sutpen's life, for instance—the white boy's humiliating dismissal by a black servant; the slave revolt in Haiti; the permissiveness and promiscuity that mark Creole life in New Orleans; the violent and rapid establishment of a cotton plantation of 100 square miles; the commitment to the Confederacy and the later withdrawal from Reconstruction activity—all these events and actions not only embody but foster the peculiar characteristics and failings of Sutpen's South: hierarchy, race, class, caste, fratricide, self-destruction. The very attributes that Sutpen swiftly demands to establish his family, and his family line, require a long, irreversible, and unavoidable decline and defeat. "You get born and you try this and you dont know why, . . . and it cant matter, you know that."[2] Faulkner knew that, too. Conceiving almost simultaneously the title of *Absalom, Absalom!* for his chief study of Sutpen and the vision of family heritage, he wrote to his New York editor Harrison Smith in early 1934

1

about the family of Sutpen as the house of Sutpen. "The one I am writing now will be called DARK HOUSE or something of that nature. It is the more or less violent breakup of a household or family from 1860 to about 1910. . . . The story is an anecdote which occurred during and right after the civil war; the climax is another anecdote which happened about 1910 and which explains the story. Roughly, the theme is a man who outraged the land, and the land then turned and destroyed the man's family."[3] But if the tenor seemed new to Faulkner—actually, it anticipates in many ways the McCaslin family story in focusing on the rape of physical and human nature—the vehicle remained consistent with Faulkner's earlier work in its understanding and analysis of Yoknapatawpha through "fathers, sons, generation, and lines of descent," as Peter Brooks has it.[4]

In *Absalom, Absalom!*, Faulkner matches the passionate and visionary need of Thomas Sutpen with what Cecil Day Lewis, in reviewing the book in 1937 for the London *Daily Telegraph*, called the "continuity and inescapableness of ancestral guilt."[5] But the scope is extraordinary, even for Faulkner. David Minter writes that *Absalom, Absalom!* "reaches back into the early nineteenth century, when Yoknapatawpha was 'still frontier.' Through its French architect it reaches back to Europe. Through Thomas Sutpen's family it reaches back both to the splendor of Tidewater Virginia and to the simplicity of a primitive Appalachian community. Through Sutpen's slaves it reaches back to the West Indies and Africa. It provides, therefore, a sense not only of the people and history of Yoknapatawpha, but of its sources." All of this is accomplished, he points out, through "the entangled relations among several generations of several doomed families."[6] Ilse Dusoir Lind sees Sutpen's story as a matter of historical import as much as temporal and spatial; she notes that the fratricidal Sutpen conflict especially mirrors in miniature the larger fratricidal conflict of the Civil War, and Sutpen's inhumanity that bred by a plantation culture based in a slave economy.[7]

But the sheer forcefulness of Sutpen's story lies not merely in the panoramic or representational qualities of his acts; his power comes as well in the way in which his singular life contracts the more dispersed generations of Sartorises, Compsons, and McCaslins in Faulkner's other works. Indeed, Sutpen seems to draw them into himself and so conquer them: he joins Colonel Sartoris's regiment in the Civil War and then succeeds him in his command; the one day he leaves battle, he returns to Jefferson to see General Compson in his law office and to search, in a single compressed (and so baffling, baffled) conversation, the shape of his design for life and his need to know where it went wrong. But if Sutpen, in this sense, incorporates the bravery of Sartoris and the wisdom of Compson into his own career, he is more evenly matched, as he knows, with Goodhue Coldfield. Because Sutpen realizes (intuitively, perhaps) more surely than either Sartoris or Compson that the underside of aristocracy is wealth and the basis of class is money, his life aligns itself, naturally, with that of Coldfield; both are characterized by dealing, bargaining, buying and selling, making "arrangements." The boy Thomas, initially dispossessed of everything, constructs a life of accumulated possessions. That this is an outlook Sutpen and Coldfield share at some deep level of understanding is made clear by the planter's relationship to the Methodist steward and merchant. Sutpen's career in Yoknapatawpha begins with a financial arrangement with Coldfield—with their joint investment in Sutpen's Hundred—and it ends with his taking over Coldfield's occupation, merchandizing, in his own little country crossroads store following the Civil War. Linked in life, these two become forged together in the town's collective memory; "Sutpen and Coldfield" as "old blood" are paired with "Sartoris and Stevens, Compson and McCaslin" in the county's history as it is disclosed in full in *Requiem for a Nun*,[8] while in later years, in the time of Mr. Compson, the two are forever fading. Jason Compson III, we are told in the "Compson Appendix" of 1946, "bred for a lawyer," "kept an office upstairs above the Square" in Jefferson, "where entombed in dusty filingcases some of the oldest names in the county—Holston and Sutpen, Grenier and Beauchamp and Coldfield—faded year by year among the bottomless labyrinths of chancery."[9] The moral rigor of Coldfield (who incarcerates himself for his abolitionist beliefs) and the stern determination of Sutpen (who forces Wash Jones to kill him) is a shared willfulness in which each brings about his own death rather than compromise with his fortune. Only apparently outward looking in their trade, both Sutpen and Coldfield are inwardly stubborn, hostages alike to the bargains they insist on making with themselves.

Warwick Wadlington has memorably termed this myopia, when it stretches through the Sutpen clan, "clandestine solidarity."[10] In fact, such solidarity binds five generations of Sutpens described by Faulkner and identified by E. O. Hawkins:

I. Thomas Sutpen's father and mother were Scotch-Irish mountaineers. The mother died when Sutpen was 10, and the father returned to the Tidewater area.

II. Thomas Sutpen (1807–69) married (1) a Haitian woman known later as Eulalia Bon and (2) Ellen Coldfield (1817–63).

III. Charles Bon (1831–65) was Sutpen's son by Eulalia Bon. Henry (1939–1909) and Judith (1941–84) were Sutpen's children by Ellen Coldfield. Clytemnestra (1835–1909) was fathered by Sutpen on a Negro slave.

IV. Charles Etienne St. Valery Bon (1859–84) was Charles Bon's son by an octoroon mistress. He married a Negress (1879).

V. Jim Bond (1881—) was the son of Charles Etienne Bon. He is, ironically, the Sutpen "heir" at the end of the book.[11]

But the sense we have of Sutpen and his extended family is not one of dispersal over generations but one of obsession and contraction that obliterates difference. Thus Rosa's intense fixation, which opens *Absalom, Absalom!*, seems absorbed into the greater fixation of Thomas, while Henry's repulsion at miscegenation is no more extreme than his father's and of considerably shorter duration. If Rosa more closely resembles her father in her staunch stoicism and determination, "She would have acted as Sutpen would have acted with anyone who tried to cross him" (p. 96); they also think so much alike they can communicate without talking (p. 96). Sutpen also identifies with Bon in that both are dismissed from the Great House and both identify with Henry and Judith too when Charles and Judith agree to marry: "the four of them had just reached as one person that point where something had to be done" (p. 222). When the crisis erupts, in Henry's murder of Charles, the three survivors share a strange lack of passion, an inviolable determinism.

In such a tightly constricted family, incest becomes the natural consequence, both as fact and metaphor.[12] While Henry may realize that his love for Judith is incestuous, we know well before he does that his attraction to Charles is also incestuous desire, just as Judith's love for Charles is a way of loving Henry and Charles's love of Henry is expressed in his affection for Judith. At the same time, Charles's apparent lack of concern for his partner in New Orleans, whom he easily displaces with Judith, only replicates his father's apparently easy dismissal of Eulalia for the more socially desirable Ellen and, in time, he replaces Ellen with Milly Jones. Such similarities cause the Sutpens, Bons, and Coldfields, both loving and hating each other, to enclose themselves in a constraining, diminishing circle of forces. It is just such a constriction, in fact, that Quentin and his father recognize when, out quail hunting, they come upon a private cemetery where five graves bring the Sutpen, Bon, and Coldfield family tightly together for eternity: Ellen's tombstone, brought from Italy by Sutpen in 1864; Sutpen's own stone, got at the same time; Charles's stone, bought by Judith when she sold her father's store (thus bringing him into Sutpen's design whether he is wanted or not); Charles Etienne Bon's stone, partly paid for by Judith; and Judith's stone supplied by Rosa (who, once in the circle, never really leaves it). It is little wonder, then, that Judith finds nursing Charles Etienne so natural and satisfying or that Judith, Rosa, and Clytie hoeing cotton together become, to any spectator's eyes, indistinguishable.

Indeed, the seemingly wide dissemination of Sutpen's story—in "Wash," "An Odor of Verbena," "The Old People," "The Bear," "The Courthouse," "The Jail," *The Town*, and *The Reivers* (as well as in "Evangeline," "Big Shot," and "Dull Tale")—only contracts as we study it, retreating into the same repetitive dialectic between aristocracy and mercantilism, between the wealth of land and the accumulation of money and possessions. In the opening chapter of *Requiem for a Nun*, "The Courthouse," we are given the fullest memorial reconstruction of Sutpen: Ratliffe and Holston, open for business in the early days of Jefferson, see "a man named Sutpen who had come into the settlement that same spring—a big gaunt friendless passion-worn untalkative man who walked in a fading aura of anonymity and violence like a man just entered a warm room or at least a shelter, out of a blizzard, bringing with him thirty-odd men slaves even wilder and more equivocal than the native wild men, the Chickasaws" (p. 37). Sutpen also brings a "tame Parisian architect—or captive rather, . . . a man no larger than Pettigrew, with humorous sardonic undefeated eyes which had seen everything and believed none of it" (pp. 37–38). This sullen and silent man will not only create "at Sutpen's Hundred something like a wing of Versailles glimpsed in a Lilliput's gothic nightmare" (p. 40) but supply the bricks and kiln for Jefferson's courthouse and other buildings on the main square of the village; in "The Jail," we learn that they still have "the old plans of his architect and even the architect's molds" (p. 238). Sutpen himself seems to expand, too, by joining Compson and Sartoris in financing, even in absentia, Jefferson's Female Institute (p. 45). But by the time of "The Bear," he has become "old Thomas Sutpen" who made bargains with Major DeSpain (pp. 101, 255). Sutpen is for young Bayard Sartoris almost talismanic. He encapsulates the grand vision.

"But nobody could have more of a dream than Colonel Sutpen," I said. He had been Father's second-in-command in the first regiment and had been elected colonel when the regiment deposed Father after Second Manassas, and it was Sutpen and not the regiment whom father never forgave. He was underbred, a cold ruthless man who had come into the country about thirty years before the War, nobody knew from where except Father said you could look at him and know he would not dare to tell. He had got some land and nobody knew how he did that either, and he got money from somewhere— Father said they all believed he robbed steamboats, either as a card sharper or as an out-and-out highwayman—and built a big house and married and set up as a gentleman. Then he lost everything in the War like everybody else, all hope of descendants too (his son killed his daughter's fiancé on the eve of the wedding and vanished) yet he came back home and set out singlehanded to rebuild his plantation. He had no friends to borrow from and he had nobody to leave it to and he was past sixty years old, yet he set out to rebuild his place like it used to be; they told how he was too busy to bother with politics or anything; how when Father and the other men organised the night riders to keep the carpet baggers from organising the Negroes into an insurrection, he refused to have anything to do with it. Father stopped hating him long enough to ride out to see Sutpen himself and he (Sutpen) came to the door with a lamp and did not even invite them to come in and discuss it; Father said, "Are you with us or against us?" and he said, "I'm for my land. If every man of you would rehabilitate his own land, the country will take care of itself" and Father challenged him to bring the lamp out and set it on a stump where they could both see to shoot and Sutpen would not. "Nobody could have more of a dream than that."

Still for Drusilla Hawk Sartoris, now Colonel Sartoris's wife, such a dream was spoiled at its inception. "Yes. But his dream is just Sutpen. John's is not. He is thinking of this whole country which is trying to raise by its bootstraps, so that all the people in it, not just his kind nor his old regiment, but all the people, black and white, the women and children back in the hills who don't even own shoes—Don't you see?" (pp. 255–56). As the "sheets of glass taller than a man and longer than a wagon and team, pressed intact in Pittsburgh factories" replace the old brick which Sutpen and his architect used ("The Jail," p. 244), even the Sutpen legend gets forcefully displaced. In time it withers away: we learn in a still later reference, in *The Reivers*, that "Thomas Sutpen's doomed baronial dream and the site of Major de Spain's hunting camp is now a drainage district" and "even Wyott's Crossing is only a name" (p. 72). Thus the vision, the *material* dream, was always, like Coldfield and Sutpen themselves, subject to decay and doom: misremembered, forgotten, vanished like the architect who had come to build a grand edifice like the wing of Versailles—but for Lilliputians.

The story of Thomas Sutpen and his family comes to us more indirectly and hypothetically than that of any other of the major families who together make up Faulkner's composite portrait of Yoknapatawpha, and of the American South. Sutpen, his forebears, and those who follow him are all revealed to us through narrative filters, implied truths, and self-imposed screens and silences. Even the best written testimonials are indirect letters: Charles's letter to Judith which she gives later to Mrs. Compson for safekeeping; Mr. Compson's letter to Quentin announcing Rosa's death. Yet none of these partial admissions or tentative interpretations can finally match the communal oversimplification, distortion, and final effacement of Sutpen, of Sutpen's Hundred, and of all who went there. Except for Jim Bond, in fact, all those who are at Sutpen's Hundred when Clytie sets it on fire (Henry, Clytie, Rosa) are dead in the later chapters of *Absalom, Absalom!* Only Jim Bond survives, his idiocy an example and a consequence of an often misconstrued and misconstructed family.

Yet Faulkner's own determined purpose in *Absalom, Absalom!* is to define the Sutpens as fully and carefully as possible, for the life of Thomas himself sharply encapsulates Faulkner's own sense of the history of the South—its rise and fall within a caste and class system that is both geographically authentic and imaginatively realizable. To write about Sutpen at the height of his creative powers as a novelist—to write about him through the death of his younger brother, the near-collapse of his marriage, and his partially self-imposed isolation in the detested Hollywood studios—is a measure of Faulkner's own passionate obsession that, in retrospect, would seem to rival that of his characters. Sutpen's concern with his drunken father clearly reflects Faulkner's concern with his father Murry; and Sutpen's design resonates from Faulkner's increased worry, now that he was entering middle age, of the purpose of his own life; it was also the time, in an unhappy conjuncture, that Hal Smith gave him an autographed copy of André Malraux's *Man's Fate*, a story of the absurdity of life.

Indeed, one of Sutpen's few admissions about himself—so directly presented in the novel that the actual narrative screens seem to fall away in its presence—is his sense of life governed by personal design. To know the design and its fate, he implies, is to know and understand him. Ralph Behrens is one of many who have taken up that challenge.

> At least four possible theories may be advanced to account for the failure of Sutpen's design and the collapse of his dynastic dreams. The first key to understanding the collapse may lie in Sutpen's innocence of the ways of the society in which he attempts to carry out his design: or, his failure may be due to a kind of hubris, similar to that of the heroes of Greek tragedy; or again the failure may lie in the very society itself which he attempts to join and emulate, the pre–Civil War South of the plantation system with its concomitant evils; or, finally, and most satisfactorily, the failure may be equated with the failure of dynasties of ancient times illustrated in the prophetic books of the Old Testament, where failure appears to lie in the dynastic concept itself.[13]

This last possibility is echoed in the novel's title, a pattern that no character in *Absalom, Absalom!* is able to recognize. Faulkner may have been alerted to the story of King David and his children in 2 Samuel by "Tamar," a poem by Robinson Jeffers that may be used earlier in *The Sound and the Fury* and later in *The Wild Palms*.[14] In the Bible, David's life is transformed when he leaves his father Jesse's sheep to deliver gifts to King Saul; like the incredible heroism assigned to Thomas in Haiti, the young David in his turn incredibly defeats Goliath; both are rewarded women in marriage whom they later reject. With such analogies in place to Pettibone and Eulalia, it seems natural to find originals of Charles, Henry, and Judith in Amnon, killed by his brother Absalom because of his rape of their sister (actually Amnon's half sister), Tamar. If David officially must punish Absalom, he is personally not displeased at the death of Amnon; later, when Absalom dies in rebellion against his father, David—unlike Thomas Sutpen—mourns for the death of his son with an anguished cry that gives Faulkner the title for his novel but which Thomas Sutpen himself never utters. For Faulkner, this Old Testament story of rape and revenge, alongside the centrality of inheritance through family lines, unites the South of Yoknapatawpha with the history of Hebrew tribes.

We can entertain such allusions because they constitute a pattern, and Faulkner, primarily concerned in his fiction with families and family lines, is America's premiere novelist of patterns, even when such patterns seem inconsistent, incomplete, or contingent. Thus Michael Millgate locates another familiar Yoknapatawphan pattern when he sees "that Sutpen's history—his somewhat suspect purchase of the land from its Indian owners, his erection of a plantation and a great house at the cost of the sweat of his Negro slaves, his determination to found a dynasty—was only an exceptionally rapid and concentrated version of the history of virtually all Southern families."[15] This essential traditionalism, in which Thomas takes his cue from communal mores, explains why he is at first accepted by the people of Jefferson, who generally find his odd ways amusing, who gamble with him, and who attend his raree shows with blacks. It can also obscure some of Thomas's more "admirable qualities" as James H. Justus has it: "His refusal to accept neighborly favors when he cannot return them, his practical demonstrations of superiority over his slaves by sportsmanlike contests, his steadfast though puzzled search for personal fault rather than the easier act of blaming fate"[16] or bad luck or bad counsel. He is, in fact, the very epitome of the American pioneer, the self-reliant man who refuses to take a loan from General Compson, who refuses support he does not enlist, and who, not once or twice but three times—in Haiti and in Yoknapatawpha before and after the War—picks himself up and starts over.

In a brilliant aperçu, Richard Poirier contends that "Sutpen's story might well be about his opportunities for becoming human."[17] But here his very abilities and attributes, which he mistakenly ascribes to his "dream," a dream validated by Yoknapatawpha, betray him. There is his empowerment in Haiti, for instance, according to Quentin and Shreve; Ellen Ruth Rifkin notes that "an amazing thing happens during the episode of the Haitian rebellion. A man walks into the heart of darkness and emerges not only alive, but victorious. . . . Sutpen's victory is like a miracle."[18] His astonishing and searching vision to create a civilized plantation on ten square miles of forest and bottomland along the Tallahatchie, succeeding, shames the Compsons; in answering the call to protect the Confederacy, he shames the Sartorises. Unlike them, he is forced to *pursue* his fortune. Rewards have come to the Sartorises by trading in patrilineal reputation and to the Compsons by practicing law. Both means are far more subtle than the open merchandising of Coldfield, to which the straightforward Sutpen is most drawn, by default bringing to Yoknapatawpha neither established ancestry nor an admired profession. Sutpen by necessity is drawn to a set of rules that govern investment and gain, arrangements of self-interest that are, at base, no different from theirs, however. That is why revenge does not occur to Sutpen but individual responsibility does—he has made a bad investment. Sutpen's relationship with Goodhue Coldfield reveals his fundamental nature: it explains how Sutpen's Hundred was (yet in some unexplained way) financed; it explains why Goodhue married Ellen off to him (although she thought it a "bad deal" from the start), and why Rosa, after a lifetime bereft of the simple commodities of life, finds such attraction in his vision of Southern life and prosperity. When Sutpen recounts his own story of his American Dream it hones closely to the ends, and perhaps even the means, of Sartorises and Compsons, were they honest with him and with themselves (pp. 211–13).

But with his own eye fixed so firmly on his own personal scheme, Sutpen fails to see more particularized consequences—such as the imprisonment of the French architect who, upon his escape, is hunted down like an animal, or the fact that dragging precious tombstones in a commandeered wagon as far as Gettysburg jeopardizes the life of his own Confederate troops. More incredibly, if Cleanth Brooks's supposition is correct, Sutpen's failure to recognize the black Charles Bon at all would—should Henry agree—guarantee by Yoknapatawphan custom the security of his dream of a white family and of white male issue that he fails to take up.[19] He thus exposes himself by exposing the limitations of his literal mind: his dream, after all, is an imitation rather than a creation, and he is best at gambling, investing, and bargaining, all literal means rather than visionary ends. His wife, Ellen, true daughter to the successful merchant Goodhue, shares his sense of events and people as so many commodities. Thus Ellen, we are told, speaks "of Bon as if he were three inanimate objects in one or perhaps one animate object for which she and her family would find three concordant uses: a garment which Judith might wear as she would a riding habit or a ball gown, a piece of furniture which would complement and complete the furnishing of her house and position, and a mentor and example to correct Henry's provincial manners and speech and clothing"; this, like Sutpen's daily activities, "encompassed time" (p. 59). Similar attention to the daily commerce and rounds of life is what characterizes both of Thomas Sutpen's daughters, Judith and Clytie. Tight-lipped, dutiful, and resigned to their purchase on life, they become coconspirators in Sutpen's design. Even Henry, who unlike his sisters seems to defy Thomas, is at first attracted to the sheer exotic materiality of Charles Bon. In time Henry makes use of Bon, exploiting their friendship—according to Quentin and Shreve—in order to secure his sister Judith's presence, to buy incest at the price of pure and unrivaled fraternity. And the more conventional materiality of Sutpen himself is what attracts Wash Jones's unquestioning loyalty as well, we are told, while Milly is seduced by such trinkets as beads and ribbons (pp. 226, 228).

It is this serious attraction to the concrete that betrays Sutpen's plan, and Sutpen himself. He is unable to see not what is concrete—the plantation, the slaves, the wife, the fine furnishings, the offspring—but what is abstract. He does not see that in his hasty carriage rides into Jefferson he duplicates the situation of his own childhood terror when carriages of the wealthy, driven recklessly, threatened his sister's life (p. 187). He does not see that in shutting the door against the black Charles (replicated in the black Clytie's refusal to admit the white Wash Jones) he duplicates the "monkey nigger" (p. 186) who refuses him at Pettibone's front door. Nor does he even see that, in his later days when lying in a barrel stave hammock on Sundays with Wash to serve him drinks, he even becomes the hated Pettibone himself!

Of all the Sutpens and Coldfields only Rosa—deprived as a child from material goods and even the money she should have to shop for food; who spends life as an adult living on the handouts of others—understands the corruption of commerce. Having effaced Goodhue even while he was above her in the attic by writing odes honoring those Confederate soldiers he rebels against, she later manages to efface Thomas Sutpen from historical record altogether in her inscription on Judith's tombstone: *"Judith Coldfield Sutpen. Daughter of Ellen Coldfield. Born October 3, 1841. Suffered the Indignities and Travails of this World for 42 Years, 4 Months, 9 Days, and went to Rest at Last February 12, 1884. Pause, Mortal; Remember Vanity and Folly and Beware"* (p. 171). Rosa alone in *Absalom, Absalom!* uses a concrete, material marker to voice a more abstracted sense of suffering, betrayal, and justice.

Even the more flamboyant Charles Bon is primarily interested in the luxuriance of Creole and Catholic custom that for him characterizes a material New Orleans rather than revenge on Sutpen. The effeminate, catlike Charles (according to Quentin and Shreve) moving from "the hot equatorial groin of the world" (p. 92) to a "labyrinthine mass of oleander and jasmine, lantana and mimosa" (p. 90), is at home in a world of opulence and sexuality. Although Charles denies "installing a counter or a scales or a safe in a store or business for a certain percentage of the profits" (pp. 92–93), he too traffics in human flesh. He deals in "creatures taken at childhood, culled and chosen and raised more carefully than any white girl, any nun, than any blooded mare even, by a person who gives them the unsleeping care and attention which no mother ever gives. For a price, of course, but a price offered and accepted or declined through a system more formal than any that white girls are sold under since they are more valuable as commodities than white girls" (p. 93). Charles comes so intuitively to a business arrangement—his marriage to Judith might have been just that, too—because he is, at base, his father's son. About this Faulkner could not be clearer: he suggests that before he comes to Sutpen's Hundred, Charles too has a son by an octoroon mistress whom he cannot acknowledge. Indeed, that son, Charles Etienne Saint-Valery Bon, an object disowned by *his* father in part because of his race (just as Charles is by Sutpen), is so disturbed by his need for a clear racial identity that he marries "a coal black and ape-like woman" (p. 166). His petty crimes and beatings before and after marriage suggest that Charles Etienne finds no solace at Sutpen's Hundred even though Judith sought him out in New Orleans and Clytie in her turn fetched him—as the missing member of the family, "theirs" brought home where "he belongs." At the Sutpen plantation, there is no economy to manage Charles Etienne, as there had been none for his father, whose only prolonged residence at Sutpen's Hundred is after his death. Instead, Charles Etienne's position is distinctly anomalous—again, materially—the trundle bed, the one object that is *his*, midway between Judith's bed and Clytie's pallet,[20] where he is disposed by them both.[21] And the economy here is prophetic, according to Shreve, for when blacks and whites do not finally balance out in the Sutpen lineage, the object left over, both white and black, is Jim Bond, made idiotic in the process.

Alone in *Absalom, Absalom!* Rosa's singular dismissal of her father and Thomas Sutpen suggests the superiority of her ledger of morality to theirs of avarice. But this is perhaps the deepest and darkest secret of *Absalom, Absalom!* For a childhood of deprivation which she alone in the larger family line shares with Thomas Sutpen is no mere coincidence: it is Faulkner, the novelist of patterns, suggesting we look for deeper similarities between Rosa and Thomas that make them secret sharers too. Their compensation for a pinched life is to watch others at a distance; as Thomas forges the means to imitate Pettibone, so Rosa dreams of being the lady of Sutpen's Hundred. When her father's abolitionism frustrates that dream, Sutpen's heroism on the Confederate battlefields sustains and reinvigorates them both. In time, she would match her passion with his potency, eliminating on their common balance sheet his coldness and her barrenness. Both, however, are highly personalized, highly selective visionaries, concerned more about role and personal satisfaction than, in effect, coupling and combining resources. Both are stubborn and persistent in what motivates most their self-preservation.[22] Both are given to excess: his hundred square miles is, in some suitable way, an equivalent to her thousand or more odes to the Confederate forces. There is, furthermore, much to support Rosa's own realization of this uncomfortable relationship, which helps to explain her long-standing bitterness toward both her mercantile father and the plantation owner to whom she later bargains her very self, and her desire to eliminate them both from her seared memory through the exorcism of confessing to Quentin. Rosa suffers a further need, however, to call on Quentin to take her to Sutpen's Hundred in 1909 and later to return, at some very real danger to herself, to reclaim her nephew. She *will*, one way or another, will herself a Sutpen—both her triumph and her defeat—just as she must know that, in her desire to possess her nephew and perhaps his property, she already is one. She claims, protesting too much, that she holds no brief for Sutpen or Ellen (p. 12 and passim). It is literally true: she holds no brief in the specific legal sense— that would be a Compson notion. What she holds is a suit against Sutpen, suing him for damages; and an obligation, having pledged herself as a kind of promissory note during the Civil War, to Sutpen's material dream. In the penetrating studies of families which are to follow this one, Faulkner will show how such materiality, such a sense of possession and of wealth, corrupts both an aristocratic line like the McCaslins and a mercantile line like the Snopeses. But their first major conjunction, which masks greed and avarice as pride and self-justification, is here, with the Sutpens, Coldfields, and Bons.

Such comments also point to the historical dimension of Faulkner's fictions of family; our understanding of his work is incomplete without recognizing, as he always did, the broader contexts for which his families serve as the central synecdoche. As Elizabeth Kerr has noted, Faulkner's historic references are sometimes inaccurate, but " 'historic' facts relating to Jefferson usually have a historic basis."[23] It is helpful to know that Sutpen's arrival in Yoknapatawpha in 1833 comes just after the Treaty of Pontotoc, signed on 20 October 1832, by which the Chickasaw Indians ceded all their land in northern Mississippi to the United States government—Rosa's accusation that he "took from a tribe of ignorant Indians" the land for Sutpen's Hundred, that he raped both Indians and land, is part of her accusations of the man she later demeans (p. 10)—and the formal establishment of Lafayette County, on which Yoknapatawpha is largely based, is on 9 February 1836, when the Mississippi legislature made provisions for twelve new counties from the cession. The point is that Sutpen is not a late arrival in Yoknapatawpha but one of its first settlers; the Sartorises and Compsons are not his predecessors but his contemporaries. According to Book A of the Lafayette County Deeds Record, there were some 120 families who settled at this time, including such families as the Butlers (Faulkner's maternal ancestors), the Shegogs (whose ancestral home Faulkner would later purchase), the Shipps (whose home may be the model for the old Frenchman place of Grenier), the Sneeds, and the Tankersleys (whose plantation home, still extant although remodelled, is roughly on land marked by Faulkner's map as Sutpen's Hundred): there was nothing singular about Sutpen's arrival except the dimensions of his dream. But even this must be put in context. Jonathan P. Sneed, for instance, who arrived in Lafayette County at about the time Sutpen comes to Yoknapatawpha, became a leading citizen and prominent business man within six years, dying in 1842. He purchased three sections, each 640 acres, in the College Hill section of Lafayette—the land Faulkner assigns to Sutpen—for $4,200. Such a large price suggests rich plantation land; and from the inventory of Sneed's estate made in 1842, his situation is not dissimilar to Sutpen's:

73 negro slaves

100 "killing hogs"

200 sows and shoats

150 head of cattle

4000 pounds of bacon

1000 bushels of corn

3000 bushels of potatoes

100 bales of cotton

13 mules

8 horses

3 Indian ponies

Open accounts totaling $1,650

Cash to the amount of $3,574.63

Notes with total face value of $5,306[24]

But Lafayette County grew quickly: the census for 1840 reveals 3,676 whites—2,018 male, 1,658 female—and 2,842 slaves; by 1850 those numbers had increased to 7,846 whites—4,466 males and 3,380 females—and 5,723 blacks, all but four of them slaves. By 1860, the number of slaves was broken down by household, showing only five families in the county owned between 100 and 200 slaves. Although we never know the number of Sutpen's slaves—it is land that most impresses the people of Yoknapatawpha—his holding must have been substantial considering his acreage, even if part of it was wooded.

Rosa herself is silent on the matter of race, but her violent reaction toward Clytie in her visit to Sutpen's Hundred with Quentin and Clytie's later destruction of Sutpen's Hundred when Rosa arrives there a second time suggests that race is, as it was generally then in Lafayette County, a matter both of instinct and custom. In Yoknapatawpha as in Lafayette, a drop of black blood made a person black. But this was not reciprocated; a drop of white blood never made one white. It was a system of class and caste distinctions that created further property—for the most part, whites owned blacks and measured their prosperity in the number they owned. Blacks in turn had their own caste system based on their mixed blood. Terms like octoroon and quadroon to signify one-eighth or one-fourth black blood, "companion to words like *mulatto* (of the same root as 'mule')," Robert Dale Parker writes, admit "a trace of the obsessively classifying language that reached American English from other slave cultures in the Caribbean and South and Central America."[25] The cause of mixed blood, miscegenation, Kerr claims, "is the self-created horror Southern men [sought] to efface from their consciousness by [an] elaborate system which is designed to prevent Negro men from doing to the white race what the white race has done to the black and which is based on the unproved assumption that Negro men desire to do so" (p. 165).

This powerful force in the lives of the Sutpens, Coldfields, and Bons is divided, disseminated, and refracted by the alternative racial and social distinctions created first in the West Indies and later in New Orleans some time before the settlement of Yoknapatawpha by whites. "Haiti looms in the background of *Absalom, Absalom!* as an exaggeration of the Mississippi South and an embodiment of American slaveholders' fear of revolt, justice, and revenge," Parker observes (pp. 106–7), prompting a Jim Crow system of repression. So important is the potency and fear of race, in fact, that for the story of the Sutpens, Faulkner changed the actual date of the Haitian rebellion—by which Toussaint-Louverture brought slavery to a bloody end in 1803, four years before Sutpen is born—to sometime around 1831–32; that Faulkner clearly had this coup in mind is suggested by his borrowing from the battle the name of the chief military officer of the government, Charles Etienne. Parker also notes that "Sutpen finds the architect in Martinique, another French Caribbean colony where slavery and the sugar crop were still going strong in the 1830s and there were major slave uprisings in 1815, 1822, and 1848" (p. 107).

The liberal Haitian attitude toward miscegenation, before and after the slavery revolt, was exported from that exotic French island to the French city of New Orleans where Eulalia Bon is thought to bring her son Charles. In *Absalom, Absalom!* Mr. Compson calls New Orleans "a place created for and by voluptuousness, the abashless and unabashed senses" (p. 91); when Faulkner was living there in the mid-1920s, his mentor Sherwood Anderson was calling it "the most civilized place I've found in America."[26] There, under a practice called *placage*, wealthy Creoles maintained mulatto mistresses and promised to support any child that resulted from the relationship.[27] Harriet Martineau describes for us the famous "quadroon balls" of New Orleans where meetings first took place:

> The quadroon girls of New Orleans are brought up by their mothers to be what they have been; the mistresses of white gentlemen. . . . The girls are highly educated, externally, and are, probably, as beautiful and accomplished a set of women as can be found. Every young man early selects one, and establishes her in one of those pretty and peculiar houses, whole rows of which may be seen in the Ramparts. The connection now and then lasts for life; usually for several years. In the latter case, when the time comes for the gentleman to take a white wife, the dreadful news reaches his quadroon partner, either by letter entitling her to call the house and furniture her own, or by the newspaper which announces the marriage. The quadroon women are rarely known to form a second connection. Some men continue the connection after marriage. Every quadroon woman believes that her partner will prove an exception to the rule of desertion. Every white lady believes that her husband has been an exception to the rule of seduction.[28]

Faulkner doubtless learned of this tradition during his earlier residence in New Orleans, but in 1928 his friend Lyle Saxon also described it in his *Fabulous New Orleans*.

> Now it must not be assumed that these women were prostitutes—they were not. They were reared in chastity, and they were as well educated as the times would permit. These were for the greater part the illegitimate daughters of white men and their quadroon mistresses. They were "free women"—not slaves. Their chastity was their chief stock in trade, in addition to their beauty. Their mothers watched them as hawks would watch chickens, accompanied them to the balls where only white men were admitted, and did not relinquish

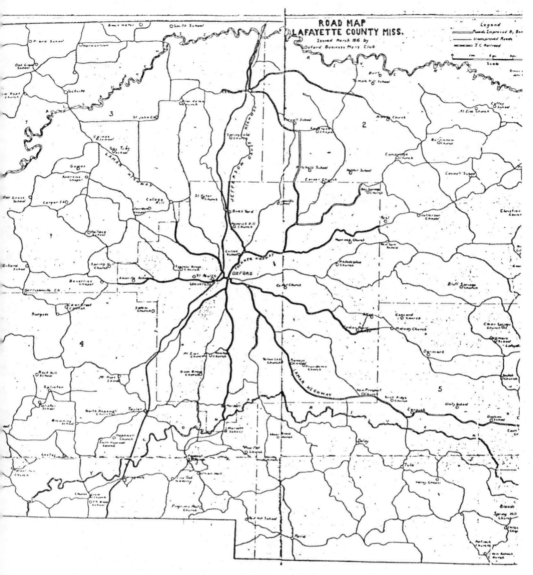

Map of Lafayette County - 1916

Official map of Lafayette County, Mississippi, in 1916, on which Faulkner based
the map of Yoknapatawpha County published with *Absalom, Absalom!*
Photograph by Arthur F. Kinney

Deed of Richard R. Corbin for the purchase of plantation land from John
Chisholm, John D. Martin, and John I. Craig for $1535.00 in Lafayette County,
Mississippi, on June 17, 1839. This is the land Faulkner's map calls Sutpen's
Hundred. From County Deed Book B. *Photograph by Arthur F. Kinney*

Formal gardens Faulkner had designed by an architect for Rowan Oak, similar to those Sutpen has designed for Sutpen's Hundred. *Photograph by Arthur F. Kinney*

Corbin's property today. *Photograph by Eva Miller*

View of Tallahatchie from ridge where Faulkner places Sutpen's mansion.
Photograph by Arthur F. Kinney

Cotton field today on land assigned to Sutpen's Hundred on Faulkner's map.
Photograph by Arthur F. Kinney

Cabin on land where Faulkner places Sutpen's Hundred, similar to the one in which Wash Jones would have lived. *Photograph by Arthur F. Kinney*

The Tankersley Plantation Home at College Hill in the late nineteenth century, the only mansion still standing in the area given as Sutpen's Hundred when Faulkner wrote *Absalom, Absalom! Photograph courtesy the Tankersley family and Skipwith Historical and Genealogical Society, Oxford, Mississippi*

The Tankersley home today, much as Faulkner would have known it best. *Photograph by Arthur F. Kinney*

*Oxford, Miss. Dec 17th 188_*

Pettis & Stowers,

BOUGHT OF

Mr. P. D. Tankersley

			Bale	Cotton.			@			
X	1			Bale Cotton.	Dan Alma	441	@ 9½	41 89		
X	1			"	Alf	555	9½	52 72		
90/	108			"	J. H. John	470	9½	44 65		
				"	Hen Lagen	476	9½	45 22		
X	1			"	John Lagen	484	10	4840		
X	1			"	".. "	513	10	51 30		
	1			"	".. "	468	10	4680	330 9

Credit his acct 330 98

E. & O. E.   Pettis & Stowers,

Plantation bill dated December 17, 1884, from the Tankersley plantation to a
business in Oxford. *Photograph by Arthur F. Kinney*

Alexander Hamilton Pegues, part of the model for Thomas Sutpen. *Photograph by Arthur F. Kinney, courtesy Skipwith Historical and Genealogical Society, Oxford, and the Pegues family and Guy Turnbow*

Rebecca Ann Evans Pegues, a putative model for Rosa Coldfield. *Photograph by Arthur F. Kinney, courtesy the Pegues family and Guy Turnbow*

Members of the Buford family in the mid-nineteenth century. The inset photograph of Goodloe Warren Buford is one putative model for Henry Sutpen. *Photograph by Arthur F. Kinney, courtesy Skipwith Historical and Genealogical Society, Oxford*

The town square of Oxford in the mid-nineteenth century. *Photograph by Eva Miller*

The exterior and interior, respectively, of stores similar to Goodhue Coldfield's in Oxford in the middle of the nineteenth century. *Photographs by Arthur F. Kinney, courtesy Skipwith Historical and Genealogical Society*

The home of Faulkner's mother, Maud Butler Falkner, near where Faulkner places the home of Rosa Coldfield. *Photograph by Arthur F. Kinney*

Shiloh Battlefield. *Photograph by Arthur F. Kinney*

Shiloh cemetery. Many stones for the Union forces are blank; Confederate
troops were buried in mass graves. *Photograph by Arthur F. Kinney*

A small private graveyard of the nineteenth century on land Faulkner's map
designates as Sutpen's Hundred and similar to the graves of Ellen and Judith
Sutpen and Charles and Charles Etienne St.-Valery Bon. *Photograph by
Arthur Kinney*

Goodmans Station July 3rd/64

Dear Sister

The Regiment arrived at this place a few minutes ago. we have camped here to day for the purpose of cooking rations. we suppose we are going up to the Mobile & Ohio R. Road. to Reinforce Genl. Forrest. we hope so at all events. the Boys are very anxious once more to meet the enemy on the Battle field we have all learned by experience that there is no fun in fighting. but we do not like to remain inactive. whi our. comrades. in arms. are. contending with this hated foe. I regret very much that I could not be at your Grand concert. I trust though you had a nice time as you most assuredly did. the young gentlemen were very entertaining & attentive. you no no that Longstreet Branch and was in route to the Southern Confederacy to join the army yankees. will fall now fly scored. and this little mess we have been trying to stop for so long will cease immediately. so in trust

The only extant letter of Robert Shegog, written during the Civil War to his sister. Shegog contributed to the portrait of Thomas Sutpen; Faulkner later bought his antebellum home, renaming it Rowan Oak. *Photograph by Arthur F. Kinney, courtesy Cynthia Shearer, curator of Rowan Oak* him not to doubt in this dreadful war though no doubt he has brought over with him a coat of Mail bullet proof & impenetrable by the heaviest Bomb shells the enemy can invent. but how can he live on Bacon and Corn Bread a week old. do you think he could endure it, dont be angry with me now for speaking of the Foreign Gentleman in the above manner. for you know he is very dear to me, & would like very much to see him,. Miss Annie Moseley sends her love to you and says you must not forget her, I had a pleasant time with her. while we were encamped there she sent me apples. butter & milk every day. of course I fell in love with her! how could I help it dont write to me the news from the plantation —

Tell Riley to take good care of my Horse & will give him a present when I come home I must close this epistle Give my love to all Please write every chance

Yours Brother
R. B. Skaggs

The mass grave of Confederate dead from Shiloh and other battles, located on the campus of the University of Mississippi in Oxford. *Photograph by Arthur F. Kinney*

Country store at College Hill when Faulkner was writing *Absalom, Absalom!*, on land near that given as Sutpen's Hundred and similar to the country store Sutpen manages at the end of his life. *Photograph by Eva Miller*

their chaperonage until the daughter found a suitable "protector." The protector was usually a young Creole gentleman with enough money to support the quadroon girl in fitting style. The "little houses along the ramparts" were not houses of ill-fame, but domiciles of these women and the white men who "protected" them. And the women were proverbially faithful, just as the young white girls of the colony were proverbially innocent. For the quadroon's future depended upon pleasing the man with whom she lived. Sometimes the liaisons lasted for years—occasionally for life. But more often than not they were broken off when the young man married.[29]

If Charles Bon's magnolia-faced wife is the result of *placage*, then both by law and custom he has every right to leave her to court Judith Sutpen. Section 323 of the General Provisions of the State Law of Louisiana on miscegenation reads, "The marriage of a white person with a negro or mulatto, or person who shall have one-eighth or more negro blood, shall be unlawful and void." Mr. Compson knows this, too, when he says that Charles's relationships in New Orleans are insufficient to explain why Henry killed him (p. 80). Knowledge and acceptance of *placage* may also explain why neither Judith nor Clytie seems offended by Charles's past, and why they feel the need to "protect" Charles's New Orleans family as he was pledged to do since it was a Sutpen who shot Charles. Indeed, the very fact that Charles' liaison has no legal matrimonial bond argues that bigamy cannot be a cause of the male Sutpens' disapproval—it is, as Charles tells Henry at Shiloh, a matter of race. *"I'm the nigger that's going to sleep with your sister. Unless you stop me, Henry"* (p. 286). Race alone finally causes fratricide and brings down the house of Sutpen.

Like exotic *placage*, miscegenation, and slavery, the War Between the States hangs heavy over the story of the Sutpen family. The War is the first motive Quentin Compson attributes to Rosa to explain why she has required his presence in her tomb-like home in the late summer of 1909. *"It's because she wants it told* he thought *so that people whom she will never see and whose names she will never hear and who have never heard her name nor seen her face will read it and know at last why God let us lose the War: that only through the blood of our men and the tears of our women could He stay this demon and efface his name and lineage from the earth"* (p. 6). For us, this is a striking revelation not of Rosa—who has not so much as hinted of the War—as it is of Quentin, who is suffused with the War and its legacy. He is already *"a barracks* filled with stubborn back-looking ghosts" (p. 7), "the Quentin Compson preparing for Harvard in the South, the deep South dead since 1865 and peopled with garrulous outraged baffled ghosts" (p. 4). Quentin tries to displace this self-assessment by blaming Rosa for all that has happened—and in doing so, he deflects precisely what Shreve will, in the end, force him to confront: the fratricide of Henry and Charles which, writ large as white against black in the South and brother against brother in the War between the States, is precisely what does keep Quentin's mind and attitude stuck in 1865 (as Thomas Sutpen's was not, nor Rosa's, nor any of their surviving relatives). As a reminder of this failure on the parts of Thomas and Henry to accept a sense of the brotherhood of humanity, Faulkner keeps making references to the War throughout *Absalom, Absalom!*, the large number of which Joseph Alexander Wigley has traced in detail.[30]

To be sure, the Civil War—still the single most important event in the history of Mississippi—is essential to placing and fully understanding the Sutpen story. Mississippi was one of the first Southern states to secede from the Union—by a vote of 84–15 on 9 January 1861, almost a month before the founding of the Confederate States of America in a convention at Montgomery, Alabama, on 4 February, and some three months before the Confederate forces attacked Fort Sumter in Charleston Harbor on 12 April and President Lincoln issued a call for a Union force of 75,000 volunteers on 14 April. Although Mississippi had a population of 70,295 white males in 1860 between 18 and 45, before the War concluded, she would have supplied 78,000 men to the Confederate forces. But Lafayette County and its county seat of Oxford (on which Jefferson is based) had long been supportive of rebellion. In late November 1860, the *Oxford Intelligencer* published a story entitled "Must the South Wait" in which the newspaper asked,

> Must the people of the South "wait" until they are totally disabled—until they are bound hand and foot—before they are to be justified in taking action to resist the threatened onslaught of these lawless hordes of half-demented fanatics? Must they defer action until it is *too late to act*? Must they wait till the thousands of John Browns come down upon us with fire and sword, backed up with all the power of the Government? In one word, is the "overt act" they are to wait for, *the total destruction of our rights, our property and our institutions?*[31]

Such sentiment prompted the formation of local volunteer military units in Lafayette County to train for battle against Union forces: the Lamar Rifles, the University Greys; Lafayette Guards; Thompson's Cavalry; Lafayette Dragoons; Mott Guards; McClung Riflemen; Avant Southrons; Dave Rogers Rifles; Webb's Rangers; Paris Rebels; Lafayette Defenders; Company A, Fourth Regiment; Lafayette Farmers; Pegues Defenders; Lafayette Rebels; and the Lafayette Cavalry—hardly any man or boy over sixteen was exempt.

Of these companies only two saw sustained active service once war broke out. The Lamar Rifles, named in honor of L. Q. C. Lamar, was organized on 1 December 1860; according to the official history of the company by the survivors, "The members of this Company were some of them students of the University of Mississippi, and nearly all were sons of prosperous merchants, planters, and professional men, and of Revolutionary ancestors."[32] The unit was mustered into state service on 21 February 1861, and on 4 May became Company G of the Eleventh Regiment of the Mississippi Volunteer Infantry, a regiment "from the older and more developed counties in North Mississippi."[33] On 13 May, the regiment enrolled in the Confederate Army at Lynchburg, Virginia, and went on to fight in thirty battles in North Carolina, Virginia, Maryland, and Pennsylvania, including the decisive battle of Gettysburg. The University Greys, in which Henry Sutpen and Charles Bon are said to enroll in *Absalom, Absalom!*, was recruited largely (but not exclusively) from the student body of the newly created University of Mississippi; Jemmy Grant Johnson estimates that four-fifths of all the students enrolled between its founding in 1848 and 1861 enlisted in Confederate service.[34] In 1861, Maud Morrow Brown reports that the campus was populated by eighty students: "They brought their horses and carriages, their negro hostlers and valets to college with them. They brought also the independent spirit of their pioneering parents, a spirit good in its place but likely to present difficult problems for those in authority over it."[35] The first commander of the University Greys was William B. Lowry, a student who spent more time at military tactics and play than at school, and possibly one of the models for Charles Bon. A. J. Ledbetter of Crawford, Mississippi, a Confederate veteran who knew Lowry, described him at nineteen years of age as "a tall, slender built man . . . with a classical, handsome face—a courteous and refined gentleman, well-to-do and wealthy"; he brought with him to college two horses—one for himself and one for his black servant—as well as his bird dogs and guns.[36] Gentleman or not, he was known for his energy, his determined leadership of others, and his sometimes reckless heroism. On 4 May 1861, the Greys became Company A of the Eleventh Mississippi Regiment and joined the Lamar Rifles at Lynchburg to enter Confederate service. There they became part of the Army of the Shenandoah under General Joseph E. Johnston and while they did not suffer substantial losses until the Battle of Gettysburg, there all of them were either killed or wounded. The company—which also counted among its soldiers Absalom C. Hardin[37]—nevertheless managed to remain intact until Lee's vain attempt to evade Federal entrapment just prior to Appomattox, according to C. John Sobotka, Jr. (p. 34), although they continued to suffer casualties and other hardships as they made their dogged retreat through Maryland.

The first major engagement of the war, First Manassas, or Bull Run, was fought on 21 July 1861, near Manassas, Virginia, and a train ride away from nearby Washington, D.C., from which spectators came to see the skirmishing from the sidelines. Three days later, on 24 July, W. Robert Ragland wrote home to his father in Oxford:

I take this opportunity of sending you a few lines. I will have to write quick I know not when I will have to stop. All day Sunday did the army of the south and the army of the north wrestle over the planes of this place in which we have gained a complete victory but dear. You would rather hear where I was I did not get into the fight. Two companies only of our regiment had got there as we came by rail road from Piedmont and came very slow. The enemy was trying to cut us off. They got in one mile of us, we stopped the cars, got out and formed a line of battle to protect the R. Road. We got here in time to go to the field of battle with Jeff Davis but the enemy was running very fast indeed leaving behind their batteries, throwing down their guns. In fact the left nearly every thing and a great many of them stayed with us. We are now camped on the battle ground. You never read of such distruction. The Yankees are lying thick here yet, it is an awful scene, too much to describe it. It is nothing to walk over a dead man. All of ours are nicely buried. You would like for me to say how many dead. This I cannot say. You will learn soon. R . . .? ward was in the fight, he is all right. He taken one prisoner himself. Moses Ward is at Winchester and is tought he will die, he has typhoid fever. Pete got here this evening and is not very well. Imagine you could see us here in a bunch of pines, lying about some asleep and others talking about the fight. I have not had a wash for several days and have not had a clean shirt in quite a time but as for clothes I will not suffer if I can get plenty to eat I don't care. We are getting to be pretty. . . . .nate. I do not know what move will be made next. I expect we will go toward Washington.[38]

The next year the war crept to the borders of Mississippi. The Battle of Shiloh (as the North called it) or the Battle of Pittsburgh Landing (as the South preferred) was fought fewer than twenty miles north of Corinth, Mississippi, on 6–7 April 1862. Confederate forces commanded by Generals Albert Sidney Johnston and P.G.T. Beauregard made a surprise attack on General Ulysses S. Grant's Army of the Tennessee encamped on a vulnerable position where troops could be transported easily at Pittsburgh Landing, on the Tennessee River. During the first day of battle, the organized Confederates fragmented and held seriously depleted Union forces; by the end of that day, they had captured the key position of Shiloh Church and pushed the Northern troops nearly to the river's bank. Union defeat was foregone until, the next day, Grant was reinforced by General Don Carlos Buell's Army of the Ohio and a division of men led by General Lew Wallace (later the author of Ben-Hur, as Shreve knows). That day General Beauregard, having sent his field doctor to nurse his troops, was fatally wounded; his death, two hours later, heralded the Confederate's defeat late that day. It was the first major battle of memorable proportions: Union troops of 55,000 suffered 13,000 killed, wounded, or captured, while Confederate forces of 42,000 suffered 11,000 killed, wounded, or captured. This huge cost of war, as well as its proximity, sent shock waves through Lafayette County. Rebecca Ann Evans Pegues of Oxford noted in her diary for April 24:

I am up to day & improving. It has been cool again—quite cool, but has become pleasant & we had no frost. I hope there is no danger now of frost. This terrible war keeps me so uneasy. A conscription-law has just been passed by (the Confederate) Congress which calls out all men from 18 to 35 years of age. This will fall heavily on many & cause much sorrow, but I believe it is necessary. We have now to use every effort against our merciless enemy. This last battle of Shilow was not so great a victory as at first supposed. We repulsed the enemy & drove them from their camps on the 6th but they rec'd reinforcements & renewed the fight on the 7th, recovered their campes etc. We retreated, not conquered but not in a condition to fight longer. I do not know the loss exactly on either side but it was very great on both—a terribly bloody battle. Our loss of valuable officers was heavy; Gen. Johnson, Gen. Gladden & many others. We took 2 or 3—prisoners & a large number of cannon, wagons etc.

"Above the smoke & stir of this dim spot which men call earth."Milton
"Liberal not lavish, is kind nature's hand." "Of chance & change oh let not men complain." Beattie[39]

Mrs. Calvin Brown's history of Lafayette County during the war years gives more details Faulkner knew well.

The Confederate troops fell back after the fall of Fort Donelson to Corinth and the war had reached North Mississippi but not Lafayette County—yet. But Shiloh was impending. After that bloody struggle there was mourning in many Lafayette County homes, but there was little time to mourn. Word came that the University buildings would be used as a hospital for the sick and wounded of that battle. . . .

When this news reached Oxford excitement was high in the town. Many homes were stripped of mattresses, beds, cots, bedding—everything that could be spared. Cots were placed in the chapel building, pallets in its galleries so thick attendants could hardly step between them. All campus buildings were used more or less and in the magnetic observatory dead were laid awaiting burial. The Lyceum was a dispensatory; the residence of the professor of chemistry, immediately behind the Lyceum, a mess hall and kitchen. Supplies were sent from New Orleans and Vicksburg at first; later the enemy cut those communications. But supplies came mostly from Oxford and Lafayette County. Many wagon loads of provisions were sent in, some also from neighboring counties. "The ladies worked diligently and incessantly spinning, weaving, sewing, knitting, day after day, week after week, that the soldiers might not lack for clothing" both here and in the camps.

Dr. T. D. Isom, who had been in Virginia with the 17th. Mississippi Regiment, was made head surgeon with various other physicians assisting him. More than 1500 soldiers were sent to the University hospital from Shiloh. For nurses the physicians depended on the women of the county and on convalescent soldiers. Two men, a Negro and a soldier, helped the women in each ward. A few women came to nurse their own and having nursed them to recovery or death, stayed on to nurse others. The women of the county were assigned to bring food for the wards in turns and came regularly bringing soups, broth, milk, and such dainties as they could. As the soldiers became convalescent they were sent, usually by twos, to private homes to make room for others who were coming in. Miss Ella Pegues [Rebecca's daughter] mentioned this:

"My father opened his country home to them and when they recovered took others in their places [at another plantation in the vicinity of Sutpen's Hundred on the Yoknapatawpha map]. My sister at first arranged flowers for their room, thinking that among them might be some handsome young officers but they were just plain, emaciated soldiers." "War," said Miss Pegues, "was beginning to lose its glamor" in the preceding August. By now it must have lost it all.

Several hundred soldiers died in the University hospital and their bodies were prepared for burial and placed in the ground by convalescent comrades or helpers at the hospital. They were buried in the plot of ground set apart for them on the campus. Mrs. Johnson says that since all the Oxford ministers were gone to war, they must have been buried without formal religious services, which is probably true but "Aunt Jane" Wilbourn, an aged Negro still living in Oxford now (1935), says that they always had a prayer, though "they buried them in bunches just like dead chickens."[40]

"God Acres"—that mass grave of 700 dead now unknown since markers were erroneously pulled up after the Civil War and the graves leveled and grass planted—remains on the grounds of the university today, awesome in its simplicity and silence. Like Miss Pegues in College Hill, Rosa tells us that she and Judith, in roughly the same location, sewed for the soldiers, too. But the University Greys never fought at Shiloh and Quentin—who scorns Shreve for his ignorance about Pickett's Charge at Gettysburg—has got it wrong himself when he says that Henry and Charles joined those forces at the Battle of Pittsburgh Landing. Perhaps Quentin has confused the University Greys with the Mississippi Greys, Company A of the 22nd Mississippi Regiment, who did fight there, but even so Faulkner's point must be to suggest Quentin's unreliability as a narrator—and his cerebral remoteness from the real and widespread suffering in that battle and in the War.[41] As for Gettysburg, the University Greys were put at the very point of Pickett's charge as the "bloody angle" and every one of them was either killed or seriously wounded.

But such discrepancies abound between historic fact and annealing memory. The congregation at College Hill Presbyterian Church—bordering the land of Sutpen's Hundred on Faulkner's map—somehow managed to keep intact a number of records during the Civil War years, including the annual minutes for January 1863. There Will Lewis Sr. found confirmation of Mrs. Brown's documents on Oxford which, like Jefferson, lay six miles to the south:

December the 1st 1862 God in his wise but inscrutable providence permitted the enemy to enter our quiet community with a force more than thirty thousand strong. During that month they occupied College Church and its vicinity depriving the congregation the privilege long granted to it of worshipping God in his own house. . . . Before the first tent was struck or a single camp fire was lighted, from twenty to thirty were in every house appropriating to themselves such articles as gratified their fiendish dispositions. Many families when they left them were almost utterly destitute of necessary food, raiment, and bedding. While they were ravaging within, our attention was scarcely directed to what was going on without doors and to our astonishment the depredations of poultry, cattle, hogs, sheep, mules, and horses were no less distinctive. But this first evening's experience was but a faint foretaste of the ignominious treatment which we were destined to receive from their hands. They would enter dwellings at a late hour of the night, arouse the sleeping inmates, and with the most profane and blasphemous language demand money and search ladies' trunks and private dressers, and, enraged at finding nothing which they desired, they would deface and destroy furniture with their sabers and bayonets. In some instances they forced worthy citizens to leave at once their homes and then set fire to their domicles. They were regardless of the pleas of females and offered insults to the old, helpless and inoffensive and often when protection was sought from those in command, it was denied. Thus from day to day as we were subjected to the insults and cruel treatment of our insolent unprincipalled foe, they not only robbed us of all property which they could appropriate to their benefit but destroyed much which was of no use to themselves but which they knew was invaluable to us.

Further commentary approaches Rosa Coldfield's attitude and even language.

Such is a mere outline of the heavy calamity which God in his providence has seen fit to inflict upon our community. To say that there were good reasons for this in the mind of him who holds the destinies of all things in his hands is saying what the Bible and the providence of God in all past ages has taught the nations of the earth. Not only the instructions of the Bible but the dealings of God with nations and individuals teach us that the sin for which punishment is inflicted in this life is brought to our knowledge by the penalty inflicted upon us. Thus our sin, in some measure at least, is not honoring God to the full extent of our duty in that which he has committed to our charge. Then is it our duty, whatever may be our omission or commission sins in sight of God, to humble ourselves, repent . . . , plead for his mercy, his grace.[42]

Although no putative model for Wash Jones survives from the documents left in this part of Lafayette County, Jones was a common name of settlers in College Hill, and one set of letters, by and about H. W. Jones, tells us another part of the authentic story.

Columbia Tennessee at the Hospittle. March 3. 1863
Dear Mother

I am at the Hospittle in this town. I have the chills the Generals are very strick with there soldiers. If a soldier git sick he is ordered to the Hospittle. the Yanks are in 13 miles of Columbia nearly all the Cavelry has passed this place and crossing Duck River not moore than one mile from town. Starks Redgement is crossing to Day. I came to the Hospittle this morning The Ladies of Columbia & neighborhood has the management of the hospittle they seems to take an interest they say here all Day & bring something good to eat. This is the first Hospittle I ever were in & I hope it will be the last although I am treated as well as could be Expected there is too many sick for me. I have been sick nearly two weeks with cold & sore throat & last night I had a chill vandorns orders is all that goes to the Hospittle & have company horses the horses are to go on with the Redgiment & the soldiers had horses had to be farmed out about 8 miles & turned into an old field & guarded I came on a blin trail & sliped my horse in to the Livery stable not two hundred yards from here. I will take quinine tomorrow to keep of the chill & I will get on my horse & overtake the Redgement before the yanks Drop in behind take us up. . . .

Marry County Tennessee March 20—1863
Dear Mother

I will write you a few lines as I have an opportunity I dont know when I will get time to write any more. we are under marching orders with 5 Days Rashions I am not able to say in what Directions we will go. The enemy is advancing on us & I suppose we are going to meet the foe. I am out in the country getting my horse sod 20 miles from Columbia. my Command Left Camp Last night at 8 oclock I will have to overtake my Command There is a great deal of talk of peace some says peace will be made in 6 weeks. I dont believe a word I hear about it nor want till I see it. . . . There were a Livery Stable burnt Down in Columbia Last week and 60 horses burnt to Death General vandorn had 6 horses of his own burnt & all his staff horses vandorn had mare cost a 1000 Dollars. she was Lost. It is the opinion of a great many that some younion man sot the buildings on fire there good many younion men in this Section. . . . Your son till death H.W. Jones

> Camp near Brandon,
> Miss.
> August 9/63

Mrs. Susan Jones
　My Dear Madam—

It becomes my painful duty to announce to you the death of your Son my lamented & much loved friend, H. W. Jones. He died in Hospital near Machanicksburg in Yazoo County [Mississippi] on the 5th July.
　　　　　　　　Pneumonia [inserted]
after an illness of some ten days. He was buried on the plantation of Mr. Mosley near where he died. You may rest assured Madam that nothing was

left undone that could be done to add to his comfort or soothe his last moment. . . . After his death his saddle Bags were sold at auction in the Company for $24- which amt- with $15 which he had in his pocket and his Watch- & Ambrotype of his late lamented wife are in the possession of Lt. Ben Johnson Comdg our Company- His horse saddle & Bridle are also in possession of our Company officer & subject to your order- If you wish it we can sell the horse at a good price & send you the money as you know horses are very much in demand in the Service. You will command me in anything that you want done- Our present location is Brandon Miss. but it is doubtful whether we will remain here long- The possibilities are that we move in a few days for the neighborhood of Carrolton in Carroll County.

Hoping Madam that you will call on me for anything or information that you may want and that Almighty God may lighten your grief & dry your tears & temper this [?] afflicition to your spiritual good. I remain

Vy Truly Your Obed. Svt-
N. T. Nelson
Co. D 28th Miss Vols-

Nelson would return to Oxford; his family from before the war owned and managed the dry-goods store on the main square, a store that still bears their name. After the war, the statue of a Confederate soldier looking south was placed before the main south entrance to the courthouse on the square (a courthouse accurately and precisely described in *Requiem for a Nun*). The inscription carved into the base honors those who served and died "in a just and holy cause." It is there today, the city's ode to its Confederate dead.

In the period of Reconstruction that followed, many of the leading citizens of Lafayette County sold up their estates and moved on. In John Cooper Hathorn's list of Redeemers of Lafayette County there is no mention of Bowles, Price, Jones, Brown, or Fendrain—men who had been leading planters before the Civil War.[43] Taking their place were scalawags—native Southerners who had joined the Republican party. Sobotka records that one of them, Word G. Vaughn, was elected state representative in 1870, although he was accused of working against the interests of the people by the conservative Jackson *Clarion* (p. 50). Another was Robert A. Hill, born in Iredell County, North Carolina, who in 1858 was elected probate judge in Tishomingo County, Mississippi, and later moved to Oxford where he served as judge of the Federal district court until 1 August 1891. He was especially skillful in keeping at bay the Federal government's prosecution of the Ku Klux Klan, founded in Lafayette County in 1867 with the help of Nathan Bedford Forrest, who came down from Memphis especially for the purpose, in a building that later became the law offices of James Stone and Sons and, by Faulkner's time, of Phil Stone, his high school friend and mentor. The relative peace in Oxford—despite the appeals of night riders in their white robes and hoods and hidden rubber bags[44] whom Rosa recalled in *Absalom,*

Absalom!—was doubtless aided by a Federal military presence which arrived in the summer of 1868 to supervise the initial voting on the state constitution, and returned as a more permanent military contingent from 1869 to 1875.[45] But not all was quiet. T. J. Gilmer writes on 17 January 1868 that "the men who went to Kinston where you wanted to go have returned bankrupt and report the negroes entering into and plundering their houses and killing the whites- This is not an over wrought picture."[46]

Epidemics of yellow fever—which takes the lives of Judith Sutpen and Charles Etienne St. Valery Bon, whom she nurses—also threatened Oxford. In 1878, Joel Williamson records, "When a prolonged and terrifying yellow fever epidemic struck the entire Mississippi River basin" in the summer and the fall, Charlie Butler, Faulkner's maternal grandfather, who was then serving as town marshal, "hired and headed a platoon of 'quarantine guards' that sealed off the town."[47] Oxford's board of aldermen issued a proclamation establishing a quarantine against all points south of Oxford on the railroad on 12 August and extended it to include all points north on 14 August; on 30 August they asked local doctors to organize a board of health. On 3 September the mayor ordered a detail of twenty-four men to patrol the streets and prohibit anyone from entering town; in addition, four special police, one for each ward, were appointed to guard the homes of families who had already fled from the disease. Special police were ordered to shoot to kill anyone not responding to a single challenge and the board of health printed circulars on the epidemic, distributing them to every home.[48] According to Williamson, "The seriousness with which the town took these matters was indicated by the fact that C. W. Petrie, a local businessman who was away when the fever hit Oxford, was hauled into mayor's court and fined $50 for slipping into town through the quarantine lines to join his family" (p. 90). Special police were assigned to each entrance into town to prevent this from happening again while in the town, on 25 October, the board of health ordered that "should Mrs. Tomlinson die, her remains must be buried on the premises or some place selected on the University grounds."[49] She died the next day, and the board appointed a committee to supervise the procurement of a coffin and the opening of her grave although it was two more years before they allowed her remains to be transferred to the local cemetery. The quarantine itself was not lifted until 6 September 1879; but by that time, some exceptions had been made.

In 1882 it was smallpox. On 6 February, the board ordered everyone in town to be vaccinated, paying for shots given indigents, because of outbreaks of smallpox in towns along the railroad and in adjacent states; the preventive shots were completed within a month. Then the second epidemic of yellow fever arrived, in September 1888. According to Williamson, "Yellow fever was rampant again and the board [of health for the town] quickly resolved that 'the Town is hereby strictly quarenteened against the world.' Trains were not allowed to stop nor even to slow below a speed of six miles an hour when passing through Oxford. Special 'quarantine guards' were hired to block the roads and patrol the boundaries of the town, stopping all ingress. The guards, as is obvious from their family names, were respectable young men of the town, hired to serve for $1.25 a day" (p. 134). Among them were Faulkner's maternal uncle and his father, requisitioned from the registration lists of voters in alphabetical order. No public assembly was allowed, and there were curfews between 9:30 P.M. and 4 A.M. Somehow, Huldric Price, the grandson of Washington Price, who is arguably a model for Faulkner's L. C. Q. McCaslin, managed to get his family out of town near the start: they "refugeed" throughout the epidemic in Monteagle, Tennessee. But others left for a while, too. According to Ward Miner, the entire town of Oxford was evacuated and disinfected: "In November the populace returned and the schools and the university reopened on November 15th. Twelve deaths were recorded."[50] Several victims, as in the story of the hidden Sutpen graves which Quentin discovers when hunting with his father, were buried in small, private, remote cemeteries.

Louis Berrone argues that this historic event, when it reappears in Faulkner's history of the Sutpens, carries considerable metaphoric weight, since yellow fever is linked to miscegenation there.

> Miscegenation is the "Haitian disease" in Faulkner's novel. The crossing of blood leads to much anguish in Charles Bon, his son Charles Etienne St. Valery Bon, and to idiocy in the grandson Jim Bond. Faulkner's metaphors for this anguish range from the "crucifixion" of crossed blood to yellow fever which is actually the Haitian disease caused by an infectious virus that attacks the liver, causes jaundice, and turns the skin yellow. The bite of the *Aeis Aegypti* mosquito carries yellow fever from one person to another. The mosquito gets the virus by biting and sucking the blood from a person who already has the virus. Faulkner uses yellow fever as a metaphor for miscegenation because the offspring of the mixed marriages vary in degrees of pigmentation from darker to lighter colors which as they become lighter appear to be shades of cream yellow, then magnolia, and skin shades almost indistinguishable from white. The anguish that this crossbred person feels is that even though in many cases he may pass for white, he is never fully accepted by the whites because of inordinate prejudices against the few drops of Negro blood. The same person because of his light and almost white complexion, on the other hand, is often not fully accepted by the blacks. He then finds himself in a physical and social no-man's land and suffers the feverish consequences caused by that alienation. . . .
>
> Sutpen does not suffer yellow fever, himself, either literally or figuratively, but his progeny do. Even his pure white children succumb with visible traces of yellow upon them and about them. Judith, who is white, dies of the yellow jaundicing fever while nursing Etienne, who is "yellow" to begin with and is suffering from the "yellow" fever. Henry who shot his "yellow" brother Charles and who felt so much remorse that he became a shut-in tended by his "yellow" half sister Clytie at the Sutpen mansion was seen by Quentin in

a "yellowed" state: "the bed, the yellow sheets and pillow, the wasted yellow face with closed, almost transparent eyelids on the pillow, the wasted hands crossed on the breast as if he were already a corpse" (p. 298). Faulkner curiously substituted "smallpox" as the cause of Judith's death for yellow fever in his *Chronology* at the end of *Absalom*. The reason most likely is that yellow fever is not directly infectious. A mosquito that had bitten Etienne would then have had to bite Judith forthwith for Etienne to have directly passed the disease on to her as Faulkner implies in the novel.[51]

But there may be another reason for this confusion. Miscegenation might have been a legacy of the Sutpen story that was as difficult for Faulkner to deal with as it is for Quentin Compson. In his study of Faulkner, Joel Williamson argues that Faulkner's maternal grandfather, Charles Butler, the revered town marshal of Oxford—the very name *Charles* contributing to the discrepancy—may have suddenly left town for good during the Christmas season of 1887 not because he was bankrupt, as the town was told, or only because he had been pocketing some of the money he had collected as town taxes, but because he was eloping with his mistress, a mulatto. The demon of miscegenation which Quentin is unwilling to raise for so long may have been the very demon Faulkner, through the story of Sutpen, not Butler, was trying to exorcise with equally compelling urgency.

The story of the Sutpen family is also notorious for its inconsistencies, as if reflecting in its various narratives the scriptwriting conferences Faulkner was attending as he wrote the last half of the novel, as Joseph R. Urgo has so persuasively argued.[52] For instance, Mr. Compson tells Quentin that Charles Bon was "a personage who in the remote Mississippi of that time must have appeared almost phoenix-like, fullsprung from no childhood, born of no woman and impervious to time and, vanished, leaving no bones nor dust anywhere" (p. 58), although by that time, both of them have actually seen Bon's grave (p. 153). Again, Mr. Compson tells his son that Rosa moved out to Sutpen's Hundred when she was twenty, in 1864, the year her father died, and then, in the next sentence, gives her year of birth as 1845 (p. 46); was she eighteen, nineteen, or twenty at the time? Of considerably greater importance, whose picture does Judith keep in a metal case? Rosa claims she actually saw the picture: *"I saw that what she held in that lax and negligent hand was the photograph, the picture of herself in its metal case which she had given {Charles}, held casual and forgotten against her flank as any interrupted pastime book"* (p. 114). But Mr. Compson, who was not there, claims this was "the photograph of the other woman and the child" (p. 71), the octoroon Charles Bon is said to have married and their son Charles Etienne, upon whom Mr. Compson builds his whole tale of Charles's black heritage, an inconsistency Shreve notices and attempts to resolve as Charles's displacement of one picture for the other to admit to Judith his true identity

(p. 286). Other material testimony invites disparate conjectures, imaginative constructions, deconstructions, and reconstructions. Thus Thomas Sutpen fetches a single gravestone for his wife, Ellen, and has it "brought in the regimental forage wagon from Charleston, South Carolina and set above the faint grassy depression which Judith told him was Ellen's grave" (p. 100). Later, the stone becomes two tombstones "from Italy, the best, the finest to be had—his wife's complete and his with the date left blank" (pp. 153–54) which Quentin sends on a wildly imaginary itinerary as "that much bombastic and inert carven rock which for the next year was to be a part of the regiment, to follow it into Pennsylvania and be present at Gettysburg, . . . the regiment moving no faster than the wagon could . . . ; then through the Cumberland Gap and down through the Tennessee mountains, travelling at night to dodge Yankee patrols, and into Mississippi in the late fall of '64, where the daughter waited" (p. 154). Such inconsistencies may be partly owing to Faulkner's technique of borrowing from other writers—again a practice in filmwriting—and scholars have suggested Robinson Jeffers, Joseph Conrad, the trilogy of T. S. Stribling, Dosteovsky's *A Raw Youth*, Eugene O'Neill's *Mourning Becomes Electra*, and even Charlotte Brontë's *Jane Eyre*,[53] as well as from his own earlier work.[54] Such resources function in two ways in *Absalom, Absalom!*—they distract us from asking embarrassing but significant questions about the Sutpens, and they preclude direct confrontation with unwanted, or unbearable, facts. Inconsistencies function as additional screening devices; they are deliberate misdirections and unconscious deferrals or avoidances.

This is surely the case because *Absalom, Absalom!* especially and the Sutpen story generally pry into the deepest and darkest fissures of Southern culture. Equally important, but necessary because of this necessary prying, the story of the Sutpen family is arguably the most harrowing family saga for Faulkner autobiographically. Less evident than with the Sartorises, there are also resemblances between the Falkner and Sutpen clans. According to Judith Bryant Wittenberg,

> Sutpen is, like the first William Falkner, a "new man," a resourceful newcomer of unknown antecedents who appears in northern Mississippi in the early nineteenth century and rapidly rises from poverty to power and economic prosperity. In the process, he abandons his oldest son as not incremental to his design, even as Faulkner's great-grandfather gave up his [first] child John to facilitate his second marriage. Sutpen is arrogant, a figure who "contrived somehow to swagger even on a horse" (16), but he is heroic in battle, with a broken plume that signifies his splendor in defeat and recalls the Old Colonel's appellation, "Knight of the Black Plume." In civilian life, Sutpen's "lust for vain magnificence" (162) drives him to exploit slaves, to build a pretentious house, and to attempt to acquire respectability through marriage—all of which the Old Colonel did. Finally, his tendency toward violence

eventually leads to his own murder and he is, like the Old Colonel himself, buried under a tombstone he has already ordered.[55]

These reactions have been borne out by further research. In 1993 Joel Williamson noted that

> in the Ripley Cemetery there are other Falkners to whom the Colonel seemingly never publicly claimed blood kin. Less than fifty yards distant, to the right and slightly to the rear of the marble [tomb Faulkner's great-grandfather had provided for himself] are the remains of three members of the slave family, the "shadow family" that lived in his yard in 1860. They lie buried in a row—Emeline Falkner, the mother [whose name may have suggested to Faulkner that of "Evangeline"]; Delia, the oldest daughter; and Hellen, the second daughter.
>
> Emeline Falkner's grave lies between those of her two daughters. Emeline is at the center, also, of an amazing story—actually the saga of a slave woman and her children, fathered by the white men who owned her, and how they passed out of slavery and beyond into the broad stream of black life in America. . . . For several years . . . Emeline apparently bore no child who survived. However, at some point between mid-1864 and April, 1866, she gave birth to a baby girl, Fannie Forrest Falkner. Emeline's descendants have always maintained that Colonel Falkner . . . was Fannie's father (pp. 64–65)

too. He goes on, "In 1880 the census listed only one servant living in Colonel Falkner's household on Main Street, but she was a Falkner too. Her name was Lena Falkner. She was thirteen years old and mulatto. It is possible that Lena was also Emeline's daughter, born around 1867, perhaps in Pontotoc, and that Colonel Falkner was her father" as well (p. 67). Not only the maternal ancestry of William Faulkner hid the secret of probable miscegenation, then, but the paternal side assuredly did, a fact subsequently confirmed for me by some present citizens of Oxford, Mississippi.

Nor was it a matter of ancestry only: Faulkner himself was not exempt. There is the fratricide which the Sutpen family anxiously avoids and toward which their family history inexorably moves. "The killing of a brother took on intensely personal reverberations for Faulkner as he wrote *Absalom, Absalom!*," Robert Dale Parker records. "Faulkner had introduced his youngest brother, Dean, to flying, and in 1935 Dean crashed and died in a plane that Faulkner had sold him. Faulkner was devastated. He spent the days comforting his mother and Dean's pregnant wife, and in the nights he spread his manuscript on their kitchen table and carried his pain into yet more feverish work on it" (p. 155). Wittenberg speculates further that "at the deepest level, however, Dean's death served as some sort of catharsis. Confronting the actual demise of his exuberant young brother, whose physical attributes and special claims on parently affection may have evoked Faulkner's subconscious jealousy, was awful but somehow purgative" (p. 141).[56] But this striking connection may also have served to keep other connections buried. The story of Faulkner's youth, like Sutpen's, is the story of being turned away at the front door. When the Oldham family prevented his marriage to their daughter Estelle, his childhood sweetheart, he too spent years of purgatorial searching for a release—in another woman (Helen Baird), in departures from his hometown (to New York, to New Orleans, to Europe), and in writing (with a singular intensity). Like Sutpen, Faulkner would make fictions that would improve his stature, and with Faulkner, such fictions would prove the Oldhams had misjudged his talent, his apparent fecklessness. Later, when Estelle took him as her second husband—an inversion of Thomas who, failing the first time, takes a second wife—Faulkner found their relationship as teacherous, disappointing, and violent at times as Thomas's briefer relationship with Rosa. But like Thomas Sutpen, Faulkner too countered by reestablishing his own baronial dream; about the time he began writing the story of the Sutpens, he began dreaming about buying Bailey's Woods that surrounded his antebellum mansion, of enlarging his land, of increasing his own estate. It was at once arrogant and compensatory; it matched Estelle's extravagance in clothes and diminished her waywardness, to his mind, with a grander vision. Thus the Sutpen story takes on immense power and extreme intensity not only because Sutpen's story is the story of the South but because it is, in some of its most anxious and difficult moments, Faulkner's story too. And in narrating the Sutpen story, Faulkner like Quentin could be accused of hating as well as loving the South, even while forcefully denying such hatred.

But the necessary entanglement of authentic and fictive history and the unavoidable intervention of the imagination extend well beyond Faulkner's personal experiences and needs in the story of the Sutpen family. Sutpen's ostentatious property reflects mid-nineteenth-century Oxford, if not the barely described Jefferson. According to Emelda V. Capati, in 1861 the *Oxford Intelligencer* made just this point: "The advertisements in the *Intelligencer* were indicative of the economic prosperity of [the time] that allowed its residents a good measure of gracious living. Silk, lace, mantillas, embroideries, inlaid writing desks, pianos, guitars, music sheets, iron railing, and other luxury items that implied a life of leisure were offered for sale. Alongside advertisements for hardware and agricultural implements were those that offered services of book binders and stationers, subscriptions to magazines and new books. Concerts, levees, and bills of entertainment of visiting variety shows were advertised in the *Intelligencer*. Even groceries were classed as 'staple and fancy.' "[57] Perhaps in part to catch this spirit of growth and prosperity, Faulkner extended Lafayette County's 720 square miles into the 24,000 square miles of Yoknapatawpha not only so he can manage to give to Thomas Sutpen one hundred of them, Sutpen's Hundred, but also to isolate Sutpen from the others and, in that separation, to examine and understand him and his family line. The exact model for Sutpen has been a matter of some disagreement. "As Sutpen was the county's largest landowner, master of one hundred square miles of virgin bottom land lying twelve miles from Jefferson," Joseph Blotner tells us,

> so—according to Johncy Falkner [his brother]—had been Colonel Barr, who "owned nearly all the land from here to Burgess, about twelve miles to the west." The father of the Potts twins, Amodeus and Theophilus, had owned ten miles up and down the Tallahatchie, it was said. Alexander Hamilton Pegues had owned five thousand acres in the northeastern part of the county; he had not fought in the war which destroyed his home, but, like Sutpen, he had tried to summon the energy of a young man to rebuild it afterwards. His brother, Colonel Thomas Pegues, was another big landowner whose house had supposedly been built by a French architect. (A New Yorker with a French name had actually drawn the plans.) In Faulkner's childhood there were still a number of big houses out in the country—gaunt antique ruins such as the old Shipp place, eleven miles due south of town, built by Dr. Felix Grundy Shipp after his arrival with sixty-five relatives, servants, and slaves in 1833. Now the house was open and abandoned, the deep track near it still visible where the stage coach once passed by. Another landowner, listed in the 1860 census, was one Wash Jones. (Another Wash Jones, a Negro, had shot himself out of unrequited love in 1891.) The family burying ground of one such house, southwest of Oxford, shows the names Jones and Bond.[58]

To this listing Williamson adds Jacob Thompson, who built a house in town across from the Shegog house and who owned ninety-seven slaves living in twenty "slave houses," including the mulatto that attracted Charlie Butler. Shegog himself, at his death on 28 August 1860, had accumulated 6,072 acres of land in Sunflower, Panola, Tunica, and Tallahatchie counties and held eighty-eight slaves.[59]

Actually all of these may contribute to the creation of Sutpen. For, unlike those persons who seem clearly to be models for the Sartorises, Compsons, and McCaslins, the point with Sutpen is that he is a composite person, constructed and reconstructed by seven narrators and witnesses—Rosa, Mr. Compson, General Compson, Sutpen himself, Judith, Quentin, and Shreve—and in the process of sensing history as a series of trial constructions, of divergent and discrepant reconstructions, Faulkner turns openly and deliberately to several models simultaneously. There are, for instance, the Avents (or Avants). Benjamin Edward Avent, born in North Carolina in 1799, did not come to Lafayette County until 1839, bringing with him several children, including Francis Marion Avent, his oldest son, born in 1823, who was orphaned at the age of ten and at fourteen left hime to reestablish himself elsewhere (in this case, Texas), and his younger brother, Thomas Lundy Avent, born in 1833. Benjamin Avent also brought with him forty slaves.

In 1851, at the age of eighteen, Thomas Lundy Avent left to prospect for gold out west, but before leaving, he paid one last visit to the home of Wash Jones and promised, before he left, to return and marry the Jones's daughter. There were other Avants. Susan Snell, in her biography of Faulkner's life-long friend Phil Stone, notes that Stone's son Philip recalled Major Tomlin Avant, who built the house in which the Stones lived in Oxford and which Faulkner often visited, sometimes to read and write. According to young Philip, this Avant, the younger son of a Virginia gentleman, built his house too for his bride, the daughter of a wealthy Lafayette County pioneer, in the 1840s.

> As Philip knew the story from his father, Tomlin Avant had come penniless to the new territory when it opened in the 1830s. On borrowed money, he acquired "acres and acres of land" in Lafayette and Panola counties, including the site for his mansion, which he purchased from Pul-lum-ma-tubby, a Chickasaw, on 19 November 1842. A business acquaintance of Jacob Thompson (later secretary of the interior under Buchanan), Avant bought lumber from Thompson (again on credit) while carpenters were still working on the Thompson house. But twenty-four hours after receiving the last wagonload of building materials, Avant declared himself bankrupt. Thompson, without legal recourse, had to watch helplessly as Avant's slaves raised not only the big house and an overseer's cottage to the west, but also a smaller house with columns to the east, which Avant built in order to have "neighbors worthy of him." Deprived of a fief by primogeniture, the Virginian was determined to live as an aristocrat, financed if need be by "thousands of other people's dollars." Lafayette County blue bloods flocked to his balls and parties, where orchestras brought in from St. Louis, Memphis or New Orleans played for the dancers. Eventually, however, the lawsuits began, and Avant, after losing the showplace, moved into his overseer's cottage, where he died owing thousands to the more respectable gentry of North Mississippi.[60]

Other early settlers in Lafayette County who may have contributed to Faulkner's portrait of Thomas Sutpen lived in the northwest quadrant of Lafayette County, where Faulkner's map places Sutpen, and all of them are associated with the settlement of College Hill, a small community still thriving about six miles north of present-day Oxford. One of these is Goodloe Warren Buford, born in South Carolina in 1794, whose diary for the year 1850 is extant, and who, according to the 1850 census, had 630 acres of land that produced 2,500 bushels of Indian corn and 75 bales of cotton as well as 3,000 bushels of rice and 1,200 bushels of sweet potatoes. (By contrast, after the Civil War, his crops were sharply reduced to 175 bushels of Indian corn and 2 bales of cotton annually.) Four of his sons enlisted in the Civil War and two, who were wounded, were paroled and walked back to College Hill in June of 1865.[61] Another early settler in College Hill was William Davis Pettis, born in Tennessee in 1806, who came to Lafayette County in

1837. He purchased a large tract of land four miles northwest of College Hill Church, but his land, like Sutpen's, ran from College Hill north to the Tallahatchie River. Pettis built his house before marrying—it was an impressive mansion constructed of handmade bricks and lumber sawed on his land from his own timber; his house, like Sutpen's, was also known for its magnificent landscaping, with cedar trees lining the brick walk to the front. He too suffered great losses in the war. He is buried with his wife in the College Hill Church cemetery; on his marker is inscribed, "a self made man." But the largest landowner in the area—the man of 5,000 acres 7.5 miles north of Oxford and more than 150 slaves—was Alexander Hamilton Pegues, Sr. (1808–71), whose dates align closely to Sutpen's. Like Sutpen, he arrived early (in 1834, from Tennessee) and he lived many years in a log cabin as a bachelor who spent much of his time hunting wild turkey, wild deer, and birds, and not marrying until he had built his fine house in 1844. Although he did not join Confederate troops as his brother did, he nevertheless financed one of the county's companies, the Pegues Defenders.

The contiguity of the land farmed by these early settlers suggests that Sutpen's Hundred, too, may be a construction, a composite of the large plantations spreading south from the Tallahatchie and from Wyatt, the first settlement, preceding Oxford, whose site was the last port with direct river transportation to the Mississippi and to New Orleans.[62] Sutpen's mansion is built slowly and described in considerable detail, not only as it emerges out of the wilderness but in its landscaping and in its architecture; here, as nowhere else in Faulkner, we are made especially aware of place—of closed doors, of corridors, of the library where Sutpen confronts Charles Bon, of the bedroom where the emaciated Henry Sutpen lies dying, and of the stairway where Clytie fends off Rosa. The Sutpen story's last striking image is of the whole edifice torched and burnt to the ground, leaving only a howling idiot, first realized in "Evangeline," a story preceding the novel. Calvin S. Brown has provided us with the best summary of Faulkner's resources for Sutpen's plantation home.

The hundred-square-mile size of Sutpen's holdings rules out any possibility that it is closely based on any actual plantation in its area. There were large plantations like it, except for size, in the appropriate place. It was located on the old Sardis road, which crossed the IRON BRIDGE over the Tallahatchie River. This road has been shifted several times, but its general course is that of the present State Route 314, which peters out at the Sardis Reservoir. Sutpen's house would have been in the hills overlooking the creek and river bottom somewhere near the end of this road. Aunt Mitty, who cooked for my family during my childhood, had been a slave on the Corbin Place in this vicinity, and when we got a second-hand Model-T Ford about 1922 she got us to take her out to the site of the old place. There were no buildings left, but she easily found and showed us the foundations of the house, smokehouse, etc., and showed us how her master could overlook his fields in the creek and river bottom from the house. In 1972 I was unable to locate this site, but found another in the vicinity which obviously represented a very large establishment, with the sites of a main house and a large series of outbuildings behind it. The house site, with the cedars and the long sedge-grass-covered open slope leading up to it, perfectly fits the description (*Absalom*, p. 187)—but there is no way of knowing that Faulkner knew this spot, or, for that matter, that it would have fitted his description as perfectly at an earlier date. All we can say with confidence is that Faulkner placed Sutpen's in an area and with a general topography fitting the approach of Davidson's Creek to the Tallahatchie River, where there had actually been establishments like this, though by no means as large.[63]

Corbin had acquired Robert Carter's place, named Fairview, "an extensive planation situated fifteen miles west of Oxford" with a mansion of "spacious dimensions" and land both sides of the Tallahatchie "well stocked with slaves"[64] which commanded a view of the river from the main house on a ridge; this was in addition to land he had purchased from the town fathers—John Chisholm, John Martin, and John Craig—in 1838, 1839, and 1840, and from J. B. Houston in 1842.[65] There is also the Reuben Tankersley plantation home—the only one still standing in the area and so the one Faulkner might have known best, had most in mind—that was occupied in time by Reuben's son David Scott Tankersley (1829–1913), who, like Henry Sutpen, went to the local college, in 1862 enlisted in the Confederate army, and survived the war to walk back home from Charlotte, North Carolina. And there were at least two houses in Oxford which may have played a part, both of them antebellum: Jacob Thompson's mansion, "still vividly remembered in the community for its tastefully designed verandas, hand-carved furniture, and an art gallery full of 'rare and costly painting,' "[66] and, across the road, the old Bailey Place, bought in time by Faulkner and renamed Rowan Oak, which was built by slaves for Colonel Robert Shegog from bricks baked on the premises and timber from his land. The Shegog place was designed by a foreign architect—English, not French—and had formal gardens laid out by another English architect as well.

The names of Sutpen's two white children, James Hinkle has conjectured, may be derived from Judith Henry, a widow who was the first civilian casualty of the Civil War, dying at First Manassas, and known as "the widow of Manassas."[67] Henry and his half brother Charles may be modeled on brothers from College Hill who served in the Lamar Rifles, such as Goodloe W. and Thomas P. Buford, who both enlisted on 26 April 1861, were seriously wounded (and in the case of Thomas hospitalized), but who managed to make it back home, together, after the war, on 1 July 1865. Two other brothers who served in the Lamar Rifles, according to the official history, were Huldric Price, listed as a farmer, and Armead Price, listed as a student at the University of Mississippi, who enlisted together on 4 August 1862.

But the career with the most resonance belongs to the otherwise unknown John M. Allen, listed among the privates in the Lamar Rifles, who enlisted 5 September 1861 at Oxford: "Born in Mississippi, and a student at Oxford, Miss.; he was twenty-one at enlistment, and single. He was present at Seven Pines and . . . at Jones Farm, October 2, 1864. After the war he was killed in a private difficulty in Mississippi."[68] There is no such model at all for Judith.

Unlike the Sutpen family, who may be based on some combination of historic prototypes in Lafayette County history which Faulkner studied so closely, the Coldfield family seems even more generalized. Goodhue Coldfield's concentrated mercantile interests suggest many early settlers of Oxford such as James G. Trigg, a native of Kentucky who in 1847 opened the town's first clothing store, or J. M. Cook with his dry-goods store, or the merchant Asa Nix, or W. S. Neilson of Tennessee, who arrived in 1836 to open a general store that still operates on the town square as a dry-goods store. Still, the Goodhue Coldfield who is called "a man of uncompromising moral strength" (p. 65) and who is a steward of the Methodist Church in Jefferson as well as a merchant, is closest to W. B. Mitchell. An essay on early merchants prepared in 1922 by the Oxford chapter of the Daughters of the American Revolution and now housed in the archives at the University of Mississippi Library, records that Mitchell was "a local Methodist preacher [who] had a good sized tin shop . . . on the west side [of the town square]. He was also Sheriff McKee's depty and the jailor. He was one of the bravest men in the world, a stranger to any idea of fear, [who] would fight any body or any number of bodies. Then, as now, there were 'rowdies' in the town and in the county and when they drew their pistols and resisted the other officers Brother Mitchell would walk right to them, with his heavy walking cane half raised and order them to throw down their weapons and surrender and they were never known to fail to do it except in one or two cases and then they ran like quarter horses."[69] Mitchell acquired land with E. W. Smith as surety (Deed Book F, pp. 611–12) and sold land to Andrew Hopp (Book K, p. 250) and E. Andrews (Book K, pp. 380–81) in 1852 and 1866. A native of Tennessee, he was born in 1810; the 1850 census shows that at age thirty he and his wife, Sarah (twenty-five), had two children—James, five, and Sarah, one—and that they had been in Mississippi for at least five years. By 1860, Sarah had died, but he now had five more children then aged eleven, eight, five, three, and ten months.[70] The Oxford Methodist Episcopal Church, organized in 1836 on Depot (now Van Buren) Street in Oxford, built on a lot purchased for $150 from Chisholm, Martin, and Craig by the oldest congregation in Oxford, is clearly the model for the church to which Sutpen comes racing into Jefferson and where, under Goodhue Coldfield's stern eye, he married Ellen Coldfield, apparently according to their bargain.

Just as Ellen fades from the story of the Sutpens in *Absalom, Absalom!*, so too there is no clear model for her. But her sister Rosa, developed by Faulkner in more detail (and with more passion and understanding), is representative of a broad class of women who suffered at home during the Civil War. We are fortunate in having the diary of one of them, Rebecca Ann Evans Pegues, the wife of Alexander Hamilton Pegues. Rebecca Pegues, who was under five feet, never weighed 100 pounds, and had large brown eyes and severely knotted black hair, is described by her daughter Mattie Pegues Wood as one who "checked happiness on the surface with fear of depths," as one who "liked to suffer. Hers was the spirit of autumn."[71] This spirit is evident in her earliest extant diary entries:

July 21, 1834—This is my week to keep house, but my good sister won't allow me to do anything.

Sept. 1, 1834. . . . if instead of studying out and forming for ourselves correct general principals [sic] of action, we follow the impulse of the moment, how frequently are we misled from the path of prudence and moderation and thus does our conduct become to us a source of remorse and unhappiness. [December] 1842. Love is too absorbing a passion. It is too selfish in its nature. It binds our thoughts and hearts with too strong a tenure to the object of our affections.

April 10, 1846. This is Good Friday. How many devout congregations are assembled in solemn worship! This surely is a day which should inspire feelings of deepest humility. The Saviour, the Son of God suffering death for man! The thought is almost beyond our comprehension. Why was this sacrifice demanded? It was for our transgressions. "The Lord hath laid on him the inquity of us all." . . .

May 14th [1853]. Sunday. A warm sultry day. I am in rather a morbid mood today stay here so much—live such an unsocial life—that my nature is becoming contracted—mind & feelings, from want of exercise & action. I am literally shut up here in the dull low walls of this log cabin. Who is to blame—more myself than any body else. . . .

Sunday Sept. 12th [1858]. Forty two years of my life have passed away—like a shadow. All my youth, all the poetry & romance of this life—And what is it in review—Nought but vanity! How unsatisfactory!—The remaining years even should I be spared to three score & ten—what can I hope from them better than from the past!—No more bright visions of earthly good or happiness—only weariness of spirit unless I rest on more stable hopes & prospects than earth can give.—Oh! that I could be wise & spend the remnant of my life wisely—in serving God & preparing for the great future—the unseen, the eternal! In thinking of the bright & enduring rewards of Heaven & preparing myself for that pure state.

Like Rosa, she is attracted to her material goods and angry at such a self-betrayal of principle.

Jan. 5th. 1859. At present gloom hangs over me—sickness of our negroes: Mark & Burrell. And Sister Mary is here sick too—with all her family. I am very uneasy & anxious. Oh! for a brighter prospect! I ought on such occasions to exert myself & summon all my strength of mind & meet whatever comes with resignation. Supposing we lose our negroes—it is not wrong to regret it & feel distresed; but when we do all for them we can, we must not repine. Property is not the chief good in life.

Like Rosa there are sudden flashes of self-recrimination.

How I wish I were a different person—either a practical energetic business woman of strong good sense & judgment, or a cultivated elegant lady. As it is I am nothing definite.—with a taste for reading—an intellectual turn of mind my knowledge is so desultory—so imperfect, it avails me nothing in society. I am only a plain, a very plain woman. One great disadvantage I labor under is want of animal spirits—of mental or bodily activity—I am torpid—undemonstrative—cold.

There is much in Rebecca Pegues's combination of self-justification and self-pity with a deep sense of shortcoming and guilt that gives a greater richness and depth to Rosa Coldfield. Rebecca Pegues moved in the highest social circles of Oxford—with Lamar, Thompson, and Longstreet—and her husband was a distinguished lawyer and member of the state legislature; her life, moreover, was full of family and children. But it was also full of daily toil, especially during the Civil War, when she sought refuge in their town house rather than in the plantation on land where Faulkner locates Sutpen's Hundred.

Aug. 3d. [1861] Bro Kit's birthday. He is 38 years old. I spent a busy day at home making pants for the soldiers. Had a pr. of pillows & cases made & sent some dried fruit. Having crackers made all day to send off. It has been oh! so hot today. I have been sewing on thick woolen cloth & have a bad headache.
[Aug.] 13th. Mallie's birthday. I went to Oxford yesterday to a meeting of the Ladies Association—covered canteens for the A. H. PEGUES DEFENDERS who went off to Virginia this morning. . . .
Up to this time, Aug. 23d. I have made for the soldiers 9 pr. Pants, 14 pr. drawers, 2 calico shirts, 10 pr. of the drawers I gave them the cloth. I am knitting socks.

For Rebecca Pegues as for Rosa Coldfield, joy was a difficult purchase.

April 5th. 1862. One of my dark unhappy days. . . . To be so misunderstood, to have so little estimation placed on me after this long & intimate association! To be pronounced so uncharitable, so hypocritical—such a compound of vanity and deception! I must try harder to exercise self-control. To restrain my tongue from any angry or impatient words. To be as pleasant & kind & attentive as I can. This is right hard, when I am treated & judged so harshly; yet it is right & much the best way to do.

The war was especially stressful.

When the Yankies first entered Oxford, they broke in Thomas' cellar and destroyed everything. After that a guard was placed around the house. They went into Alex' house, broke every article of furniture, every piece of glass and crockery ware, broke the carriages and buggy, hauled off all his corn except from one crib, drove off all his mules, horses, oxen, sheep, hogs, etc., killed and destroyed all the poultry, and left the plantation a complete waste. The negroes, however, had not left except one boy,

Rebecca Pegues writes in an unidentified letter. Later she describes returning to her own plantation home:

When I returned to the house a few days afterwards on my way to the plantation, intending to remain, the yard was full of Yanks with wagons. They had all the wine, liquers, etc. out on a table in the yard with glasses drinking—had a wagon filled with potatoes, etc. every door wide open. The locks all broken open—everything thrown out of the bureaux and sideboard—letters and papers all over the floor. Every thing miserably torn to pieces. I stayed two nights at the plantation and then Mr Gist and I, from information we rec'd that made it doubtful whether we were safe in staying, concluded to return to town—where we all stayed about six weeks.

We can measure Rosa's determination and fortitude by Rebecca Pegues's: it puts into perspective her attempt to help Judith and Clytie, hoeing cotton beside them on Sutpen's Hundred to keep crops growing until Thomas returns; and it measures too her sense of isolation and loneliness, her stubbornness and her battles with despair.

At the close of *Absalom, Absalom!* Rosa, after forty-five years of grief and self-incarceration, makes an astonishing leap into life in an attempt to locate and rescue her criminal nephew Henry Sutpen. But the men and the ambulance she takes with her by sheer will to save him are too late.

They ran onto the gallery too, into the seeping smoke, Miss Coldfield screaming harshly, "The window! The window!" to the second man at the door. But the door was not locked; it swung inward; the blast of heat struck them. The entire staircase was on fire. Yet they had to hold her; Quentin could see it: the light thin furious creature making no sound at all now, struggling with silent and bitter fury, clawing and scratching and biting at the two men who held her, who dragged her back and down the steps as the draft created by the open door seemed to explode like powder among the flames as the whole lower hall vanished. (p. 300)

Her last hope, as Quentin tells it, her one final act of generosity, is denied her. Instead she must watch the demolition of Sutpen's Hundred, of her fate and that of the last of her relations much as Rebecca Pegues, in town, saw the destruction of Oxford when Whiskey Smith torched it for the Union army. But Rebecca had her own personal moment of horror, too. After a "winter of gloom," she records a fire in the black quarters on 29 April 1855:

> It was an awful and terrible night to me. I was aroused from my sleep with the startling tale that the negro houses were on fire and the negroes were being burned up. I ran out and saw the vivid flames and heard the terrible cries of the frantic creatures—a house just falling in and one poor woman and three children not rescued—Such a scene of confusion and dismay! I was as one speechless with awe and terror—yet feeling heavy responsibility as my husband was away and no one to direct and control the poor wild, distracted negroes—but me.—Two guests hurried to the scene—the helpless Mother and three children had perished a cruel death—nothing but scattered bones remained of them. I was almost overwhelmed.

But throughout her life as an inexplicable gethsemane, Rebecca Pegues has her family—a husband who is always returning home, especially in time of trouble, and children she will not let go of. In both, she is luckier than Rosa. For Rosa Coldfield hardly knows family: her aunt deserts her, her father departs into his own secret life (and death), her sister disappears into Sutpen's Hundred, Thomas's proposal is crude and demeaning of her and of their shared vision of Southern achievement, and Clytie willfully keeps her from any hope of family by eliminating those who remain save Jim Bond. Without family, Rosa Coldfield learns in *Absalom, Absalom!*, there is nothing.

This seems to be the larger, final meaning for others in *Absalom, Absalom!* too. "For Quentin," Patricia Tobin writes,

> the source of the South's peculiar distinction was the sanctity it accorded to the family. In its genealogical aspect, the family transmitted through its generations the traditional values of classical-Christian humanity; and through its patriarchal line of descent from father to son, it fostered an obligation to deserve the loyalty that a renowned family name would inevitably attract. In its nuclear organization, the Southern family represented the fierce and loving protection of the normal kinship relations between husband and wife, brother and brother, sister and brother.
>
> Once Quentin's resurrection in ritual identifies the Sutpen family as the whole in the part and the past in the present, he must face those truths which deny his own mythic South. He learns that the genealogical families have neither substance nor value. In his ruthless rape of the land, Thomas Sutpen is revealed as the prototype of all founders of Southern dynasties; and if this seems foreign to the genteel tradition of the planter-aristocrat, it is only because Sutpen accomplished in one generation what generally required several generations. Quentin learns the fragility of the father-son relationship, and

the tragic absurdity of a racial taboo that makes Henry's four choices—
bigamy, incest, fratricide, and miscegenation—all sins against the family.
And he learns the threat of incest to the normal brother-sister relationship.
Like Absalom, who kills his brother Amnon for having violated their sister
Tamar, Henry is also a fratricide, but his motive for murder is miscegenation.
Incest, he is willing to condone, although he views it as an indication of the
rot that is already enveloping the Southern family. In his hypothetical picture
of the Sutpens after Bon's marriage to Judith, he imagines them all "together
in torment" in a kind of family hell that parallels their damnation in life.
(pp. 347–48)[72]

At the time he kills Charles Bon, Henry Sutpen does not feel that way: he
is acting on the code of family and Southern honor. Yet he must sense a
kind of guilt, a deep repulsion, because his next act is flight. Actually, he
would not have to fear his father, who would understand and praise his
action. Nor need he fear the law that would also prevent miscegenation
where possible. The reason Henry flees must be his own stark recognition
that in killing Charles Bon, he has not only destroyed a man he admires
and perhaps loves, but, more horribly, he has fulfilled his father's inhuman
design. The last shot which he fired in the Civil War is truly a shot of
brother against brother, upholding the narrowness of vision that has already
meant defeat for the Confederacy. Barring his brother from the door, he
himself has become Pettibone too. His flight, like Coldfield's self-incarceration and Clytie's arson, suggests that a Southern family determined to preserve itself whatever the cost will only destroy itself.

The critical reception of William Faulkner is a well-known story, often told.
Despite early support from Sherwood Anderson (who helped Faulkner to
publish his first two novels, *Soldiers' Pay* and *Mosquitoes*, and advised him
to write about Mississippi for his third, *Flags in the Dust*, shortened by his
agent Ben Wasson for publication as *Sartoris* in 1929), most of his early
recognition came from scattered reviews. These were uneven; Faulkner's
work was often thought to be derivative, tangled, obscure, or morbid.
Sanctuary (1931) was his first successful novel because it was thought to be
sensational, not serious; Faulkner himself called it a "potboiler." Indeed,
throughout the 1930s, when Faulkner was publishing much of his finest
fiction, he was more admired in Europe than in his own country; Jean-Paul
Sartre's acclaim for *Sartoris* and *Sanctuary* and the early translations into
French by Maurice Edgar Coindreau are representative examples, if the most
famous. In the United States, the first important critical reception came
with two essays in 1939. In "Faulkner's Mythology," George Marion O'Donnell looked at much of Faulkner's work and found a figure in the carpet in
the conflict between the aristocratic Sartoris clan and upstart nouveau riche
such as the Snopeses. In the same year, Conrad Aiken, whom Faulkner had
admired as a poet, published an essay on "William Faulkner: The Novel as

Form," the first commentary of substance on the unique techniques and effects of Faulkner's style; his views were soon taken up by Warren Beck.[73] The same year, 1939, Faulkner was also elected to the National Institute of Arts and Letters. But he had to wait until 1946, and the publication of *The Portable Faulkner*, edited by Malcolm Cowley, before he would gain a growing, serious audience. It was Cowley's anthology—which arranged selected stories and episodes from novels into a history of Yoknapatawpha County— along with the 1949 Nobel Prize for Literature (awarded in 1950, the year Faulkner's *Collected Stories* won the National Book Award)—that led directly to his current popularity with readers, students, critics, and scholars. He is now the preeminent American writer, the subject of more criticism in English than any other author except Shakespeare. Important bibliographies of Faulkner's work and the criticism on it have been published by John Bassett and Thomas L. McHaney.[74]

The present collection brings together resources that help us to understand Faulkner's Sutpen-Bon-Coldfield family through associated texts and critical interpretations, many of them published here for the first time. Faulkner first began to work out the theme of the rejected poor white in "Wash" and of Sutpen's family in "Evangeline," but key portions of "The Big Shot," revised as "Dull Tale," also show him struggling to understand these characters. An early verion of the novel appeared as "Absalom, Absalom!" in the *American Mercury* in 1936; it is essentially chapter 1 without Quentin Compson, Faulkner's sensed need for narrative voices to tell the Sutpen story coming later in his conceptual development and the story's evolution. Older and newer work by historians in this collection and the WPA guide to the state of Mississippi frame general essays by John T. Irwin, Thadious Davis, and Andrea Dimino. More specific essays on the various lines of the Sutpen family follow, and an Appendix provides helpful guides and charts to untangling the episodes and the characters in them and, in the case of Hershel Parker, tackles the final mystery of *Absalom, Absalom!*

Readers may wish to supplement these insights with work not included here. Joseph Blotner, the authorized biographer, has the most detailed biography of Faulkner; in addition, David Minter, Frederick R. Karl, and Joel Williamson have written briefer and more specialized studies of his life.[75] Several older general studies of Faulkner's life and work are still useful. Michael Millgate has examined each novel in light of its textual history and development; Olga W. Vickery has read each novel according to theme and structure; and Cleanth Brooks has provided invaluable commentary on Faulkner's works as representative of Southern culture.[76] In addition, Richard P. Adams and Judith L. Sensibar have studied the origins of Faulkner's art, Michel Gresset and André Bleikasten have full-length studies on Faulkner's major period, 1919–36, and Michael Grimwood has written on Faulkner's writing as vocational struggle.[77] Overviews of the life and work have also been provided by Hyatt H. Waggoner, and John Pikoulis and, from the insights of Southern perspective, by John Pilkington and Walter Taylor.[78] Among important other works, John T. Irwin studies from a psychoanalytic viewpoint the Quentin Compson of *The Sound and the Fury* and *Absalom, Absalom!*; the difficulty of meaning is examined by Robert Dale Parker; Arthur F. Kinney examines the resources of Faulkner's style and technique and Joseph W. Reed, Jr., evaluates their effects.[79] There are important recent books by James A. Snead on racism in Faulkner, Minrose C. Gwin on Faulkner's feminism, and by Donald M. Kartiganer, John T. Matthews, and Warwick Wadlington using the newer critical approaches of postmodernist thought.[80] In addition, there is an array of helpful reference materials, such as glossaries and chronologies.[81]

Historical documents of Lafayette County which record the area Faulkner uses in his fiction have been published over the years by the Skipwith Historical and Genealogical Society based in Oxford, Mississippi.[82] In connection with *Absalom, Absalom!*, Gerald Langford has published a highly conjectural collation of Faulkner's manuscript; the actual documents have also been reprinted and edited by Noel Polk. The most useful recent work on the novel is by Robert Dale Parker and David Paul Ragan; Ragan has also published a useful glossary to the novel. There are also many useful essays and helpful chapters from longer books.[83]

In preparing this present collection, I am especially grateful for the advice and counsel of many readers, friends, and Faulknerians, including Howard Bahr, Martha Cofield, Cheri Friedman, Evans and Betty Harrington, Will Lewis, Jr., Ilse Dusoir Lind, Ronald Macdonald, Mark McElreath, Chester McLarty, Patricia Young; and in Oxford, to Thomas Verich, director, and the staff of the Archives and Special Collections, John Davis Williams Library, University of Mississippi; Richard and Lisa Howarth and the staff of Square Books; and the officers, editors, and authors of the Skipwith Historical and Genealogical Society.

ARTHUR F. KINNEY
University of Massachusetts, Amherst

Notes

1. Elizabeth M. Kerr, *Yoknapatawpha: Faulkner's "Little Postage Stamp of Native Soil"* (New York: Fordham University Press, 1969), 155–56.

2. *Absalom, Absalom!: The Corrected Text* (New York: Random House, Vintage ed., 1990), 100–1. All citations to the text in this Introduction are to this edition; quotations may use other editions. See the textual note.

3. William Faulkner, *Selected Letters*, ed. Joseph Blotner (New York: Random House, 1977), 78–79.

4. Peter Brooks, " 'Incredulous Narration': *Absalom, Absalom!*," *Comparative Literature* 34:3 (1982): 252.

5. Lewis, 19 February 1937, 7.

6. David Minter, *William Faulkner: His Life and Work* (Baltimore: Johns Hopkins University Press, 1980), 152–53.

7. Ilse Dusoir Lind, "The Design and Meaning of *Absalom, Absalom!*," *PMLA* 70:5 (December 1955): 908.

8. William Faulkner, "The Courthouse," in *Requiem for a Nun* (New York: Random House, 1951), 9.

9. "1699–1945: The Compsons," in *The Portable Faulkner*, ed. Malcolm Cowley (New York: Viking Press, 1946), 742.

10. Warwick Wadlington, *Reading Faulknerian Tragedy* (Ithaca: Cornell University Press, 1987), 34.

11. E. O. Hawkins, *A Handbook of Yoknapatawpha*, unpub. dissertation, Arkansas, 1961, 116–17.

12. "All the [Sutpen] family relationships are incestuous in the sense that no member of the family is free to establish a meaningful union beyond the family circle": so John Daniel Sykes, Jr., *The Romance of Innocence and the Myth of History: Faulkner's Religious Critique of Southern Culture*, unpub. dissertation, Virginia, 1986, 93.

13. Ralph Behrens, "Collapse of Dynasty: The Thematic Center of *Absalom, Absalom!*," *PMLA* 89:1 (1974): 24.

14. See Thomas L. McHaney, "Robinson Jeffers' 'Tamar' and *The Sound and the Fury*," *Mississippi Quarterly* 22 (Summer 1969): 261–63; cf. Beth B. Haury, "The Influence of Robinson Jeffers' 'Tamar' on *Absalom, Absalom!*," *Mississippi Quarterly* 25 (Summer 1972): 356–58.

15. Michael Millgate, *The Achievement of William Faulkner* (New York: Random House, 1966), 157.

16. James H. Justus, "The Epic Design of *Absalom, Absalom!*" in *William Faulkner's "Absalom, Absalom!": A Critical Casebook*, ed. Elisabeth Muhlenfeld (New York: Garland Publishing Co., 1984), 43–44.

17. William R. Poirier, " 'Strange Gods' in Jefferson, Mississippi: Analysis of *Absalom, Absalom!*" as rep. in *William Faulkner: Two Decades of Criticism*, ed. Frederick J. Hoffman and Olga W. Vickery (East Lansing: Michigan State College Press, 1954), 225. (Originally published in *Sewanee Review* 53 [Summer 1945]: 353–61.)

18. Ellen Ruth Rifken, *"Absalom, Absalom!" and the Curse of Inherited Fictions: Wherein a Student of Faulkner Reclaims her Education and Requests Title to the Deed*, unpub. dissertation, University of California, Santa Cruz, 1980, 73.

19. Cleanth Brooks, "On *Absalom, Absalom!*," *Mosaic* 7:1 (Fall 1973): 179.

20. David Paul Ragan, *William Faulkner's "Absalom, Absalom!": A Critical Study* (Ann Arbor: UMI Research Press, 1987), 97.

21. Donald M. Kartiganer, "Faulkner's *Absalom, Absalom!*": The Discovery of Values," *American Literature* 37 (November 1965): 299.

22. These ideas are derived from James E. Juergensen, Sr., *Nihilism and Religion in Faulkner's Prose*, unpub. dissertation, Kent State, 1988, 236–38.

23. Kerr, 93, n.34.

24. The Census figures are also reprinted in John Cooper Hathorn, *Early Settlers of Lafayette Co., Mississippi* (Oxford, Miss.: Skipwith Historical and Genealogical Society, Inc., 1980), 37–38. Sneed's inventory is on 73–74.

25. Robert Dale Parker, *"Absalom, Absalom!": The Questioning of Fictions* (Boston: Twayne Publishers, 1991), 133.

26. Sherwood Anderson, *Letters*, ed. H. M. Jones (Boston, 1953), 87, as quoted by W. Kenneth Holditch, "The Brooding Air of the Past: William Faulkner" in *Literary New Orleans*, ed. Richard S. Kennedy (Baton Rouge: Louisiana State University Press, 1992), 40.

27. John W. Blassingame, *Black New Orleans, 1860–1880* (Chicago: University of Chicago Press, 1973), 17.

28. Harriet Martineau, *Society in America* (New York: Doubleday and Co., 1962), 34.

29. Lyle Saxon, *Fabulous New Orleans* (New York: D. Appleton-Century Co., 1928), 181.

30. Joseph Alexander Wigley, *An Analysis of the Imagery of William Faulkner's "Absalom, Absalom!,"* unpub. dissertation, Northwestern, 1956, 109–12 et seq.; cf. Thomas Nordanberg, *Cataclysm as Catalyst: The Theme of War in William Faulkner's Fiction* (Uppsala, n.p., 1983), 97.

31. *Oxford Intelligencer*, 28 November 1860; as cited in C. John Sobotka, Jr., *A History of Lafayette County, Mississippi* (Oxford, Miss.: Rebel Press, Inc., 1976), 33; but see all of chapter 4.

32. *Lamar Rifles: A History of Company G, Eleventh Mississippi Regiment, C.S.A.* (Oxford, Miss.: n.p., 1901; rep. Topeka, Kans.: Bonnie Blue Press, 1992), 8.

33. Cited by Sobotka, 34.

34. Mrs. Jemmy Grant Johnson, "The University War Hospital," *Mississippi Historical Society Publications*, 12: 94.

35. Maud Morrow Brown, *The University Greys* (Richmond: Garrett and Massie, Inc., 1940), 3.

36. A. J. Ledbetter as quoted by Brown, 9.

37. Brown, 21.

38. *Family Ties*, Vol. II: *Old Letters* (Oxford, Miss.: Skipwith Historical and Genealogical Society, Inc., 1982), 157.

39. Typescript of the Pegues Family Papers in the private possession of Guy Turnbow, "1860–1865," 25.

40. Mrs. Calvin Brown, *Lafayette County 1860–1865: A Narrative* (Oxford, Miss.: UDC ts, 1935), 22–24, who draws on Johnson in part. Quoted by permission of The Mississippi Collection, The University of Mississippi Library, University, Miss.

41. See Scott Douglass, "Possible Sources for Faulkner's General Compson," *Resources for American Literary Study* 11:1 (Spring 1981): 114.

42. Will Lewis, Sr., *The Founding and Early History of College Hill Presbyterian Church* (Oxford, Miss.: privately printed by the church, 1985), 12–13. I have collated this transcription with copies of the original documents at the church and on film at the Oxford Public Library.

43. Hathorn, 111–14.

44. Julia Kendel, "Reconstruction in Lafayette County," *Publications of the Mississippi Historical Society*, 17: 239–40.

45. These facts are recorded by Sobotka, 50–51.

46. *Family Ties*, II, 88.

47. Joel Williamson, *William Faulkner and Southern History* (New York: Oxford University Press, 1993), 90.

48. From Thomas Webb and Louise Avent, "Oxford," in *Lafayette County Heritage* (Oxford, Miss.: Skipwith Historical and Genealogical Society, 1986), 33.

49. Quoted by Webb and Avent, 33.

50. Ward L. Miner, *The World of William Faulkner* (Durham, N.C.: Duke University Press, 1952), 59; see *Report of the Mississippi State Board of Health from 30 September 1897 to 30 September 1899* (Jacksonville, Fla.: 1900), 81–83.

51. Louis Berrone, Faulkner's *"Absalom, Absalom!" and Dickens: A Study of Time and Change Correspondences*, unpub. dissertation, Fordham, 1973, 153–54, 156–57.

52. Joseph R. Urgo, *"Absalom Absalom!*: The Movie," *American Literature* 62:1 (March 1990): 56–73.

53. A helpful summary of these sources is given by David Paul Ragan, *Absalom, Absalom! (Annotations)* (New York: Garland Publishing, Inc., 1991), xiii (Jeffers), xvi–xvii

(Dostoevsky from Kinney and Weisgarber), xiii–xiv (O'Neill from Wittenberg), and xv (Brontë from Millgate).

54.   Parker compares Joe Christmas with Charles Etienne St. Valery Bon, e.g., 93–94.

55.   Judith Bryant Wittenberg, *Faulkner: The Transfiguration of Biography* (Lincoln: University of Nebraska Press, 1979), 152.

56.   She adds, tellingly, "The theme of the dead brother-rival, a relatively dominant one in Faulkner's work up to 1935, would never recur in his fiction, except in *Intruder in the Dust*, where it appears in a subordinate way" (p. 141).

57.   Emelda V. Capati, *A Country Editor Faces Secession: The Story of the "Oxford Intelligencer": 1860–1861* (University, Miss.: Academy Press, 1961), 110.

58.   Joseph Blotner, *Faulkner: A Biography*, 2 vols. (New York: Random House, 1974), Vol. 1, 889–90.

59.   Jane Isbell Haynes, *William Faulkner: His Lafayette County Heritage: Lands, Houses, and Businesses Oxford, Mississippi* (Ripley, Miss.: Tippah County Historical and Genealogical Society, 1992), 50.

60.   Susan Snell, *Phil Stone of Oxford: A Vicarious Life* (Athens: University of Georgia Press, 1991), 23.

61.   In addition to Buford's diary, now in private hands in Oxford, Miss., memoranda for 1850 and 1851 survive that record expenses and income.

62.   Wyatt failed quickly, victim of the Panic of 1837 and the rerouting of the railroad from Holly Springs through Oxford rather than Wyatt and College Hill.

63.   Calvin S. Brown, *A Glossary of Faulkner's South* (New Haven: Yale University Press, 1976), 193–94.

64.   Gabriele Gutting, *Yoknapatawpha: The Function of Geographical and Historical Facts in William Faulkner's Fictional Picture of the Deep South* (Frankfurt-am-Main and New York: Peter Lang, 1992), 136.

65.   County Deed Book A, 327–28, 367–68; Deed Book B, 75–76, 295–96. He also deeded land back to Craig in 1839 (Deed Book B, 180–81) and to John Davidson in 1841 and to Gavin Edmond Corbin in 1844 (Book C, 42–43; Book D, 187). No other records of Corbin are now extant except as a trustee in the funding of the Oxford M.E. Church in 1836 (church history, "115 Years of Methodism in Oxford," n.p.) and as a witness to Sarah Ann Sneed's will (Adm. Book D, 6).

66.   Williamson, 126–27.

67.   James Hinkle, "Some Yoknapatawpha Names" in *New Directions in Faulkner Studies*, ed. Doreen Fowler and Ann J. Abadie (Jackson: University Press of Mississippi, 1984), 197.

68.   *Lamar Rifles*, 19.

69.   Mrs. Lee Baggett, Sr., Mrs. W. S. Leathers and Mrs. H. F. Simpson in an unpub. paper for the Daughters of the American Revolution in 1922.

70.   Mitchell's will, drawn up on 15 September 1860, is recorded in Administrative Book D, 104, packet #36.

71.   In a prefatory note to her transcription of her mother's (Rebecca Ann Evans Pegues's) nineteenth-century diary.

72.   Patricia Tobin, "The Time of Myth and History in *Absalom, Absalom!*," *American Literature* 45:2 (1973–74): 269–70.

73.   The O'Donnell and Aiken essays have frequently been anthologized. O'Donnell's work first appeared in *Kenyon Review* (Summer 1939): 285–99; Aiken's first appeared in *Atlantic Monthly* (November 1939): 650–54. Beck's work first appeared in *American Prefaces* (Spring 1941): 195–211; it was later incorporated in his *Faulkner* (Madison: University of Wisconsin Press, 1976). A fourth relatively early and influential study of Faulkner's style is Walter J. Slatoff, *Quest for Failure* (Ithaca: Cornell University Press, 1960).

74.   John Bassett, *William Faulkner: An Annotated Checklist of Criticism* (New York: David Lewis, 1972), supplemented by *Faulkner: An Annotated Checklist of Recent Criticism*

(Kent, Ohio: Kent State University Press, 1983) and *Faulkner in the Eighties: An Annotated Critical Bibliography* (Metuchen, N.J.: Scarecrow Press, Inc., 1991); Thomas L. McHaney, *William Faulkner: A Reference Guide* (Boston: G. K. Hall and Co., 1976), now being revised. The annual MLA International Bibliography, in print and on CD-ROM, is also up-to-date, but unannotated. Earlier and other works, somewhat outdated, are Beatrice Ricks, *William Faulkner: A Bibliography of Secondary Works* (Metuchen, N.J.: Scarecrow Press, Inc., 1981); Patricia E. Sweeney, *William Faulkner's Women Characters: An Annotated Bibliography of Criticism* (Santa Barbara, CA: ABC-Clio Information Services, 1985); and Irene Lynn Sleeth, *William Faulkner: A Bibliography of Criticism* (Denver: Alan Swallow, 1962).

75. Joseph Blotner, *Faulkner: A Biography*, 2 vols. (New York: Random House, 1974), revised, updated, and condensed in a one-volume edition published by Random House in 1984. In *William Faulkner: His Life and Work* (Baltimore and London: Johns Hopkins University Press, 1980), David Minter attempts to relate biography to the fiction; in *William Faulkner: American Writer* (New York: Weidenfeld and Nicolson, 1989), Frederick R. Karl informs Faulkner's life with psychoanalysis; and in *William Faulkner and Southern History* (New York and Oxford: Oxford University Press, 1993), Joel Williamson views Faulkner's life as an historian. An earlier, stimulating Freudian biography is Judith Bryant Wittenberg, *Faulkner: The Transfiguration of Biography* (Lincoln and London: University of Nebraska Press, 1979).

76. Michael Millgate, *The Achievement of William Faulkner* (New York: Random House, 1963), also in paperback; Olga W. Vickery, *The Novels of William Faulkner: A Critical Interpretation* (Baton Rouge: Louisiana State University Press, 1959; rev. 1961); Cleanth Brooks, *William Faulkner: The Yoknapatawpha Country* (New Haven and London: Yale University Press, 1963).

77. Richard P. Adams, *Faulkner: Myth and Motion* (Princeton: Princeton University Press, 1968), esp. chapter 1; Judith L. Sensibar, *The Origins of Faulkner's Art* (Austin: University of Texas Press, 1984), which is the fullest account of his early poetry and its impact on his fiction; Michel Gresset, *Fascination: Faulkner's Fiction, 1919–1936*, adapted from the French by Thomas West (Durham and London: Duke University Press, 1989); André Bleikasten, *The Ink of Melancholy: Faulkner's Novels from "The Sound and the Fury" to "Light in August"* (Bloomington: Indiana University Press, 1990); Michael Grimwood, *Heart in Conflict: Faulkner's Struggles with Vocation* (Athens: University of Georgia Press, 1987).

78. Hyatt H. Waggoner, *William Faulkner: From Jefferson to the World* (Lexington: University of Kentucky Press, 1959); John Pikoulis, *The Art of William Faulkner* (Totowa, N.J.: Barnes and Noble, 1982); John Pilkington, *The Heart of Yoknapatawpha* (Jackson: University Press of Mississippi, 1981); Walter Taylor, *Faulkner's Search for a South* (Urbana: University of Illinois Press, 1983).

79. John T. Irwin, *Doubling and Incest/Repetition and Revenge: A Speculative Reading of Faulkner* (Baltimore and London: Johns Hopkins University Press, 1975); Robert Dale Parker, *Faulkner and the Novelistic Imagination* (Urbana: University of Illinois Press, 1985); Arthur F. Kinney, *Faulkner's Narrative Poetics: Style As Vision* (Amherst: University of Massachusetts Press, 1978); Joseph W. Reed, Jr., *Faulkner's Narrative* (New Haven and London: Yale University Press, 1973).

80. James A. Snead, *Figures of Division: William Faulkner's Major Novels* (New York and London: Methuen, 1986); Minrose C. Gwin, *The Feminine and Faulkner: Reading (Beyond) Sexual Difference* (Knoxville: University of Tennessee Press, 1990); Donald M. Kartiganer, *The Fragile Thread: The Meaning of Form in Faulkner's Novels* (Amherst: University of Massachusetts Press, 1979); John T. Matthews, *The Play of Faulkner's Language* (Ithaca: Cornell University Press, 1982); Warwick Wadlington, *Reading Faulknerian Tragedy* (Ithaca: Cornell University Press, 1987).

81. Michel Gresset, *A Faulkner Chronology*, trans. Arthur B. Scharff (Jackson: University Press of Mississippi, 1985); Calvin S. Brown, *A Glossary of Faulkner's South* (New Haven and London: Yale University Press, 1976), which partly supersedes Harry Runyan, *A Faulkner*

Glossary (New York: Citadel Press, 1964); Edmond L. Volpe, *A Reader's Guide to William Faulkner* (New York: Farrar, Straus and Giroux, 1964); Dorothy Tuck, *Crowell's Handbook of Faulkner* (later *Apollo Handbook*) (New York: Thomas Y. Crowell Co., 1964).

82. The society's work has been collected in *Lafayette County Heritage* (Oxford, 1986; reissued, 1993), but see also Walker Coffey, *Lafayette County Legacy* (1990) and *Lamar Rifles* (1901; reprinted privately in 1992) listing the soldiers who fought in the Civil War from Lafayette County.

83. Gerald Langford, *Faulkner's Revision of "Absalom, Absalom!"* (Austin: University of Texas Press, 1971); Noel Polk, *William Faulkner: Manuscripts 13: "Absalom, Absalom!"—Typescript, Setting Copy and Miscellaneous Material* (New York and London: Garland Publishing, Inc., 1987). Robert Dale Parker, *"Absalom, Absalom!": The Questioning of Fictions* (Boston: Twayne Publishers, 1991), with a selective and annotated bibliography; David Paul Ragan, *William Faulkner's "Absalom, Absalom!": A Critical Study* (Ann Arbor: UMI Research Press, 1987). Ragan also has a helpful volume on the novel in *The Garland Faulkner Annotation Series* (New York and London: Garland Publishing, Inc., 1991). Three other book-length studies focus on *Absalom, Absalom!* In *Old Tales and Talking: Quentin Compson in William Faulkner's "Absalom, Absalom!" and Related Works* (Jackson: University Press of Mississippi, 1977), Estella Schoenberg traces the genesis and development of Quentin Compson in Faulkner's fiction; in *Sutpen's Design: Interpreting Faulkner's "Absalom, Absalom!"* (Charlottesville and London: University Press of Virginia, 1990), Dirk Kuyk, Jr. presents a highly individual understanding of Sutpen's secret that has not been widely accepted; and in *Faulkner and/or Writing* (Tokyo: Liber Press, 1986), Sanae Tokizane provides a number of interrelated essays on facets of the novel.

Of the dozens of essays not included in this collection, readers should consult David Kraus, "Reading Shreve's Letters and Faulkner's *Absalom, Absalom!*" in *Studies in American Fiction* 11:2 (1983): 153–69 and Ilse Dusoir Lind, "The Design and Meaning of *Absalom, Absalom!*" on the various skewed perspectives of the narrators in *PMLA* 70:5 (1955): 887–912. Among the most helpful unpublished dissertations and theses are those by John L. Dodds (Loyola University of Chicago, 1977); Maxine Smith Rose (Alabama, 1973); Idelle Sullens (Washington, 1954); and Joseph Alexander Wigley (Northwestern, 1956). More specialized work on the topics central to this volume include: For the Sutpen family—Alan Warren Friedman, *William Faulkner* (New York: Frederick Ungar Publishing Co., 1984), pp. 54–73, and Daniel Joseph Singal, *The War Within* (Chapel Hill: University of North Carolina Press, 1982), pp. 188–95. For Thomas Sutpen and his design—James Guetti, *The Limits of Metaphor* (Ithaca: Cornell University Press, 1967); William J. Sowder, *American Literature* 33:4 (1962): 485–99; and the unpublished dissertations of John Daniel Sykes, Jr. (Virginia, 1986) and Thomas William Zelman (Indiana, 1983). For the Sutpen women—Elisabeth S. Muhlenfeld, *Mississippi Quarterly* 25:3 (1972): 289–304, and the unpublished dissertation of Carol A. Twigg (State University of New York, Buffalo, 1985), pp. 80–115. For Rosa Coldfield—Jenny Jennings Foerst, *The Faulkner Journal* 4:1, 2 (1988/ 1989): 37–53; Deborah Garfield, *The Southern Literary Journal* 12:1 (1989): 61–79; Gwin, pp. 63–121; and Sally R. Page, *Faulkner's Women: Characterization and Meaning* (Deland, FL: Everett/ Edwards, Inc., 1972), pp. 102–08. For race—Frederick R. Karl, "Race, History, and Technique in *Absalom, Absalom!*" in *Faulkner and Race*, ed. Doreen Fowler and Ann J. Abadie (Jackson: University Press of Mississippi, 1987), pp. 209–21, and the unpublished dissertation by Stephen E. Agbaw (Connecticut, 1986).

New material on Faulkner and on the Sutpen family is published each year. Besides *Dissertation Abstracts* and the MLA International Bibliography, readers should consult the annual publications of papers of the Faulkner and Yoknapatawpha Conference, ed. Doreen Fowler and Ann J. Abadie for the University Press of Mississippi under various titles, *The Faulkner Journal*, and *The Faulkner Newsletter and Yoknapatawpha Review*, ed. William Boozer and published four times a year by the Yoknapatawpha Press in Oxford, Mississippi; this always carries a list of the most recent publications of note.

(PRE/POST)TEXTS

◆

Evangeline

WILLIAM FAULKNER*

I

I had not seen Don in seven years and had not heard from him in six and a half when I got the wire collect: HAVE GHOST FOR YOU CAN YOU COME AND GET IT NOW LEAVING MYSELF THIS WEEK. And I thought at once, 'What in the world do I want with a ghost?' and I reread the wire and the name of the place where it was sent—a Mississippi village so small that the name of the town was address sufficient for a person transient enough to leave at the end of the week—and I thought, 'What in the world is he doing there?'

I found that out the next day. Don is an architect by vocation and an amateur painter by avocation. He was spending his two weeks' vacation squatting behind an easel about the countryside, sketching colonial porticoes and houses and negro cabins and heads—hill niggers, different from those of the lowlands, the cities.

While we were at supper at the hotel that evening he told me about the ghost. The house was about six miles from the village, vacant these forty years. "It seems that this bird—his name was Sutpen—"

"—Colonel Sutpen," I said.

"That's not fair," Don said.

"I know it," I said. "Pray continue."

"—seems that he found the land or swapped the Indians a stereopticon for it or won it at blackjack or something. Anyway—this must have been about '40 or '50—he imported him a foreign architect and built him a house and laid out a park and gardens (you can still see the old paths and beds, bordered with brick) which would be a fitten setting for his lone jewel—"

"—a daughter named—"

"Wait," Don said. "Here, now; I—"

"—named Azalea," I said.

*From *Uncollected Stories of William Faulkner* by William Faulkner. © 1979 by Random House, Inc. Reprinted by permission of Random House, Inc. and Chatto & Windus (London). The text is from pp. 583–609. This story, first discovered in a closet in Faulkner's home in 1971, is an early draft regarding Henry and Judith Sutpen.

"Now we're even," Don said.

"I meant Syringa," I said.

"Now I'm one up," Don said. "Her name was Judith."

"That's what I meant, Judith."

"All right. You tell, then."

"Carry on," I said. "I'll behave."

II[1]

It seems that he had a son and a daughter both, as well as a wife—a florid, portly man, a little swaggering, who liked to ride fast to church of a Sunday. He rode fast there the last time he went, lying in a homemade coffin in his Confederate uniform, with his sabre and his embroidered gauntlets. That was in '70. He had lived for five years since the war in the decaying house, alone with his daughter who was a widow without having been a wife, as they say. All the livestock was gone then except a team of spavined workhorses and a pair of two year old mules that had never been in double harness until they put them into the light wagon to carry the colonel to town to the Episcopal chapel that day. Anyway, the mules ran away and turned the wagon over and tumbled the colonel, sabre and plumes and all, into the ditch; from which Judith had him fetched back to the house, and read the service for the dead herself and buried him in the cedar grove where her mother and her husband already lay.

Judith's nature had solidified a right smart by that time, the niggers told Don. "You know how women, girls, must have lived in those days. Sheltered. Not idle, maybe, with all the niggers to look after and such. But not breeding any highpressure real estate agents or lady captains of commerce. But she and her mother took care of the place while the men were away at the war, and after her mother died in '63 Judith stayed on alone. Maybe waiting for her husband to come back kept her bucked up. She knew he was coming back, you see. The niggers told me that never worried her at all. That she kept his room ready for him, same as she kept her father's and brother's rooms ready, changing the sheets every week until all the sheets save one set for each bed were gone to make lint and she couldn't change them anymore.

"And then the war was over and she had a letter from him—his name was Charles Bon, from New Orleans—written after the surrender. She wasn't surprised, elated, anything. 'I knew it would be all right,' she told the old nigger, the old one, the greatgrandmother, the one whose name was Sutpen too. 'They will be home soon now.' 'They?' the nigger said. 'You mean, him and Marse Henry too? That they'll both come back to the same roof after what has happened?' And Judith said, 'Oh. That. They were just children then. And Charles Bon is my husband now. Have you forgotten that?' And the nigger said, 'I aint forgot it. And Henry Sutpen aint forgot it neither.' And (they were cleaning up the room then) Judith says, 'They have got over that now. Dont you think the war could do that much?' And the nigger said, 'It all depends on what it is the war got to get over with.'

"What what was for the war to get over with?"

"That's it," Don said. "They didn't seem to know. Or to care, maybe it was. Maybe it was just so long ago. Or maybe it's because niggers are wiser than white folks and dont bother about *why* you do, but only about *what* you do, and not so much about that. This was what they told me. Not her, the old one, the one whose name was Sutpen too; I never did talk to her. I would just see her, sitting in a chair beside the cabin door, looking like she might have been nine years old when God was born. She's pretty near whiter than she is black; a regular empress, maybe because she is white. The others, the rest of them, of her descendants, get darker each generation, like stairsteps kind of. They live in a cabin about a half mile from the house—two rooms and an open hall full of children and grandchildren and greatgrandchildren, all women. Not a man over eleven years old in the house. She sits there all day long where she can see the big house, smoking a pipe, her bare feet wrapped around a chair rung like an ape does, while the others work. And just let one stop, let up for a minute. You can hear her a mile, and her looking no bigger than one of these half lifesize dolls-of-all-nations in the church bazaar. Not moving except to take the pipe out of her mouth: 'You, Sibey!' or 'You, Abum!' or 'You, Rose!' That's all she has to say.

"But the others talked; the grandmother, the old one's daughter, of what she had seen as a child or heard her mother tell. She told me how the old woman used to talk a lot, telling the stories over and over, until about forty years ago. Then she quit talking, telling the stories, and the daughter said that sometimes the old woman would get mad and say such and such a thing never happened at all and tell them to hush their mouths and get out of the house. But she said that before that she had heard the stories so much that now she never could remember whether she had seen something or just heard it told. I went there several times, and they told me about the old days before the war, about the fiddles and the lighted hall and the fine horses and carriages in the drive, the young men coming thirty and forty and fifty miles, courting Judith. And one coming further than that: Charles Bon. He and Judith's brother were the same age. They had met one another at school—"

"University of Virginia," I said. "Bayard attenuated 1000 miles. Out of the wilderness proud honor periodical regurgitant."

"Wrong," Don said. "It was the University of Mississippi. They were of the tenth graduating class since its founding—almost charter members, you might say."

"I didn't know there were ten in Mississippi that went to school then."

"—you might say. It was not far from Henry's home, and (he kept a pair of saddle horses and a groom and a dog, descendant of a pair of shepherds which Colonel Sutpen had brought back from Germany: the first police dogs Mississippi, America, maybe, had ever seen) once a month perhaps he would make the overnight ride and spend Sunday at home. One weekend he brought Charles Bon home with him. Charles had probably heard of Judith. Maybe Henry had a picture of her, or maybe Henry had bragged a little. And maybe Charles got himself invited to go home with Henry without Henry being aware that this had happened. As Charles' character divulged (or became less obscure as circumstances circumstanced, you might say) it began to appear as if Charles might be that sort of a guy. And Henry that sort of a guy too, you might say.

"Now, get it. The two young men riding up to the colonial portico, and Judith leaning against the column in a white dress—"

"—with a red rose in her dark hair—"

"All right. Have a rose. But she was blonde. And them looking at one another, her and Charles. She had been around some, of course. But to other houses like the one she lived in, lives no different from the one she knew: patriarchial and generous enough, but provincial after all. And here was Charles, young—" We said, "and handsome" in the same breath. ("Dead heat," Don said) "and from New Orleans, prototype of what today would be a Balkan archduke at the outside. Especially after that visit. The niggers told how after that, every Tuesday A.M. Charles' nigger would arrive after his allnight ride, with a bouquet of flowers and a letter, and sleep for a while in the barn and then ride back again."

"Did Judith use the same column all the time, or would she change, say, twice a week?"

"Column?"

"To lean against. Looking up the road."

"Oh," Don said. "Not while they were away at the war, her father and brother and Charles. I asked the nigger what they—those two women— did while they were living there alone. 'Never done nothin. Jes hid de silver in de back gyarden, and et whut dey could git.' Isn't that fine? So simple. War is so much simpler than people think. Just bury the silver, and eat what you can git."

"Oh, the war," I said. "I think this should count as just one: Did Charles save Henry's life or did Henry save Charles' life?"

"Now I am two up," Don said. "They never saw each other during the war, until at the end of it. Here's the dope. Here are Henry and Charles, close as a married couple almost, rooming together at the university, spending their holidays and vacations under Henry's roof, where Charles was treated like a son by the old folks, and was the acknowledged railhorse of Judith's swains; even acknowledged so by Judith after a while. Overcame her maiden modesty, maybe. Or put down her maiden dissimulation, more like—"

"Ay. More like."

"Ay. Anyway, the attendance of saddle horses and fast buggies fell off, and in the second summer (Charles was an orphan, with a guardian in New Orleans—I never did find out just how Charles came to be in school way up in North Mississippi) when Charles decided that perhaps he had better let his guardian see him in the flesh maybe, and went home, he took with him Judith's picture in a metal case that closed like a book and locked with a key, and left behind him a ring.

"And Henry went with him, to spend the summer as Charles' guest in turn. They were to be gone all summer, but Henry was back in three weeks. They—the niggers—didn't know what had happened. They just knew that Henry was back in three weeks instead of three months, and that he tried to make Judith send Charles back his ring."

"And so Judith pined and died, and there's your unrequited ghost."

"She did no such thing. She refused to send back the ring and she dared Henry to tell what was wrong with Charles, and Henry wouldn't tell. Then the old folks tried to get Henry to tell what it was, but he wouldn't do it. So it must have been pretty bad, to Henry at least. But the engagement wasn't announced yet; maybe the old folks decided to see Charles and see if some explanation was coming forth between him and Henry, since whatever it was, Henry wasn't going to tell it. It appears that Henry was that sort of a guy, too.

"Then fall came, and Henry went back to the university. Charles was there, too. Judith wrote to him and had letters back, but maybe they were waiting for Henry to fetch him at another weekend, like they used to do. They waited a good while; Henry's boy told how they didn't room together now and didn't speak when they met on the campus. And at home Judith wouldn't speak to him, either. Henry must have been having a fine time. Getting the full worth out of whatever it was he wouldn't tell.

"Judith might have cried some then at times, being as that was before her nature changed, as the niggers put it. And so maybe the old folks worked on Henry some, and Henry still not telling. And so at Thanksgiving they told Henry that Charles was coming to spend Christmas. They had it, then, Henry and his father, behind closed doors. But they said you could hear them through the door: 'Then I won't be here myself,' Henry says. 'You will be here, sir,' the colonel says. 'And you will give both Charles and your sister a satisfactory explanation of your conduct': something like that, I imagine.

"Henry and Charles explained it this way. There is a ball on Christmas eve, and Colonel Sutpen announces the engagement, which everybody knew about, anyway. And the next morning about daylight a nigger wakes the colonel and he comes charging down with his nightshirt stuffed into his britches and his galluses dangling and jumps on the mule bareback (the mule being the first animal the nigger came to in the lot) and gets down to the back pasture just as Henry and Charles are aiming at one another with pistols.[2] And the colonel hasn't any more than got there when here comes Judith, in her nightdress too and a shawl, and bareback on a pony too. And what she didn't tell Henry. Not crying, even though it wasn't until after the war that she gave up crying for good, her nature changing and all. 'Say what he has done,' she tells Henry. 'Accuse him to his face.' But still Henry wont tell. Then Charles says that maybe he had better clear off, but the colonel wont have it. And so thirty minutes later Henry rides off, without any breakfast and without even telling his mother goodbye, and they never saw him again for three years. The police dog howled a right smart at first; it wouldn't let anybody touch it or feed it. It got into the house and got into Henry's room and for two days it wouldn't let anybody enter the room.

"He was gone for three years. In the second year after that Christmas Charles graduated and went home. After Henry cleared out Charles' visits were put in abeyance, you might say, by mutual consent. A kind of probation. He and Judith saw one another now and then, and she still wore the ring, and when he graduated and went home, the wedding was set for that day one year. But when that day one year came, they were getting ready to fight Bull Run. Henry came home that spring, in uniform. He and Judith greeted one another: 'Good morning, Henry.' 'Good morning, Judith.' But that was about all. Charles Bon's name was not mentioned between them; maybe the ring on Judith's hand was mention enough. And then about three days after his arrival, a nigger rode out from the village, with a letter from Charles Bon, who had stopped tactfully you might say, at the hotel here, this hotel here.

"I dont know what it was. Maybe Henry's old man convinced him, or maybe it was Judith. Or maybe it was just the two young knights going off to battle; I think I told you Henry was that sort of a guy. Anyway, Henry rides into the village. They didn't shake hands, but after a while Henry and Charles come back together. And that afternoon Judith and Charles were married. And that evening Charles and Henry rode away together, to Tennessee and the army facing Sherman. They were gone four years.

"They had expected to be in Washington by July fourth of that first year and home again in time to lay-by the corn and cotton. But they were not in Washington by July fourth, and so in the late summer the colonel threw down his newspaper and went out on his horse and herded up the first three hundred men he met, trash, gentles and all, and told them they were a regiment and wrote himself a colonel's commission and took them to Tennessee too. Then the two women were left in the house alone, to 'bury the silver and eat what they could git.' Not leaning on any columns, looking up the road, and not crying, either. That was when Judith's nature began to change. But it didn't change good until one night three years later.

"But it seemed that the old lady couldn't git enough. Maybe she wasn't a good forager. Anyway, she died, and the colonel couldn't get home in time and so Judith buried her and then the colonel got home at last and tried to persuade Judith to go into the village to live but Judith said she would stay at home and the colonel went back to where the war was, not having to go far, either. And Judith stayed in the house, looking after the niggers and what crops they had, keeping the rooms fresh and ready for the three men, changing the bedlinen each week as long as there was linen to change with. Not standing on the porch, looking up the road. Gittin something to eat had got so simple by then that it took all your time. And besides, she wasn't worried. She had Charles' monthly letters to sleep on, and besides she knew he would come through all right, anyway. All she had to do was to be ready and wait. And she was used to waiting by then.

"She wasn't worried. You have to expect, to worry. She didn't even expect when, almost as soon as she heard of the surrender and got Charles' letter saying that the war was over and he was safe, one of the niggers come running into the house one morning saying, 'Missy. Missy.' And she standing in the hall when Henry came onto the porch and in the door. She stood there, in the white dress (and you can still have the rose, if you like); she stood there; maybe her hand was lifted a little, like when someone threatens you with a stick, even in fun. 'Yes?' she says. 'Yes?'

" 'I have brought Charles home,' Henry says. She looks at him; the light is on her face but not on his. Maybe it is her eyes talking, because Henry says, not even gesturing with his head: 'Out there. In the wagon.'

" 'Oh,' she says, quite quiet, looking at him, not moving too. 'Was— was the journey hard on him?'

" 'It was not hard on him.'

" 'Oh,' she says. 'Yes. Yes. Of course. There must have been a last . . . last shot, so it could end. Yes. I had forgot.' Then she moves, quiet, deliberate. 'I am grateful to you. I thank you.' She calls then, to the niggers murmuring about the front door, peering into the hall. She calls them by name, composed, quiet: 'Bring Mr Charles into the house.'

"They carried him up to the room which she had kept ready for four years, and laid him on the fresh bed, in his boots and all, who had been killed by the last shot of the war. Judith walked up the stairs after them, her face quiet, composed, cold. She went into the room and sent the niggers out and she locked the door. The next morning, when she came out again, her face looked exactly as it had when she went into the room. And the next morning Henry was gone. He had ridden away in the night, and no man that knew his face ever saw him again."

"And which one is the ghost?" I said.

Don looked at me. "You are not keeping count anymore. Are you?"

"No," I said. "I'm not keeping count anymore."

"I dont know which one is the ghost. The colonel came home and died in '70 and Judith buried him beside her mother and her husband, and the nigger woman, the grandmother (not the old one, the one named Sutpen) who was a biggish girl then, she told how, fifteen years after that day, something else happened in that big decaying house. She told of Judith living there alone, busy around the house in an old dress like trash would wear, raising chickens, working with them before day and after dark. She told it as she remembered it, of waking on her pallet in the cabin one dawn to find her mother, dressed, crouched over the fire, blowing it alive. The mother told her to get up and dress, and she told me how they went up to the house in the dawn. She said she already knew it, before they got to the house and found another negro woman and two negro men of another family living three miles away already in the hall, their eyeballs rolling in the dusk, and how all that day the house seemed to be whispering: 'Shhhhhh. Miss Judith. Miss Judith. Shhhhhh.'

"She told me how she crouched between errands in the hall, listening to the negroes moving about upstairs, and about the grave. It was already dug, the moist, fresh earth upturned in slowly drying shards as the sun mounted. And she told me about the slow, scuffing feet coming down the stairs (she was hidden then, in a closet beneath the staircase); hearing the slow feet move across overhead, and pass out the door and cease. But she didn't come out, even then. It was late afternoon when she came out and found herself locked in the empty house. And while she was trying to get out she heard the sound from upstairs and she began to scream and to run. She said she didn't know what she was trying to do. She said she just ran, back and forth in the dim hall, until she tripped over something near the staircase and fell, screaming, and while she lay on her back beneath the stairwell, screaming, she saw in the air above her a face, a head upside down. Then she said the next thing she remembered was when she waked in the cabin and it was night, and her mother standing over her. 'You dreamed it,' the mother said. 'What is in that house belongs to that house. You dreamed it, you hear, nigger?' "

"So the niggers in the neighborhood have got them a live ghost," I said. "They claim that Judith is not dead, eh?"

"You forget about the grave," Don said. "It's there to be seen with the other three."

"That's right," I said. "Besides those niggers that saw Judith dead."

"Ah," Don said. "Nobody but the old woman saw Judith dead. She laid out the body herself. Wouldn't let anybody in until the body was in the coffin and it fastened shut. But there's more than that. More than niggers." He looked at me. "White folks too. That is a good house, even yet. Sound inside. It could have been had for the taxes anytime these forty years. But there is something else." He looked at me. "There's a dog there."

"What about that?"

"It's a police dog. The same kind of dog that Colonel Sutpen brought back from Europe and that Henry had at the university with him—"

"—and has been waiting at the house forty years for Henry to come home. That puts us even. So if you'll just buy me a ticket home, I'll let you off about the wire."

"I dont mean the same dog. Henry's dog. Henry's dog howled around the house for a while after he rode off that night, and died, and its son was an old dog when they had Judith's funeral. It nearly broke up the funeral. They had to drive it away from the grave with sticks, where it wanted to dig. It was the last of the breed, and it stayed around the house, howling. It would let no one approach the house. Folks would see it hunting in the woods, gaunt as a wolf, and now and then at night it would take a howling spell. But it was old then; after a while it could not get very far from the house, and I expect there were lots of folks waiting for it to die so they could get up there and give that house a prowl. Then one day a white man found the dog dead in a ditch it had got into hunting food and was too weak to get out again, and he thought, 'Now is my chance.' He had almost got to the porch when a police dog came around the house. Perhaps he watched it for a moment in a kind of horrid and outraged astonishment before he decided it wasn't a ghost and climbed a tree. He stayed there three hours, yelling, until the old nigger woman came and drove it away and told the man to get off the place and stay off."

"That's fine," I said. "I like the touch about the dog's ghost. I'll bet that Sutpen ghost has got a horse, too. And did they mention the ghost of a demijohn, maybe?"

"That dog wasn't a ghost. Ask that man if it was. Because it died too. And then there was another police dog there. They would watch each dog in turn get old and die, and then on the day they would find it dead, another police dog would come charging full-fleshed and in midstride around the corner of the house like somebody with a wand or something had struck the foundation stone. I saw the present one. It isn't a ghost."

"A dog," I said. "A haunted house that bears police dogs like plums on a bush." We looked at one another. "And the old nigger woman could drive it away. And her name is Sutpen too. Who do you suppose is living in that house?"

"Who do you suppose?"

"Not Judith. They buried her."

"They buried something."

"But why should she want to make folks think she is dead if she isn't dead?"

"That's what I sent for you for. That's for you to find out."

"How find out?"

"Just go and see. Just walk up to the house and go in and holler: 'Hello. Who's at home?' That's the way they do in the country."

"Oh, is it?"

"Sure. That's the way. It's easy."

"Oh, is it."

"Sure," Don said. "Dogs like you, and you dont believe in haunts. You said so yourself."

And so I did what Don said. I went there and I entered that house. And I was right and Don was right. That dog was a flesh-and-blood dog and that ghost was a flesh-and-blood ghost. It had lived in that house for forty years, with the old negro woman supplying it with food, and no man the wiser.

III

While I stood in the darkness in a thick jungle of overgrown crepe myrtle beneath a shuttered window of the house, I thought, 'I have only to get into the house. Then she will hear me and will call out. She will say "Is that you?" and call the old negress by her name. And so I will find out what the old negress' name is too.' That's what I was thinking, standing there beside the dark house in the darkness, listening to the diminishing rush of the dog fading toward the branch in the pasture.

So I stood there in the junglish overgrowth of the old garden, beside the looming and scaling wall of the house, thinking of the trivial matter of the old woman's name. Beyond the garden, beyond the pasture, I could see a light in the cabin, where in the afternoon I had found the old woman smoking in a wirebound chair beside the door. "So your name is Sutpen too," I said.

She removed the pipe. "And what might your name be?"

I told her. She watched me, smoking. She was incredibly old: a small woman with a myriadwrinkled face in color like pale coffee and as still and cold as granite. The features were not negroid, the face in its cast was too cold, too implacable, and I thought suddenly, 'It's Indian blood. Part Indian and part Sutpen, spirit and flesh. No wonder Judith found her sufficient since forty years.' Still as granite, and as cold. She wore a clean calico dress and an apron. Her hand was bound in a clean white cloth. Her feet were bare. I told her my business, profession, she nursing the pipe and watching me with eyes that had no whites at all; from a short distance away she appeared to have no eyes at all. Her whole face was perfectly blank, like a mask in which the eyesockets had been savagely thumbed and the eyes themselves forgotten. "A which?" she said.

"A writer. A man that writes pieces for the newspapers and such."

She grunted. "I know um." She grunted again around the pipe stem, not ceasing to puff at it, speaking in smoke, shaping her words in smoke for the eye to hear. "I know um. You aint the first newspaper writer we done had dealings with."

"I'm not? When——"

She puffed, not looking at me. "Not much dealings, though. Not after Marse Henry went to town and horsewhupped him outen he own office, out into the street, wropping the whup around him like a dog." She smoked, the pipe held in a hand not much larger than the hand of a doll. "And so because you writes for the newspapers, you think you got lief to come meddling round Cunnel Sutpen's house?"

"It's not Colonel Sutpen's house now. It belongs to the state. To anybody."

"How come it does?"

"Because the taxes haven't been paid on it in forty years. Do you know what taxes are?"

She smoked. She was not looking at me. But it was hard to tell what she was looking at. Then I found what she was looking at. She extended her arm, the pipe stem pointing toward the house, the pasture. "Look yonder," she said. "Going up across the pahster." It was the dog. It looked as big as a calf: big, savage, lonely without itself being aware that it was lonely, like the house itself. "That dont belong to no state. You try it and see."

"Oh, that dog. I can pass that dog."

"How pass it?"

"I can pass it."

She smoked again. "You go on about your business, young white gentleman. You let what dont concern you alone."

"I can pass that dog. But if you'd tell me, I wouldn't have to."

"You get by that dog. Then we'll see about telling."

"Is that a dare?"

"You pass that dog."

"All right," I said. "I'll do that." I turned and went back to the road. I could feel her watching me. I didn't look back. I went on up the road. Then she called me, strongvoiced; as Don said, her voice would carry a good mile, and not full raised either. I turned. She still sat in the chair, small as a big doll, jerking her arm, the smoking pipe, at me. "You git out of here and stay out!" she shouted. "You go on away."

That's what I was thinking of while I stood there beside the house, hearing the dog. Passing it was easy: just a matter of finding where the branch ran, and a hunk of raw beef folded about a half can full of pepper. So I stood there, about to commit breaking and entering, thinking of the trivial matter of an old negress' name. I was a little wrought up; I was not too old for that. Not so old but what the threshold of adventure could pretty well deprive me of natural judgment, since it had not once occurred to me that one who had lived hidden in a house for forty years, going out only at night for fresh air, her presence known only to one other human being and a dog, would not need to call out, on hearing a noise in the house: "Is that you?"

So when I was in the dark hall at last, standing at the foot of the stairs where forty years ago the negro girl, lying screaming on her back, had seen the face upside down in the air above her, still hearing no sound, no voice yet saying, 'Is that you?' I was about ready to be tied myself. I was that young. I stood there for some time, until I found that my eyeballs were aching, thinking, 'What shall I do now? The ghost must be asleep. So I wont disturb her.'

Then I heard the sound. It was at the back of the house somewhere, and on the ground floor. I had a seething feeling, of vindication. I thought of myself talking to Don, telling him "I told you so! I told you all the time." Perhaps I had mesmerised myself and still had a hangover, because I imagine that judgment had already recognized the sound for that of a stiff key in a stiff lock; that someone was entering the house from the rear, in a logical flesh-and-blood way with a logical key. And I suppose that judgment knew who it was, remembering how the uproar of the creekward dog must have reached the cabin too. Anyway, I stood there in the pitch dark and heard her enter the hall from the back, moving without haste yet surely, as a blind fish might move surely about and among the blind rocks in a blind pool in a cave. Then she spoke, quietly, not loud, yet without lowering her voice: "So you passed the dog."

"Yes," I whispered. She came on, invisible.

"I told you," she said. "I told you not to meddle with what aint none of your concern. What have they done to you and yo'n?"

"Shhhhh," I whispered. "If she hasn't heard me yet maybe I can get out. Maybe she wont know——"

"He aint going to hear you. Wouldn't mind, if he did."

"He?" I said.

"Git out?" she said. She came on. "You done got this far. I told you not to, but you was bound. Gittin out is too late now."

"He?" I said. "He?" She passed me, without touching me. I heard her begin to mount the stairs. I turned toward the sound, as though I could see her. "What do you want me to do?"

She didn't pause. "Do? You done done too much now. I told you. But young head mulehard. You come with me."

"No; I'll——"

"You come with me. You done had your chance and you wouldn't take it. You come on."

We mounted the stairs. She moved on ahead, surely, invisible. I held to the railing, feeling ahead, my eyeballs aching: suddenly I brushed into her where she stood motionless. "Here's the top," she said. "Aint nothing up here to run into." I followed her again, the soft sound of her bare feet.

I touched a wall and heard a door click and felt the door yawn inward upon a rush of stale, fetid air warm as an oven: a smell of old flesh, a closed room. And I smelled something else. But I didn't know what it was at the time, not until she closed the door again and struck a match to a candle fixed upright in a china plate. And I watched the candle come to life and I wondered quietly in that suspension of judgment how it could burn, live, at all in this dead room, this tomblike air. Then I looked at the room, the bed, and I went and stood above the bed, surrounded by that odor of stale and unwashed flesh and of death which at first I had not recognised. The woman brought the candle to the bed and set it on the table. On the table lay another object—a flat metal case. 'Why, that's the picture,' I thought. 'The picture of Judith which Charles Bon carried to the war with him and brought back.' Then I looked at the man in the bed—the gaunt, pallid, skull-like head surrounded by long, unkempt hair of the same ivory color, and a beard reaching almost to his waist, lying in a foul, yellowish nightshirt on foul, yellowish sheets. His mouth was open, and he breathed through it, peaceful, slow, faint, scarce stirring his beard. He lay with closed eyelids so thin that they looked like patches of dampened tissue paper pasted over the balls. I looked at the woman. She had approached. Behind us our shadows loomed crouching high up the scaling, fishcolored wall. "My God," I said. "Who is it?"

She spoke without stirring, without any visible movement of her mouth, in that voice not loud and not lowered either. "It's Henry Sutpen," she said.

IV

We were downstairs again, in the dark kitchen. We stood, facing one another. "And he's going to die," I said. "How long has he been like this?"

"About a week. He used to walk at night with the dog. But about a week ago one night I waked up and heard the dog howling and I dressed and come up here and found him laying in the garden with the dog standing over him, howling. And I brought him in and put him in that bed and he aint moved since."

"You put him to bed? You mean, you brought him into the house and up the stairs by yourself?"

"I put Judith into her coffin by myself. And he dont weigh nothing now. I going to put him in his coffin by myself too."

"God knows that will be soon," I said. "Why dont you get a doctor?"

She grunted; her voice sounded no higher than my waist. "He's the fourth one to die in this house without no doctor. I done for the other three. I reckon I can do for him too."

Then she told me, there in the dark kitchen, with Henry Sutpen upstairs in that foul room, dying quietly unknown to any man, including himself. "I got to get it off my mind. I done toted it a long time now, and now I going to lay it down." She told again of Henry and Charles Bon like two brothers until that second summer when Henry went home with Charles in turn. And how Henry, who was to be gone three months, was back home in three weeks, because he had found It out.

"Found what out?" I said.

It was dark in the kitchen. The single window was a pale square of summer darkness above the shagmassed garden. Something moved beneath the window outside the kitchen, something big-soft-footed; then the dog barked once. It barked again, fulltongued now; I thought quietly, 'Now I haven't got any more meat and pepper. Now I am in the house and I cant get out.' The old woman moved; her torso came into silhouette in the window. "Hush," she said. The dog hushed for a moment, then as the woman turned away from the window it bayed again, a wild, deep, savage, reverberant sound. I went to the window.

"Hush," I said, not loud. "Hush, boy. Still, now." It ceased; the faint, soft-big sound of its feet faded and died. I turned. Again the woman was invisible. "What happened in New Orleans?" I said.

She didn't answer at once. She was utterly still; I could not even hear her breathe. Then her voice came out of the unbreathing stillness. "Charles Bon already had a wife."

"Oh," I said. "Already had a wife. I see. And so—"

She talked, not more rapidly, exactly. I dont know how to express it. It was like a train running along a track, not fast, but you got off the track, telling me how Henry had given Charles Bon his chance. Chance for what, to do what, never did quite emerge. It couldn't have been to get a divorce; she told me and Henry's subsequent actions showed that he could not have known there was an actual marriage between them until much later, perhaps during or maybe at the very end, of the war. It seemed that there was something about the New Orleans business that, to Henry anyway, was more disgraceful than the question of divorce could have been. But what it was, she wouldn't tell me. "You dont need to know that," she said. "It dont make no difference now. Judith is dead and Charles Bon is dead and I reckon she's done dead down yonder in New Orleans too, for all them lace dresses and them curly fans and niggers to wait on her, but I reckon things is different down there. I reckon Henry done told Charles Bon that at the time. And now Henry wont be living fore long, and so it dont matter."

"Do you think Henry will die tonight?"

Her voice came out of the darkness, hardly waisthigh. "If the Lord wills it. So he gave Charles Bon his chance. And Charles Bon never took it."

"Why didn't Henry tell Judith and his father what it was?" I said. "If it was reason enough for Henry, it would be reason enough for them."

"Would Henry tell his blooden kin something, withouten there wouldn't anything else do but telling them, that I wont tell you, a stranger? Aint I just telling you how Henry tried other ways first? and how Charles Bon lied to him?"

"Lied to him?"

"Charles Bon lied to Henry Sutpen. Henry told Charles Bon that them wasn't Sutpen ways, and Charles Bon lied to Henry. You reckon if Charles Bon hadn't lied to Henry, that Henry would have let Charles Bon marry his sister? Charles Bon lied to Henry before that Christmas morning. And then he lied to Henry again after that Christmas morning; else Henry wouldn't have never let Charles Bon marry Judith."

"How lied?"

"Aint I just told you how Henry found out in New Orleans? Likely Charles Bon took Henry to see her, showing Henry how they did in New Orleans, and Henry told Charles Bon, 'Them ways aint Sutpen ways.' "

But still I couldn't understand it. If Henry didn't know they were married, it seemed to make him out pretty much of a prude. But maybe nowadays we can no longer understand people of that time. Perhaps that's why to us their written and told doings have a quality fustian though courageous, gallant, yet a little absurd. But that wasn't it either. There was something more than just the relationship between Charles and the woman; something she hadn't told me and had told me she was not going to tell and which I knew she would not tell out of some sense of honor or of pride; and I thought quietly, 'And now I'll never know that. And without it, the whole tale will be pointless, and so I am wasting my time.'

But anyway, one thing was coming a little clearer, and so when she told how Henry and Charles had gone away to the war in seeming amity and Judith with her hour old wedding ring had taken care of the place and buried her mother and kept the house ready for her husband's return, and how they heard that the war was over and that Charles Bon was safe and how two days later Henry brought Charles' body home in the wagon, dead, killed by the last shot of the war, I said, "The last shot fired by who?"

She didn't answer at once. She was quite still. It seemed to me that I could see her, motionless, her face lowered a little—that immobile, myriad face, cold, implacable, contained. "I wonder how Henry found out that they were married," I said.

She didn't answer that either. Then she talked again, her voice level, cold, about when Henry brought Charles home and they carried him up to the room which Judith had kept ready for him, and how she sent them all away and locked the door upon herself and her dead husband and the picture. And how she—the negress; she spent the night on a chair in the front hall—heard once in the night a pounding noise from the room above and how when Judith came out the next morning her face looked just like it had when she locked the door upon herself. "Then she called me and I went in and we put him in the coffin and I took the picture from the table and I said, 'Do you want to put this in, Missy?' and she said, 'I wont put that in,' and I saw how she had took the poker and beat that lock shut to where it wouldn't never open again.

"We buried him that day. And the next day I took the letter to town to put it on the train—"

"Who was the letter to?"

"I didn't know. I cant read. All I knew, it was to New Orleans because I knowed what New Orleans looked like wrote out because I used to mail the letters she wrote to Charles Bon before the war, before they was married."

"To New Orleans," I said. "How did Judith find where the woman lived?" Then I said: "Was there—There was money in that letter."

"Not then. We never had no money then. We never had no money to send until later, after Cunnel had done come home and died and we buried him too, and Judith bought them chickens and we raised them and sold them and the eggs. Then she could put money in the letters."

"And the woman took the money? She took it?"

She grunted. "Took it." She talked again; her voice was cold and steady as oil flowing. "And then one day Judith said, 'We will fix up Mr Charles' room.' 'Fix it up with what?' I said. 'We'll do the best we can,' she said. So we fixed up the room, and that day week the wagon went to town to meet the train and it come back with her in it from New Orleans. It was full of trunks, and she had that fan and that mosquito-bar umbrella over her head and a nigger woman, and she never liked it about the wagon. 'I aint used to riding in wagons,' she said. And Judith waiting on the porch in a old dress, and her getting down with all them trunks and that nigger woman and that boy—"

"Boy?"

"Hers and Charles Bon's boy. He was about nine years old. And soon as I saw her I knew, and soon as Judith saw her she knew too."

"Knew what?" I said. "What was the matter with this woman, any-way?"

"You'll hear what I going to tell you. What I aint going to tell you aint going to hear." She talked, invisible, quiet, cold. "She didn't stay long. She never liked it here. Wasn't nothing to do and nobody to see. She wouldn't get up till dinner. Then she would come down and set on the porch in one of them dresses outen the trunks, and fan herself and yawn, and Judith out in the back since daylight, in a old dress no better than mine, working.

"She never stayed long. Just until she had wore all the dresses outen the trunks one time, I reckon. She would tell Judith how she ought to have the house fixed up and have more niggers so she wouldn't have to fool with the chickens herself, and then she would play on the piano. But it never suited her neither because it wasn't tuned right. The first day she went out to see where Charles Bon was buried, with that fan and that umbrella that wouldn't stop no rain, and she come back crying into a lace handkerchief and laid down with that nigger woman rubbing her head with medicine. But at suppertime she come down with another dress on and said she never seed how Judith stood it here and played the piano and cried again, telling Judith about Charles Bon like Judith hadn't never seed him."

"You mean, she didn't know that Judith and Charles had been married too?"

She didn't answer at all. I could feel her looking at me with a kind of cold contempt. She went on: "She cried about Charles Bon a right smart at first. She would dress up in the afternoon and go promenading across to the burying ground, with that umbrella and the fan, and the boy and that nigger woman following with smelling bottles and a pillow for her to set on by the grave, and now and then she would cry about Charles Bon in the house, kind of flinging herself on Judith and Judith setting there in her old dress, straightbacked as Cunnel, with her face looking like it did when she come outen Charles Bon's room that morning, until she would stop crying and put some powder on her face and play on the piano and tell Judith how they done in New Orleans to enjoy themselves and how Judith ought to sell this old place and go down there to live.

"Then she went away, setting in the wagon in one of them mosquito-bar dresses too, with that umbrella, crying into the hankcher a while and then waving it at Judith standing there on the porch in that old dress, until the wagon went out of sight. Then Judith looked at me and she said, 'Raby, I'm tired. I'm awful tired.' "

"And I'm tired too. I done toted it a long time now. But we had to look after them chickens so we could put the money in the letter every month—"

"And she still took the money? even after she came and saw, she still took it? And after Judith saw, she still sent it?"

She answered immediately, abrupt, levelvoiced: "Who are you, questioning what a Sutpen does?"

"I'm sorry. When did Henry come home?"

"Right after she left, I carried two letters to the train one day. One of them had Henry Sutpen on it. I knowed how that looked wrote out, too."

"Oh. Judith knew where Henry was. And she wrote him after she saw the woman. Why did she wait until then?"

"Aint I told you Judith knew soon as she saw that woman, same as I knew soon as I saw?"

"But you never did tell me what. What is there about this woman? Dont you see, if you dont tell me that, the story wont make sense."

"It done made enough sense to put three folks in their graves. How much more sense you want it to make?"

"Yes," I said. "And so Henry came home."

"Not right then. One day, about a year after she was here, Judith gave me another letter with Henry Sutpen on it. It was all fixed up, ready to go on the train. 'You'll know when to send it,' Judith said. And I told her I would know the time when it come. And then the time come and Judith said, 'I reckon you can send that letter now' and I said 'I done already sent it three days ago.'

"And four nights later Henry rode up and we went to Judith in the bed and she said, 'Henry. Henry, I'm tired. I'm so tired, Henry.' And we never needed no doctor then and no preacher, and I aint going to need no doctor now and no preacher neither."

"And Henry has been here forty years, hidden in the house. My God."

"That's forty years longer than any of the rest of them stayed. He was a young man then, and when them dogs would begin to get old he would leave at night and be gone two days and come back the next night with another dog just like um. But he aint young now and last time I went myself to get the new dog. But he aint going to need no more dog. And I aint young neither, and I going soon too. Because I tired as Judith, too."

It was quiet in the kitchen, still, blackdark. Outside the summer midnight was filled with insects; somewhere a mockingbird sang. "Why did you do all this for Henry Sutpen? Didn't you have your own life to live, your own family to raise?"

She spoke, her voice not waisthigh, level, quiet. "Henry Sutpen is my brother."

V

We stood in the dark kitchen. "And so he wont live until morning. And nobody here but you."

"I been enough for three of them before him."

"Maybe I'd better stay too. Just in case. . . ."

Her voice came level, immediate: "In case what?" I didn't answer. I could not hear her breathe at all. "I been plenty enough for three of them. I dont need no help. You done found out now. You go on away from here and write your paper piece."

"I may not write it at all."

"I bound you wouldn't, if Henry Sutpen was in his right mind and strength. If I was to go up there now and say, 'Henry Sutpen, here a man going to write in the papers about you and your paw and your sister,' what you reckon he'd do?"

"I dont know. What would he do?"

"Nummine that. You done heard now. You go away from here. You let Henry Sutpen die quiet. That's all you can do for him."

"Maybe that's what he would do: just say, 'Let me die quiet.' "

"That's what I doing, anyway. You go away from here."

So that's what I did. She called the dog to the kitchen window and I could hear her talking to it quietly as I let myself out the front door and went on down the drive. I expected the dog to come charging around the house after me and tree me too, but it didn't. Perhaps that was what decided me. Or perhaps it was just that human way of justifying meddling with the humanities. Anyway, I stopped where the rusted and now hingeless iron gate gave upon the road and I stood there for a while, in the myriad, peaceful, summer country midnight. The lamp in the cabin was black now, and the house too was invisible beyond the cedartunnelled drive, the massed cedars which hid it shaggy on the sky. And there was no sound save the bugs, the insects silversounding in the grass, and the senseless mockingbird. And so I turned and went back up the drive to the house.

I still expected the dog to come charging around the corner, barking. 'And then she will know I didn't play fair,' I thought. 'She will know I lied to her like Charles Bon lied to Henry Sutpen.' But the dog didn't come. It didn't appear until I had been sitting on the top step for some time, my back against a column. Then it was there: it appeared without a sound, standing on the earth below the steps, looming, shadowy, watching me. I made no sound, no move. After a while it went away, as silent as it came. The shadow of it made one slow dissolving movement and disappeared.

It was quite still. There was a faint constant sighing high in the cedars, and I could hear the insects and the mockingbird. Soon there were two of them, answering one another, brief, quiring, risinginflectioned. Soon the sighing cedars, the insects and the birds became one peaceful sound bowled inside the skull in monotonous miniature, as if all the earth were contracted and reduced to the dimensions of a baseball, into and out of which shapes, fading, emerged fading and faded emerging:

"And you were killed by the last shot fired in the war?"

"I was so killed. Yes."

"Who fired the last shot fired in the war?"

"Was it the last shot you fired in the war, Henry?"

"I fired a last shot in the war; yes."

"You depended on the war, and the war betrayed you too; was that it?"

"Was that it, Henry?"

"What was wrong with that woman, Henry? There was something the matter that was worse to you than the marriage. Was it the child? But Raby said the child was nine after Colonel Sutpen died in '70. So it must have been born after Charles and Judith married. Was that how Charles Bon lied to you?"

"What was it that Judith knew and Raby knew as soon as they saw her?"

"Yes."

"Yes what?"

"Yes."

"Oh. And you have lived hidden here for forty years."

"I have lived here forty years."

"Were you at peace?"

"I was tired."

"That's the same thing, isn't it? For you and Raby too."

"Same thing. Same as me. I tried too."

"Why did you do all this for Henry Sutpen?"

"He was my brother."

VI

The whole thing went off like a box of matches. I came out of sleep with the deep and savage thunder of the dog roaring over my head and I stumbled past it and down the steps running before I was good awake, awake at all, perhaps. I remember the thin, mellow, farcarrying negro voices from the cabin beyond the pasture, and then I turned still half asleep and saw the facade of the house limned in fire, and the erstblind sockets of the windows, so that the entire front of the house seemed to loom stooping above me in a wild and furious exultation. The dog, howling,[3] was hurling itself against the locked front door, then it sprang from the porch and ran around toward the back.

I followed, running; I was shouting too. The kitchen was already gone, and the whole rear of the house was on fire, and the roof too; the light, longdried shingles taking wing and swirling upward like scraps of burning paper, burning out zenithward like inverted shooting stars. I ran back toward the front of the house, still yelling. The dog passed me, fulltongued, frantic; as I watched the running figures of negro women coming up across the redglared pasture I could hear the dog hurling itself again and again against the front door.

The negroes came up, the three generations of them, their eyeballs white, their open mouths pinkly cavernous. "They're in there, I tell you!" I was yelling. "She set fire to it and they are both in there. She told me Henry Sutpen would not be alive by morning, but I didn't—" In the roaring I could scarce hear myself, and I could not hear the negroes at all for a time. I could only see their open mouths, their fixed, whitecircled eyeballs. Then the roaring reached that point where the ear loses it and it rushes soundless up and away, and I could hear the negroes. They were making a long, concerted, wild, measured wailing, in harmonic pitch from the treble of the children to the soprano of the oldest woman, the daughter of the woman in the burning house; they might have rehearsed it for years, waiting for this irrevocable moment out of all time. Then we saw the woman in the house.

We were standing beneath the wall, watching the clapboards peel and melt away, obliterating window after window, and we saw the old negress come to the window upstairs. She came through fire and she leaned for a moment in the window, her hands on the burning ledge, looking no bigger than a doll, as impervious as an effigy of bronze, serene, dynamic, musing in the foreground of Holocaust. Then the whole house seemed to collapse, to fold in upon itself, melting; the dog passed us again, not howling now. It came opposite us and then turned and sprang into the roaring dissolution of the house without a sound, without a cry.

I think I said that the sound had now passed beyond the outraged and surfeited ear. We stood there and watched the house dissolve and liquefy and rush upward in silent and furious scarlet, licking and leaping among the wild and blazing branches of the cedars, so that, blazing, melting too, against the soft, mildstarred sky of summer they too wildly tossed and swirled.

VII

Just before dawn it began to rain. It came up fast, without thunder or lightning, and it rained hard all forenoon, lancing into the ruin so that above the gaunt, unfallen chimneys and the charred wood a thick canopy of steam unwinded floated. But after a while the steam dispersed and we could walk among the beams and plank ends. We moved gingerly, however, the negroes in nondescript outer garments against the rain, quiet too, not chanting now, save the oldest woman, the grandmother, who was singing a hymn monotonously as she moved here and there, pausing now and then to pick up something. It was she who found the picture in the metal case, the picture of Judith which Charles Bon had owned. "I'll take that," I said.

She looked at me. She was a shade darker than the mother. But there was still the Indian, faintly; still the Sutpen, in her face. "I dont reckon mammy would like that. She particular about Sutpen property."

"I talked to her last night. She told me about it, about everything. It'll be all right." She watched me, my face. "I'll buy it from you, then."

"It aint none of mine to sell."

"Just let me look at it, then. I'll give it back. I talked to her last night. It'll be all right."

She gave it to me then. The case was melted a little; the lock which Judith had hammered shut for all time melted now into a thin streak along the seam, to be lifted away with a knifeblade, almost. But it took an axe to open it.

The picture was intact. I looked at the face and I thought quietly, stupidly (I was a little idiotic myself, with sleeplessness and wet and no breakfast)—I thought quietly, 'Why, I thought she was blonde. They told me Judith was blonde. . . .' Then I came awake, alive. I looked quietly at the face: the smooth, oval, unblemished face, the mouth rich, full, a little loose, the hot, slumbrous, secretive eyes, the inklike hair with its faint but unmistakable wiriness—all the ineradicable and tragic stamp of negro blood. The inscription was in French: *A mon mari. Toujours. 12 Aout, 1860.*[4] And I looked again quietly at the doomed and passionate face with its thick, surfeitive quality of magnolia petals—the face which had unawares destroyed three lives—and I knew now why Charles Bon's guardian had sent him all the way to North Mississippi to attend school, and what to a Henry Sutpen born, created by long time, with what he was and what he believed and thought, would be worse than the marriage and which compounded the bigamy to where the pistol was not only justified, but inescapable.

"That's all there is in it," the negro woman said. Her hand came out from beneath the worn, mudstained khaki army overcoat which she wore across her shoulders. She took the picture. She glanced once at it before closing it: a glance blank or dull, I could not tell which. I could not tell if she had ever seen the photograph or the face before, or if she was not even aware that she had never seen either of them before. "I reckon you better let me have it."

Notes

1. Cf. "Elly," which also deals with the murdered bridegroom.
2. In the first draft, this duel takes place within or near the house.
3. Cf. howling of Jim Bond at the conclusion of *Absalom, Absalom!*
4. 1859 in early draft, where Raby is named Sukey.

[Sutpen I]

WILLIAM FAULKNER*

After Govelli departs he [Martin] still sits in the chair, motionless, with that immobility of country people, before which patience is no more than a sound without any meaning. He was born and raised on a Mississippi farm. Tenant-farmers—you know: barefoot, the whole family, nine months in the year. He told me about one day his father sent him up to the big house, the house of the owner, the boss, with a message. He went to the front door in his patched overalls, his bare feet: he had never been there before; perhaps he knew no better anyway, to whom a house was just where you kept the quilt pallets and the corn meal out of the rain (he said 'outen the rain'). And perhaps the boss didn't know him by sight; he probably looked exactly like a dozen others on his land and a hundred others in the neighborhood.

Anyway the boss came to the door himself. Suddenly he—the boy—looked up and there within touching distance for the first time was the being who had come to symbolise for him the ease and pleasant ways of the earth: idleness, a horse to ride all day long, shoes all the year round. And you can imagine him when the boss spoke: "Dont you ever come to my front door again. When you come here, you go around to the kitchen door and tell one of the niggers what you want." That was it, you see. There was a negro servant come to the door behind the boss, his eyeballs white in the gloom, and Martin's people and kind, although they looked upon Republicans and Catholics, having never seen either one, probably, with something of that mystical horror which European peasants of the fifteenth century were taught to regard Democrats and Protestants, the antipathy between them and negroes was an immediate and definite affair, being at once biblical, political, and economic: the three compulsions—the harsh unflagging land broken into sparse intervals by spells of demagoguery and religio-neurotic hysteria—which shaped and coerced their gaunt lives. A mystical justification of the need to feel superior to someone somewhere, you see.

*From *Uncollected Stories of William Faulkner* by William Faulkner. © 1979 by Random House, Inc. Reprinted by permission of Random House, Inc. Excerpted from "Big Shot," pp. 507–13 and note, p. 707. This story may contain Faulkner's first sketch of Thomas Sutpen; a subsequent story, "Dull Tale," a revision of "Big Shot," adds the element of suicide.

He didn't deliver the message at all. He turned and walked back down the drive, feeling the nigger's teeth too in the gloom of the hall beyond the boss' shoulder, holding his back straight until he was out of sight of the house. Then he ran. He ran down the road and into the woods and hid there all day, lying on his face in a ditch. He told me that now and then he crawled to the edge of the field and he could see his father and his two older sisters and his brother working in the field, chopping cotton, and he told me it was as though he were seeing them for the first time.

But he didn't go home until that night. I dont know what he told them, what happened; perhaps nothing did. Perhaps the message was of no importance—I cant imagine those people having anything of importance capable of being communicated by words—or it may have been sent again. And people like that react to disobedience and unreliability only when it means loss of labor or money. Unless they had needed him in the field that day, they probably had not even missed him.

He never approached the boss again. He would see him from a distance, on the horse, and then he began to watch him, the way he sat the horse, his gestures and mannerisms, the way he spoke; he told me that sometimes he would hide and talk to himself, using the boss' gestures and tone to his own shadow on the wall of the barn or the bank of a ditch: "Don't you never come to my front door no more. You go around to the back door and tell hit to the nigger. Dont you never come to my front door no more" in his meagre idiom that said 'ye' and 'hit' and 'effen' for 'you' and 'it' and 'if', set off by the aped gestures of that lazy and arrogant man who had given an unwitting death-blow to that which he signified and summed and which alone permitted him breath. He didn't tell me, but I believe that he would slip away from the field, the furrow and the deserted hoe, to lurk near the gate to the big house and wait for the boss to pass. He just told me that he didn't hate the man at all, not even that day at the door with the nigger servant grinning beyond the other's shoulder. And that the reason he hid to watch and admire him was that his folks would think he ought to hate him and he knew he couldn't.

Then he was married, a father, and proprietor of a store at the crossroads. The process must have been to him something like the bald statement: suddenly he was grown and married and owner of a store within long sight of the big house. I dont think he remembered himself the process of getting grown and getting the store anymore than he could remember the road, the path he would traverse to reach the gate and crouch in the brush there in time. He had done it the same way. The actual passing of time, the attenuation, had condensed into a forgotten instant; his strange body—that vehicle in which we ride from one unknown station to another as in a train, unwitting when the engine changes or drops a car here and takes on one there with only a strange new whistle-blast coming back to us—had metamorphosed, inventing for him new minor desires and compulsions to be obeyed and cajoled, conquered or surrendered to or bribed with the small change left over from his unflagging dream while he lay in the weeds at the gate, waiting to see pass the man who knew neither his name nor his face nor that implacable purpose which he—the man—had got upon that female part of every child where ambition lies fecund and waiting.

So he was a merchant, one step above his father, his brothers mesmerised still to the stubborn and inescapable land. He could neither read nor write; he did a credit business in spools of thread and tins of snuff and lap-links and plow-shares, carrying them in his head through the day and reciting them without a penny's error while his wife transcribed them into the cash book on the kitchen table after supper was done.

Now the next part he was a little ashamed of and a little proud of too: his man's nature, the I, and the dream in conflict. It emerged from his telling as a picture, a tableau. The boss was an old man now, gone quietly back to his impotent vices. He still rode about the place a little, but most of the day he spent in his sock feet lying in a hammock between two trees in the yard—the man who had always been able to wear shoes all day long, all year long. Martin told me about that. "That's what I had made up my mind," he said. "Once I had believed that if I could just wear shoes all the time, you see. And then I found that I wanted more. I wanted to work right through the wanting and being able to wear shoes all the time and come out on the other side where I could own fifty pairs at once if I wanted and then not even want to wear one of them." And when he told me that he was sitting in the swivel chair behind the desk, his stocking feet propped in an open drawer.

But to get back to the picture. It is night, an oil lamp burns on an up-ended box in a narrow cuddy; it is the store-room behind the store proper, filled with unopened boxes and barrels, with coils of new rope and pieces of new harness on nails in the wall; the two of them—the old man with his white stained moustache and his eyes that dont see so good anymore and his blue-veined uncertain hands, and the young man, the peasant at his first maturity, with his cold face and the old habit of deference and emulation and perhaps affection (we must love or hate anything to ape it) and surely a little awe, facing one another across the box, the cards lying between them—they used wrought nails for counters—and a tumbler and spoon at the old man's hand and the whiskey jug on the floor in the shadow of the box. "I've got three queens," the boss says, spreading his cards in a palsied and triumphant row. "Beat that, by Henry!"

"Well, sir," the other says, "you had me fooled again."

"I thought so. By Henry, you young fellows that count on the luck all the time. . . ."

The other lays his cards down. His hands are gnarled, plow-warped; he handles the cards with a certain deliberation which at first glance appears stiff and clumsy, so that a man would not glance at them again: certainly not a man whose eyes are dim in the first place and a little fuddled with drink in the second. But I doubt if the liquor was for that purpose, if he depended on it alone. I suspect he was as confident of himself, had taken his slow and patient precautions just as he would have got out and practised with an axe before undertaking to clear up a cypress bottom for profit by the stick. "I reckon I still got it," he says.

The boss has reached for the nails. Now he leans forward. He does it slowly, his trembling hand arrested above the nails. He leans across the table, peering, his movement slowing all the while. It is as though he knows what he will see. It is as though the whole movement were without conviction, as you reach for money in a dream, knowing you are not awake. "Move them closer," he says. "Damn it, do you expect me to read them from here?" The other does so—the 2, 3, 4, 5, 6. The boss looks at them. He is breathing hard. Then he sits back and takes in his trembling hand a cold chewed cigar from the table-edge and sucks at it, making shaking contact between cigar and mouth, while the other watches him, motionless, his face lowered a little, not yet reaching for the nails. The boss curses, sucking at the cigar. "Pour me a toddy," he says.

That's how he got his start. He sold the store and with his wife and infant daughter he came to town, to the city. And he arrived here at just exactly the right time—the year three A. V. Otherwise the best he could have hoped for would have been another store, where at sixty perhaps he could have retired. But now, at only forty-eight (there is a certain irony that oversees the doings of the great. It's as though behind their chairs at whatever table they sit there loom leaning and partisan shadows making each the homely and immemorial gesture for fortune and good luck and whose triumphant shout at each coup roars beneath his own exultation, tossing it high—until one day he turns suddenly himself aghast at the sardonic roar), now at forty-eight he was a millionaire, living with the daughter—she was eighteen; his wife had lain ten years now beneath a marble cenotaph that cost twenty thousand dollars among the significant names in the oldest section of the oldest cemetery: he bought the lot at a bankrupt sale—in four or five acres of Spanish bungalow in our newest subdivision, being fetched each morning by his daughter in a lemon-colored roadster doing forty and fifty miles an hour along the avenue to the touched caps of the traffic policemen, in to the barren office where he would sit in his sock feet and read in the *Sentinel* with cold and biding delusion the yearly list of debutantes at the Chickasaw Guards ball each December.

The Spanish bungalow was recent. The first year they had lived in rented rooms, the second year they moved into—the compulsion of his country rearing—the biggest house he could find nearest the downtown, the street cars and traffic, the electric signs. His wife still insisted on doing her own housework. She still wanted to go back to the country, or, lacking that, to buy one of those tiny, neat, tight bungalows surrounded by infinitesimal lawns and garden plots and aseptic chicken-runs on the highways just beyond the city limits.

But he was already beginning to affirm himself in that picture of a brick house with columns on a broad, faintly dingy lawn of magnolias; he could already tell at a glance the right names—Sandeman, Blount, Heustace—in the newspapers and the city directory. He got the house, paid three prices for it, and it killed his wife. Not the overpurchase of the house, but the watching of that man who heretofore had been superior to all occasions, putting himself with that patient casualness with which he used to hide in the brush near the gate to the big house, in the way of his neighbors, establishing a certain hedge-top armistice with the men while their wives remained cold, turning in and out of the drives in their heavy, slightly outmoded limousines without a glance across the dividing box and privet.

So she died, and he got a couple—Italians—to come in and keep house for him and the girl. Not negroes yet, mind you. He was not ready for them. He had the house, the outward shape and form, but he was not yet certain of himself, not yet ready to affirm in actual practise that conviction of superiority; he would not yet jeopardise that which had once saved him. He had not yet learned that man is circumstance.

The bungalow came five years ago, when he practically gave the house away—he had begun to learn then—and built the new one, the stucco splendor of terraces and patios and wrought iron like the ultimate sublimation of a gasoline station. Perhaps he felt that in this both himself and them—the peasant without past and the black man without future—would have at least a scratch start from very paradox.

This house was staffed by negroes, too many of them; more than he had any use for. He could not bring himself to like them, to be at ease with them: the continuous sad soft murmur of their voices from the kitchen always on the verge of laughter harked him back despite himself, who was saying "Hit aint" for "it is not" and dipping his cheap snuff in the presence of urban politicians and judges and contractors with no subjective qualms whatever, to that day when, feeling the nigger's teeth and eyeballs in the dusky hall, he tramped with stiff back down the drive from the big house and so out of his childhood forever, paced by the two voices, the one saying "You cannot run" and the other "You cannot cry."

[*Ed. note:*

Like "Mistral," "Snow," and "Evangeline," this story employs a first-person narrator and a confidant named Don who shares the narrative function. Don was probably based on William Spratling, the New Orleans friend with whom Faulkner traveled in 1925 to Europe, the scene of the first two stories mentioned above. "The Big Shot" was submitted unsuccessfully to The American Mercury at some time prior to 23 January 1930 and subsequently to four other magazines. The style suggests that it was written after the stories Faulkner wrote in New Orleans but before more mature writing of the later 1920's such as Sartoris. *Elements in this story would appear in several later works.* . . . *Dal Martin is remarkable in his foreshadowing of elements in characters as disparate as Thomas Sutpen, Wash Jones, and Flem Snopes. The slight he receives at the hands of the plantation owner whose tenant his father is anticipates Sutpen's similar traumatic experience, which similarly motivates Sutpen in his determination to acquire possessions which will permit him to rise in the world. Martin's relationship to the plantation owner, particularly as the latter lies in a hammock and drinks toddies mixed by Martin, suggests several scenes between Wash Jones and Thomas Sutpen in* Absalom, Absalom! . . . For further commentary, see Beatrice Lang, "An unpublished Faulkner Story: 'The Big Shot,' " *The Mississippi Quarterly*, XXVI (Summer 1973), 312–24.—*Joseph Blotner*]

[William Faulkner's *Revolt in the Earth*]

Bruce F. Kawin*

In order to assess Faulkner's strengths and weaknesses as a screenwriter, and to discover whatever connections he might have perceived between the aesthetics of film and of fiction, I would now like to examine two of his screenplays in depth. The first, *Revolt in the Earth*, is a loose adaptation of the montage novel, *Absalom, Absalom!* The second, *Dreadful Hollow*, is an original horror film. Neither of these has yet been discussed in print—the first, no doubt, because it is so bad, and the second because no one besides Hawks and myself has seen it. Taken together, these scripts resolve many of the paradoxes of Faulkner's two careers.

By all rights, *Revolt in the Earth* ought to have been a masterpiece. Faulkner's collaborator, Dudley Murphy, was an experimental filmmaker with distinct interests in montage (he photographed Fernand Léger's *Ballet Mécanique* in 1924), in Jungian archetype (he directed the film of O'Neill's *Emperor Jones* in 1933), and in race conflict—all of which are basic to *Absalom*. So for once Faulkner was in a position to collaborate with a filmmaker who might have been receptive to the montage aesthetic of his fiction, and one must wonder at their decision not even to attempt to adapt *Absalom*'s techniques for the screen. Even though *Revolt* is not the average linear script, and includes some interesting experiments with superimposition, visual symbolism, and subjective sound, it is in no way comparable to *Absalom*—not in technique, not in thematic integrity, and hardly even in plot.

In 1934 Faulkner had published the story "Wash," in which he described the relationship between Colonel Thomas Sutpen and the white-trash squatter on his plantation who becomes (after Sutpen is ruined by the Civil War) his drinking companion and storeclerk. When Sutpen impregnates Wash's granddaughter, Wash assumes he will do right by her; it develops, however, that Sutpen is interested in Milly only if she gives birth to a son (so that his estate and lineage will not perish; Sutpen's son, Henry, had been killed in the war). When she delivers a daughter, Sutpen insults and rejects her; Wash kills Sutpen with a scythe. When a posse arrives,

* Reprinted with permission of the author from *Faulkner and Film* (New York: Frederick Ungar Publishing Co., 1977), 126–35. © 1977, 1993 by Bruce F. Kawin. All rights reserved.

Wash kills Milly and the infant, then rushes at the men with his scythe, forcing them to shoot him.

This story formed the germ of *Absalom, Absalom!*, which was published in 1936. In his novel Faulkner explored the reasons for Sutpen's compulsion to have a son survive him, and established that Sutpen himself was of hillbilly origins, an "innocent" like Wash. Sutpen came down from the mountains like the Biblical David, confronted the power structure (a big house from whose door he is turned away by a black servant), and decided that the only way to negate his shame would be to make himself as powerful as the unseen aristocrat: to found and dominate a "House." This obsession, which he calls his "design," leads him first to the Indies, where he sires Charles Bon. When he discovers that Bon's mother is part black, he rejects both of them and returns to the South, where he lays claim to a hundred square miles of forest and swamp ("Sutpen's Hundred"), builds a mansion, and marries the white and respectable Ellen Coldfield. Ellen bears him a son, Henry, and a daughter, Judith. Complications arise when Bon shows up in New Orleans, befriends Henry, and pays court to Judith—all with the intention of forcing Sutpen to acknowledge him as his son. Since Bon, as the eldest, would be heir (and, as part-black, unrespectable), Sutpen instead places on Henry the burden of sending Bon away. The war intervenes, but all three men survive. Henry, who has very little idea of Bon's parentage, shoots him in order to prevent miscegenation; he then flees, leaving Sutpen with the problem of getting another son. By this time Ellen has died, so Sutpen propositions her sister, Rosa Coldfield. When Rosa realizes that he intends to marry her only if their child is male, she rejects him. Eventually, Milly accepts the (perhaps unstated) terms of Sutpen's offer. As in "Wash," Sutpen's rejection of yet another innocent leads to his death.

The figure of Sutpen continues to obsess Rosa, who in 1909 tells her version of this story to Quentin Compson. Quentin, who is in the grips of his loss of Caddy, and who is described as on the verge of becoming a "ghost" himself—of surrendering to his doom, and to the force of the past—identifies with Henry and seeks out the rest of the story from his own father (who tells it rather differently). Quentin and Rosa go out to Sutpen's Hundred, where Clytie (Sutpen's half-black daughter) has been hiding Henry for years; Henry and Quentin meet, in a scene which is delayed till the novel's final chapter. At Harvard, Quentin tells the story to his roommate, Shreve, after he has received a letter from his father informing him of the deaths of Rosa, Clytie, and Henry. Quentin and Shreve then spend a long night filling in the gaps in the story, each spurred on by an identification with both Bon and Henry, and by some power in Sutpen's story that compels itself to be told and uses the boys as its mediums. By the end of the night, Quentin is a mass of ambivalence, and his forthcoming suicide has been much more dynamically motivated than it ever was in *The Sound and the Fury*.

The basic device in *Absalom* is that of a voice turned against itself:

Quentin arguing with ghost-Quentin, Quentin telling and inventing with Shreve, Quentin and Shreve dialectically engaging the power of the self-telling story, and so on. The novel is characterized by an agonized, compulsive rhetoric, and projects the tension of absolute unresolution. In every sentence, Faulkner tries to reflect, restate, and intensify the dialectic of all these forces—"to say it all in one sentence, between one Cap and one period." Although there is not the sudden cutting between past and present that characterizes *The Sound and the Fury*, there is an omnipresent sense of conflict-through-juxtaposition; it is appropriate, then, to call this a montage novel, even if the rhetoric's intent is to transcend fragmentation. The brilliance of the novel depends, in fact, on Faulkner's awareness that such transcendence is impossible, and his consequent attempt to construct the novel for maximum unresolution. His compulsion to "say it all" resembles Sutpen's obsession with his design, Rosa's with Sutpen, and Quentin's with the story; all of them begin with this undifferentiated compulsive stream, find it breaking into fragments (words and scenes) when they try to express it, surge forward in spite of their awareness of necessary failure, and stop only at the point of exhaustion—at which point the tension renews itself, and they try again.

It *would* be possible to tell this story on film, by cutting between the talkers and what they know or invent, by letting the contradictions accumulate, and by exploiting the inherently dialectical nature of classical montage. It would not, however, have been possible to sell such an idea to Warner Brothers in 1942, and that is really the only excuse *Revolt in the Earth* might have. The crucial point about *Revolt* is that it makes it appear unlikely that Faulkner considered film as serious a medium as fiction. Although he might have been aware of the connections between what he and Eisenstein were doing (as *The Wild Palms* suggests), he evidently felt that there was no point in attempting to tell so complex a story on film: or perhaps he simply did not know how to do it. In any case, *Revolt* depends on a condensation and simplification of *Absalom* that is so radical and so downright inane that it might be better to call it an amplification of "Wash."

Whereas Faulkner described *Absalom* to his publisher as "the story of a man who wanted a son through pride, and got too many of them and they destroyed him," he described it to Nunnally Johnson as simply "about miscegenation." Neither is an adequate description, but the latter indicates what Faulkner considered that aspect of the story which could be sold to Hollywood. *Revolt* is not even particularly about miscegenation; its main concern is with voodoo.

Dudley Murphy's *Emperor Jones* had used drumbeats, chants, and double exposure to dramatize the way Jones is hounded by his past—both by his deeds and by his racial unconscious. It is a fairly powerful film, and the odds are that Murphy's directing could have made the voodoo drums, galloping horsebeats, and demonic laughter that punctuate *Revolt* function effectively. Faulkner had already explored (with Nunnally Johnson in *Slave Ship*) the organizing device of the curse: the slave ship begins in blood and must end in blood, as a convenient "old man" prophesies—in person, at the start of that screenplay, and voice-over, at its conclusion. *Revolt*'s entire text, it should be noted, is consistent in style and typography with the rest of Faulkner's Hollywood writings; it is likely that Murphy and Faulkner discussed the project together, but that Faulkner did all the writing.

Revolt has a fairly promising beginning: a fade-in on a marble statue of Colonel Sutpen, banked by "formal yet lush shrubbery. In the background a broad sweep of grounds and colonial mansion. As CAMERA BEGINS TO RETREAT, the sound of a galloping horse begins. The CAMERA PICKS UP Clytie, a child of twelve, a mulatto, who is watching the statue with a grave, rapt, still gaze. Accompanying the hooves, the wraith of a horse and rider crosses the scene between Clytie and the statue. It is gone, but the sound of the galloping hooves continues on through [a] DISSOLVE INTO: INTERIOR OF A NEGRO CABIN." (This is similar to Faulkner's description of Wash's meditation on Sutpen: " . . . thinking went slowly and terrifically, fumbling, involved somehow with a sound of galloping hooves, until there broke suddenly free in mid-gallop the fine proud figure of the man on the fine proud stallion . . .") In the cabin, Clytie has just been born. She is apparently not Sutpen's child, but the devil's, as an old black woman intones. Sutpen, who has stopped in to pay his respects, discounts the idea that "my family is under the displeasure of nigger witch doctors one jump from Africa, eh?" but the old woman's curse is apparently a reflection of the truth: "When de devil spawns on Sutpen land dey'll be a revolt in earth till Sutpen land has swallowed Sutpen birth." What is apparently satanic here is miscegenation; as soon as Sutpen fails to destroy the child, the curse takes hold.

The next scene (which may be in Clytie's memory, or simply a flashback) shows Sutpen's pleasure at the birth of a calf, and his subsequent rejection of Milly's child. Wash attacks Sutpen with a jug, but is beaten back; Wash's whole family, then, survives this encounter, and Wash's great-granddaughter goes on in her turn to have a son, also named Wash.

It is soon established that Sutpen has two legitimate children, Henry and Judith, and that Judith is being courted by Bon (who is no kin to Sutpen). When Henry discovers that Bon has a mulatto mistress and child (as in the novel), he kills Bon so that Judith cannot marry him. Soon afterwards, both Henry and Sutpen are killed in the war. Throughout most of this, a tom-tom has been beating on the soundtrack; now it blends with the drumming of shellfire. The scene of Sutpen's death (with Henry in his arms) dissolves to a voodoo ceremony. Faulkner then cuts to the Sutpen house, which is being overtaken by "jungle," and to the servants' discussion of the "drums in de earth." Upstairs, Judith walks "frantically back and forth to the rhythm of the drums . . . finding each time that she is walking in the rhythm, discovering this with increasing horror each time she breaks her stride." Eventually she runs out to a battlefield, takes a pistol from a dead soldier, and fires at a Yankee officer who "symbolizes the murderer of her father." She misses, and (believe it or not) they marry:

He grasps her, takes the weapon away from her, and holds her. Judith is hysterical. We hear the drums again, and she looks over her shoulder as if she feared they were behind her.

JUDITH: Take me away!

She is in the officer's arms; this pose is electrified into a photograph of the same people in wedding dress. The laughter carries over the—

DISSOLVE TO:

CLYTIE

—again standing looking up at the statue. It has begun to be overgrown and stained. The laughter begins to die away. A musical theme enters. It is martial, and perhaps we hear the bugle call to cease firing which denotes the end of the war. A black man approaches, and the music has in it something of sadness and fortitude. The man tries to attract Clytie's attention, but she doesn't respond. Tom-toms grow out of the music as she continues to watch the statue. . . . Then suddenly Clytie turns with a rhythmic movement almost in time to the music and she and the negro embrace.

DISSOLVE TO:

SOUND OF TOM-TOMS CONTINUES
Out of fading dissolve come the separate birth cries of three children.

The children are born to Milly's daughter, to Clytie, and to Judith. Judith hears tom-toms in the delivery room, and the doctor insists that her Yankee husband take her to Europe. He does so, and Judith becomes a great lady. Clytie gets letters and photos from her, and watches as her own grandson taunts Milly's grandson (Wash) with his disinheritance. Wash, staring at the houseboat where the first Wash lived (a shack, in *Absalom*), becomes obsessed with the notion of carrying out the curse. (He is, of course, a Sutpen too.) Wash grows into a version of Conrad's Mr. Kurtz and makes himself the head of a voodoo cult. He sends his evil influence across the Atlantic and lures the only other surviving Sutpen—Judith's granddaughter, Miriam—back to the old plantation, to her doom.

Miriam, who is the cliché heroine-in-distress, has just married Eric, who exceeds all clichés in his irritating stupidity. Eric wants to study voodoo and takes Miriam back to the States. Judith, hearing the news in the middle of the night, falls down a staircase to her death. A great deal of parallel cutting establishes that Wash is responsible for all this; dissolves and more complex optical effects establish that Clytie is telepathic. At this point Faulkner downplays the fact that Clytie is the "devil's scrub" whose birth occasioned the whole problem and shows her attempts to save Miriam from Wash—mainly by threatening him with the bleeding rib of a pig. Eventually

Miriam is "swallowed" by quicksand, Wash drowns while attempting to get away from Clytie, and Eric loses *some* of his obtuseness. Now that there are no more Sutpens, a snake slides away from the Colonel's statue, and the screenplay ends.

Aside from the fact that *Revolt* does no justice to *Absalom*, it is also an extremely poor horror film. One could make up an interesting analysis of it as "Faulkner's *Heart of Darkness*" or as a "drama of the conflict between the white and half-white Sutpens" or as a "Jungian treatment of racial and generational trauma"—but the screenplay will not support it. Even if by some chance Faulkner had all that on his mind (and the Wash/Kurtz connection seems likely), he made a botch of it. There seems little point in delaying Wash's vengeance on Sutpen with such complex apparatus. When Faulkner showed him the screenplay, Robert Buckner of Warner Brothers wrote him a "private and confidential" telegram; he thanked him, but went on: "Quite frankly, Bill, I cannot imagine your having had any share in it. I think it is a very badly conceived story with no possibilities whatever for a motion picture. I hope if you had nothing to do with it that you will not let it get around with your name on it. Please forgive me if I seem too presumptuous about this, but I have so high a regard for you as a writer that I refuse to be disillusioned."[7] It should be emphasized that Buckner is not reacting to the theme of miscegenation, or the failure of the screenplay to live up to *Absalom*, or any kind of box-office pressure, and that he writes from a position of respect. I see no reason to disagree with his judgment here. *Revolt* has some interesting visual effects and is significant as Faulkner's most formally experimental screenplay; nevertheless, the story *is* badly conceived, the dialogue is ludicrous, and the whole effort has more loose ends than the jungle-growth around Sutpen's statue.

(CON)TEXTS

◆

[The Myth of the Cavalier]

W. J. Cash*

Most of the Virginians who counted themselves gentlemen were [after 1700] still, in reality, hardly more than superior farmers. Many great property-holders were still almost, if not quite, illiterate. Life in the greater part of the country was still more crude than not. The frontier still lent its tang to the manners of even the most advanced, all the young men who were presently to rule the Republic having been more or less shaped by it. And, as the emergence of Jeffersonian democracy from exactly this milieu testifies, rank had not generally hardened into caste.

But this Virginia was not the great South. By paradox, it was not even all of Virginia. It was a narrow world, confined to the areas where tobacco, rice, and indigo could profitably be grown on a large scale—to a relatively negligible fraction, that is, of the Southern country. All the rest, at the close of the Revolution, was still in the frontier or semi-frontier stage. Here were no baronies, no plantations, and no manors. And here was no aristocracy nor any fully established distinction save that eternal one between man and man.

In the vast backcountry of the seaboard states, there lived unchanged the pioneer breed—the unsuccessful and the restless from the older regions; the homespun Scotch-Irish, dogged out of Pennsylvania and Maryland by poverty and the love of freedom; pious Moravian brothers, as poor as they were pious; stolid Lutheran peasants from northern Germany; ragged, throat-slitting Highlanders, lusting for elbow-room and still singing hotly of Bonnie Prince Charlie; all that generally unpretentious and often hard-bitten crew which, from about 1740, had been slowly filling up the region. Houses, almost without exception, were cabins of logs. Farms were clearings, on which was grown enough corn to meet the grower's needs, and perhaps a little tobacco which once a year was "rolled" down to a landing on a navigable stream. Roads and trade hardly yet existed. Life had but ceased to be a business of Indian fighting. It was still largely a matter of coon-hunting, of "painter" tales and hard drinking.

Westward, Boone had barely yesterday blazed his trail. Kentucky and Tennessee were just opening up. And southward of the Nashville basin, the great Mississippi Valley, all that country which was to be Alabama, Mississippi, western Georgia, and northern Louisiana, was still mainly a wasteland, given over to the noble savage and peripatetic traders with an itch for adventure and a taste for squaw seraglios.

Then the Yankee, Eli Whitney, interested himself in the problem of extracting the seed from a recalcitrant fiber, and cotton was on its way to be king. The despised backcountry was coming into its own—but slowly at first. Cotton would release the plantation from the narrow confines of the coastlands and the tobacco belt, and stamp it as the reigning pattern on all the country. Cotton would end stagnation, beat back the wilderness, mow the forest, pour black men and plows and mules along the Yazoo and the Arkansas, spin out the railroad, freight the yellow waters of the Mississippi with panting stern-wheelers—in brief, create the great South. But not in a day. It was necessary to wait until the gin could be proved a success, until experience had shown that the uplands of Carolina and Georgia were pregnant with wealth, until the rumor was abroad in the world that the blacklands of the valley constituted a new El Dorado.

It was 1800 before the advance of the plantation was really under way, and even then the pace was not too swift. The physical difficulties to be overcome were enormous. And beyond the mountains the first American was still a dismaying problem. It was necessary to wait until Andrew Jackson and the men of Tennessee could finally crush him. 1810 came and went, the battle of New Orleans was fought and won, and it was actually 1820 before the plantation was fully on the march, striding over the hills of Carolina to Mississippi—1820 before the tide of immigration was in full sweep about the base of the Appalachians.

From 1820 to 1860 is but forty years—a little more than the span of a single generation. The whole period from the invention of the cotton gin to the outbreak of the Civil War is less than seventy years—the lifetime of a single man. Yet it was wholly within the longer of these periods, and mainly within the shorter, that the development and growth of the great South took place. Men who, as children, had heard the war-whoop of the Cherokee in the Carolina backwoods lived to hear the guns at Vicksburg. And thousands of other men who had looked upon Alabama when it was still a wilderness and upon Mississippi when it was still a stubborn jungle, lived to fight—and to fight well, too—in the ranks of the Confederate armies.

The inference is plain. It is impossible to conceive the great South as being, on the whole, more than a few steps removed from the frontier stage at the beginning of the Civil War. It is imperative, indeed, to conceive it as having remained more or less fully in the frontier stage for a great part— maybe the greater part—of its antebellum history. However rapidly the plantation might advance, however much the slave might smooth the way, it is obvious that the mere physical process of subduing the vast territory which was involved, the essential frontier process of wresting a stable foothold from a hostile environment, must have consumed most of the years down to 1840. . . .

How account for the ruling class, then? Manifestly, for the great part, by the strong, the pushing, the ambitious, among the old coon-hunting population of the backcountry. The frontier was their predestined inheritance. They possessed precisely the qualities necessary to the taming of the land and the building of the cotton kingdom. The process of their rise to power was simplicity itself. Take a concrete case.

A stout young Irishman brought his bride into the Carolina upcountry about 1800. He cleared a bit of land, built a log cabin of two rooms, and sat down to the pioneer life. One winter, with several of his neighbors, he loaded a boat with whisky and the coarse woolen cloth woven by the women and drifted down to Charleston to trade. There, remembering the fondness of his woman for a bit of beauty, he bought a handful of cotton seed, which she planted about the cabin with the wild rose and the honeysuckle—as a flower. Afterward she learned, under the tutelage of a new neighbor, to pick the seed from the fiber with her fingers and to spin it into yarn. Another winter the man drifted down the river, this time to find the halfway station of Columbia in a strange ferment. There was a new wonder in the world— the cotton gin—and the forest which had lined the banks of the stream for a thousand centuries was beginning to go down. Fires flared red and portentous in the night—to set off an answering fire in the breast of the Irishman.

Land in his neighborhood was to be had for fifty cents an acre. With twenty dollars, the savings of his lifetime, he bought forty acres and set himself to clear it. Rising long before day, he toiled deep into the night, with his wife holding a pine torch for him to see by. Aided by his neighbors, he piled the trunks of the trees into great heaps and burned them, grubbed up the stumps, hacked away the tangle of underbrush and vine, stamped out the poison ivy and the snakes. A wandering trader sold him a horse, bony and half-starved, for a knife, a dollar, and a gallon of whisky. Every day now—Sundays not excepted—when the heavens allowed, and every night that the moon came, he drove the plow into the earth, with uptorn roots bruising his shanks at every step. Behind him came his wife with a hoe. In a few years the land was beginning to yield cotton—richly, for the soil was fecund with the accumulated mold of centuries. Another trip down the river, and he brought home a mangy black slave—an old and lazy fellow reckoned of no account in the ricelands, but with plenty of life in him still if you knew how to get it out. Next year the Irishman bought fifty acres more, and the year after another black. Five years more and he had two hundred acres and ten Negroes. Cotton prices swung up and down sharply, but always, whatever the return, it was almost pure velvet. For the fertility of the soil seemed inexhaustible.

When he was forty-five, he quit work, abandoned the log house, which had grown to six rooms, and built himself a wide-spreading frame cottage. When he was fifty, he became a magistrate, acquired a carriage, and built a cotton gin and a third house—a "big house" this time. It was not, to be truthful, a very grand house really. Built of lumber sawn on the place, it was a little crude and had not cost above a thousand dollars, even when the marble mantel was counted in. Essentially, it was just a box, with four rooms, bisected by a hallway, set on four more rooms bisected by another hallway, and a detached kitchen at the back. Wind-swept in winter, it was difficult to keep clean of vermin in summer. But it was huge, it had great columns in front, and it was eventually painted white, and so, in this land of wide fields and pinewoods it seemed very imposing.

Meantime the country around had been growing up. Other "big houses" had been built. There was a county seat now, a cluster of frame houses, stores, and "doggeries" about a red brick courthouse. A Presbyterian parson had drifted in and started an academy, as Presbyterian parsons had a habit of doing everywhere in the South—and Pompeys and Caesars and Ciceros and Platos were multiplying both among the pickaninnies in the slave quarters and among the white children of the "big houses." The Irishman had a piano in his house, on which his daughters, taught by a vagabond German, played as well as young ladies could be expected to. One of the Irishman's sons went to the College of South Carolina, came back to grow into the chief lawyer in the county, got to be a judge, and would have been Governor if he had not died at the head of his regiment at Chancellorsville.

As a crown on his career, the old man went to the Legislature, where he was accepted by the Charleston gentlemen tolerantly and with genuine liking. He grew extremely mellow in age and liked to pass his time in company, arguing about predestination and infant damnation, proving conclusively that cotton was king and that the damnyankee didn't dare do anything about it, and developing a notable taste in the local liquors. Tall and well made, he grew whiskers after the Galway fashion—the well-kept whiteness of which contrasted very agreeably with the brick red of his complexion—donned the long-tailed coat, stove-pipe hat, and string tie of the statesmen of his period, waxed innocently pompous, and, in short, became a really striking figure of a man.

Once, going down to Columbia for the inauguration of a new Governor, he took his youngest daughter along. There she met a Charleston gentleman who was pestering her father for a loan. Her manner, formed by the Presbyterian parson, was plain but not bad, and she was very pretty. Moreover, the Charleston gentleman was decidedly in hard times. So he married her.

When the old man finally died in 1854, he left two thousand acres, a hundred and fourteen slaves, and four cotton gins. The little newspaper which had recently set up in the county seat spoke of him as "a gentleman of the old school" and "a noble specimen of the chivalry at its best"; the Charleston papers each gave him a column; and a lordly Legaré introduced resolutions of respect into the Legislature. His wife outlived him by ten years—by her portrait a beautifully fragile old woman, and, as I have heard it said, with lovely hands, knotted and twisted just enough to give them character, and a finely transparent skin through which the blue veins showed most aristocratically.

[Forms of Plantation Acculturation]

Ulrich Bonnell Phillips*

Two contrasting types of plantations developed upon American soil through the adapting of European institutions to the new geographical conditions. In the West Indies the policy of the Spaniards was to exploit the land through the forced labor of the subjugated natives.[1] Large gangs of Indian slaves were compelled to work in the mines, upon the roads, and in the sugar cane fields. The system of slavery was so extremely harsh that within a few decades the native population of the West Indies had become diminished to within perhaps a tenth of its original numbers. Distressed by this terrible state of things, the Spanish priest Las Casas suggested, about 1518, that negro slaves be imported from Africa to relieve the unbearable hardships of the natives. In quick acceptance of this idea, thousands of negroes were rapidly poured into the West Indies, where they were largely employed in sugar production. When the English settled Barbados, in 1625, and captured Jamaica, in 1655, they borrowed from the Spaniards the system of plantations which the Spaniards had already developed.

These plantations in the English West Indies were of the commercial type, where the predominating purpose of the planter was to get money, and to get it as rapidly as possible. West Indian planters lived in the islands merely for the time being. When they had established their plantations upon a paying basis, they usually left them to overseers and went back to England to spend their income. While the men were making their fortunes in the tropics their mothers and wives and children were mostly at home in England; English families as a rule did not establish English homes upon the West Indian plantations. The proportion of whites in the population of Jamaica and Barbados remained very small; for instance, in 1768 Jamaica had about 17,000 whites and 167,000 negroes. The negroes were not in close enough touch with the whites to be able to adopt their civilization with any degree of rapidity. There were few white families to set examples for the blacks; and in consequence polygamy, paganism, and other savage customs were long continued among the West Indian negroes. . . .

*From *The Slave Economy of the Old South: Selected Essays in Economic and Social History* by Ulrich Bonnell Phillips. © 1968 by Louisiana State University Press. Used with permission. Originally pp. 83–87; originally titled: "The Plantation as a Civilizing Factor." First published in *Sewanee Review* 12 (July 1904): 257–67.

In the colony of Virginia the resort to white indentured servants and the discovery of the value of tobacco production caused the development of the system of patriarchal plantations before the negro became a factor in the situation. The plantation there was not borrowed from the Spaniards, but was developed as a modification of the old English institution of the manor. Involuntary labor was used because labor of any sort was profitable, and hired labor was not to be had so long as there was abundance of free land on the outskirts of settlement. The chief desire of the substantial men of Virginia was to live as English gentlemen lived. They soon found that by resorting to indentured white servants, and later to negro slaves, instead of to serfs, hired labor, and manorial tenants they could establish themselves in something very much like the English manor system, and could gain an honest competence as landowners and managers of agricultural labor.

Negroes gradually replaced the white servants in this system, without causing any substantial change in the general organization. The desire of the planters was not so much to make money and vaunt it in England like the nabobs of the Indies, but to live in comfort as English gentlemen. The Virginians early became noted for generosity, hospitality, and kindliness; and their virtues were not shown to their white guests exclusively. The planters and their families were in close personal association with a large proportion of their servants; and these negroes in the Virginia system of patriarchal plantations had an extraordinary opportunity to acquire habits of industry and the forms of English civilization. A very instructive consideration is that, whereas in the West Indies among able-bodied slaves a freshly imported African would bring about the same price as a negro born and reared upon a sugar plantation, in Virginia even before the eighteenth century a home-grown negro was considered nearly twice as valuable as a fresh African. This contrast gives forcible illustration of the efficiency of the Virginia training school.

Note

1   H. C. Lea, "The Indian Policy of Spain," *Yale Review* (VIII), 119.

[Myth Against History: The Case of Southern Womanhood]

Sarah N. Evans*

Until recent years the idea of "womanhood" in the South was inextricably linked in both history and fiction with the notion of the "southern lady" or her younger counterpart, the "southern belle." Few southern women actually lived the life of the lady or fully embodied her essential qualities: innocence, modesty, morality, piousness, delicacy, self-sacrificial devotion to family, and . . . whiteness. Yet all southern women have been affected by the fusion of sexual imagery with the racial caste system. Southern colonists brought with them the fundamental Western myths about female nature which embodied a polarization between the virgin, pure and untouchable, and the prostitute, dangerously sexual. This dichotomy, associated with images of light and dark, good and evil, gradually took on concrete reality with the emergence of a white planter class based upon a racial slave labor system.

The role of the white lady which emerged in the eighteenth and nineteenth centuries and the dual imagery of the black woman as whore and mammy revealed more about the needs of white planters than about the actual lives of women, white or black. The white lady, revered and sexually repressed, guaranteed the purity of the white race and the future of white civilization. As the symbol of white men's power she was carefully placed on a moral pedestal within the privacy of the home, well out of the realm of politics and public power. Sexual relations between white women and black men violated the most potent social taboo in southern culture. On the other hand, the white man's guilt-ridden sexual access to black women represented a reenactment of the power relationships of slavery. Yet responsibility for the rape of black women was laid at the feet of the victim, who, it was said, was naturally promiscuous. Finally, the black mammy became the nurturant, all-giving mother figure, beloved because she threatened neither hierarchy of race nor sex.

By the middle of the nineteenth century the myth of the Southern lady had become a pillar of the southern defense of slavery. Thus the fusion of

* "Women" by Sarah N. Evans, from *The Encyclopedia of Southern History*, ed. David C. Roller and Robert W. Twyman. © 1979 by Louisiana State University Press. Used with permission. Excerpted.

race and sex created a southern version of the Victorian Cult of True Woman-hood. These dual images of black and white women, which served to maintain the racial caste system and a hierarchical social order, persisted into the twentieth century. Defense of the lady justified racial violence and possibly served as an expiation of white male guilt. And rigid enforcement of the most conservative definitions of sex roles ensured that women would not extend their moral duties beyond the home.

Such myths, clearly, obscured as much as they revealed. The reproductive roles of housewife and mother defined all women, whether they were slaves, wives of yeoman farmers, industrial workers, or plantation mistresses. Yet such roles did not separate them significantly from the basic work of economic production in an economy which remained primarily rural and agrarian from the earliest colonization to World War II.

As slaves, black women provided much of the field labor which enriched Southern society, and they furnished most of the household labor on which the upper-class life-style depended. At the same time they were the central figures in creating and maintaining a unique form of black family structure geared to the exigencies of life under slavery. While they tended the children of the white planter class, they also provided their own children with the emotional support and social skills required for survival and passed on a rich subcultural heritage. Long-term monogamous relationships, highly valued if rare, were characterized by a degree of sexual equality unknown in white society. Southern black women were probably an important source of resistance to the values of white society, and in a few striking cases, such as Harriet Tubman and the Underground Railroad, they led active resistance to the slave system.

Most adult white women before the Civil War were the wives of yeoman farmers. Their families owned few if any slaves. Like black women their lot was one of constant hard work. "Women's work" included gardening, caring for cows and poultry, spinning, weaving, sewing, baking, preserving, and cheese making as well as the routine duties of meal preparation, house-cleaning, and child-rearing. Though field work was considered unseemly for a white woman, such social taboos often weakened in the face of grim necessity. . . .

Ladies of the upper classes had little time for leisure. Most sewed, cooked, cleaned, gardened, tended the sick. On large plantations they administered and supervised the work of an army of household servants. Though they were denied access to a true education and had few legal or political rights, their domestic domain lay at the heart of southern economic life, the plantation. Their administrative duties required the constant exercise of authority in the home while from their pedestals they pretended ignorance of the miscegenation around them.

During and after the carnage of the Civil War women took over and ran farms, shops, and plantations and flocked to cities where they provided a significant war-industry labor force. With a new sense of competence, many would be reluctant to yield to patriarchal authority at the war's end. During the Reconstruction era, while upper-class white men attempted to regain social and political control of southern society through political pressure and KKK terrorism, women directed much of the actual work of "reconstructing" the ravaged economy. On many plantations and farms, war widows had no choice but to forge ahead alone. On others, women simply continued to act with the assurance and authority gained during the wartime experience. Thus white women's self-perceptions diverged increasingly from the prescriptions of delicacy and submission despite the resurrection of a romanticized "Old South" after 1880.

[Southern Women, Southern Households]

Elizabeth Fox-Genovese*

The plantation South would never have existed, much less expanded, had it not been for the capitalist world market. From its origins in the tobacco economy of the seventeenth-century Chesapeake until the development of the cotton belt of the nineteenth-century Deep South, the plantation system grew apace with the development of and demand for staple crops exchanged in the world market. The dimension of change over time is critical. Expansion of the South entailed the extension of slaveholding into newly opened territories. Yet some of the older areas, although they remained in the slaveholding sphere, remained out of or withdrew from the international staple market in favor of greater communal self-sufficiency. The profitability of slavery is not at issue. Although individual planters might withstand depressions in the market by virtue of credit extended by merchants or kin, the system as a whole required profits to survive and expand. At issue remains the nature of the social formation and the characteristic productive relations that produced the staples. The most telling characteristic of southern political economy may well have been that the decisive social relations of production were contained within the household rather than outside it, for the household constituted the dominant unit of production throughout the antebellum era. Not all southern households were plantations or even farms, not all southern households included slaves, and not all slaveholding southern households followed the same economic strategies, but the slave system and the household reinforced each other to discourage capitalist development. . . .

The figure of the lady, especially the plantation mistress, dominated southern ideals of womanhood. That slaveholding ladies were massively outnumbered by nonslaveholding or small-slaveholding women challenges any easy assumptions about the relation between the ideal and reality but does not undermine the power of the ideal. The temptation to demystify the figure of the lady has proved almost irresistible. It has been argued that the plantation mistress closely resembled slave women in being the victim of the double burden of patriarchy and slavery. According to this view,

*Reprinted from *Within the Plantation Household: Black and White Women of the Old South*, by Elizabeth Fox-Genovese. © 1988 by The University of North Carolina Press. Used by permission of the author and publisher.

southern ladies, isolated on plantations and condemned to bear many children, endured husbands who whored in the slave quarters and slaves who combined sauciness with sloth and indifference. It has been, if anything, more seductive to reason that ladies, who themselves suffered male domination, were the primary, if secret, critics of their society—nothing less than closet feminists and abolitionists who saw slavery as a "monstrous system." "Poor women, poor slaves," in the widely quoted words of Mary Boykin Chesnut. But most ladies, like Mary Chesnut herself, were hardly prepared to do without slaves and enthusiastically supported secession. Above all, they did not advance an alternate model of womanhood. The North, too, had its ladies and fashionable women, but northern society preferred to celebrate the virtues of domesticity over those of privilege. . . .

The history of slave women, like that of the women of other oppressed groups, races, nations, and classes, demonstrates how dangerous it can be to study women in isolation from the interlocking systems of class, gender, and race relations that constitute any society. By modern feminist standards, slave women did escape some of the fetters of privilege that imprisoned white northern women. But surely they did not escape the larger constraints imposed by life in a slave society. Nor is there any reason to believe that they, any more than their men, escaped a heavy dose of cultural domination, even though they might appropriate, reinterpret, and turn to their own advantage those distinct elements of white culture that they could assimilate into an Afro-American culture of their own making. What can be the political and cultural moral of the story of slave women's purported independence? Did that independence materially free them from their own enslavement? From the perspective of Afro-Americans as a people, should the independence of women be interpreted as a collective gain, or merely as the confirmation of slave men's weakness relative to white men? Nothing can be gained by pretending that these complexities do not exist. Even the recognition of black women's "double" oppression and their uniquely creative solutions to the problems that confront all women cannot explain away the consequences of the enslavement of black men for black women's identities. . . .

[Miscegenation]

SIDNEY KAPLAN*

A little before Christmas of 1863 there appeared for sale on newsstands in New York City a seventy-two-page pamphlet, costing a quarter and bearing the enigmatic title, *Miscegenation: The Theory of the Blending of the Races, Applied to the American White Man and Negro.*[1] This pamphlet, a curious hash of quarter-truths and pseudo-learned oddities, was to give a new word to the language and a refurbished issue to the Democratic Party—although its anonymous author, for good reason perhaps, never came forward to claim his honors. In the welter of leaflets, brochures, cards, tracts and cartoons struck off by all parties during the Civil War, it stands out as centrally significant.

Miscegenation is a disorganized piece of work, difficult to summarize briefly.[2] With a flourish of scholarship on his very first page the pamphleteer defines the "new words" he finds necessary to coin in order to present his argument. The first is *miscegenation* (from the Latin *miscere*, to mix, and *genus*, race) with its derivatives, *miscegen*, *miscegenate* and *miscegenetic*; the second—a more precise neologism—is *melaleukation* (from the Greek *melas*, black, and *leukos*, white) with its derivatives, *melaleukon* and *melaleuketic*, "to express the idea of the union of the white and black races."[3]

Having disposed of his definitions, the author gets his argument rapidly under way. Science and Christianity have proved beyond doubt "that all the tribes which inhabit the earth were originally derived from one type." Dr. Draper of New York University, Camper of Gröningen, Aristotle, Galen, Dr. Pritchard and Baron Larrey have established the "physiological equality of the white and colored races." Furthermore, if "any fact is well established in history, it is that the miscegenetic or mixed races are much superior, mentally, physically, and morally, to those pure or unmixed." Don Felix De Azara, Pallas, Moodie, Laurence, Dr. Hancock, Dallas and Walker have confirmed this fact. The English are great because they are composite; the French—who invented divorce—were originally a blend; they intermarried and decayed; thus the two most brilliant writers France can boast of are "the

*Excerpted from Sidney Kaplan, "The Miscegenation Issue in the Election of 1864," in *Journal of Negro History*, 34, no. 3 (1949): 277–84; the essay is copyright and reprinted with permission from the Association for the Study of Afro-American Life and History.

97

melaleukon, Dumas, and his son, a quadroon." The peoples of Sicily and Naples have inbred, and are therefore "probably the lowest people, except the Irish, in the scale of civilization in Europe . . . brutal, ignorant and barbarous," while the "most promising nation in Europe is the Russian, and its future will be glorious, only because its people represents a greater variety of race than any other in Europe." American vitality comes "not from its Anglo-Saxon progenitors, but from all the different nationalities" of the melting-pot. "All that is needed to make us the finest race on earth is to engraft upon our stock the negro element; the blood of the negro is the most precious because it is the most unlike any other that enters into the composition of our national life."

The truth is that "no race can long endure without commingling of its blood with that of other races." Human progress itself depends on miscegenation and "Providence has kindly placed on the American soil . . . four millions of colored people" for that purpose. It will be "our noble prerogative to set the example of this rich blending of blood."

> It is idle to maintain that this present war is not a war for the negro . . . it is a war, if you please, of amalgamation . . . a war looking, as its final fruit, to the blending of the white and black. . . . Let the war go on . . . until church, and state, and society recognize not only the propriety but the necessity of the fusion of the white and black—in short, until the great truth shall be declared in our public documents and announced in the messages of our Presidents, that it is desirable the white man should marry the black woman and the white woman the black man—that the race should become melaleuketic before it becomes miscegenetic.

The next step is to open California to the swarming millions of eastern Asia. The patience and skill of the Japanese and Chinese in the mechanic arts must be blended into "the composite race which will hereafter rule this continent."

The Indian has shown—and the physiologists have affirmed—that copper is the permanent American skin-color; indeed, the "white race which settled New England will be unable to maintain its vitality as a blonde people." The proof is that tuberculosis in "our Eastern States is mainly confined to the yellow-haired and thin-blooded blondes. . . ." Ultimately, black will absorb white; it is a truth of nature. The conquest of Britain by Rome illustrates the fact that all the "noted ancient and modern wars of Europe may be traced to the yearning of the brunette and blonde to mingle." Americans must become "a yellow-skinned, black-haired people—in fine . . . miscegens. . . ."

How solve the mystery of the Pyramids? What answer give to the question of the Sphynx? It is the "principle of Miscegenation in ancient Egypt"; civilization, science and art are the creations of "the miscegenetic mind developed upon the banks of the Nile, by Asiatics and Africans." The Jews themselves "were partly of Abyssinian or negro origin." The conclusion is clear: "Let us then embrace our black brother" in America. Perfect religion and perfect mankind will be the results, for "the ideal or type man of the future will blend in himself all that is passionate and emotional in the darker races, all that is imaginative and spiritual in the Asiatic races, and all that is intellectual and perceptive in the white races." He will be "brown, with reddish cheeks, curly and waving hair, dark eyes, and a fullness and suppleness of form not now dreamed of by any individual people." Adam and Christ were type-men, or miscegens, red or yellow.

Furthermore, the mutual love of black and white is based on the natural law of the attraction of opposites. For example, the "sympathy Mr. Greeley feels for the negro is the love which the blonde bears for the black . . . stronger than the love they bear to women." The Abolitionist leaders furnish additional examples: his complexion "reddish and sanguine," Wendell Phillips is one of the "sharpest possible contrasts to the pure negro." Theodore Tilton, "the eloquent young editor of the Independent, who has already achieved immortality by advocating enthusiastically the doctrine of miscegenation, is a very pure specimen of the blonde." That black loves blonde is shown also by the number of "rape cases in the courts and by the experience of Southern plantations." The only remedy is "legitimate melaleuketic marriage." Give nature a free course and men and women, "whether anti-slavery or pro-slavery, conservative or radical, democratic or republican, will marry the most perfect specimens of the colored race. . . ." This natural passion is "the secret of the strange infatuation of the Southern woman with the hideous barbarism of slavery. Freedom, she knows, would separate her forever from the colored man. . . . It is idle for Southern woman to deny it; she loves the black man, and the raiment she clothes herself with is to please him. . . ."

All this is only preparation. For it is with the specific relationship of the Irish working-people and the Negro—the New York draft riots of the previous summer were fresh in the memory of the country—that the pamphleteer is especially concerned. "Notwithstanding the apparent antagonism which exists between the Irish and negroes on this continent"

> there are the strongest reasons for believing that the first movement towards a melaleuketic union will take place between these two races. Indeed, in very many instances it has already occurred. Wherever there is a poor community of Irish in the North they naturally herd with the poor negroes . . . connubial relations are formed between the black men and white Irish women . . . pleasant to both parties, and were it not for the unhappy prejudice which exists, such unions would be very much more frequent. The white Irishwoman loves the black man, and in the old country . . . the negro is sure of the handsomest among the poor white females. . . . The fusion, whenever it takes place, will be of infinite service to the Irish. They are a more brutal race and

lower in civilization than the negro . . . coarse-grained, revengeful, unintellec-
tual . . . below the level of the most degraded negro. Take an equal number
of negroes and Irish from among the lowest communities of the city of New
York, and the former will be found far superior to the latter in cleanliness,
education, moral feelings, beauty of form and feature, and natural sense. . . .

The "prognathous skull, the projecting mouth, the flat and open nostril"
are characteristic of the "inhabitants of Sligo and Mayo." With education
"and an intermingling with the superior black, the Irish may be lifted up
to something like the dignity of their ancestors, the Milesians. . . ." There
is only one correct course: the Irish should put aside prejudice toward their
"dark-skinned fellow-laborers and friends and proclaim intermarriage with
the Negro as a solution to their problem."

Do the Irish object to this prognosis? They ought not. Observe the
noblemen produced by nature in the Southern aristocracy. Yet the "truth
may as well be understood, that the superiority of the slaveholding classes
of the South arises from their intimate communication, from birth to death,
with the colored race. . . ." It is notorious that, "for three generations back,
the wealthy, educated, governing class of the South have mingled their blood
with the enslaved race." The "emotional power, fervid oratory and intensity
which distinguishes all thoroughbred slaveholders is due to their intimate
association with the most charming and intelligent of their slave girls." In
fact, "legal melaleukation will be first openly adopted in the slave States."
The large cities of the South, New Orleans especially, even now swarm
with mulattoes, quadroons and octoroons, and the "unions producing these
mixtures will be continued under the sanctions of public opinion, law, and
religion."

His preamble completed, the pamphleteer is now ready for his main
point. What is the meaning, he asks, of all these "scientific" and "historical"
data for 1864, the fateful year in which the North must choose a new
president? Only this—emancipation means amalgamation: the party of Abo-
lition is "the party of miscegenation." True, the "people do not yet understand" the point and the "party as a whole" will not admit it. But there is
still hope that opinion will change, for the "leaders of Progress"—among
them Phillips and Tilton—"urge miscegenetic reform" and the "people are
ripe to receive the truth." What must be recognized is that the Republican
Party "will not perform its whole mission till it throws aloft the standard
of Miscegenation."

Yet examine the platform of the Chicago Convention—how meager it
is on this vital subject. Nowhere does it acknowledge the fact that "miscegenation reform should enter into the approaching presidential contest." Is it,
however, too late to add the miscegenation plank to the platform? Not at all,
maintains the pamphleteer in a grand finale: let Abraham Lincoln candidly
proclaim that "the solution of the negro problem will not have been reached

in this country until public opinion sanctions a union of the two races . . . that in the millenial future, the most perfect and highest type of manhood will not be white or black but brown, or colored, and that whoever helps to unite the various races of man, helps to make the human family the sooner realize its great destiny. . . ." And although the Democrats attempt "to divert discussion to senseless side issues, such as peace, free speech, and personal and constitutional rights," let the motto of "the great progressive party of this country be Freedom, Political and Social Equality; Universal Brotherhood."

Excerpts from "amalgamationist" speeches delivered by Theodore Tilton and Wendell Phillips in May and July of 1863, a few lines from a book review of Wilson's *Prehistoric Man*, a selection from an article in the *Independent* on the "intermingling of Colors and Sexes at Oberlin University," and a quotation from Harriet Beecher Stowe's novel *Dred*—a description of Harry and Lisette under the title of "Pen-Portrait of a Miscegenetic Woman and Man"—bring the pamphlet to a close.

So much for the pamphlet itself. The author, apparently an impassioned— even learned—Abolitionist, preferred to remain anonymous. Yet he was proud of his work. So, on Christmas Day, 1863, he mailed out complimentary copies of his little tract to a number of prominent anti-slavery leaders throughout the country. Tucked into each copy was a warm and friendly letter which, after noting that the doctrine of miscegenation might be "in advance of the times," asked the distinguished recipient for an opinion of its merits. There was nothing unusual in the practice; so Emerson had discovered Whitman. Replies were to be addressed to the "Author of 'Miscegenation,' " in care of his Nassau Street publishers.

Now the curious thing about this ostensibly Abolitionist tract was that it was *not* written by an Abolitionist at all. As a matter of fact it was conceived by two clever journalists in the offices of Manton Marble's violently anti-Abolitionist New York *World*—a newspaper which, in the words of the historian Rhodes, was "the ablest and most influential Democratic journal in the country, the organ of the high-toned Democrats of New York City and State. . . ."[4] David Goodman Croly, managing editor of this quasi-Copperhead sheet, and his young friend, George Wakeman, a reporter on its staff, were the joint, forever unconfessed, authors of the pamphlet, *Miscegenation*. Croly himself footed the printing bill.[5]

Notes

1. New York, 1863; hereinafter referred to as *Miscegenation*.
2. The quotations in the summary that follows are taken *passim* from the pamphlet.
3. The current expression, *amalgamation*, was, according to the author, a "poor word"

since it properly referred to the "union of metals with quicksilver, and was, in fact, only borrowed for an emergency, and should now be returned to its proper signification." Said the London *Morning Herald* of November 1, 1864: "Whatever good or evil the authors of 'Miscegenation' may have done in a political way, they have achieved a sort of reflected fame on the coining of two or three new words—at least one of which is destined to be incorporated into the language. Speakers and writers of English will gladly accept the word 'Miscegenation' in the place of the word amalgamation. . . ." A *Dictionary of American English* makes a curious typographic error in one of the historical citations attached to its definition of *miscegenation*. The citation—an excerpt from M. Schele De Vere's *Americanisms* (1872), 288–289—is printed in the *DAE* as follows: "I was one . . . who first publicly used the illshapen word miscegenation, and openly dared to advocate the expediency of favoring, by every agency of State and Church, the mingling of the black and white races." Can this mean that De Vere (Professor of Modern Languages at the University of Virginia in 1872) was a miscegenationist—a startling thought, since a reading of his book reveals him as an unreconciled champion of the Confederacy. The matter is clarified by an examination of De Vere's text, where, following a partisan definition of scalawags as the "evidently dishonest among the Southerners, who went over to the dominant party, and unblushingly lived on their conquered friends and neighbors," the citation in question appears as follows: "It was one of this class, rather than the eloquent advocate of Women's Rights [Wendell Phillips] often charged with the crime, who first publicly used the illshapen word miscegenation, and openly dared to advocate the expediency of favoring, by every agency of State and Church, the mingling of the black and white races." De Vere, of course, was wrong. *Miscegenation* originated in the pamphlet of that title in 1863, as is recognized by the *New English Dictionary*; its brother word, *melaleukation*, did not "take" from the start.

4.   James Ford Rhodes, *History of the United States* (New York, 1906), IV, 471. In its editorial box, the *World* described itself as "a sound Democratic newspaper" with 100,000 subscribers and half a million readers.

5.   *The Dictionary of American Biography*, Sabin's *Dictionary* and the Library of Congress catalogue err in listing one E. C. Howell as a third author. Howell (whose correct initials are S. C.) was city editor of the *World* while Croly was managing editor but probably took no part in writing the pamphlet. (*Real Estate Record & Builders Guide*, XLIII [May 4, 1889], 613–614.)

[The War for States' Rights]

THE SURVIVORS' ASSOCIATION OF LAMAR RIFLES*

Again, as early as 1793, Mr Pickering, a member of Washington's Cabinet, and subsequently a United States Senator from Massachusetts, proposed that the New England States, New York, Pennsylvania, and New Jersey, should form a Northern Confederacy. No one objected, but it was finally not considered expedient to do so, and the subject was dropped.

Again, the Hartford Convention, called at the instance of Massachusetts in the year 1814, was for the purpose of considering the propriety of the New England States seceding from the Union, and forming a Northern or Eastern Confederacy. Some of these States not only refused to comply with the request for men and means to carry on the war, then in progress with Great Britain, but actually gave aid and comfort to the enemy. This was practical secession. But the war soon terminated successfully for the United States and the purpose of forming a Northern Confederacy was again abandoned.

During these movements to form a separate government by the New England States their abstract and constitutional right to do so was not denied by any of the other States of the Union, or by the general Government. Indeed, until about 1830 the right of the States to withdraw from the Union was never questioned by any statesman, North or South. From that time down to 1860 the question was not a subject of political discussion, but as late as 1844 Massachusetts, by resolution of its Legislature, threatened to secede if Texas was admitted into the Union as a slave State. Texas was so admitted, but Massachusetts did not secede.

Finally in 1860, after the South had endured heavy tariffs for the protected industries of the North for a generation; after thirteen of the Northern States had enacted "Personal Liberty Laws" in conflict with the Federal Constitution, and in violation of the terms and spirit and purpose for which the Union had been formed; and after the election of a Northern President upon a strictly sectional issue, one who declared that the Union could not continue "half free and half slave," thereby indicating a desire to abolish slavery in the face of the Constitution that authorized and protected

*Reprinted with permission from *Lamar Rifles: A History of Company G, Eleventh Mississippi Regiment, C. S. A.* (Oxford, Miss.: n.p., 1901; rep. Topeka: Bonnie Blue Press, 1992), 10–11.

it; eleven of the Southern States, acting upon their inherent and reserved right of sovereignty, withdrew from the Union and formed a separate government. Whereupon, the North inaugurated the most cruel and relentless war of invasion, spoliation, and subjugation against the South—a war in which every usage and custom of civilized warfare was violated, and barbarities perpetrated that would have disgraced the Apache Indians of forty years ago.

The fundamental purpose of the North in this war was to preserve and increase her commercial interests. The South at that time was strictly an agricultural country; the North, and especially New England, was largely a manufacturing section; and if the South had been allowed to exercise her constitutional right to independence, and establish a separate government, she would have opened free trade with the markets of Europe, and this would have tended to paralyze, if not pauperize the manufacturing establishments of the North. And this was more than Northern cupidity and Northern lust for power could bear. Hence the war of invasion and subjugation by the North.

After four years of gallant resistance in defense of her constitutional and inherent right to independence, the South was overwhelmed by the superior numbers and resources of the North, aided by the world, upon which she drew largely for both men and material. And thus the beautiful principle asserted in the Declaration of Independence, "That governments derive their just powers from the consent of the governed," was stricken down and annihilated, and a doctrine of force enthroned in its stead, and which doctrine is still dominant, as illustrated in the recent history and present condition of Porto Rico and the Philippine Islands.

(SUB)TEXTS

◆

Early Understandings

♦

Witchcraft in Mississippi

Bernard DeVoto*

Mr. Faulkner's new fantasia [*Absalom, Absalom!*] is familiar to us in every-thing but style. Although the story is told in approximations which display a magnificent technical dexterity—more expert than Mr. Dos Passos's, and therefore the most expert in contemporary American fiction—and although the various segments are shredded and displaced, it is not a difficult story to follow. It is not, for instance, so darkly refracted through distorting lenses as "The Sound and the Fury." Though plenty of devices are employed to postpone the ultimate clarification, none are introduced for the sole purpose of misleading the reader, and in an access of helpfulness, Mr. Faulkner has included not only an appendix of short biographies which make clear all the relationships, but also a chronological chart which summarizes the story. If you study both of them before beginning the book, you will have no trouble.

Thomas Sutpen, the demon of this novel, has a childhood racked by the monstrous cruelties to which all Faulkner children are subjected. He has immeasurable will—like evil, will is always immeasurable in Faulkner. He forms a "design": to found a fortune and a family. In pursuit of it he marries the daughter of a Haitian planter, has a son by her, discovers that she has Negro blood, abandons her, and rouses in her a purpose of immeasurable revenge. He takes some Haitian slaves to Mississippi, clears a plantation, becomes rich, marries a gentlewoman, and begets Henry and Judith. At the

*Reprinted from *Saturday Review of Literature* 15 (31 October 1936): 3–4, 14.

University Henry meets his mulatto half-brother, Charles Bon, who has been sent there by his vengeful mother, who knows the secret of his parentage, and who is married to a New Orleans octoroon. Henry worships Charles at sight and helps to effect his engagement to Judith. Thomas Sutpen inconceivably does nothing to prevent the engagement till, just before the Civil War, he tells Henry the secret of Bon's birth, though not (and here again the motive is what Mr. Faulkner would call unmotive) that of his Negro blood. Through four years of war Henry remains jubilant about the contemplated incest, but when his father at last reveals the secret he cannot accept incestuous miscegenation, and so shoots Bon when he goes to claim his bride. Henry then disappears and Thomas Sutpen, still demonic, comes back to rehabilitate both his estate and his posterity. He informs the sister of his dead wife (who also was tortured in childhood and hates all men, though she contrives to desire two of them) that if he can succeed in begetting a male child on her, he will marry her. Being a Southern gentlewoman, she declines, and Sutpen begets a child on the fifteen-year old granddaughter of a poor-white retainer. The child is a daughter and so Sutpen's design is ruined forever. The grandfather kills him with a scythe, kills the granddaughter and the child with a butcher's knife, and rushes happily into the arms of the lynchers. The relicts then send for Charles Bon's son and raise him, a mulatto, with further tortures. He rebels, marries a coal-black wench, and begets a semi-idiot, the last of the Sutpens who gives a tragic twist to the title of the novel. The horror which Quentin Compson has to undergo occurs many years later, when Henry Sutpen has crept back to die in the ruined mansion, cared for by the shrivelled Clytie, another mulatto of Thomas's get. Henry and Clytie are burned up in the final holocaust, the ritualistic destruction of the house of hell and doom that is in part repeated from "Light in August."

Mr. Faulkner, in fact, has done much of this before. This off-stage hammering on a coffin—Charles Bon's coffin this time—was used to make us liquefy with pity in "As I Lay Dying" where it was Addie Bundren's coffin. And when Addie's coffin, with the corpse inside, slid off the wagon into the flooded river, the effect then gained discounted the scene in "Absalom, Absalom!" where the mules bolt and throw Thomas Sutpen's corpse and coffin into the ditch. Much of Henry Sutpen's ambiguous feeling for his sister Judith was sketched in Quentin Compson's attitude toward Candace. When Charles Bon forces Henry Sutpen to shoot him, moved by some inscrutable inertia of pride and contempt and abnegation (or moved by unmotive)—he is repeating whatever immolation was in Popeye's mind when he refused to defend himself against the murder charge of which he was innocent, near the end of "Sanctuary." These are incidental repetitions, but many fundamental parts of "Absalom, Absalom!" seem to come straight out of "Light in August." It is not only that Etienne Bon undergoes in childhood cruelties as unceasing as those that made Joe Christmas the most persecuted child since Dickens, not only that he is moved by the same necessity to wreak both revenge and forgiveness on both black and white that moved Joe, not only that he commits some of the same defiances in the same terms, and not only that the same gigantic injustices are bludgeoned on the same immeasurable stubbornness and stupidity in the same inexplicable succession. It is deeper than that and comes down to an identity of theme. That theme is hardly reducible to words, and certainly has not been reduced to words by Mr. Faulkner. It is beyond the boundary of explanation: some undimensional identity of fear and lust in which a man is both black and white, yet neither, loathing both, rushing to embrace both with some super-Tolstoian ecstasy of abasement, fulfillment, and expiation.

The drama of "Absalom, Absalom!" is clearly diabolism, a "miasmal distillant" of horror, with clouds of sulphur smoke billowing from the pit and flashes of hellish lightning flickering across the steady phosphorus-glow of the graveyard and the medium's cabinet. And it is embodied in the familiar hypochondria of Mr. Faulkner's prose, a supersaturated solution of pity and despair. In book after book now he has dropped tears like the famed Arabian tree, in a rapture of sensibility amounting to continuous orgasm. The medium in which his novels exist is lachrymal, and in "Absalom, Absalom!" that disconsolate fog reaches its greatest concentration to date. And its most tortured prose. Mr. Faulkner has always had many styles at his command, has been able to write expertly in many manners, but he has always been best at the phrase, and it is as a phrase-maker only that he writes well here. Many times he says the incidental thing perfectly, as "that quiet aptitude of a child for accepting the inexplicable." But, beyond the phrase, he now—deliberately—mires himself in such a quicksand of invertebrate sentences as has not been seen since "Euphues." There have been contentions between Mr. Faulkner and Mr. Hemingway before this; it may be that he is matching himself against the Gertrude-Steinish explosions of syntax that spattered "Green Hills of Africa" with bad prose. If so, he comes home under wraps: the longest Hemingway sentence ran only forty-three lines, whereas the longest Faulkner sentence runs eighty lines and there are more than anyone will bother to count which exceed the thirty-three line measure of his page. They have the steady purpose of expressing the inexpressible that accounts for so much of Mr. Faulkner, but they show a style in process of disintegration. When a narrative sentence has to have as many as three parentheses identifying the reference of pronouns, it signifies mere bad writing and can be justified by no psychological or esthetic principle whatever.

It is time, however, to inquire just what Mr. Faulkner means by this novel, and by the whole physiography of the countryside which he locates on the map of Mississippi in the vinicity of a town called Jefferson. This community is said to be in the geographical and historical South, and the Sutpens, together with the Compsons and the Sartorises and the Benbows and the Poor Whites and the Negroes, are presented to us as human beings.

Yet even the brief summary I have made above shows that if we are forced to judge them as human beings we can accept them only as farce. Just why did not Thomas Sutpen, recognizing Charles Bon as his mulatto son, order him off the plantation, or bribe or kill him, or tell Judith either half of the truth, or tell Henry all of it? In a single sentence toward the end of the book, Mr. Faulkner gives us an explanation, but it is as inadequate to explain the tornadoes that depend on it as if he had tried to explain the Civil War by the annual rainfall at New Granada. Not even that effort at explanation is made for most of the behavior in the book. Eulalia Bon's monotone of revenge is quite inconceivable, and her demonic lawyer is just one more of those figures of pure bale that began with Januarius Jones in "Soldiers' Pay" and have drifted through all the novels since exhaling evil and imitating the facial mannerisms of the basilisk. Miss Rosa (another Emily, without rose) is comprehensible neither as a woman nor as a maniac. Why do the children suffer so? Why did Rosa's father treat her that way? Why did Sutpen treat Henry and Judith that way? Why did Judith and Clytie treat Etienne that way? Just what revenge or expiation was Etienne wreaking on whites and Negroes in that Joe Christmas series of attempts at self-immolation? Just what momentary and sacrificial nobility moved Wash Jones to kill three people? Just what emotion, compulsion, obsession, or immediate clairvoyant pattern of impotence plus regeneration plus pure evil may be invoked to explain the behavior of Charles Bon, for which neither experience nor the psychology of the unconscious nor any logic of the heart or mind can supply an explanation?

Well, it might answer everything to say that they are all crazy. As mere symptomatology, their behavior does vividly suggest schizophrenia, paranoia, and dementia precox. But that is too easy a verdict, it would have to be extended to all the population of Jefferson, the countryside, New Granada, and New Orleans, and besides the whole force of Mr. Faulkner's titanic effort is expended in assuring us that this is not insanity.

A scholarly examination might get us a little farther. This fiction of families destroyed by a mysterious curse (beginning with the Sartorises, there has been one in every novel except "As I Lay Dying" and "Pylon"), of ruined castles in romantic landscapes, of Giaours and dark "unwill," may be only a continuation of the literature of excessive heartbreak. The Poe of "Ligeia" and kindred tales, Charles Brockden Brown, Horace Walpole, and Mrs. Radcliffe suggest a clue to a state of mind which, after accepting the theorem that sensation is desirable for itself alone, has moved on to the further theorem that the more violent sensation is the more admirable, noble, and appropriate to fiction. Surely this reek of hell and the passage to and fro of demons has intimate linkages with Eblis; surely Vathek saw this ceaseless agony, this intercellular doom, and this Caliph's heart transparent as crystal and enveloped in flames that can never be quenched. Surely; and yet that tells us very little.

Much more central is the thesis advanced in these columns a couple of years ago, that Mr. Faulkner is exploring the primitive violence of the unconscious mind. Nothing else can explain the continuity of rape, mutilation, castration, incest, patricide, lynching, and necrophilia in his novels, the blind drive of terror, the obsessional preoccupation with corpses and decay and generation and especially with the threat to generation. It is for the most part a deliberate exploration, Mr. Faulkner is at pains to give us Freudian clues, and he has mapped in detail the unconscious mind's domain of horrors, populated by anthropophagi, hermaphrodites, Hyppogypi, acephalites, and cynocephalites. It is the world of subliminal guilt and revenge, the land of prodigy which D. H. Lawrence thought was peopled exclusively by beautiful, testicular athletes, but which is inhabited instead by such races as Mandeville and Carpini saw. These are the dog-faced men, the men whose heads do grow beneath their shoulders, who feed on corpses, who hiss and bark instead of talking, whose custom it is to tear their own bowels. A far country, deep under the mind's frozen ocean. In Mr. Faulkner's words, a "shadowy miasmic region," "amoral evil's undeviating absolute," "quicksand of nightmare," "the seething and anonymous miasmal mass which in all the years of time has taught itself no boon of death."

Haunted by the fear of impotence and mutilation and dismemberment, hell-ridden by compulsions to destroy the mind's own self and to perpetuate a primal revengeful murder on the old, cataleptic in the helplessness of the terrified young, bringing the world to an end in a final fantasy of ritual murder and the burning house—the inhabitants of the prodigy-land of the unconscious are also fascinated by those other primal lusts and dreads, incest and miscegenation. In Joe Christmas and Etienne Bon, neither white nor black, repudiating both races, inexplicably ecstatic with love of both, mysteriously dreading both, mysteriously wreaking revenge and expiation on both, we face a central preoccupation of Mr. Faulkner, a central theme of his fiction, and, I think, an obligation to go beyond the psycho-analytical study of his purposes. In spite of his enormous labor to elucidate these two mulattoes and their feelings and their symbolism in society, they are never elucidated. What is it that bubbles through those minds, what is it that drives them, what are they feeling, what are they trying to do, what do they mean? You cannot tell, for you do not know. A fair conclusion is that you do not know because Mr. Faulkner does not know. I suggest that on that fact hinges the explanation of his fiction.

It is a fact in religion. For the energy derived from primitive sources in the mind projects a structure of thought intended to be explanatory of the world, and this is religious, though religious in the familiar reversal that constitutes demonology and witchcraft. William James has told us how it comes about. The simple truth is that Mr. Faulkner is a mystic. He is trying to communicate to us an immediate experience of the ineffable. He cannot tell us because he does not know—because what he perceives cannot be known, cannot therefore be told, can never be put into words but can only be suggested in symbols, whose content and import must forever be in great part missed and in greater part misunderstood. This is a mysticism, furthermore, of what James called the lower path. There are, James said, two mystical paths, the one proceeding out of some beatitude of spiritual health which we may faintly glimpse in the visions of the saints. It is from the lower path, the decay of the vision, that witchcraft always proceeds. And witchcraft, like all magic, is a spurious substitute for fundamental knowledge.

The crux of the process by which witchcraft came to substitute for the ordinary concerns of fiction in Mr. Faulkner's work may be observed in "Sartoris." His first book, "Soldiers' Pay," introduced the overwhelming despair finding expression in lachrymation and the creatures of unadulterated evil that have appeared in all his later books—curiously combined with the glibness and tight technique of magazine fiction. His second book, "Mosquitoes," was his "Crome Yellow" effort, and had in common with his other work only a pair of lovers moving on some manic errand through a nightmare world. With "Sartoris" (which was published, if not written, before "The Sound and the Fury"), he became a serious novelist in the best sense of that adjective. He undertook to deal fairly with experience, to articulate his characters with a social organism, and to interpret the web of life in terms of human personality. Wherever he was factual and objective— in Loosh, Miss Jenny (who is his best creation to date), the unmystical Negroes, the crackers, the old men, Dr. Alford—he imposed a conformable and convincing world of his own on a recognizable American experience, in symbols communicative to us all. But he failed in the principal effort of the novel. What he tried to do, with the Sartorises themselves, was to deliver up to us the heart of a mystery—to explain the damnation, the curse, of a brilliant, decayed, and vainglorious family doomed to failure and death. And he did not do it. They were a void. We did not know them and he could not tell us about them. They were without necessity, without causation. When he faced the simple but primary necessity of the novelist, to inform us about his characters, he backed away.

He has been backing away ever since. All the prestidigitation of his later technique rests on a tacit promise that this tortuous narrative method, this obsession with pathology, this parade of Grand Guignol tricks and sensations, will, if persevered with, bring us in the end to a deeper and a fuller truth about his people than we could get otherwise. And it never does. Those people remain wraiths blown at random through fog by winds of myth. The revelation remains just a series of horror stories that are essentially false—false because they happen to grotesques who have no psychology, no necessary motivation as what they have become out of what they were. They are also the targets of a fiercely rhetorical bombast diffused through the brilliant technique that promises us everything and gives us nothing, leaving them just wraiths. Meanwhile the talent for serious fiction shown in "Sartoris" and the rich comic intelligence grudgingly displayed from time to time, especially in "Sanctuary," have been allowed to atrophy from disuse and have been covered deep by a tide of sensibility.

Poe in Mississippi

MALCOLM COWLEY*

Among all the empty and witless tags attached to living American authors, perhaps the most misleading is that of Southern Realist as applied to William Faulkner. He writes about one section of the South—that much is true— and he writes in what often seems to be a mood of utter distaste. But critics have no excuse for confusing realism with revulsion, or rather with the mixture of violent love and violent hatred that Faulkner bears toward his native state. No, there is only one possible justification for classing him with the novelists who try to copy the South without distortion. It lies in the fact that he can and does write realistically when his daemon consents. He can and does give us the exact tone of Mississippi voices, the feel of a Mississippi landscape, the look of an old plantation house rotting among sedge-grown fields. On occasion he even gives us Mississippi humor (like the scene between Uncle Bud and the three madams, in "Sanctuary") that is as broad and native as anything preserved from the days of the steamboat gamblers. But Faulkner's daemon does not often permit him to be broadly humorous or to echo the mild confusions of daily life. The daemon forces him to be always intense, to write in a wild lyrical style, to omit almost every detail that does not contribute to a single effect of somber violence and horror.

And this gives us a clue to Faulkner's real kinship. He belongs with the other writers who try to produce this single and somber effect—that is, with the "satanic" poets from Byron to Baudelaire, and with the "black" or "terrifying" novelists from Monk Lewis and the Hoffman of the "Tales" to Edgar Allan Poe. The daemon that haunts him is the ghost of the haunted castle—though it is also Poe's raven and Manfred's evil spirit. And the daemon is especially prominent in his new novel.[1] Not only is "Absalom, Absalom!" in many ways the strongest, the most unified and characteristic of his twelve books, but it is also the most romantic, in the strict historical sense of the word.

Thomas Sutpen, in 1833, comes riding into a little Mississippi town with twenty coal-black Negroes straight from the jungle. He despises his new neighbors, who in turn regard him as Satan in the flesh. He is the

*Reprinted with permission of *New Republic* 89 (4 November 1936): 22.

lonely Byronic hero with his mind coldly fixed on the achievement of one design. And the plantation house built with the help of his naked slaves— the great mansion literally hewn from the swamps—is the haunted castle that was described so often in early nineteenth-century romances. Like other haunted castles, Sutpen's Hundred is brooded over by a curse. Years ago in the West Indies, Thomas Sutpen had deserted his wife and his infant son after discovering that they had Negro blood. He now marries again; he has two children and a hundred square miles of virgin land; but in the midst of his triumph the curse begins to operate: the deserted son reappears and tries to marry his own half-sister. Here the note of incest suggests Byron, but elsewhere it is Poe whose spirit seems closest to the story—especially at the end, where Sutpen's Hundred collapses like the House of Usher. And indeed one might say that Faulkner is Poe in Mississippi—Poe modernized with technical and psychological devices imported from Joyce's Dublin and Freud's Vienna.

But this is a great deal different from saying with Granville Hicks that Faulkner is "in danger of becoming a Sax Rohmer for the sophisticated." It is different from saying that "he is not primarily interested in representative men and women; certainly he is not interested in the forces that have shaped them." Hicks's judgment seems to be based on the false theory that romantic authors are always trying to evade the life of their own times. The truth is that they know and can write about nothing else. The men and women they present in romantic disguises are their own selves, with their friends, mistresses and enemies. The issues they deal with are derived from their own lives and are frequently social as well as personal or pathological. And the general result is that romantic novels are likely to be written on two planes, with one subject below, in the foreground, and above it another subject that is half-revealed by conscious or unconscious symbolism.

In Faulkner's new book, the second or hidden subject is the decline of the South after the Civil War. Sutpen's Hundred, the mansion that rotted and finally burned, is obviously a symbol of Southern culture. Thomas Sutpen himself seems to represent the Southern ruling caste, though here the symbolism is confused by the fact that he also represents the proud Byronic hero hated by his fellow men. But it is clear enough that Sutpen's curse is a result of his relations with Negroes, and that he is finally murdered by a poor white. Forty years later, when his mansion collapses in flames, the only survivor among his descendants is Jim Bond, a half-witted mulatto. And one of the other characters tells us, on the last page, "I think that in time the Jim Bonds are going to conquer the western hemisphere. . . . In a few thousand years I who regard you will also have sprung from the loins of African kings."

But Faulkner is not presenting this picture as the reasoned conclusion of an essay on the South. He is not arguing that Southern society was ruined by its own injustice toward the Negroes, nor again that a mixed race will survive after the heirs have vanished from the great plantations. He is not arguing anything whatever. He is giving us perceptions rather than ideas, and their value is not statistical but emotional. To the critic their importance lies in the fact that they explain a great deal not only about "Absalom, Absalom!" but also about Faulkner's earlier novels. His violence here and elsewhere is not a means of arousing pointless horror: it is an expression of a whole society which the author sincerely loves and hates and which he perceives to be in a state of catastrophic decay.

But Faulkner's new book falls considerably short of the powerful mood that it might have achieved. Possibly this is because he has failed to find a satisfactory relationship between the horror story in the foreground and the vaster theme that it conceals: the two subjects interfere with each other. But the partial failure of "Absalom, Absalom!" is chiefly explained by the style in which his daemon forced him to write it—a strained, involved, ecstatic style in which colloquialisms and deliberate grammatical errors are mingled with words too pretentious even for Henry James. Too often it seems that Faulkner, in the process of evoking an emotion in himself, has ignored the equally important task of evoking it in the reader.

Note

1. *Absalom, Absalom!* by William Faulkner (New York: Random House, 1936).

[The Itinerary of an Ideological Dream]

PHILIP RAHV*

The rise and catastrophic end of a plantation family, the Civil War, the defeat that peopled the ravaged land with "garrulous outraged baffled ghosts" whose fear and pride and glory you live and breathe, a thing that you, the outsider, cannot understand, for "you would have to be born there"—all this is the classic avowal and exhortation of the peculiar trauma induced by the heritage of the Confederate South. The old ghost-tides come to life in a tide of events and emotions and in men and women as peculiar to Faulkner as the Karamazovs to Dostoevsky. Tom Sutpen, who bursts out of the wilderness to father a domain and a race, his son, Henry, the incestuous lovers Judith and Charles, the illicit drop of Negro blood in the family swirling and boiling till it rises like the very flood of fate to engulf the scene of crime and evil and single insane purpose—all placed within the pattern of an imagination as absolute and exacting as any in modern fiction.

Only, the book actually makes dull reading. What has happened is that his pattern and imagery have been impaired and dispersed by an unsuccessful method of presentation. This method, however, has not been arbitrarily chosen; and the clue, I think, lies in the language, which is formal, prolix, tortuous, running over into passages of psychological theorizing that arrest the dramatic development. In a writer who depends so much on drama to carry him forward, anything that blocks the dramatic movement is bound to disintegrate his structure. The language, in its turn, is shaped by a narrative form that, instead of recreating the story for the reader, laboriously pieces it together and interprets it for him through several narrators who all speak in the same voice, the monotonous and sorrowful voice of the author's contemplation of his world. The material is not explored objectively to provide the vision; it is manipulated to illustrate and fit the vision, which is preconceived. Thus the language becomes a function of the author's metaphysics, of spiritual relations, and of reverie: it no longer sticks to the object, but to the author's idea of the object. And as Eliot once observed, language can only be healthy when it directly presents the object, when "it is so close to the object that the two are identified"; otherwise it becomes morbid and unreal.

*Excerpted and reprinted from *New Masses* (24 November 1936): 20–21.

The form this narrative takes suggests that Faulkner is following the itinerary of an ideological dream, rather than that of history. And since to him the historic process is a mystery of human fate doomed by a "sickness somewhere at the prime foundation of this factual scheme," his reproduction of this process in creative terms is always in danger of degenerating into mystification, is ever on the brink of the dilettantism of horror. It is at this point that his actual qualities as a novelist are directly penetrated by his ideology, whose matrix, it seems to me, is to be located in his tortured consciousness of the defeat of the Old South and the annihilation of its way of life. But inasmuch as on this and other grounds he implicitly rejects the industrial civilization that replaced the Old South, and at the same time his mind still runs absolutely counter to materialist ideas, the final sum of his thought is a kind of social despair distended to hold the scheme of things entire. And the best symbol I can think of to represent the bond that ties him to the South he so desperately loves and hates is the very symbol he has himself inscribed into his novel. That symbol is incest. For is not Faulkner's relation to his incestuous lovers, and to the land whose agony they bear, as sterile and desolate, though at times inspired by the grandeur of defiance and death, as their relation among themselves?

Mr. Faulkner Adds a Cubit

PAULA SNELLING*

. . . *Absalom, Absalom!* centers around a man, Sutpen, whose silence concerning his past (and his present and future) and whose singleminded and at times ruthless pursuit of his uncommunicated ambition shroud him in unholy mystery in the eyes of Jefferson people of the early and middle nineteenth century; so that now, in 1909, when most of the victims of the drama and destruction which came to those closely associated with Sutpen have died and the survivors are not willing or not able to unravel all the threads of mystery, the attempt to reconstruct the story resolves itself frequently into the speculations of first one and then another. The section in which Rosa Coldfield relieves her part (tenuous, yet the core of her life and sufficient to make of her a poet and philosopher) is perhaps the richest section of the book. It would be unfair to summarize baldly a story whose value is derived largely from the significance and overtones which accrue as the reader learns first one incomplete part, then another tantalizing fragment and gradually arrives, as he does in life, at as full a comprehension as is permitted him. But it touches on several matters which have, at intervals, troubled man's sleep: ambition, conflicts of personalities, murder, poverty, war, gossip, courage, miscegenation, hate, love, marriage without love, sympathy, slavery, incest, friendship, blood ties, family pride, torture, reputation, loyalty, inadequacy, hope, imbecility, wealth, betrayal, suspense, loneliness . . . ; and is well worth anyone's reading.

*Reprinted from *Pseudopodia* 4 (Fall 1936): 16, by permission from International Thompson Publishing Services Ltd. on behalf of Routledge.

Reviewing Reviews

SATURDAY REVIEW OF LITERATURE*

The question whether our leading novelists are supposed to make their books readable or not has been taken out for an airing in recent reviews of William Faulkner's "Absalom, Absalom!" and James T. Farrell's "A World I Never Made." Van Gelder in *The Times* wrote that "Absalom, Absalom!" is "worth all the effort required to read it. That is not faint praise." Other reviewers were almost unanimous in agreeing at least that an effort was required, but divided into two schools of thought when it came to praise. "Falls considerably short of the powerful mood that it might have achieved," wrote Malcolm Cowley in *The New Republic*; "The partial failure of 'Absalom, Absalom!' is chiefly explained by . . . a strained, involved, ecstatic style." "The vogue for William Faulkner and his literary style is one of the affectations of the present day," said Dorothea Lawrence Mann in the Boston *Transcript*; and the Detroit *Free Press* summed it up thus: "he can qualify any time as the Gypsy Rose Lee among authors, a strip-tease artist worthy of glorification." "Occasionally there are passages of great power and beauty," wrote Harold Strauss in the *Times Book Review*. ". . . . There are other passages which, while hardly communicative, drop into a pure blank verse and are estimable for their sheer verbal music. For the rest, 'Absalom, Absalom!' must be left to those hardy souls who care for puzzles." No critical point, however, can be carried without dissent; thus we find Harry Hansen writing, in the *World-Telegram*, "The prose is a triumph."

*Reprinted from *Saturday Review of Literature* 15 (5 December 1936): 58.

The Sutpen-Bon-Coldfield Family

◆

[Sutpen and Southern History]

MELVIN BACKMAN*

Thomas Sutpen, who transplanted his slaves from Haiti to the Mississippi wilderness and transformed the wilderness to a plantation, was part of a large historical movement. He was part of the movement of slavery from the islands to the mainland and from the Eastern seaboard to the Southwest. Paradoxically, slavery was to find its most aggressive defenders in the Southern democrats of the United States. The very aggressiveness of the defense was related to various factors. For the Western world the nineteenth century was a century of industrial progress and intellectual liberalism, but for the South it was a century of resistance to the tide of liberalism and progress. Isolated, feeling itself threatened by a growing and hostile North, and harboring a bad conscience over its peculiar system, the South grew more ready to turn to violence. C. Vann Woodward, the Southern historian, has commented upon the South's state of mind immediately prior to the Civil War:

> The South had been living in a crisis atmosphere for a long time. It was a society in the grip of an insecurity complex, a tension resulting from both rational and irrational fears. One cause of it was the steady, invincible expansion of the free-state system in size and power, after the Southern system had

*Reprinted with permission from Melvin Backman, *Faulkner: The Major Years: A Critical Study* (Bloomington: Indiana University Press, 1966), 101–12.

reached the limits of its own expansion. The South, therefore, felt itself to be menaced through encirclement by a power containing elements unfriendly to its interests, elements that were growing strong enough to capture the government. The South's insecurity was heightened by having to defend against constant attack an institution it knew to be discredited throughout the civilized world and of which Southerners had once been among the severest critics. Its reaction was to withdraw increasingly from contact with the offending world, to retreat into an isolationism of spirit, and to attempt by curtailing freedom of speech to avoid criticism.[1]

"Much of the South's intellectual energy," Woodward continues, "went into a desperate effort to convince the world that its peculiar evil was actually a 'positive good,' but it failed even to convince itself. It writhed in the torments of its own conscience until it plunged into catastrophe to escape."[2] According to Woodward, the South, beset by a bad conscience, turned guilt and frustration into aggression and destruction. Woodward may be exaggerating the role played by conscience. We must remember that in the generation preceding the outbreak of the Civil War, the South was expanding: the frontier was being pushed westward and southward, the Cotton Kingdom was growing into the chief economic and social fact of the South's existence, and political power was shifting from Virginia and the Carolinas to the Deep South. The men who were making this expansion were caught up in the grip of their own ambitions and interests. They were passionate rather than reflective, doers rather than thinkers. Simply and fiercely they identified themselves and their interests with the South. Their proneness to violence was probably due less to bad conscience than to the fact that violence had played an important role in their frontier background and in their making of a plantation. It was a time when the South chose not a Thomas Jefferson but a Jefferson Davis as its leader. It was a time of Thomas Sutpens, not Quentin Compsons.

In the 1830's the men who would later become the leaders of the South in the Civil War were men on the make, men who had yet to achieve their dream. It was a "dream of grim and castlelike magnificence" (38) which Thomas Sutpen, with the help of his slaves and the captured French architect, built into the great house itself. With an assist from the puritan, Goodhue Coldfield, he acquired the appropriate furnishings for his baronial dream: the chandeliers, rugs, mahogany, and "the stainless wife" (51). The marriage of Thomas Sutpen to Ellen Coldfield signifies the union of frontiersman and puritan, a union which would give birth to the very character of the South. Frontier violence would be yoked to fundamentalist religion, frontier individualism would be wedded to the puritan's conscience. Superimposed on the marriage was the plantation system, with another set of values and with its Peculiar Institution.

In Mississippi the planter-to-be had no time to waste. Out of the virgin land Sutpen "tore violently a plantation" (9), and out of the virgin wife "without gentleness begot" (9) a son and daughter. He was hurrying his dream into shape. Even the names of his offspring and possessions reflect the dream. Charles and Henry might have come from English and Norman royalty, Judith from the Old Testament, Clytemnestra from the Greeks, and Rob Roy (his thoroughbred stallion) from Sir Walter Scott. By the 1850's Sutpen had become the biggest landowner and planter of Yoknapatawpha. "He acted his role too—a role of arrogant ease and leisure" (72), while his wife "moved, lived, from attitude to attitude against her background of chatelaine to the largest, wife to the wealthiest, mother of the most fortunate" (69). Dream had become actuality. "Now he would take that boy in where he would never again need to stand on the outside of a white door" (261). He had riven himself free from the brutehood of his past, made himself part of the proud and privileged class of the South, and had planted the heir who would perpetuate the achievement. So it seemed—until the Christmas of 1859 when retribution knocked on the white door of Sutpen's great house, and the past he had put away walked back into his life in the person of his first son, Charles Bon.

Charles Bon. Charles Good. In station and manners and breeding he was the elegant New Orleans scion, fortunate member of the planter class and an elite Latin culture. In personality he was "gentle sardonic whimsical and incurably pessimistic" (129). In his heart he was the son whose life had been "enclosed by an unsleeping cabal bent apparently on teaching him that he had never had a father" (313), he was "that mental and spiritual orphan whose fate it apparently was to exist in some limbo" (124), he was that "forlorn nameless and homeless lost child" (267) who came knocking on the white door of Sutpen's house. He wanted no inheritance; he wanted but a word, a sign, a look, a touch from Sutpen which would say you are my son. He got no acknowledgment, he got nothing. Even the love he got from his brother Henry turned into ashes when Henry learned that Bon was "the nigger that's going to sleep with your sister" (358). For all his sophistication, Bon remained only the orphan (he never really had a mother since, warped by paranoiac hatred of Sutpen, she had lost the power to love) who never found the father he sought: that was his fate. So it was that he lived as if something had gone out of him, as if he did not really want to live.

The story of Charles Bon is a richly ironic fable of the Old South. Bon embodies both the most favored of whites, a New Orleans scion, and the lowliest of blacks, the white man's bastard. He is the intelligent, cultivated young gentleman who must be shot by a Mississippi clodhopper because the nigger signifies a subhuman threat to white womanhood. Like his father, he cannot acknowledge his son by a colored woman. These ironies are part of a system; beneath these ironies rest other parts of the system's foundation. In the Old South the Negro slave had generally no father and little mother. Under a system that made human beings into chattels, the Negro woman, when she did not labor in the fields, served as the breeder of stock and as the instrument for the white man's sexual pleasure. The Negress was a kind of mare, the Negro a stud. The effect was to destroy or warp the institution of the family among a whole people. In removing sex from its familial role, the system did violence to the morality of both whites and blacks.[5] It made sex for the Negro into an irresponsible animal relationship; it made sex for the white man into a guilty, dishonest one. A schism, a kind of unconscious hypocrisy, embedded itself deeply into the soul of the South. For the white man the Negress was the female animalized and the white woman was the female spiritualized. It was as if the planter were trying to make up to his white woman for his faithlessness and duplicity.[4] Reality was two families by the planter, white and black. Reality was a brother who was not a brother, a sister who was not a sister, a wife who was not a wife. Southerners knew of this reality, accepted it, lived with it, even though it violated what they thought they believed in: honor, pride, the family, and the decencies of life. This reality underlies the story of the House of Sutpen.

All the relationships in the Sutpen family are invested with a peculiar irony, doom, and tragedy, as if a curse had been placed on them like the curse of the House of Oedipus. Incest, fratricide, and the fall of a family are all aspects of both curses. Moreover, like several characters in *Oedipus Rex*, the Sutpens, for the most part, did not know the full truth about themselves and could not realize their identity and humanity. Henry and Charles were brothers, yet not brothers; Judith and Charles were sister and brother, yet not sister and brother; Sutpen and Charles were father and son, yet not father and son. They seem compelled as by a Greek fate—such is the power of the system—to repudiate or destroy one another; they seem compelled as by the Old Testament God to suffer for the sins of their father. It was the father, the nucleus of the culture, who determined the fate and character of the others. He signifies an elemental force, a heroic *hybris*, in the Southern culture; he is the archetype of the Southern planter. There is a grandeur to the man who hammers out his "design" in the face of God's and nature's opposition. Yet there is a fatal defect too: his Adamic innocence, like that of other American barons on the make, had hardened into moral blindness, and the egoism and energy generated by his rejection and dream of vindication had become ultimately a force for destruction of himself, his family, and his society. In attempting to build a dynasty, he had lost a family; in making himself into the image of the Southern planter, he had lost part of his humanity; in displacing conscience by pride, he had lost the power to see into himself. Since he was "incapable of that rending of the self and tearing out of pride which forms the tragic element,"[5] his life ended not in tragic affirmation but in gross deterioration and unheroic death.

Ironically, the lowliest of the whites is the instrument of retribution. For Wash Jones the Colonel signified all that was best in the planter: courage, honor, paternalism, and authority. For Wash the Colonel was a god.

. . . on the week days he would see Sutpen (the fine figure of the man as he called it) on the black stallion, galloping about the plantation, and Father said how for that moment Wash's heart would be quiet and proud both and that maybe it would seem to him that this world where niggers, that the Bible said had been created and cursed by God to be brute and vassal to all men of white skin, were better found and housed and even clothed than he and his granddaughter—that this world where he walked always in mocking and jeering echoes of nigger laughter, was just a dream and an illusion and that the actual world was the one where his own lonely apotheosis (Father said) galloped on the black thoroughbred, thinking maybe, Father said, how the Book said that all men were created in the image of God and so all men were the same in God's eyes anyway, looked the same to God at least, and so he would look at Sutpen and think *A fine proud man. If God Himself was to come down and ride the natural earth, that's what He would aim to look like.* (282)

In spite of the blind contradiction in Wash's belief that the Bible could be used as authority for both the Negro's enslavement and man's equality, there is something touching about Wash's faith in the planter who had sprung from the same brute origins but who in the span of several decades had become the poor white's apotheosis. By 1869, however, the ravages of the War and Reconstruction had eaten so deeply into the planter and his "design" that his power was being broken and his ruthlessness exposed. The breaking point came when Sutpen, having attended the mare that had just foaled a colt to his stallion, entered Wash's cabin to see whether he had bred a son by Milly, Wash's granddaughter. Bending over the pallet where she lay with her newborn daughter, he said, " 'Well, Milly; too bad you're not a mare too. Then I could give you a decent stall in the stable' " (286). The earth seemed to fall away from beneath Wash's feet. He confronted the planter. Like the Grim Reaper, he raised the rusty scythe; the planter's whip lashed twice across his face, and then the scythe came down.

Although the poor white has been depicted as the instrument of the planter's demise, the deterioration of Sutpen's will and character, wrought by the inroads of the War and Reconstruction, contributed also to his downfall. The planter's confidence and power had been deeply shaken by the loss of the War; nevertheless, the Southern people did not actually repudiate their leaders until much later. Toward the end of the nineteenth century they did begin to turn to other leaders, to those who made the Negro the scapegoat for the Lost Cause and the current ills. The Negro, who had once been inviolate as the planter's chattel, became fair game for any white. Providing an outlet for the people's frustration and resentment, racism became the official policy of the South. In effect, Faulkner was right: the poor white eventually did turn on the planter.

What survived from Sutpen's "design"? There was the heir apparent, Henry Sutpen, who vanished for a generation, only to reappear at the beginning of the next century like a futile ghost out of a dead but lingering past.

And there were the three women: Judith, Clytie, and Rosa Coldfield. Judith had been intended *"by the tradition in which Thomas Sutpen's ruthless will had carved a niche to pass through the soft insulated and unscathed cocoon stages: bud, served prolific queen, then potent and soft-handled matriarch of old age's serene and well-lived content"* (156). Instead, she had become *"the bowed and unwived widow kneeling"* (138) beside her lover's corpse. She lived on in the empty and rotting house, scraping out a meager existence by doing a man's labor. In silent, stoic joylessness she survived the privations of the War and Reconstruction. Her mulatto sister, Clytie, continued long beyond Judith's death as the guardian of her master's house. Clytie represents the Negro family servant so involved with her white folks that she could make no life of her own. Finally there was Miss Rosa. Conceived in her parents' old age, as Gail Hightower had been, she passed from a warped childhood to a spinster's dream world and became a writer of odes to Confederate heroes. But the emotional thrust of her life derived from her hatred of Sutpen, a hatred which stemmed mainly from his matter-of-fact proposal "that they try it first and if it was a boy and lived, they would be married" (284). Faulkner's characterization of Miss Rosa is generally rendered in broad paradox and sly irony. She is both the chaste Southern woman and warped old maid; the romantic defender of the South and paranoiac hater of its supreme representative, Thomas Sutpen; vicarious bride in her dreams to Charles Bon and hater of the Negro. So shielded had she been from the realities of the Old South, Rosa Coldfield never knew she had loved the "nigger" son of Thomas Sutpen.

The true heir of the grand "design" was Charles Etienne Saint-Valery Bon, only child of Thomas Sutpen's elder son. Neither black nor white, living in a much less fortunate time and having less than his father, he became the classic mulatto pariah. He struggled to find his identity by marrying a coal-black woman and living a Negro's life; but he could only express himself by destroying himself, by "treading the thorny and flintpaved path toward Gethsemane [sic] which he had decreed and created for himself, where he had crucified himself and come down from his cross for a moment and now returned to it" (209). "With a furious and indomitable desperation" (202) he flung the gage of his apparently futile challenge in the white world's face and turned from his "emancipation" to death.

As the nineteenth century yielded to the twentieth, there survived the rotting house, its slave guardian, the death-in-life heir (Henry), and the last Sutpen descendant—the idiot, Jim Bond. It had taken two generations for Bon to become Bond, good to become slave.[6] Not much was left of the planter's baronial dream. Like the planter's mansion, the dream kept rotting. In December 1909 the house of Sutpen went up in smoke. Only the idiot remained. The others were dead. Dead was the planter with his double family, black and white; dead were the Coldfields, with the shopkeeper's barren puritanism and the spinster's barren gentility; and dead was the poor white family of Wash Jones.

A mood of despair and futility pervades this story of the South. Even the most decent of men, General Compson, could only conclude when touched by the misery and destructiveness of Valery Bon's life, " 'Better that he were dead, better that he had never lived' " (205). Yet the despair has been quickened by a kind of fierce, underground idealism. Valery Bon destroyed himself not only because he would rather be dead but because he felt compelled to make a protest against the system which denies his people their human rights. Even Wash Jones's life ended in protest. From an outraged and anguished heart Faulkner has cried out in *Absalom* against an evil implanted in his South.

Faulkner has presented Sutpen as the source of the evil, but he has presented him too as the only heroic figure in the story. Sutpen is both the pride and the shame of the South. For a Quentin Compson the ambivalence of his feelings about his heritage is further complicated by the reality of the present. His heritage is peculiarly compounded of accomplishment and defeat, innocence and guilt, pride and defensiveness. The ruthless planter-backwoodsman who built his house upon slavery and lived as if the evil were a positive good is dead and gone. For his descendants accomplishment has often become but a memory, pride has become delusion, and innocence has become unacknowledgeable guilt. As loyalty to the Old South has turned into savage racism, the planter's power to act has deteriorated for his twentieth-century descendants into a stasis of will.

For Quentin, as for his father, Sutpen represented another time when men were "simpler and therefore, integer for integer, larger, more heroic and the figures therefore more heroic too, not dwarfed and involved but distinct, uncomplex who had the gift of loving once or dying once instead of being diffused and scattered creatures drawn blindly limb from limb from a grab bag and assembled" (89). Out of his sense of impotence and alienation, Quentin, like Bon himself, seemed to turn to the godlike Sutpen for the power and virility he lacked, for the father who would solve the son's dilemma. But the giant, rising out of the past like a swiftly growing djinn from Aladdin's lamp, threatened to consume rather than renew the puny summoner. The vision of the South which Quentin invoked left him shivering, "panting in the cold air, the iron New England dark; *I dont. I dont! I dont hate it! I dont hate it!*" (378). Even in the alien air of New England the South was too much with him. The burden of its history lay heavy upon Quentin Compson. Torn by loyalty and guilt, by the desire to defend and the need to expiate, by the desire to suppress and the need to confess, he could only cry out against his burden. And this is how the novel ends—with the sins of the past unexpiated and the dilemma of the present irresoluble.

Notes

1. C. Vann Woodward, *The Burden of Southern History*, p. 62.
2. Ibid., pp. 20–21.
3. It is of course difficult to appraise the moral and psychological damage done to the Negro in the process of enslaving him. One can suggest, however, some historians and commentators who provide information and insight: Frederick Bancroft, *Slave Trading in the Old South* (New York, Ungar, 1959); E. Franklin Frazier, *The Negro Family in the United States* (New York, Dryden, 1948); John Hope Franklin, *From Slavery to Freedom*; W. E. Burghardt Du Bois, *Black Folk: Then and Now*; Frank Tannenbaum, *Slave and Citizen: The Negro in the Americas* (New York, Knopf, 1947); Daniel P. Mannix, in collaboration with Malcolm Cowley, *Black Cargoes: A History of the Atlantic Slave Trade* (New York, Viking, 1962); Frederick Douglass, *Narrative of the Life of Frederick Douglass, an American Slave, Written by Himself*, edited by Benjamin Quarles (Cambridge, Belknap, 1960); and Stanley M. Elkins, *Slavery* (Chicago, University of Chicago, 1959).
4. W. J. Cash, *The Mind of the South* (New York, Knopf, 1969), pp. 97–98.
5. Irving Howe, *William Faulkner: A Critical Study* (New York, Random House, 1951), p. 164.
6. I am indebted to Konrad Hopkins for this idea.

[Fathers and Sons]

John T. Irwin*

The doctrine of the equality of men is at odds with the patriarchal principle that fathers are inherently superior to sons, for obviously the doctrine of equality is the doctrine of a son. The son, finding himself powerless in relation to the father, yet desiring power, admits that mastery inheres in the role of the father but disputes the criteria that determine who occupies that role. The doctrine of the son is simply the doctrine of the son's equality of opportunity to assume the role of the father through a combat with the father that will show who is the better man. But that doctrine of equality the father must reject, for from the father's point of view the authority which he holds as the father is not open to dispute; it is not subject to trial by combat because that authority is not something that the father could ever lose, it is not accidental to fatherhood, it inheres in its very nature. That authority is something which has been irrevocably conferred on the father by the very nature of time, for the essence of the authority, the mastery, that a father has over his son is simply priority in time—the fact that in time the father always comes first. And against that patriarchal authority whose basis is priority in time, the son's will is impotent, for the will cannot move backwards in time, it cannot alter the past. In his rivalry with the father for the love of the mother, the son realizes that no matter how much the mother loves him, she loved the father *first*. Indeed, the son carries with him in the very fact of his own existence inescapable proof that she loved the father first and that the son comes second. Any power that the son has, he has not in his own right, but by inheritance from the father, by being a copy of the father, who has supreme authority because he comes first, who has power because of the very nature of time. No wonder, then, that the envy of the son for the father takes the form of the revenge against time.

When Nietzsche speaks of the "envy of your fathers," the phrase is intentionally ambiguous, for it is not just the envy that a son feels for his father, it is as well the envy that the son inherits from his father, who was himself a son once. The targets of Sutpen's revenge for the affront that he suffered as a boy are the artificial advantages of high birth and inherited

*Reprinted with permission from *Doubling and Incest/Repetition and Revenge: A Speculative Reading of Faulkner* (Baltimore/London: Johns Hopkins University Press, 1975).

wealth (or the artificial disadvantages of low birth and inherited poverty), that is, generation and patrimony—those modes of the son's dependence on his father, those expressions of the fact that whatever the son is or has, he has received from his father and holds at the sufferance of the father. But again we confront the paradox of Sutpen's solution—that he seeks revenge on the artificial standards that make one man inferior to another, not by trying to do away with those standards, but rather by founding a dynasty, by establishing that same artificial standard of superiority for his family and bequeathing it to his son. Put in that way, the paradox seems clearer: it is the paradox that sons turn into fathers by trying to forget (albeit unsuccessfully) that they were once sons. When Sutpen began his quest for revenge, his quest to supplant the father, his attitude was that of a son: that the authority and power of the father obey the rule of power, that they are subject to a trial by combat, and if the son's will proves the stronger, belong to the son not as a gift or inheritance (which would entail his dependence on the father) but as a right, a mark of his independence. Yet (and here is the paradoxical shift) the proof of the son's success in his attempt to become the father will be the son's denial of the attitude of the son (the rule of power) in favor of the attitude of the father. The proof that Sutpen has achieved his revenge, that he has become the father, will be his affirmation that the authority and power of the father obey not the rule of power but the rule of authority, that is, that they are not subject to dispute or trial by combat since they belong irrevocably to the father through priority in time, that to oppose the father is to oppose time, that authority and power cannot be taken from the father by the son but can only be given as a gift or inheritance by the father to the son. We see why Sutpen's revenge requires that he found a dynasty, for the proof that he has succeeded in becoming the father will finally be achieved only when he bequeaths his authority and power to his son as an inheritance (a gift, not a right), thereby establishing the son's dependence on his father and thus the father's mastery. That proof, of course, Sutpen never achieves, though he dies trying. His is the paradoxical fate of one who tries to seize authority and power by one rule and then hold them by another, the fate of a man who wants to be God. Or we could say, shifting the focus slightly, that Sutpen sets out to vindicate the right of every poor white boy to an equal opportunity to become the rich planter, but that once he has vindicated that right by becoming the rich planter, he immediately denies that same right to black boys, specifically, to his black son Charles Bon. We can also see why Faulkner equated Sutpen's attempt to establish that one man cannot be inferior to another through artificial standards or circumstances with his attempt to prove that man is immortal, for if the former attempt aims at toppling that traditional power of the father over the son's life that is implicit in the inherited advantages of position and wealth (or the inherited disadvantages of poverty and lack of position), and if that aim involves the son's challenging that authority of the father whose basis is priority in time so that the son's will directly opposes itself to the nature of time, then that aim can be successful only if the son is able to free himself from the grip of time, only if man can free himself from time's final sanction—death, that inevitable castration of the son by Father Time—only if man can become immortal.

When Sutpen returns from the Civil War to find one son dead and the other gone, he starts over a third time in his design to found a dynasty, to get the son who will inherit his land and thereby prove, through his dependence, that Sutpen has succeeded in his quest to be the son who seized the power of the father and then, as the father, kept that power from being seized by his own son in turn. For Sutpen can only prove that he is a better man than his father if he proves that he is a better man than his son, since Sutpen's father would have been defeated by his son in that very act. In Sutpen's final attempt to achieve his design, the battle against time receives its most explicit statement: "He was home again where his problem now was haste, passing time, the need to hurry. *He was not concerned,* Mr. Compson said, *about the courage and the will, nor even about the shrewdness now. He was not for one moment concerned about his ability to start the third time. All that he was concerned about was the possibility that he might not have time sufficient to do it in, regain his lost ground in*" (p. 278). But then, *"he realized that there was more in his problem than just lack of time, that the problem contained some super-distillation of this lack: that he was now past sixty and that possibly he could get but one more son, had at best but one more son in his loins, as the old cannon might know when it had just one more shot in its corporeality*" (p. 279). The problem is not just too little time; it is also the physical impotence that time brings, a physical impotence symbolic of Sutpen's "old impotent logic" (p. 279), of the impotence of the son's will in the face of the "it was" of time. Rosa says that when Sutpen gave her dead sister's wedding ring as a sign of their engagement it was "as though in the restoration of that ring to a living finger he had turned all time back twenty years and stopped it, froze it" (p. 165).

Sutpen's concern that he might be able to get only one more son leads him to suggest to Rosa that they try it first, and if the child is a male, that they marry. That suggestion drives Rosa from Sutpen's home and leads Sutpen to choose for his partner in the last effort to accomplish his design the only other available woman on his land, Milly Jones, the granddaughter of the poor-white Wash Jones, and that choice brings Sutpen to the final repetition of the traumatic affront. In fact, Sutpen had reenacted that affront from the very start of his relationship with Wash Jones, never allowing Jones to approach the front of the mansion. When Sutpen seduces Milly and when her child is a daughter rather than the required son, Sutpen rejects mother and child as he had rejected his first wife and child. He tells Milly that if she were a mare he could give her a decent stall in his stable—a remark that Wash Jones overhears and that makes Jones realize for the first time

Sutpen's attitude toward him and his family. Jones confronts the seducer of his granddaughter and kills him with a scythe. The irony of Sutpen's final repetition of the affront is that, though he delivers the affront in the role of a father rejecting his child, in order to get that child he had to assume the role of the son; and Wash Jones, the poor white who had been the object of Sutpen's paternalism, now assumes the role of outraged father in relation to Sutpen. It is emblematic of the fate of the son in his battle against time that Sutpen, struggling in his old age to achieve his revenge, must again become the son and in that role be struck down by an old man with a scythe. . . .

In this mechanism of a repetition in which the active and passive roles are reversed, we have the very essence of revenge. But we must distinguish between two different situations: in the ideal situation, the revenge is inflicted on the same person who originally delivered the affront—the person who was originally active is now forced to assume the passive role in the same scenario; in the other situation, the revenge is inflicted on a substitute. This second situation sheds light on Sutpen's attempt to master the traumatic affront that he suffered as a boy from the man who became his surrogate father, to master it by repeating that affront in reverse, inflicting it on his own son Charles Bon. This scenario of revenge on a substitute sheds light as well on the connection between repetition and the fantasy of the reversal of generations and on the psychological mechanism of generation itself. The primal affront that the son suffers at the hands of the father and for which the son seeks revenge throughout his life is the very fact of being a son— of being the generated in relation to the generator, the passive in relation to the active, the effect in relation to the cause. He seeks revenge on his father for the generation of an existence which the son, in relation to the father, must always experience as a dependency. But if revenge involves a repetition in which the active and passive roles are reversed, then the very nature of time precludes the son's taking revenge on his father, for since time is irreversible, the son can never really effect that reversal by which he would become his father's father. The son's only alternative is to take revenge on a substitute—that is, to become a father himself and thus repeat the generative situation as a reversal in which he now inflicts on his own son, who is a substitute for the grandfather, the affront of being a son, that affront that the father had previously suffered from his own father. We can see now why Nietzsche, in connecting the revenge against time with the "envy of your fathers" (that envy which the son feels for his father and which the son has inherited from his father, who was himself a son), says, "What was silent in the father speaks in the son; and often I found the son the unveiled secret of the father."

When Sutpen takes revenge on a substitute for the affront that he received as a boy, he takes revenge not just on Charles Bon but on Henry as well. For if the primal affront is the very fact of being a son, then acknowledgment and rejection, inheritance and disinheritance are simply the positive and negative modes of delivering the affront of the son's dependency on the father. Further, we can see the centrality of the notion of revenge on a substitute to the figure of the double. The brother avenger and the brother seducer are, as I have pointed out, substitutes for the father and the son in the Oedipal triangle, but if the revenge which the father inflicts on the son is a substitute for the revenge that the father wishes to inflict on his own father, then the brother avenger's killing of the brother seducer becomes a double action: the avenger's murder of the seducer (son) is a symbolic substitute for the seducer's murder of the avenger (father). This adds another dimension to Henry's murder of Bon. Henry is the younger brother and Bon the older, and the killing of the older brother by the younger is a common substitute for the murder of the father by the son. Thus, when Henry kills Bon, he is the father-surrogate killing the son, but since Henry, like Bon, is also in love with their sister Judith, he is as well the younger brother (son) killing the older brother who symbolizes the father, the father who is the rival for the mother and who punishes incest between brother and sister, son and mother. The multiple, reversible character of these relationships is only what we would expect in a closed system like the Oedipal triangle, and it is precisely this multiple, reversible character that gives the Oedipal triangle a charge of emotional energy that becomes overpowering as it cycles and builds. The very mechanism of doubling is an embodiment of that revenge on a substitute which we find in generation, for it is the threat from the father in the castration fear that fixes the son in that secondary narcissism from which the figure of the double as ambivalent Other springs. When the bright self (the ego influenced by the superego) kills the dark self (the ego influenced by unconscious), we have in this murder of the son as related to his mother by the son as related to his father the reversed repetition of that repressed desire which the son felt when he first desired his mother and was faced with the threat of castration—the desire of the son to murder his father. For the psychologically impotent son who cannot have a child, the act of generating a double is his equivalent of that revenge on the father through a substitute which the potent son seeks by the act of generating a son.

[The Sutpens and the Blacks]

Thadious M. Davis*

Major black figures emerge out of conceptions of blacks accommodating themselves to the white world. They evolve out of two rather conventional literary images of blacks; significantly both involve mixed-bloods. One is the free mulatto during pre- and postwar years who, envisioned as searcher, occupies the tragic "noplace" in southern life; the second is the slave daughter of the master who remains on the family plantation in an ambiguous maternal role as member and non-member of the family. In fact, all of the blacks in *Absalom* who are given names and delineated in detail are mixed-bloods, or presumed to be by the narrators. Clytie and the Bon men are representative characters. Whereas the Bons are obviously crucial to the resolution of the novel, Clytie reveals the most about Faulkner's art and the Negro in this novel.

Throughout the work, Clytie is the felt black presence that pervades the South. She embodies this presence much more than Charles Bon, the abstraction who is made "nigger" in order to complete the pattern of the legend. She, more than any other character, reveals the ultimately inexplicable nature of human motivation. Both the tension of her existence and the obscurity of her involvement in the lives of others manifest Judith Sutpen's metaphor: " 'You get born and you try this and you dont know why only you keep on trying it and you are born at the same time with a lot of other people, all mixed up with them, like trying to, having to, move your arms and legs with strings only the same strings are hitched to all the other arms and legs and the others all trying and they dont know why either except that the strings are all in one another's way' " (127). The process of life, as Judith describes it, means that Clytie is irrevocably connected to other individuals, so that her very existence, not merely her actions, affects and is affected by others.

Clytie is symbolically and literally a fusion of the two worlds of southern life; yet like the other mixed-bloods in the novel, Clytie does not experience the black world as a black person. Nonetheless, like Charles Bon and his son, Charles Etienne St. Valery, Clytie knows what it is to be treated as

*From *Faulkner's "Negro": Art and the Southern Context* by Thadious M. Davis. © 1983 by Louisiana State University Press. Used with permission. From pp. 197–209, 211–13.

"nigger" in the white world. She is, for instance, greeted differently by Sutpen upon his return from the war. Instead of the kiss and touch he gives Judith, Sutpen merely "looked at Clytie and said, 'Ah, Clytie' " (159). And Rosa Coldfield, who recoils from Clytie's "nigger" touch on the day of Charles Bon's death, has from childhood "instinctively" feared her and shunned objects she has touched (140).

Bereft of all that gave meaning to black life, Clytie is denied access to the only two institutions available to blacks—the family and the church. . . . But Clytie is not simply a member of the Sutpen household. She is a member of the family, marked, according to all accounts, with the Sutpen face. She has no connections with individuals who are not Sutpens; her mother, one of Sutpen's original band of slaves, is not even given to her as a memory in the novel. Legally chattel before the war and an institution afterwards, Clytie is a coffee-colored Sutpen. She is defined mainly in terms of her Sutpen heritage and blood. In terms of traditional place and order, then, she is where she belongs. There are no possibilities suggested for her living apart from Sutpen's Hundred; she has no alternative form of existence.

Clytie's singular position may initially suggest a realistic mode of characterizing blacks; however, the fictional method by which she achieves life, primarily through Rosa Coldfield's imaginative construction of her, is a break with conventional portraits. Clytie's presence, unlike Dilsey's, is not intended to provide ethical certainty or emotional comfort. Instead it evokes the duality of human nature. Whereas Dilsey lacks close personal identification with any member of the Compson family, Clytie is closely identified with both her half-sister Judith and her father Sutpen. Described as "at once both more and less Sutpen" (140), she is an extension of the physical selves of Judith and Sutpen, as well as an imaginative projection by the narrators of some dark essence of the Sutpen being. Whatever reality Clytie attains as a character, she attains in the minds of her narrators, but that reality primarily reinforces their central visions. All that readers know of her is filtered through the consciousness of others. . . .

Although Judith and her brother Henry are described as "that single personality with two bodies" (9–10), the description is even more fitting when applied to Clytie and Judith. Except for physical coloring, the two could be twins. They appear together initially, and from that first appearance, they are twin, silent, and calm figures of strength. Both frequently are called "inscrutable," "impenetrable," and "serene." As they age, they become more alike and gradually assume the status of living legends in the Jefferson community. Clytie is the shadowy complement of her white sister. In a sense, she is Judith's double, functioning to complete Judith's fragmented self. For example, after Bon's death Judith tells the Compsons that she will not commit suicide because " 'somebody will have to take care of Clytie' " (128). Yet because a Clytie who needs Judith's care is never visible, the reader may speculate that she is instead another part of Judith's own self which cannot be denied as long as there is some external manifestation of it. Symbolically, Clytie represents both Judith's inner self and the social environment in which Judith functions and exists.

Because Clytie is Judith's complementary part, she follows out to conclusion the pattern of action established by Judith and supported by the two of them while Judith lived. She pays for Judith's and Charles Etienne's tombstones, raises Jim Bond, and harbors Henry. Her final action, the burning of the Sutpen mansion, is a desperate attempt to preserve the house and the family from violation by outsiders because the Sutpens have earned that right. As she observes, " 'Whatever he done, me and Judith and him have paid it out' " (370).

Clytie, as black twin to Judith, becomes a subtle statement of the oneness of humankind. The common bonds of temperament, interests, duty, and affection unite the two women in a sisterhood that transcends race. Their relationship is a more sustained and meaningful version of that between Henry and Charles. Because Clytie and Judith relate to each other as "womenfolk" first, then as "daughter" and "sister," they partly escape the racial burden placed on their brothers. Their personal relationship provides a model of sibling cooperation and harmony in the novel, and by extension it suggests the possibility of a different order of social interaction between races in the South. . . .

The relationship between Clytie and Judith is critical to the meaning of the novel because it achieves a level of communication and kinship across social barriers, but also because it precipitates the destructive cycle of Charles Etienne St. Valery Bon, the son of Charles Bon and a New Orleans octoroon. Charles Etienne's story moves the Sutpen legend into the postwar period and enlarges its social significance. Clytie prevents the boy on his first visit to Sutpen's Hundred from playing with a black youth. Even after Charles Etienne arrives to live on the plantation, he is not allowed to have contact with blacks or whites. By watching him with a "brooding fierce unflagging jealous care" (200),[1] Clytie virtually isolates him from members of either race. It seems that as long as she can keep him on Sutpen's Hundred, Clytie believes that she can protect Charles Etienne from the knowledge that barriers exist between races and that those barriers are socially real. She knows that the plantation is a self-contained world sustained only by Judith and herself, for whom racial distinctions no longer have social meanings. Clytie—not Judith—is the boy's guardian and protector. She becomes "the fierce, brooding woman" (197), who in a "curious blend of savageness and pity, of yearning and hatred" (198) cares for Charles Etienne. Clytie's efforts, nevertheless, lead the boy to a much more painful and premature knowledge: the awareness that the barriers between races and individuals are psychically real. Sutpen's legacy to his rejected black son, Charles Bon, is thus perpetuated in the next generation.

When taken abruptly from the "padded and silken vacuum cell" (199) of his life in New Orleans, Charles Etienne encounters the "gaunt and barren" (197) world in which Clytie and Judith live. Once he crosses the threshold of Sutpen's Hundred, his "very silken remaining clothes, his delicate shirt and stockings and shoes which still remained to remind him of what he had once been, vanished, fled from arms and body and legs as if they had been woven of chimaeras or of smoke" (197). His silk clothing is symbolic of more than the white world;[2] it represents the hedonistic, cosmopolitan world of New Orleans, "where pigmentation had no more moral value than the silk walls . . . and the rose-colored . . . shades, where the very abstractions which he might have observed—monogamy and fidelity and decorum and gentleness and affection—were as purely rooted in the flesh's offices as the digestive processes" (199). The city with less rigid racial codes and more indulgent mores forms a contrast to the closed world of the plantation and Jefferson. Compared to the delicate, mythical existence Charles Etienne experiences in New Orleans, Sutpen's Hundred (as introduced by Clytie and the denim jumper) is the abrasive, "actual world"; Mr. Compson envisions Charles Etienne as "produced complete . . . in that cloyed and scented maze of shuttered silk as if he were the delicate and perverse spirit symbol, immortal page of the ancient immortal Lilith, entering the actual world not at the age of one second but twelve years, the delicate garments of his pagehood already half concealed beneath that harsh and shapeless denim cut to an iron pattern and sold by the millions—that burlesque of the Sons of Ham" (196).

When Clytie covers Charles Etienne with a coarse denim jumper, she burdens him with a second existence without explanation. She begins the process of alienating the boy and destroying the world he knows to be real. Neither Clytie nor Judith recognizes that Charles Etienne is a "lonely child in his parchment-and-denim hairshirt" (204). He is irretrievably an outsider—alien to Sutpen's Hundred and lost to the two women who, in their simplicity, fail to realize that he does not understand (indeed has no basis for understanding) his new life, the two women themselves, or their awkward protective gestures. Clytie and Judith, for all their strength and endurance, are extremely naïve women; they are, like their father and brother, independent country people. Thus, they are unable to see the beginning of Charles Etienne's dividedness. Their naïveté and ignorance compound the boy's problem with identity and place. Both women fail Charles Etienne; he, in turn, fails them and himself. These joint failures emphasize the reciprocal nature of the tragedy resulting from defining human beings in terms of race and caste. The tragedy is social as much as private; it affects whites as well as blacks.

Charles Etienne rejects the white world, which he mistakenly perceives as being peopled by the two stern, shadow women, Judith and Clytie, who seem to need only each other. By their inability to express their feelings for him in terms he can clearly comprehend, his two Sutpen "aunts" propel

Charles Etienne into a constant battle with racial barriers, which are mainly presented as social restrictions against open, public display of interracial activities. (He is reminiscent of Joe Christmas, who is similarly propelled by a restrictive Puritan disciplinarian into a rootless, embattled life.)

Charles Etienne marries a "coal black and ape-like woman" who "existed in that aghast and automaton-like state" (205). He makes his wife, a "black gargoyle" (209), an external projection of his black self. He abuses his wife's humanity, even though Faulkner presents her as physically grotesque and inhuman ("resembling something in a zoo," 209). By his treatment of the helpless woman, he dehumanizes himself and alienates himself from the rest of humanity. After a period of moving through a series of cities and towns as if driven by a fury, Charles Etienne returns to Sutpen's Hundred, rents a parcel of land on shares, and lives in an old slave cabin on the place. Nonetheless, he does not penetrate the black world. He remains as alienated from it as he is from his black wife and the Sutpen women.

Clytie and Judith succeed in making not race alone Charles Etienne's albatross, but in making his Sutpen blood heritage (figuratively Sutpen's Hundred) his private prison. The two women do not intend to alienate their ward; both love him according to their capacities as human beings. However, the problem for Judith and Clytie is that as Sutpen "twins" they do not need words, or even gestures, to communicate with each other. The two women, Clytie in particular, mistakenly rely upon Charles Etienne's sharing their kinship and their *"rapport of communal blood"* (159); he cannot. His blood is strongly rooted in the foreign environment of New Orleans, and the silken cocoon of his mother's existence there, even though his exact orientation to the city disintegrates along with the physical disintegration of his silk clothing. Their inability to understand different worlds and perceptions is akin to their father's; Sutpen, insulated from a larger experience of life, could not understand Charles Bon or his way of seeing the world.

Clytie's fierce guardianship of Charles Etienne corresponds to mythical allusions evoked by her name, "Clytemnestra." According to Mr. Compson, Sutpen "named her himself" (61), though perhaps "he intended to name Clytie, Cassandra, prompted by some pure dramatic economy not only to beget but to designate the presiding augur of his own disaster, and . . . he just got the name wrong through a mistake natural in a man who must have almost taught himself to read" (62). Mr. Compson seems inaccurate here because Clytie is not so much Cassandra, mad prophetess of doom, as she is Clytemnestra, fiercely maternal wife-mother figure of vengeance. (Rosa Coldfield appears to be the Cassandra figure.)

The allusions to the name "Clytemnestra" seem appropriate, if not precisely so. Clytemnestra is wife-mother, who out of complex motives brings disaster to her children and herself by willfully exacting revenge for her daughter Iphigenia's death. Despite the reference to Clytie's "fierceness," she does not seem to be a personality motivated by a personal fury (such as revenge). However, the mythical Clytemnestra is responsible for Cassandra's death; their two visions of reality and duty fatally conflict. Clytie is related to the mythical Clytemnestra in this sense, because she finally thwarts Rosa's efforts to control the Sutpens by taking charge of Henry. She burns the mansion rather than have Rosa remove Henry and assume responsibility for him. Shortly thereafter, Rosa dies, somehow mortally wounded by her last encounter with Clytie. Clytie's action represents a kind of dual expiation on the part of both races in the South and particularly on the part of the planter class. In burning Sutpen's Hundred with herself and Henry inside, Clytie destroys the two surviving Sutpens, who along with Judith are similar to the mythical Orestes in their attempts to expiate the old crimes, their own sins and those they inherit from their father. . . .

When Rosa and Clytie confront each other on the stairs of Sutpen's Hundred after Charles Bon's murder, they participate in one of the most dramatic, and revealing, scenes in the work.[3] At the moment of their meeting, Rosa sees Clytie as an extension of Sutpen and as her own twin sister because of their joint connection to him: "the two of us joined by that hand and arm which held us like a fierce rigid umbilical cord, twin sistered to a fell darkness which had produced her" (140). Though Rosa, like Charles Etienne, rails against the order of things in her world, she recognizes the complex nature of human interconnectedness (thereby accentuating one of Faulkner's major themes). She describes herself as well as Clytie as "sentient victim" and admits the private, mysterious connection to Sutpen, who is Clytie's biological father and who gives Rosa life (that is, provides her with a *raison d'etre* which in its negative capacity links her even more closely to the negative aspect of Sutpen's indefatigable and undefeated will to duplicate himself). At the same time, Rosa acknowledges the connection between two individuals who share a deeply felt experience: "*we seemed to glare at one another not as two faces but as the two abstract contradictions which we actually were, neither of our voices raised, as though we spoke to one another free of the limitations and restrictions of speech and hearing*" (138). Rosa and Clytie are yoked so that their differences are grossly exaggerated, even though the very intensity of their union destroys ordinary impediments to communication. This yoking of "abstract contradictions" is central to the structural and thematic progress of the novel. For instance, it is one way of approaching Quentin and Shreve as creators, or Henry and Charles as friends. It is a process repeated in the narrative shared by the southerner and the Canadian as they attempt to form meaning and significance out of the legend.

Rosa's meeting with Clytie is a central scene because it reverberates all the tensions between black and white, between classes and races that have been used to define the South and to establish the major concerns of the novel. One of the most starkly honest scenes in the Faulkner canon, this meeting probes the psychological and cultural realities of race and kinship. It suggests all of the dramatic meetings which take place in *Absalom* (Sutpen and the monkey nigger, Charles Bon and Henry, even Shreve and Quentin). Superseded in intensity only by Quentin's encounter with Henry, it is the single extended narration of a confrontation between black and white in a work clearly dependent upon a series of such confrontations for meaning.

Rosa, in her moments of knowing, her "epiphany," encounters Clytie as "Negro" and "woman" but also, paradoxically, as "sister": *"we stood there joined by that volitionless . . . hand, . . . I cried 'And you too? And you too, sister, sister?' "* (140). Prior to this moment, Rosa has neither recognized nor accepted Clytie as Sutpen's daughter, sister to Judith and metaphorically sister to Rosa herself. Still, Clytie is not a person to Rosa. She is "nigger" and a sphinxlike presence invented by Sutpen solely to confound Rosa; she is *"the Sutpen face . . . already there, rocklike and firm . . . waiting there . . . in his own image the cold Cerberus of his private hell"* (136).

Clytie's presence reminds Rosa that she is cut off from significant areas of life, particularly from family participation, just as the Negro, symbolically represented by the "balloon face" and the "monkey nigger," serves to remind Sutpen of his poor-white origins. It is not only that Rosa is not a wife, but that finally she is not sister, daughter, aunt, or niece. She is and remains an outsider. Begrudgingly, Rosa recognizes her own inadequacies, Clytie's essential harmony with her world, and their psychological union. But she does so by making Clytie not merely like Sutpen, a demon, but the personification of all that has prevented her full participation in life. Clytie becomes an *"immobile antagonism,"* *"that presence, that familiar coffee-colored face"* (137), which Rosa "sees" as both an object blocking her passage up the stairs and as a force confounding her entire life.

Clytie stands for Sutpen's continuing reality and his insult to the spinster who hurls herself into: *"that inscrutable coffee-colored face, that cold implacable mindless (no, not mindless: anything but mindless, his own clairvoyant will tempered to amoral evil's undeviating absolute by the black willing blood with which he had crossed it) replica of his own which he had created and decreed to preside upon his absence, as you might watch a wild distracted nightbound bird flutter into the brazen and fatal lamp"* (138). Clytie is the proof (and for the sight-oriented Rosa, the visible therefore incontrovertible proof) of Sutpen's sexual activity, in particular his mating with someone other than "wife," with someone more animal than human, with the "black willing blood" of one of the original "wild niggers." It is an insult to the spinster that Sutpen, who represented her one opportunity for marriage (here specifically sex and children), would "grace" *even a nigger* but would deny her. Thus, Sutpen himself, not Clytie, has condemned Miss Rosa to ignorance and blind, futile thrusting. Sutpen is, paradoxically, "clairvoyant," and Clytie is a "brazen and fatal lamp," while Rosa is "a wild distracted nightbound bird." For all their negative capacity drawn by Miss Rosa, Sutpen and Clytie symbolize vision and light for her. On the other hand, Rosa with ironic aptness sees herself as a sightless bird enmeshed in darkness and fluttering blindly into destruction.

Clytie's command, " 'Dont you go up there, Rosa' " (138), causes Rosa to assert the authority of her race and the superiority of her position as white woman in the South: " 'Rosa? . . . 'To me? To my face?' " (139). Yet even while speaking the words, Rosa knows "it was not the name, the word the fact that she had called me Rosa" (139); Rosa believes that "while we stood face to face . . . she did me more grace and respect than anyone else I knew; . . . to her of all who knew me I was no child" (139). She infers that Clytie recognizes her as "woman," intuits her female urges and sexual drives. Perhaps Clytie alone, with her "brooding awareness and acceptance of the inexplicable unseen, inherited from an older and a purer race" (138), understands Rosa's frustrated sexual energy, understands that Rosa is denied access to marriage and familial intimacy (and in this instance specifically, denied access as well to the knowledge and experience of life and death she seeks in the upper regions of the Sutpen house).

Nonetheless, Rosa perverts the meeting into a racial confrontation; she is otherwise unable to cope with its implications (that is, Clytie as a Sutpen "belongs" at Sutpen's Hundred and has a natural place in the affairs of the family, whereas Rosa, though white, is relegated to a lower, nonprivileged status). Rosa's tactic reiterates the ultimate tragedy of the Sutpen legend: the son's meeting with the father is reduced to a racial confrontation; kinship, whether physical or spiritual, may be denied when one party is "Negro."

Clytie's reactions to this meeting are not provided; she remains as nonverbal as she has been throughout the novel; however, her presence, as a mixed-blood placed within the Sutpen family, suggests that either race or kinship must be denied if caste and color are to continue to sustain fixed meanings in a changing world. Clytie's involvement in the lives of other characters forwards the conclusion that in order to avoid self-destruction, and perhaps ultimately social disintegration, bonds of kinship on every level must be honored, even if they exist across racial lines (or most especially when they do, as Faulkner suggests both with the resolution of Absalom, Absalom! and with a later novel, Go Down, Moses). This idea of kinship, most apparent in the portraits of Clytie and Charles Bon, is, in one sense, an insightful development of the idea of family (both white and black) Faulkner first employs in Flags in the Dust and uses more intensively in The Sound and the Fury; it partakes, too, of the conception of "blood" and racial definitions from Light in August. Blood and family become in Absalom, Absalom! human kinship and interconnection[4]—larger abstractions—which Faulkner presents as confused and conflicting, but by means of them he aims toward a more comprehensive way of portraying the divided world of his South.

Notes

1. The drawing of Clytie in these terms suggests Callie Barr, whose sharp tongue and watchful presence have been recorded by the Faulkner brothers. John, for instance, reveals, "I am sure when our time comes, she will demand an explanation even of Him if we are denied admittance Up There, and as sure that her staunch vehemence will bring for each of us at least a resigned 'All right, Let them in.' " *My Brother Bill*, 52.

2. Nilon limits the interpretation of Charles Etienne's clothing—the silk to the white world and the denim to the black. *Faulkner and the Negro*, 95.

3. One measure of the importance of the encounter between Rosa and Clytie is the care Faulkner took in revising the scene. According to Gerald Langford, there were four stages of revision apparent in Faulkner's presentation of the meeting between the two women. The manuscript shows that much of Faulkner's rewriting of the scene involves emphasizing the dramatic impact of the confrontation. Specifically, Faulkner added to the section in such a way as to extend the significance of the touch, of Clytie's coffee-colored hand on Rosa's white woman flesh. *Faulkner's Revision of "Absalom, Absalom!": A Collation of the Manuscript and the Published Book* (Austin: University of Texas Press, 1971), 29–31.

4. Faulkner threads the theme of human kinship and interconnection throughout the narratives. Several of the most prominent statements of this theme are: Judith's idea that people are all "hitched to one another by strings" (127); Mr. Compson's belief that in assimilating the fragments of the past "we see dimly people . . . in whose living blood and seed we ourselves lay dormant and waiting" (101); Quentin's notion that no thing or person happens once "but like ripples . . . on water after the pebble sinks, the ripples moving on, spreading, the pool attached by a narrow umbilical water-cord to the next pool" (261); and the omniscient narrator's view that Quentin and Shreve are "connected . . . in a sort of geographical transubstantiation by the Continental Trough" (258), that they are "two of them, then four" (345) because they are compounded in Henry and Charles, so that ultimately "it was not even four now but compounded still further since now both of them were Henry . . . both were Bon" (351).

Fathers and Strangers:
From Patriarchy to Counterfamily
in Faulkner's *Absalom, Absalom!*

ANDREA DIMINO*

William Faulkner's *Absalom, Absalom!* is not about one family, but two. The first is a patriarchal family headed by Thomas Sutpen; the second, which I shall call the counterfamily, is engaged in erasing the name of the father as its origin and center of power, substituting instead a complex series of fluid, dynamic, and temporary coalitions. In spite of the fact that many of its members also belong to the first Sutpen family, the counterfamily transgresses patriarchal boundaries and creates new forms of human affiliation.

The narrators of the novel are engaged, moreover, in a turbulent dialogue about the meaning of "family" itself. At times, families seem to embody in an essentialist way the stamp of the father; but elsewhere they function somewhat mechanistically as conduits for larger social and cultural forces. As an example of essentialism, Sutpen's patriarchal force—his founding of the figurative "House of Sutpen"—is reified in the plantation, Sutpen's Hundred, and in the actual house, the grandiose symbol of the dynastic design. The house and plantation are strongly identified with Sutpen's literal body—in Mr. Compson's words, "as though houses actually possess a sentience . . . begotten upon the wood and brick by the man or men who conceived and built them" (p. 67).[1] A character's membership in the Sutpen family seems like another irreducible essence strongly linked to the power and to the body of the patriarch. Mr. Compson sees Judith as a " 'Sutpen with the ruthless Sutpen code of taking what it wanted' " (p. 95); Miss Rosa Coldfield, the sister of Sutpen's wife Ellen, perceives Clytie Sutpen's face as a *"coffee-colored . . . replica"* of her father's (p. 110), and speaks of *"the house which {Sutpen} had built, which some suppuration of himself had created about him"* (p. 111). When Sutpen recounts his past life to Grandfather Compson during the hunt for the architect, his body appears metaphorically as the individualistic force that determines his family's future: "he said he thought how there was something about a man's destiny (or about the man) that caused the

*This essay was written especially for this volume and is published here for the first time by permission of the author.

destiny to shape itself to him like his clothes did, like the same coat that new might have fitted a thousand men, yet after one man has worn it for a while it fits no one else" (p. 198).[2]

In other episodes, however, the narrators view the family as an agent of the larger society. Sutpen's desire for a particular kind of family, his dynastic design, is often portrayed as a basically economic activity. While he is building his mansion, Sutpen drinks his guests' whiskey "with a sort of sparing calculation as though keeping mentally, General Compson said, a sort of balance of spiritual solvency between the amount of whiskey he accepted and the amount of running meat which he supplied to the guns" (p. 30). Quentin Compson remembers his grandfather's similes as he tells his Harvard roommate Shreve of Sutpen's talk with General Compson during the Civil War. General Compson perceives in Sutpen's search for the flaw in his design " 'that innocence which believed that the ingredients of morality were like the ingredients of pie or cake and once you had measured them and balanced them . . . it was all finished' " (pp. 211–12). Even though the entire town of Jefferson sees Sutpen's association with his storekeeper father-in-law Mr. Coldfield as highly incongruous, these repeated references to measuring link him to a similarly mercantile kind of quantification. This undercuts the putative social division between storekeepers and wealthy planters.[3] Finally, Sutpen's role as a colonel in the Civil War extends the quantifying aspect of his dynasty-building: he keeps his men alive *"in order to swap them blood and flesh for the largest amount of ground at its bargain price"* (p. 277). We see in Sutpen's urge to measure and quantify a basic stance that links his morality, his family life, and his place in a larger economy.

On an even more basic level, one with strong symbolic overtones, the Sutpens are tied to larger cultural dynamics in that the family repeatedly enacts the basic process that transforms nature into culture. Clytie Sutpen, the daughter of Thomas Sutpen and a slave, seems to Miss Rosa *"like the indolent and solitary wolf or bear (yes, wild: half untamed black, half Sutpen blood: and if 'untamed' be synonymous with 'wild' then 'Sutpen' is the silent unsleeping viciousness of the tamer's lash)"* (p. 126). When Sutpen arrives at Wash Jones's cabin to find out whether Milly Jones has borne him the son he desires, he appears as the arbiter of the passage between brutehood and humankind, barring Milly's entrance to his family. He asks the black midwife, " 'Well? Damn your black hide: horse or mare?' " (p. 229).

We see the most striking link between the family and the wider culture in the war metaphor that is largely developed by Mr. Compson. From an ironic distance, he finds in Henry and Judith "a curious relationship: something of that fierce impersonal rivalry between two cadets in a crack regiment" (p. 62). The metaphor turns into black humor when Quentin remembers his father describing Sutpen's courtship as an assault on Miss Rosa's *"embattled spinsterhood . . . with . . . ruthless tactical skill"*; but Sutpen's aging body has become a decrepit instrument of war: *"he was now past sixty and . . . possibly he could get but one more son, had at best but one more son in his loins, as the old cannon might know when it has just one more shot in its corporeality"* (pp. 223–24). The earliest chronological appearance of this war metaphor is the young Sutpen's loss of innocence after the planter's servant insults him; he conceives of his dynastic design as the result of an inner " 'explosion' " that reinterprets his life as a " 'combat' " between social classes (p. 192).

If this pervasive war metaphor helps us to gauge the wide-ranging role of the patriarchal family in reproducing a culture awash in contradictions, our awareness is further intensified by Faulkner's development of what I would call "boundary situations": episodes in which characters enter or leave the Sutpen family, or change their roles within the family. These boundary situations not only foreground the destructiveness of Sutpen's power, but also remind us that Sutpen's definition of his family is reductive. In 1870 Charles Etienne, the son of Charles Bon, is brought from New Orleans to Sutpen's Hundred, and learns what his blackness means within the boundaries of the Sutpen family: "he . . . crossed that strange threshold, that irrevocable demarcation . . . into that gaunt and barren household where his very silken remaining clothes . . . fled from arms and body and legs as if they had been woven of chimaeras or of smoke" (p. 160). In 1865 Charles Bon himself is killed by Henry Sutpen when he reaches the boundary of the gate to Sutpen's Hundred. Quentin encounters in his turn the disturbing aura of Sutpen's Hundred as a child, when he tries to enter the decaying Sutpen house. Frightened by Clytie, he hurls himself over the plantation fence, *"and then the earth, the land, the sky and trees and woods, looked different again, all right again"* (p. 174).

Finally, the portrayal of women and black people within the Sutpen family also helps the reader to perceive the family as a contradictory entity in flux. In this context we can see Mr. Compson articulating the ideology behind Sutpen's dynastic appropriation of women and blacks. For example, Mr. Compson will often describe women characters as absences; Judith is " 'just the blank shape, the empty vessel' " in which the relationships between Bon and Henry, " 'seducer and seduced,' " is played out (p. 95). Miss Rosa confirms that Sutpen has a similar attitude toward women; in proposing to his sister-in-law he does not want *"my being, my presence: just my existence"* (p. 134). Mr. Compson also highlights women's exchange value for Sutpen in a masculine economy rather than their identities as human subjects.[4] His perception covers women of all races and social classes; in the same paragraph we see Sutpen choose his women's slaves " 'with the same care and shrewdness with which he chose the other livestock' " and put off buying furniture and courting a wife because " 'he had at the time nothing to exchange for it them or her' " (p. 48).

Since *Absalom, Absalom!* appeared in 1936, Thomas Sutpen has remained a compelling figure for readers and critics, for we are still engaged in the cultural discourse of fathers. But in the current critical climate, for those who work with deconstruction, poststructuralist thought, feminism, politically engaged criticism, and postmodernism, who are primed to see contradiction, subtext, subversion, and multiplicity when they engage a literary text, another kind of family emerges in Faulkner's novel. I have tentatively called this a "counterfamily," but I shall develop the concept with the understanding that the argument will eventually call into question any use of the term "family" at all. As I have noted, the counterfamily is not a unit like the patriarchal family, but rather a system of fluid and temporary affiliations.

The counterfamily in *Absalom, Absalom!* takes two basic forms: the first is embodied in designs that counter or mirror Sutpen's patriarchal dynasty. One such design is Shreve's invention of the protomilitary campaign mounted by Eulalia Bon (to avenge Sutpen's rejection) and by her scheming lawyer (to extort his wealth). Henry Sutpen also wrenches power from Sutpen because of his love for Bon, overturning the forms of primogeniture; he refutes Bon's statement that " ' "No son of a landed father wants an older brother," ' " and he later abjures his birthright when Sutpen tells him that Charles is in fact his brother (pp. 253, 237). And by imposing a "probation" during the war, when he tries to accept the possibility of incest between Bon and Judith, Henry makes a desperate attempt to forge a counterdesign (p. 276).

The second, more significant form of counterfamily involves the creation of new structures that embody a relative freedom from patriarchal design. This possibility erupts during Mr. Compson's narrative, when he recounts Judith Sutpen's gift of Bon's final letter to Grandmother Compson. This unexpected gift to a relative stranger opens radical possibilities for relationship, functioning within an entirely different system of values than Sutpen's design. When Mrs. Compson asks if she should keep the letter, Judith replies:

> Yes. . . . Or destroy it. As you like. Read it if you like or dont read it if you like. Because you make so little impression, you see. You get born and you try this and you dont know why only you keep on trying it and you are born at the same time with a lot of other people, all mixed up with them, like trying to, having to, move your arms and legs with strings only the same strings are hitched to all the other arms and legs and the others all trying and they dont know why either except that the strings are all in one another's way like five or six people all trying to make a rug on the same loom . . . then all of a sudden it's all over and all you have left is a block of stone with scratches on it. (pp. 100–1)

No mention here of Sutpen's dream of freedom from brutehood; for Judith time is not informed by the meaningful succession of genealogy. In the face of a world that does not even contain family, but simply a "lot of other people," a world in which nothing seems to matter, Judith substitutes for the monumental authority of the father the desperate but significant gesture of giving a scrap of paper to a stranger.[5]

At the heart of Judith's counterfamily lies the substitution of the "umbilical" of language—in the words of Grandfather Compson, the " 'meagre and fragile thread . . . by which the little surface corners and edges of men's secret and solitary lives may be joined for an instant now and then' "—for the rigid umbilical that binds people to the father in a reverie of Quentin's (pp. 202, 210). When we see Judith with Sutpen, she is almost silent; with Grandmother Compson, a relative stranger, she voices a passionate quest for meaning. And the letter from Charles Bon that she gives to Mrs. Compson is similarly divested of the basic forms of orientation of conventional society. Unlike the familial and "familiar" letter from Mr. Compson over which Quentin broods during much of his collaboration with Shreve, Charles's letter is " 'without date or salutation or signature' " (pp. 141, 102).[6]

Judith's discourse of the stranger acts as a catalyst for the two other major attempts in the novel to create new counterfamilial structures of human affiliation: Miss Rosa's monologue in chapter 5 and Quentin and Shreve's re-creation of the Sutpen story at Harvard, which culminates in their "happy marriage of speaking and hearing" (pp. 115, 253).[7] The power of Rosa's speech in her monologue wrenches her away from her conventional relationship to the Sutpen family as undervalued spinster sister and aunt and rejected fiancée to Sutpen himself. Rosa's monologue is marked by turbulence and contradiction, to the point where some of her utterances just do not make sense. Like a tectonic plate shaking up the novel roughly midway through, the earthquake of chapter 5 substitutes disturbing and flamboyant new forms for Sutpen's rigid language and sense of meaning.

Rosa's acknowledgement of her own sexuality enables her to claim a new line of descent separate from that of her hated father, a purely female line: *"had I not heired too from all the unsistered Eves since the Snake?"* (p. 115). One's gender, then, can be a counterfamily. This stance is contradicted, however: during her summer of wisteria, the sexual awakening triggered by the mysterious bond between Charles Bon and Judith, she transgresses the gender boundaries decreed by patriarchy. Rosa lives out the summer not as a woman *"but rather as the man which I perhaps should have been . . . I became all polymath love's androgynous advocate"* (pp. 116–17). In contrast to Sutpen's dynastic marriage, with its insistence on the specificity and purity of " 'stainless' " names, Miss Rosa experiences *"one anonymous climaxless epicene and unravished nuptial . . . a world filled with living marriage like the light and air which she breathes"* (pp. 39, 116).

As an outburst of language, Rosa's chapter 5 encodes energy, exuberance, and transgression; in relation to traditional conventions of meaning and to familiar social relationships, it is an arena of confusion. When Miss Rosa tries to explain her relationship with Judith and Clytie at Sutpen's

Hundred during the war, she is unable to clarify why she stays with two women whom she does not understand. This is not, then, the harmonious "community of women" evoked as an ideal by feminist criticism; even though Judith is *"blood kin,"* her actions disturb Rosa to the point where Rosa does not even wish to understand her (p. 123).[8] Rosa describes Clytie as *"so foreign to me and to all that I was that we might have been not only of different races . . . but of different species, speaking no language which the other understood"* (p. 123). Nevertheless, when Clytie grasps her arm after Bon's death, the women are *"twin sistered"* by the touch of *"flesh . . . with flesh"* (p. 112). In these paradoxical assertions of the greatest difference and the greatest closeness— for Judith's link with Bon nurtures Miss Rosa's burgeoning self—lies the nature of Miss Rosa's troubling counterfamily, a community of strangers.

In contrast to Sutpen's rigid social, racial, and gender distinctions, the three women transgress these boundaries in some respects. They live *"amicably, not as two white women and a negress, not as three negroes or three whites, not even as three women, but merely as three creatures"* (p. 125). The turbulent linguistic world of chapter 5 allows Miss Rosa to utter something that in other contexts would be unthinkable: Judith, Rosa, and Clytie as "three negroes"? "three whites"? And ultimately even the boundaries between individuals are eroded: *"It was as though we were one being, interchangeable and indiscriminate"* (p. 125).[9] The relationship stands as a challenge to Thomas Sutpen's obsession with quantifying, with names, and with the individuality of his design. We find an equally radical challenge to Sutpen in Miss Rosa's claim to what could be called an androgynous "fathering" of Charles Bon himself; she says of Bon's face, which she has never actually seen, *"so who will dispute me when I say, Why did I not invent, create it?"* (p. 118).

Together with Judith Sutpen's discourse of the stranger and her gift of Bon's letter to Grandmother Compson, Miss Rosa's transformative cosmos in chapter 5 opens up crucial possibilities for counterfamilial links in Quentin and Shreve's narrative partnership later in the novel. At the height of their collaboration, the roommates, like Miss Rosa, belong to the patriarchal Sutpen family and to the counterfamily at the same time. In a complex sharing of the existences of Henry and Charles, the roommates exist as two young men, then four, and then "both of them were Henry Sutpen and both of them were Bon" (p. 280). The sharing is expressed as a literal "blood" relation (p. 237). This is a shifting counterfamily of the most radical kind; Sutpen could not act as a quantifying social arbiter here, since we can't even count the family members.

Faulkner's portrayal of the counterfamily in *Absalom, Absalom!* raises some difficult questions about his own cultural and historical identity. If we broadly sketch out the cultural possibilities for the depiction of the family in modern literature, we see a field bounded on one side by the classic nineteenth-century novel, with its linear stories of fathers and sons. At the far reaches of this field of cultural possibilities, we can read the counterfamilial elements in *Absalom, Absalom!* as a move in the direction of a radical counterculture, like the one Gilles Deleuze discusses in responding to Nietzsche's *On the Genealogy of Morals.* For Deleuze, Nietzsche is the only modern thinker "who makes no attempt at recodification" when confronted with the breaking down of codes in our societies—codes embodied in law, contracts, philosophic discourse, literature, and, of course, institutions like the family.[10] Nietzsche expresses instead "something that can not be codified, confounding all codes"; something that Deleuze calls "nomad thought" (p. 143). This cultural possibility challenges Faulkner's readers to consider how far we want to go in codifying the play of forces that I have called the "counterfamily" in terms of particular concepts and structures.

Thus the counterfamily in *Absalom, Absalom!* does not constitute a negation of the family, a *"retroactive severance of the stream of event"* that displaces a relatively coherent though contradictory old system in favor of a confusing new one (p. 127). Reading the novel, we respond to family and counterfamily at the same time. In terms of the history of Faulkner criticism, our ability to see counterfamilial patterns of opposition, subversion, and dynamic affiliation is an element in our own conceptual lenses—as I have noted, an element that has been shaped by contemporary realms of discourse. Nevertheless the term "counterfamily" preserves the historical mark of our past and present fascination with Faulkner's families. My use of this umbrella term thus signals that the novel's subversive coalitions of characters and narrators represent for us a liberating multiplicity that has been given many names, but not yet a monolithic one.

Notes

1. *Absalom, Absalom!* (New York: Vintage, 1990); hereafter cited in the text.

2. Though Sutpen himself can be seen as an example of individualism in the public sphere, his family diverges from the individualistic "democratic family"—the term is de Tocqueville's—that became increasingly prevalent in nineteenth-century America (see Steven Mintz and Susan Kellogg, *Domestic Revolutions: A Social History of American Family Life* [New York: Macmillan, Free Press, 1988], chapter 3). As a private place marked by the values of love and mutuality, the "democratic family" provided a counterweight to the values of the marketplace (p. 44). But as Mintz and Kellogg note, nineteenth-century Southern families tended to uphold older notions of patriarchy and a "code of honor" that stressed "hierarchy . . . and family allegiance"; this was particularly evident in the Southern conception of womanhood" (p. 267).

3. As James A. Snead argues, Faulkner's novels show connection, merging, and reversal in the face of a social rhetoric that tries to impose divisions; see *Figures of Division: William Faulkner's Major Novels* (New York: Methuen, 1986). In fact, Sutpen does become a storekeeper in the desperate years after the war.

4. For a wide-ranging discussion of Faulkner's portrayal of woman as "other," outside of male cultural dialogue, see Philip M. Weinstein, *Faulkner's Subject: A Cosmos No One Owns* (New York: Cambridge University Press, 1992), chapter 1. Minrose C. Gwin examines women's resistance to their role as a commodity in patriarchal culture, including Miss Rosa's

"hysterical text" in chapter 5 (*The Feminine and Faulkner: Reading (Beyond) Sexual Difference* [Knoxville: University of Tennessee Press, 1990], 72).

5. We could, in fact, see the "block of stone" in Judith's outburst to Grandmother Compson as a veiled reference to Sutpen himself. Miss Rosa compares Sutpen's boastful proposal of marriage to writing carved in stone (p. 132), and during the war Sutpen's soldiers give the name " ' "Colonel" ' " to one of the tombstones that the regiment has been dragging around (p. 154).

6. In Olga Scherer's view, Judith's long speech to Grandmother Compson, quoted above, represents a dialogue with Bon's letter and affirms the value of the dialogic ("A Polyphonic Insert: Charles's Letter to Judith," in *Intertextuality in Faulkner*, ed. Michel Gresset and Noel Polk [Jackson: University Press of Mississippi, 1985], 168–77). A number of recent critics (Stephen Ross, Warwick Wadlington, John Matthews) associate Sutpen with rigid language and with the "monologic"; the dialogic is linked to the values of the counterfamily.

7. Judith's evocation of the "stranger" also resonates with Faulkner's own comments about his relation to his reader, the "stranger" who will look at his writing "100 years later"; in general Faulkner's comments shift between quasi-patriarchal conceptions of his literary authority (the godlike creation of a "cosmos of my own") and potentially "counterfamilial" conceptions like the stranger-reader. (See his interview with Jean Stein vanden Heuvel, *Lion in the Garden: Interviews with William Faulkner*, ed. James B. Meriwether and Michael Millgate [Lincoln: University of Nebraska Press, 1980], 253–55).

8. Nina Auerbach discusses a wide range of familial and nonfamilial communities in *Communities of Women: An Idea in Fiction* (Cambridge: Harvard University Press, 1978).

9. This blurring of the individual extends to the problem of narrative voice in Rosa's chapter 5. I have argued elsewhere that the narrator cannot literally be Miss Rosa, who as a gentlewoman would not utter these tortured revelations in public. An analysis of narrative voice and of the chapter's relation to the novel's spatial settings, narrative structure, and themes, suggests that we hear in this chapter an intermingling of the voices of Miss Rosa, Quentin, Shreve, and the third-person narrator. The italic form of the chapter is the most visible sign of this complex narrative voice. See " 'A Time Altered to Fit the Dream': Narrative Indeterminacy," a chapter in my unpublished book-length study, *Faulkner's Hunt for the Present*.

10. Gilles Deleuze, "Nomad Thought," in *The New Nietzsche: Contemporary Styles of Interpretation*, ed. David B. Allison (New York: Dell, 1977), 143; hereafter cited in the text.

Thomas Sutpen

♦

[The Significance of Thomas Sutpen]

CAROLYN PORTER*

Sutpen's career reconstitutes the very class structure, the very artificial standards it is designed to invalidate. With Sutpen, then, Faulkner cuts through the multilayered myths of the Old South to confront the entrepreneurial designs which had actually created the Cotton Kingdom, and in so doing, reveals the explosive consequences of understanding the slaveowning planter for the capitalist entrepreneur he was.[1] . . .

This, in any case, would seem to be Faulkner's view of the matter in *Absalom, Absalom!*, where he presents us with a man who acts in the service of a dream of paternal authority which is sufficiently grandiose to merit the analogy with King David implied by the novel's title. Sutpen embodies that paternalism embraced by Andrew Jackson in the service of capitalist expansion and his fate reflects the contradictions at the core of that paternalism. As Faulkner explained, Sutpen was "a man who wanted sons and got sons who destroyed him," as a result of his failure to recognize that he was "a member . . . of the human family." Herein lies the central irony of Sutpen's dream of founding a dynasty. In the name of his patriarchal design, Sutpen ruthlessly violates the bonds of love and of blood with stunning consistency. He repudiates one wife and refuses to recognize his eldest son; he makes a

*Reprinted from *Seeing and Being: the Plight of the Participant Observer in Emerson, James, Adams and Faulkner*. © 1984 by Carolyn Porter, Wesleyan University Press. By permission of University Press of New England.

bargain for a second wife whose attractions are entirely a matter of her irrefutable respectability; he turns one son into the murderer of the other, making—as Rosa Coldfield never tires of repeating—a widow of his daughter before she can become a bride; he offers Rosa a contract for copulation and Milly Jones an insult for her failure to emulate his horse in producing male offspring. Needless to say, these are not the acts of a benign paternalistic planter in a panama hat and a white suit; these are the acts of a character of mythic dimensions in whose career is inscribed the history of America itself, revealing, for one thing, the irony of a paternal authority in the name of which Indian tribes were broken up and Africans enslaved. For when Sutpen refuses to recognize his own son, he exhibits the logical, if self-contradictory, consequence of a paternalism generated in the interest of Capital, a paternalism which logically dictates that fathers exile and repudiate their sons.[2] . . .

The contradiction within paternalism is not the only feature of America's history which Sutpen's career exposes. In his desire to demonstrate, once and forever, the Declaration of Independence's opening assertion, he acts in the name of America's revolutionary rejection of the European past, its assertion that the "artificial standards" and "circumstances" of class will have no place in American society. Sutpen's aim is to lay waste to the class structure so that future generations will be "riven forever free from brute-hood," recognized as free men, no matter what their social origins. Yet in his effort to vindicate the principle of social equality, Sutpen reconstitutes the very class structure he set out to oppose. Once again, he is the victim of his own design; in order to prove that any little boy can live in the big white house, he must acquire the house itself and all that goes with it, and in so doing, he rises above and finally refuses recognition to the man who mirrors Sutpen's own origins—Wash Jones. In denying Jones the social recognition he demands and deserves, Sutpen brings his own life to a violent end, and provokes Jones himself to suicide and the massacre of his offspring, as a result of the realization that there is no place for him in this society, that it would be "better if his kind and mine too had never drawn the breath of life on this earth" than to live without the respect owed by free men to one another. Facing the fact which Sutpen himself had once faced at the planter's front door, that he is precisely the insignificant creature for which Sutpen's slaves have always taken him, Wash Jones sees "his whole life shredded from him and shrivel away like a dried shuck thrown into the fire."[3]

Wash Jones's apocalyptic despair not only mirrors Sutpen's as a boy but also reflects the fragility of an identity dependent upon the political concepts of freedom and equality as asserted in the Declaration of Independence. For as Karl Marx remarks, this freedom "is not founded upon the relations between man and man, but rather upon the separation of man from man," and this equality amounts to the claim that "every man is equally regarded as a self-sufficient monad." In the conditions of the politically emancipated state, identity is grounded in difference. Sutpen himself constitutes the pure case of such identity. He regards everyone as a self-sufficient monad like himself, as the bearer of atomized social freedom. In realizing his freedom, egoistic man necessarily denies his relation to other men, since his liberty as a free man is founded on his separation from them. In *Absalom, Absalom!*, that separation is always revealed by its denial of the human family. Thus, joined at last by a blood relation to Sutpen as a result of Milly's newborn child, Wash Jones sees that relation denied and is forced to recognize that it means nothing at all. Faulkner thereby exposes a world in which the identity of a free man depends upon his separation from, rather than his relation to, all other free men.[4]

Wash's identity also, of course, depends upon another difference of crucial significance in American history—that between free and unfree men, between white and black. Perhaps the most harrowing of the contradictions exposed by Sutpen's life is that between American freedom and American slavery. As Edmund Morgan has pointed out, it was the labor of slaves which produced the tobacco on which "the position of the United States depended not only in 1776 but during the span of a long lifetime thereafter." "King Tobacco Diplomacy" was to be followed by King Cotton, the economic and political significance of which is well known. Sutpen's design faithfully replicates the corrupt society which first provoked it, a society at whose political birth slavery served as midwife, and whose economic prosperity in the nineteenth century heavily depended upon slave labor. Politically, this meant that white freedom was forged by the denial of black freedom, a fact whose social consequences are registered in Wash Jones's tenuous hold on his social identity as a free man. But what adds resonance to Jones's suicidal despair are the revelations harbored within Sutpen's career regarding the contradiction between white freedom and black slavery as an implicit feature of America's noblest ideal. In pursuing his design, Sutpen asserts the principles of freedom and equality; herein lies the source of his heroic stature. At the same time, however, Sutpen's career exposes the source of that design's implicit doom—its denial of the flesh-and-blood bond between the black, whose labor is exploited to support the white, and the white, whose freedom and equality is secured by that labor. That denial is no more accidental in Sutpen's career than it was accidental in America's. Faulkner exposes this contradiction in American society by confronting us with what James Baldwin once called the "savage paradox" at its heart—that which binds the white slaveowner to the African slave he exploits in a love/hate relationship secured by the bonds of flesh and blood. By denying those bonds, Sutpen exposes their power. In repudiating his black son, he alienates his white one as well, and thereby, in one fell swoop, turns brother against brother, son against father, and black against white. His assertion of freedom compels him to deny his relation to all others, black and white, who are all members of one human family. The blood-and-flesh bonds of that family reassert their power by yielding the black dynasty which Sutpen in fact founds. But this ironic outcome is already implicit in a design which derives American freedom from American slavery.[5]

By emphasizing the ways in which Faulkner exploits Sutpen's career as a register of American history and his design as a mirror of the contradictions inherent in a capitalist society, I do not mean to dismiss as unimportant those features of *Absalom, Absalom!* which focus on the South. The South, as Faulkner acknowledged to Cowley, provided his "material." But he went on to say that this material "is not very important to me. I just happen to know it, and don't have time in one life to learn another one and write at the same time. Though the one I know is probably as good as another, life is a phenomenon but not a novelty, the same frantic steeplechase toward nothing everywhere and man stinks the same stink no matter where in time." As Shreve's responses in *Absalom, Absalom!* indicate, Faulkner knew that the South was regarded as an alien land, a fabled country whose legends were "better than Ben-Hur." But as his narrative use of Shreve also indicates, Faulkner knew how to exploit the South's image in the service of larger purposes than merely those of representing it to outsiders. It is Rosa Coldfield, after all, who seeks in Sutpen an explanation for the Lost Cause; Faulkner was pursuing bigger game. Among other narrative purposes, Faulkner set out to trace, in the rise of an American entrepreneur, the tragic fate implicit in the American dream. Although Faulkner did not have to import such an entrepreneur into the South, it may well be that his experience as a Southerner enabled him to treat this figure with more telling results than he could have done otherwise. If we compare Sutpen to that other archetypal American hero, Jay Gatsby, whose career also serves to embody the American dream, it becomes clear that Faulkner's historical vision makes a significant difference.[6]

Like Gatsby, Sutpen is the child of shiftless people, one who rises to entrepreneurial splendor through shady means. Both Gatsby and Sutpen are self-made men who refuse to recognize the failure of their designs, maintaining to the end of their lives a belief that it is never too late to try again; both are in thrall to the future and the hopes invested in it—Gatsby's hopes to win Daisy back, and Sutpen's hopes for a son; both are underbred parvenus who have come from nowhere; both believe in schedules, in calculation and planning. Finally, both are doomed to failure; not only are their dreams shattered, but they are both murdered by men who mirror their own social origins. A general holocaust marks the end of their lives, reflecting a similar emphasis on violence in the two novels. Yet in Faulkner's hands, the failure of the American dream embodied in Sutpen's rise and fall is treated as a social phenomenon rooted in history rather than as a romantic ideal betrayed by history. Sutpen's design is not born of any Platonic self-conception; it is born of a social affront, and thus originates in history rather than in spite of it.

Notes

1. Frederick L. Gwynn and Joseph L. Blotner, eds., *Faulkner in the University* (New York: Vintage, 1965), p. 35.

2. Faulkner, *Absalom, Absalom!* (New York: Vintage, 1936), pp. 73, 80. Note this is the 1936 typesetting, but the Vintage edition was published later in 1964; the mistake is Porter's.

3. Gwynn and Blotner, p. 35; Faulkner, *Absalom, Absalom!*, pp. 290–91.

4. T. B. Bottomore, ed. and trans., *Karl Marx: Early Writings* (New York: McGraw-Hill, 1963), pp. 24–25.

5. James Baldwin, "Many Thousands Gone," in Baldwin, *Notes of a Native Son* (Boston: Beacon Press, 1955), p. 42; Edmund Morgan, *American Slavery, American Freedom*; Gwynn and Blotner, p. 81.

6. "To Malcolm Cowley," November 1944 in *Selected Letters of William Faulkner*, ed. Joseph Blotner (New York: Random House, 1977), p. 185; Faulkner, *Absalom, Absalom!*, p. 217.

[Sutpen as Patriarch]

ANDRÉ BLEIKASTEN*

Southern society was almost from the outset a family-centered society. Indeed, in the Old South the patriarchal family typified to a large extent the proper relations between ruler and ruled and so supplied the primal model for social organization and political government. Father and master in one, the slaveholding planter of the prewar South was the source and locus of power: as *paterfamilias*, he claimed full authority over wife and children; as "massa," he felt entitled to demand filial subservience from his slaves. He thus presided over an extended family, white and black, and, as Eugene D. Genovese has demonstrated persuasively in his reevaluation of Southern slave society, this sense of extended family came to inform the whole network of race and class relations.[1] The planters, it is true, were only a minority, and one should beware of oversimplification: the social order of the ante-bellum South was more complex and more fluid than well-established stereotypes would have us believe. Yet the plantation system conditioned all of Southern life, and the patriarchal and paternalistic values of the ruling class permeated Southern society at large. Whether paternalism mitigated the evil of slavery will long remain a matter of dispute among historians, but there can be no question that the father metaphor played a major role in the rhetoric of white male power, nor can it be denied that it had become a key concept—or rather a key fantasy—in the ideology of the South.

The *Väterdämmerung* set in after the Civil War, when the socioeconomic foundations of autocratic father rule began at last to crumble. The defeat of the Confederacy meant the end of slavery. Paternalism no doubt survived for many years among the remnants of the plantation system, and so did the patriarchal family structure till the early decades of the twentieth century. But the lordly father image associated with the planter ideal had become an image of the past.[2] In the impoverished South of the Reconstruction years, fathers surely had as many responsibilities as ever, and their tradition-hallowed authority allowed them to keep control over the family. In the upper

---

*Reprinted with permission from *The Fictional Father: Lacanian Readings of the Text*, ed. Robert Con Davis (Amherst: The University of Massachusetts Press, 1981), 121–22, 139–43. © 1981 by The University of Massachusetts Press.

classes, however, their field of power had shrunk irretrievably. Compared to that of their predecessors, theirs was indeed a diminished role and one they must have filled the more self-consciously as they could not help but feel dwarfed by the formidable ghosts of their forefathers.

Out of the nostalgic memories of a lost world and out of the nightmare of a lost war, an imaginary South had arisen, as if to obliterate the real one—a collective mirage in which the old Cavalier legend blended into the Confederate myth born from the exploits of Lee, Jackson, Stuart, Forrest, and all the lesser heroes who had bravely fought and died for the Southern cause. And out of this compelling mirage grew Southern shintoism and its wistful rituals. Probably nowhere else in America, not even in New England, was the ancestor ever held in so much reverence as he then was in the South, nor had he ever been such a powerful and omnipresent phantom.

Fatherland had become a haunted and haunting ghostland, and so the Southern father image was bound to become a divided one, at least in those families—generally of the upper middle-class—that had a sense of continuity and tradition. On the one hand, there was the glorious ancestor, the idolized dead father, safely enshrined in myth, intact and intangible in his godlike remoteness and the more indestructible for being timeless; on the other hand, the human, all too human, progenitor, the hopelessly prosaic real father, born into a time and place in which there was no longer use for the dazzling deeds of heroic gentlemen. How, then, could he be expected to serve as a model to his son? And with whom was the son most likely to identify in his youthful search for an ideal self if not his grandfather or his great-grandfather? . . .

In no other of Faulkner's novels is fatherhood surrounded with so much of a mythic aura, and in his tremendous energy, in his indomitable will, and in his ruthless pursuit of the "design," Sutpen is assuredly the most virile and most heroic of the novelist's father figures. But *Absalom, Absalom!* is no celebration of the father myth, and as we learn in chapter 7 Sutpen's grand "design" is in fact but a plan of revenge for the affront he suffered as a boy, when he was ordered by a "monkey nigger" to the back door of a Tidewater mansion. Sutpen had then considered killing the plantation owner, but eventually chose to become like him: "So to combat them you have got to have what they have that made them do what the man did. You got to have land and niggers and a fine house to combat them with."[3] Instead of rebelling against the Southern ruling class, young Sutpen decides to join it by becoming as rich and powerful as the planter who insulted him. His career begins like any other Oedipal "family romance": in betraying his class and in repudiating his family, Sutpen rejects his poor "white trash" father to pay allegiance to one of better birth. Supplanting the feckless real father, the planter becomes his ideal father, the model of mastery on whom he will pattern his life.[4]

Born of the memory of outrage and of the furious need for self-vindication, Sutpen's "design" is to acquire land, to build a stately mansion, to found a dynasty, i.e., to appropriate all the attributes that defined social leadership in the Old South. Yet his "wild braggart dream"[5] should not be mistaken for the vulgar ambitions of the parvenu. Social success and prestige are only means and signs, the metaphorical objects of an impossible and appallingly "innocent" desire: the desire to defeat time, to free the self from the bondage of flesh and death and to achieve absolute permanence. To Sutpen it is not merely a matter of replacing one father by another, but of having no father at all, of being both one's own father and one's own son—*causa sui*, self-generated, self-enclosed, and self-sufficient. Sutpen is no god, but he would be god. Autogenesis. Sutpen fantasizes it as a purely masculine filiation: the son born of the father, the father reborn in the son. *Et pas de mère alors.* No earthy Eve, no "natural" generation to compromise the design. No (m)other to obstruct the reproduction of the same. Sutpen will need a wife, of course, but only "incidentally."[6] And his children will be his, with faces that are "replicas of his face."[7] To Sutpen fatherhood and sonship are in fact only complementary modes of his ideal self, which means that for him the begetting of a male heir is a symbolic act transcending the procreative urge. Contrary to appearances, his is not the dynastic dream of a genealogy unfolding in time, as what he aims at is not biological perpetuation, but ontological self-expansion. So just as he denied his father, he must deny his sons, for if he acknowledged them as sons he would have to abide by the law of patrilineal succession and to envision the transmission of his power to his descendants. In other words, he would have to face the ineluctability of his death, the very necessity that his "design" is intended to negate.

In *The Sound and the Fury* the father-son relationship fails because of the father's incapacity to exercise his prerogatives; in *Absalom, Absalom!* it is blocked because of his reluctance ever to yield his authority to anyone. Much like Sutpen's wives, his sons are only there to be used in the pursuit of his egotistical scheme, and once they have ceased to be "adjunctive and incremental to [his] design"[8] they are promptly discarded—hence Sutpen's repeated refusal to *recognize* his first-born son. Although Charles Bon poses no threat whatever to Sutpen's design in social terms, his very existence represents for Sutpen the scandal of an irreducible *otherness:* Bon is the reminder of the other race as well as of the other sex (he is "black" like his mother); he is a rem(a)inder, too, of another time, of a past which Sutpen, the indefatigable rebeginner, the "self-made" man forever in the making, has vainly sought to erase from his life. To Sutpen "blackness," first encountered in the face of the liveried "monkey nigger" who stood at the forbidden door of the planter's mansion, is not so much a matter of a race as a private symbol of outrage and frustration; it means to him what "whiteness" meant to Captain Ahab: the inscrutable blankness of reality and its stubborn resistance to man's conquering will.[9] In denying recognition to Bon—and so repeating in reverse the rejection he had himself suffered as a boy—Sutpen refuses once again to acknowledge that the world is not, and cannot be made into, the imperium of his megalomaniac self.

As for Henry, the younger son, he never breaks out of the iron circle of paternal rule. His extravagant triangular fantasies about Bon, Judith, and himself may no doubt be interpreted as a circuitous counterplot, an unconscious attempt to thwart his father's design. It is with Sutpen's will, however, that he identifies in the end, for in killing his half-brother he acts as the father's appointed avenger. Henry thus becomes Sutpen's instrument of retaliation against his first-born. Whether he has ever been more to him than an instrument we do not know for sure, but as there is no hint whatever of a personal feeling on Sutpen's part after Henry's disappearance, it seems safe to assume that Sutpen is just as indifferent to the loss of his second son as to the death of the first.

In the last resort, then, neither son is properly acknowledged.[10] The father-son relationship, exemplified by Sutpen and his male off-spring, is of such a nature as to preclude the very possibility of an act of recognition. In a sense it is no relationship at all: the son is doomed either to be *absorbed* (like Henry, who spends the rest of his life as a recluse in the father's house) or to be *expelled* (like Bon, his masochistic son, or Bond, his idiot grandson: the rejected residues of Sutpen's scheme); either he becomes the father's double or dissolves into nothingness. As in all unmediated dual relationships, twoness finally reverts to oneness.[11]

In Sutpen's world there is indeed only room for *one*—one desire, one will, one power, one "imperial self."[12] Sutpen is the absolute father, an arresting reincarnation of the archaic paternal figure postulated in Freud's anthropological speculations, the *Urvater* who "was lord and father to the entire horde and unrestricted in his power,"[13] and who "loved no one but himself, or other people only in so far as they served his needs."[14] According to Freud, the ferocious and jealous father of prehistoric times was eventually killed, dismembered, and devoured by his sons, and out of their sense of guilt and need for atonement arose the systems of totems and taboos, of substitutions and prohibitions which govern the symbolic order of all human societies. Before being murdered, the "father of the primal horde" *was* the law, absolutely; in death, he came to *represent* the law, metaphorically, thus allowing the unrestricted violence of primitive paternal power to be replaced by the rules of patriarchal authority. In *Absalom, Absalom!* there are a number of striking parallels to Freud's "scientific myth," yet the differences are perhaps even more significant. Patricide here is preceded by fratricide: "[Sutpen's] sons destroyed one another and then him."[15] And since he was the instigator of fratricide, the "original sin" is his. In this novel as in all of Faulkner's works, the primal crime is not patricide;[16] the first figure of guilt, the originator of evil is never the son. Filial guilt is always inherited guilt, and the curse that afflicts generation after generation always begins with the misdeeds of a "primal father."

Faulkner's fiction thus seems to reverse the Freudian pattern, since what it places at the origin is not the murder of the father but the father's sin. It seems to, yet it does not, for, as *Absalom, Absalom!* reveals, before Sutpen, the arrogant, ruthless father, there was Sutpen, the weak, affronted son. The son is always father to the man, and the father's sins are the son's revenge. In the novel, Sutpen appears no doubt as a beginner and begetter (and he thinks of himself precisely in these terms); he strikes us as a demiurgic figure of tremendous power, but as such he is largely a retroactive creation of the narrators' (especially Rosa's) myth-making. Sutpen is not (at) the origin or, rather, he is a false origin, a *proton pseudos*, an origin (re)constructed from its traces and effects. What he stands for is the quintessential *phallacy:* the omnipotence of infantile desire as projected onto the father. In contradistinction to the powerless living fathers of the present, Sutpen and his analogues in Faulkner's novels apparently possess the prerogatives of the strong father, but if they refer us back to the dreaded and envied rival of the primary Oedipal relation, they never come to function as the symbolic agencies of its dissolution. To put the matter into Lacanian terms, they never come to act the role of the "dead father" who guarantees the law. Faulkner's great ancestral figures, we might say, are essentially "ghostly fathers."[17] The trouble with them is that they are dead, but not dead enough to allow their descendants to live.

Absalom, Absalom! is Faulkner's most sustained invocation of the father, conjuring up his spectral presence with a power and intensity unmatched in Faulkner's other novels. Yet the novelist's involvement with fathers and sons hardly diminished in his later works, and in this respect two at least would deserve close scrutiny: *Go Down, Moses* and *A Fable.*

Notes

1. See Eugene D. Genovese, *Roll, Jordan Roll: The World the Slaves Made* (New York: Random House, 1974), pp. 73–75, 133–49, and passim.

2. Despite the gallantry of the Southern armies, the experience of defeat could hardly fail to damage the Southern male self-image. On the other hand, the Civil War had taught Southern women to take many responsibilities which had previously been considered outside their "sphere," and this change in social roles was bound to alter their sense of themselves in relation to their husbands and fathers. On this point, see Anne Firor Scott's fine study, *The Southern Lady: From Pedestal to Politics 1830–1930* (Chicago: University of Chicago Press, 1970).

3. *Absalom, Absalom!*, (New York: Random House, 1936), p. 237.

4. It is worth noting that in "Family Romances" Freud illustrates his point in terms recalling Sutpen's experience at the planter's mansion: ". . . the child's imagination becomes engaged in the task of getting free from the parents of whom he now has a low opinion and of replacing them by others, who, as a rule, are of a higher social standing. He will make use in this connection of any opportune coincidences from his actual experience, such as his becoming acquainted with the Lord of the Manor or some landed proprietor if he lives in

the country or with some member of the aristocracy if he lives in town" (*SE*, chapter 9 [pp. 238–39]).

5. *Absalom, Absalom!*, p. 165.

6. *Absalom, Absalom!*, p. 263.

7. *Absalom, Absalom!*, p. 23.

8. *Absalom, Absalom!*, p. 240.

9. On Ahab and Sutpen, see James Guetti, *The Limits of Metaphor: A Study of Melville, Conrad, and Faulkner* (Ithaca, N.Y.: Cornell University Press, 1967), pp. 82–85, 95, 103.

10. The only evidence to the contrary is Sutpen's outcry in the scene (reconstructed by Quentin and Shreve) of his encounter with Henry during the war: "—Henry . . .—My son" (*Absalom, Absalom!*, p. 353). Sutpen's words closely echo David's in the Bible (cf. 2 Samuel 18: 33); yet, contrary to David's, they do not express grief. At this point, it should be remembered, Henry still stands for the hope that Sutpen's design will be fulfilled.

11. In this respect the father-son relationship in *Absalom, Absalom!* suggests the pre-Oedipal relationship between mother and child, which the father normally is assumed to transform into a triangular pattern. Sutpen might also be defined as a phallic mother, gathering in himself all parental attributes, just as Addie Bundren does in *As I Lay Dying*.

12. I borrow the phrase from Quentin Anderson's book, *The Imperial Self: An Essay in Literary and Cultural History* (N.Y.: Random House, 1971). Focusing on Emerson, Whitman, and Henry James, Anderson contends that in their over-emphasis on the claims of the individual self and their utter disregard for the needs of communal life, these writers exemplify a major trend of American culture. While Anderson's study is heavily biased, it provides a number of valid insights into the regressive and narcissistic tendencies of American romanticism and American literature at large. It fails, however, to give proper credit to those American writers, from Hawthorne and Melville through Fitzgerald and Faulkner, who have exposed the devastating effects of self-centered "innocence." As a fictional hero, Thomas Sutpen belongs with such strong-willed men of design as Colonel Pyncheon, Hollingsworth, Ahab, and Jay Gatsby. There has been much needless discussion as to Sutpen's representative character, based on the dubious assumption that he had to be either a typical Southern planter or a typical non-Southern American. In fact, even though Sutpen lacks the social graces of the gentleman-planter, there can be no question that he embodies to some extent the feudal dream of the ante-bellum South. But this dream, one might argue, was itself a paradoxical version of the American dream, even as the latter was an outgrowth of the Promethean fantasies of post-Renaissance Western Culture.

13. Freud, *Moses and Monotheism*, in *SE*, chapter 23 (p. 81).

14. Freud, *Group Psychology and the Analysis of the Ego*, in *SE*, chapter 18 (p. 123).

15. *Faulkner in the University*, ed. Frederick L. Gwynn and Joseph L. Blotner (Charlottesville: University Press of Virginia, 1959), p. 35.

16. Significantly, while there are many symbolic and displaced forms of patricide in Faulkner's novels, there is no direct representation of it as in Dostoevski's *Brothers Karamazov*.

17. The paradigm of the ghostly father in Western literature is Hamlet's father, murdered "in the blossoms of [his] sin." In terms of sonship and fatherhood, the archetypes of Faulkner's fiction seem to be Hamlet and his father rather than Oedipus and Laius. Oedipus had no complex: he killed his father, married his mother, and then paid the debt. Hamlet commits neither patricide nor incest, though he is obsessed by both. Contrary to that of Oedipus, his is the tragedy of unfulfilled desire and of the unpaid debt. Consider Faulkner's guilt-ridden and helpless sons: they are all Hamlets.

A Brief for Thomas Sutpen

WOODROW STROBLE*

The forceful figures that are Faulkner's villains testify to the power of their creator's imagination. Indeed, the accomplishment is so effective that it can lead to distorted responses among not only fictional characters but readers as well. Nothing is so easy as condemning his villains and nothing so difficult as finding in them redeeming virtues. But finding in Faulkner's scoundrels only unmitigated evil is to find only two-dimensional characters, straw figures, which conceals the fullness of their creator's imagination. Critical treatment of Thomas Sutpen focuses on the hostilities not only of his fellow fictional characters but also of the reader. As one of Faulkner's most powerfully imagined creations, Thomas Sutpen deserves better.

For instance, it is a mistake to believe that Sutpen fails in life because he is unscrupulous; on the contrary, he is too scrupulous. Had he been as ruthless as his detractors claim, he would easily have solved his difficulties. He might have arrived in Jefferson a wealthy man who had only to order that his plantation be erected while he waited in comfort to occupy it. And when his son of tainted blood arrived, he might have preserved what he had by simply denouncing the child to his face, either in private or, if necessary, in public. That he chose otherwise testifies to stronger motives than self-interest. In recounting the night of the Haitian rebellion, Sutpen reveals that until he was married, he was a virgin, an astonishing instance of his rigorous, even ascetic, moral code in service to "the design which I had in my mind."[1] To ignore Sutpen's ethical character is to distort his fullness as a character.

Sutpen's mistake is believing in an ethical value called integrity—which Irving Howe acutely separates from honor because the latter is a public value.[2] Of his integrity only Sutpen can be judge. He confesses to Grandfather Compson, regarding the proposed marriage between Bon and Judith, that he might allow it since to the public it would be normal, but cannot because it would "be a mockery and a betrayal of that little boy who approached that door fifty years ago and was turned away" (p. 274). This is an expression of integrity. Sutpen, if he is innocent, is innocent in the sense that his

*This essay was written especially for this volume and is published here for the first time by permission of the author.

idealism is inadequate among men who live by acts of accommodation and compromise. His refusal to sully the reputation of his first wife by revealing her Negro blood is a crucial decision that eventuates in his world crumbling about his ears.

In the summer of 1860 Sutpen confirms, by visiting New Orleans, the identity of Charles Bon. But he cannot discover whether Bon knows it as well. This gap in his information complicates his scrupulous care to protect the reputation of his first wife by now requiring a second choice—to protect also his first son against the ignominy not only of being discovered to carry Negro blood, but, worse, of having it discovered by the father who abandoned him. Because the speculations of three generations of Compsons obscure his words and motives, it is too easy for readers to understand Sutpen's first choice—like his second choice—to be between pursuing his design or surrendering it. But these aren't the horns of his dilemma. About his first choice he remarks, "I was faced with condoning a fact which had been foisted upon me without my knowledge during the process of building toward my design, which meant the absolute and irrevocable negation of the design; or in holding to my original *plan for the design* in pursuit of which I had incurred this negation" (p. 27; emphasis added).[3] Sutpen sees his options not as design or no design, but as principle or no principle.

The distinction is important, for he means by it that he either abandons his dream of becoming a plantation aristocrat with descendants of unsullied racial lineage or he fulfills his dream by violating his plan to achieve it by scrupulous means. He chooses the dishonorable course of renouncing his wife and child, but tries to ameliorate the consequences: " 'I made to the fullest what atonement lay in my power for whatever injury I might have done in choosing' " (p. 273). When Judith's espousal to Bon calls for a second choice, Sutpen sees his options—to acknowledge Bon as his son or not to acknowledge him—as the same alternatives he had had to choose between when he made his first choice.

A remark Sutpen makes to Grandfather Compson concerning the vengeful motive that had originated his design reveals the anguish Sutpen must feel when he contemplates his alternatives in 1864:

> Telling Grandfather that the boy-symbol at the door wasn't it because the boy-symbol was just the figment of the amazed and desperate child; that now he would take that boy in where he would never again need to stand on the outside of a white door and knock at it: and not at all for mere shelter but so that that boy, that whatever nameless stranger, could shut that door himself forever behind him on all that he had ever known, and look ahead along the still undivulged light rays in which his descendants who might not even ever hear his [the boy's] name, waited to be born without even having to know that they had once been riven forever free from brutehood just as his own [Sutpen's] children were—. (p. 261)

This passage confounds critics who argue that Sutpen is not a tragic figure because he learns nothing. Peter Swiggart, on the other hand, contends that by making this remark Sutpen is only creating a glamorous moral image with which to pet his ego, but that the irony of the boy actually arriving in the form of his part-Negro son betrays its empty pretentiousness.[3] In fact, Bon's arrival at Sutpen's Hundred does test Sutpen's sincerity. Yet Sutpen's choices are not as simple as Swiggart believes. He is faced with a dilemma of opposing ideals—it is right to take in the boy at his door, but also right to protect the boy from knowing his taint. Sutpen, in opening his door, might be opening it to an insult far greater than any given by its remaining closed.

Sutpen, in desperation, tries a middle road by explaining to Henry why the marriage must not occur, hoping that Henry, because of his influence with Bon, will somehow be able to dissuade Bon from marrying Judith without Bon's learning the reason. Of course, by resorting to Henry, the desperate father sets in motion a series of events that eventuates in the horror of fratricide.

Sutpen's essential flaw is deep in his personality, and a symptom of it surfaces in the episode of the French architect, which nicely complements the disclosure by Sutpen of his past. The dispassionate manner in which he pursues a human being is at first the seemingly inhuman act of a monster. But his arrangement with the architect is unknown and his pursuit of the escapee could be explained as Sutpen's insistence that the architect live up to his obligation according to the terms of an unrevealed agreement. No one suggests the architect was under unlawful durance or that he appealed for help to Sutpen's neighbors, who surely would not have tolerated a white man's being enslaved. The rigors of frontier life and incessant toil seem to have been more than the architect had bargained for, but bargain he had, and Sutpen's values insist that a bargain be kept, no matter what burden it imposes. In fact, victims of a bad bargain are frequent in Faulkner's fiction, and they are always expected to live up to its terms as faithfully as they would enforce the terms of a good bargain. That the right is with Sutpen is implicit in Jefferson's citizens participating in the pursuit, not even Grandfather Compson taking exception to it.

Sutpen has an adolescent's exaggerated sense of justice, so that to him the Golden Rule is founded not upon a principle of love but a more nearly Draconian code akin to the principle of an eye for an eye. He naïvely believes—and in this sense Grandfather Compson's judgment of "innocence" is correct—that human relationships can be conducted as bargains, the conditions of which are inviolable. In this respect Sutpen's ethics are much like Goodhue Coldfield's, but without the metaphysical sanction. Sutpen expects that a man has only to strike a balance between kindnesses done and kindnesses received in order to exact fair measure for one's principled restraint and self-discipline in his relationships with his fellows. His drinking habits during his first five years in Jefferson are the perfect example of this morality.

One of the judgmental legacies inherited by Quentin Compson regarding Sutpen is that Sutpen was " 'fog-bound by his own private embattlement of personal morality: that picayune splitting of abstract hairs.' " Grandfather Compson admiringly contrasts this with the youthful penchant for reacting " 'to a single simple Yes and a single simple No as instantaneous and complete and unthinking as a snapping on and off of electricity' " (pp. 271–72). This opinion is flawed not because it is untrue of Sutpen, but because it refers only to his old age.

In fact, it describes Sutpen since he was a boy of fourteen. His predilection for the splitting of abstract hairs begins with his reflections on the proper response to the insult received at Pettibone's door. He decides then that he could lie in hiding to ambush Pettibone, but rejects this because it would be a kind of "single simple Yes" and most wrong because *simple*. He can already recognize the complex issues of identity and self-esteem inherent in the insult.

Grandfather Compson points to this quality in Sutpen's character when he explodes in response to Sutpen's mention of conscience in his renunciation of his first wife: "Conscience? Conscience? Good God, man, what else did you expect? . . . Didn't the dread and fear of females which you must have drawn in with the primary mammalian milk teach you better? What kind of abysmal and purblind innocence could that have been which someone told you to call virginity? what conscience to trade with which would have warranted you in the belief that you could have bought immunity from her for no other coin just justice?" (p. 265).

Grandfather Compson betrays in this outburst some of his son's misogyny, but essentially he describes the human factor that Sutpen's design doesn't recognize—that side of the human coin that doesn't operate in terms of justice or conscience, that is instead irrational and passionate. Grandfather Compson understands that the Yes or No options by which ordinary men operate are *single* and *simple* because motivated by self-interest. "Sutpen confesses that after the fatal insult in Virginia, he saw his own father and sisters and brothers as the owner, the rich man (not the nigger) must have been seeing them all the time—as cattle, creatures heavy and without grace, brutely evacuated into a world without hope or purpose for them" (p. 235). The brute image is powerful in Sutpen's imagination, for, as witnessed above, he uses it when he explains to Grandfather Compson that he would not repeat Pettibone's insult, that he would admit a little boy at his door in order that the boy and his descendants might be "riven forever free from brutehood" (p. 261).

Readers who deny Sutpen tragic status because he learns nothing overlook not only his remark in Grandfather Compson's office in 1864, but also forget his conduct upon returning from the war to a plantation that is, and can be, only a vestige of its former splendor. Edmond Volpe, for instance, believes that Sutpen's attempt to rebuild is evidence of his Southerner's creed: "He never loses his conviction because, like the Southerners he represents, he cannot understand that his downfall is caused by the violation of a design for human existence far more basic than the design of plantation aristocracy."[4] Olga Vickery makes a similar point by seeing Sutpen as "a mirror image of the South, for his career in Jefferson merely repeats in a foreshortened form the rise of many families whose longer tenure of the land has given them respectability."[5] But Sutpen is not a representative figure. Vickery's assessment denies Sutpen the many indications of his individuality, and particularly ignores his unique position in Jefferson's society. No small part of Sutpen's difficulty in life is his solitariness in a society that resents him. Although his separateness is as much the result of his own choice as it is imposed, it gives him the stature that raises him above his fellows—he attempts to control his life despite the help or hindrance proffered or threatened by his fellow men. Consequently, those about him are intimidated and snipe at him by deliberately misrepresenting or, through a constitutional disability, misconstruing his character and motives.

Even though, when he begins to rebuild, he no longer dreams of living in antebellum splendor, Rosa Coldfield recalls the night Sutpen confronts a "deputation" of night riders who threaten him because he refuses to join them:

and he refused, declined, offered them (with no change of gaunt ruthless face nor level voice) defiance if it was defiance they wanted, telling them that if every man in the South would do as he himself was doing, would see to the restoration of his own land, the general land and South would save itself: and ushered them from the room and from the house and stood plain in the doorway holding the lamp above his head while their spokesman delivered his ultimatum: "this may be war, Sutpen," and answered, "I am used to it." (pp. 161–62)

Although his dream vanished in the war, his character did not. He still trails the mountain man's cloud of self-reliance. In announcing that night his simpler hope to salvage what remains and in renouncing the empty pomp of the antebellum South, Sutpen learns at last from the tribulations of war and human suffering simply to cultivate his own garden.

Thus the glory and the grandeur of the South erode. Yet Sutpen does not surrender all hope. Instead he persists in his desperate attempt to produce a male heir. But this time, unwilling to gamble in his final effort to sire an heir, Sutpen elects to get a son first, then to give it his name. However, he drives off his sister-in-law with his immodest proposal and finally settles upon the granddaughter of Wash Jones. It is uncertain whether the choice is merely random or fortuitous. In his reduced circumstances, Sutpen must recognize the ironic aptness of his attempting to get the hoped-for son upon the granddaughter of Wash Jones. While his neighbors can only interpret his conduct with Milly Jones as a haughty and unfeeling exercise of the *droit du seigneur*, Sutpen surely sees in the male issue of the relationship the quintessential achievement of his nearly lifelong ambition—he will raise from brutehood not only his progeny, but Wash Jones's as well. The salvation that Milly's son will represent will be Sutpen's and Jones's, too.

But before Milly gives birth, Sutpen discovers a perilous fault in his latest design: in it, he repeats the Pettibone sin. When Grandfather Compson one day enters the country store run by Sutpen and Wash, he overhears a telling exchange between the two men concerning Sutpen's gift of a dress to Milly. Wash says that he has let Milly keep the dress because Sutpen is "different":

> "How different?" and Grandfather said how Wash did not answer and that he called again now and neither of them heard him; and then Sutpen said: "So that's why you are afraid of me?" and Wash said, "I aint afraid. Because you are brave. It aint that you were a brave man at one second or minute or hour of your life and got a paper to show hit from General Lee. But you are brave, the same as you are alive and breathing. That's where it's different. Hit don't need no ticket from nobody to tell me that. And I know that whatever your hands tech, whether hit's a regiment or men or a ignorant gal or just a hound dog, that you will make hit right." Then Grandfather heard Sutpen move, sudden and sharp, and Grandfather said he reckoned, thought just about what he imagined Wash was thinking. But all Sutpen said was, "Get the jug."—"Sho, Kernel," Wash said. (p. 284)

But the aborted violence Sutpen threatens against Wash betrays the impact upon him of Wash's speech. It speaks volumes about what happens in his mind and prepares for the circumstances of his death.

Wash Jones's quietly spoken admiration of his "kernel" illuminates for Sutpen the moral peril that his plan for an heir creates. Although living in severely reduced circumstances, he is Thomas Sutpen, landowner, Civil War hero, respected if not admired for being a man of principle. And Wash Jones is poor white without hope of being anything better, except for the attention Sutpen bestows upon him. But in the instant that Sutpen is raised to anger by Wash's daring to insinuate that he could have any but honorable intentions toward the granddaughter, he also recognizes its truth. He is already bitterly aware that he has "teched" his own children and been utterly helpless "to make hit right." His reaction is the typically ambivalent response of a man whose conduct is neither purely virtuous nor vile. In that instant Sutpen learns how near he is to playing Pettibone to Wash Jones. Until the war destroyed his design, and he lost his sons, Sutpen had lived by a rigorous code of conduct. But after he returns to his ruined home and family, he resorts repeatedly to callous and selfish acts. The first is the shameful proposition he makes to Rosa Coldfield. And failing in that, he threatens with an unforgivable insult a man whose meager portion of self-esteem is based upon a selfless loyalty. Suddenly the little boy is at *his* front door, but the "boy" is an old man in his seventies, and Sutpen is perilously close to repeating the fateful insult. Sutpen must now see the circle his seduction of Milly completes. Yet the circle can be broken, for his intention is to legitimize the seduction by marriage *if* Milly bears him a son. And so he waits, with his fate held in balance by a pregnant, fifteen-year-old girl.

Because Faulkner seldom lets Sutpen speak, the events surrounding his death pose no difficulty for Jefferson's citizens. But when he does speak, he betrays an active intelligence and a moral nature that, while narrow, is nevertheless intense. Consequently, his death is more subtly meaningful than any of the novel's narrators can appreciate. In believing he had inherited a lack of human worth, Sutpen as a boy commits an error that has lifelong consequences. Only at last does he realize that one does not inherit identity from his father nor, as a father, bestow identity upon his children. In an existential universe, legacies are myths for both fathers and sons.

In the moments of silence immediately following the midwife's announcement that Milly's child is a girl, Sutpen understands how little his life has meant and how little its failure will matter. Had Sutpen known when he stood insulted at Pettibone's front door what he learns in the cabin of Wash Jones, his design never would have been born. But because of his innocence in an existential world, because he believes that in the insult is the essence that by preceding his existence defines it, he is both agent and victim of enormous suffering that eventuates finally in his standing defeated in the forlorn cabin of Wash Jones, which is the symbolic alpha and omega of his life. Sutpen's remark to Wash's granddaughter—"Well, Milly; too bad you're not a mare too. Then I could give you a decent stall in the stable" (p. 286)—is intended to force the hand of the girl's grandfather. Sutpen arranges his death and thereby expiates the guilt he only finally learns is his. But he has done the greatest injury not to his executioner, but to himself, for he has led his life not in bad faith but in mistaken faith. Still, he achieves limited grace because—regardless of how misguided—in living and especially in dying he acts with integrity. It is the only grace a man can achieve in Yoknapatawpha county.

Notes

1. William Faulkner, *Absalom, Absalom!* (New York: Modern Library, 1951), 248.

2. Irving Howe, *William Faulkner: A Critical Study* (New York: Random House, 1951), 103.

3. Peter Swiggart, *The Art of Faulkner's Novels* (Austin: University of Texas Press, 1962), 161.

4. Edmond L. Volpe, *A Reader's Guide to William Faulkner* (New York: Farrar, Straus, and Giroux, 1964), 204.

5. Olga W. Vickery, *The Novels of William Faulkner: A Critical Interpretation* (Baton Rouge: Louisiana State University Press, 1964), 93.

Sutpen's Children

♦

"We have waited long enough": Judith Sutpen and Charles Bon

ELISABETH MUHLENFELD*

Given the fact that *Absalom, Absalom!* is Thomas Sutpen's novel, a very large proportion of the narrative is devoted to the triangle between Judith, Bon, and Henry. . . . I do not wish to suggest that Judith and Bon are the central characters in *Absalom*—though unquestionably their proposed marriage is the deciding factor which leads inevitably to the crumbling of Sutpen's design—but Mr. Compson is right to consider this relationship one of the keys to the Sutpen story, and the relationship is worth examining in far more detail than has heretofore been given it: is it possible to determine, from the evidence in the novel itself, what kind of people Judith and Bon were and whether they did in fact love one another? I intend to limit my investigation to an examination of the *facts* which Faulkner provides, considering those remarks and events which are the products of the imaginations of the narrator-characters only when such remarks or events seem probable or shed light on the facts as we know them. . . .

There is, however, a cluster of "givens" in the novel—facts and other pieces of evidence available to Quentin and Shreve—which ought not to be ignored. Foremost among these is Bon's letter, the only surviving document

*Reprinted from *Southern Review* N. S. 14, no. 1 (1978): pp. 66–80, with permission of the author. A passage on pp. 66–68 has been deleted, as well as two concluding paragraphs.

attributable to one of the key participants in the events. As we shall see, Mr. Compson gives considerable weight to the letter, finds it puzzling, and has apparently pondered it at length. Quentin and Shreve, on the other hand, do not speculate about it, indeed dismiss it, and there is no evidence in the novel that Rosa even knew of its existence. Except for the letter, almost everything we learn about Bon is exclusively the product of someone's imagination; thus it must be of crucial importance for our understanding of him. The only other documentary evidence in *Absalom* is that of the tomb-stones, and to these both Mr. Compson and Quentin attach significance as clues to the emotions and motives of Judith. Even armed with this set of givens, though, being objective about Judith and Bon requires constant care, for we are bombarded with highly stylized and colored descriptions of them before we understand the extent and nature of the biases of the narrators themselves. Judith, for example, is first mentioned by Rosa in mythic or biblical terms as being *"begot"* by Sutpen, *"without gentleness,"* and our first view of her and her brother is rather horrifying: "the ogre-shape which . . . resolved out of itself before Quentin's eyes the two half-ogre children."

In Chapter I, we learn from Rosa about two episodes in Judith's child-hood: her wild delight at riding to church behind the runaway horses followed by her fury when deprived of this thrill, and her calm observance of her father's savage and ritualistic fight with the slave. Both these episodes may be accepted as fact: both were witnessed and seem to be common knowledge among the townspeople. Neither episode tells us much about the mature Judith, but together they indicate that, as a child, she was willful, passionate, and inclined to defy authority. Further, they bear witness to the close emo-tional ties she has with her father (in the horse-racing episode, she deliberately apes him) and to her intense determination to *experience* rather than retreat from life.

We know nothing more about Judith's upbringing, except that she occasionally saw Rosa and her grandfather, and as she entered adulthood, often went shopping and visiting with her mother, always seemingly uninter-ested, distracted. Mr. Compson describes her in very abstract terms and, because he could not have known first hand, his description must not be taken as necessarily true. Nevertheless, all of the townspeople would have seen her at this time, and thus the passage suggests that, in fact, her behavior did change markedly between childhood and adolescence. He says Judith had entered

> that transition stage . . . that state where, though still visible, young girls appear as though seen through glass and where even the voice cannot reach them; where they exist (this the hoyden who could—and did—outrun and outclimb, and ride and fight both with and beside her brother) in a pearly lambence . . . not in themselves floating and seeking but merely waiting, parasitic and potent and serene, drawing to themselves without effort the

post-genitive upon and about which to shape, flow into back, breast; bosom, flank, thigh.

This description probably says more about Mr. Compson than about Judith, but Richard Adams, in *Faulkner: Myth and Motion*, suggests very plausibly that the passage represents "one of Faulkner's earlier efforts to present a direct impression of a young woman moving so harmoniously with the motion of life that no motion can be seen." While in this waiting, serene state, Judith first meets Charles Bon, a university friend of her brother.

The scant facts surrounding the courtship of Judith and Bon do not allow us to reach any conclusions regarding its intensity. We know only that Bon visited at Christmas for two weeks and again at the beginning of the summer for a few days. Judith's mother, Ellen, apparently favored the match to the extent that she bought a trousseau before any hint of engagement had passed between the two. At some point Bon gave Judith his picture (which Rosa saw) and began to write her regularly. On the occasion of Bon's third visit to Sutpen's Hundred, an interview between Henry and his father terminated with Henry repudiating his birthright and the two young men departing for New Orleans. Surely some understanding existed between Judith and Bon at this time, for she waited quite patiently for four years before she heard from him again. Mr. Compson finds the "entire queerly placid course of [the] courtship" very puzzling, and speculates that the absence of any formal trappings of engagement indicates Bon's indifference. But it need not be so interpreted. Earlier we have seen Sutpen, with a new hat and coat and a "cornucopia of flowers," propose quite formally—but without love.

If Rosa and the townspeople know little about Bon, Quentin and Mr. Compson know very little more. Bon is a fascinating figure to Mr. Compson, who endows him with a Byronic personality. Quentin apparently does not challenge his father's basic premise that Bon was a fatalistic, doomed soul, but he and Shreve do expand and modify the portrait. We as readers know that he is Sutpen's son—a fact which Quentin apparently learned at Sutpen's Hundred, and which we can verify by reference to Faulkner's appended chronology. Thus Bon, son of a Haitian heiress and probably raised in New Orleans, grew up knowing that he was fatherless. The evidence of the octoroon's picture found on Bon's body, and of Charles Etienne's presence at Sutpen's Hundred, indicates that at some point prior to his departure for the university, Bon "married," after the New Orleans fashion, an octoroon and had a son by her. We know that at the time he studied law with Henry, he was considerably older than his classmates, and that he presented a sophisticated, even elegant appearance. We know further that he joined the university's regiment with Henry, that he promptly received a commission, and that he was wounded. Finally we know that near the end of the war Henry had an interview with his father, and shortly thereafter Bon wrote a long letter to Judith announcing his intention to return to her. Outside the gates of Sutpen's Hundred, he was killed.

Mr. Compson finds these facts to be very suggestive, and he devotes several pages of his narrative to probing beneath them to find the "real" Bon. Particularly interesting to Mr. Compson is the impression that Bon seemed always out of place, "that mental and spiritual orphan whose fate it apparently was to exist in some limbo halfway between where his corporeality was and his mentality and moral equipment desired to be." He assumes, correctly I think, that Bon must have had some motive for attending the university at Oxford—an unlikely place for a wealthy, cosmopolitan young man to go: "this man miscast for the time and knowing it, accepting it for a reason obviously good enough to cause him to endure it and apparently too serious or at least too private to be divulged to what acquaintances he now possessed."

We do *not* know one very crucial thing: whether Bon was aware that his father was Thomas Sutpen. Quentin and Shreve imagine very moving scenes in which Bon longs for recognition from Sutpen, and by the time the two Harvard students begin their cold night of speculation, Quentin has already been to Sutpen's Hundred with Rosa and has learned all he will ever know—almost certainly he has been told by either Clytie or Henry that Bon was Sutpen's son. Nevertheless, Quentin makes a very curious statement to Shreve which suggests that he has not been given any insight into Bon's motives for marrying Judith: "nobody ever did know if Bon ever knew Sutpen was his father or not, whether he was trying to revenge his mother or not at first and only later fell in love"; then he adds "whether Bon wanted revenge or was just caught and sunk and doomed too, it was all the same."

Whether Bon sought revenge or merely fell in love may in the end be "all the same" in the sense that he died at Henry's hands in any case, but the distinction is an important one for the reader. If Bon was merely using Judith to force recognition from his father, then all Judith's years of waiting, of devotion, of care for his son offer a very dark commentary on faith and love, and she becomes just one more victim—like so many others in the novel—of her own illusions. If, on the other hand, she and Bon do truly love one another, then her actions can be read as an affirmation of a powerful, real force—a human force antithetical to Sutpen's design.

All that we know about the adult Judith testifies to her devotion to duty as she sees it, and her conception of duty is neither meaningless nor rigid. Although not always successful, everything she does is constructive, aimed at alleviating human suffering. Apparently without knowing the reasons for her father's objection to her marriage, she behaves toward Sutpen as if nothing had happened. After her father goes off to war, she and Clytie live alone. Her mother, prostrate since the shock of the dissolved engagement, requires "the unremitting attention of a child," and Judith cares for her until her death, while doing the best she can to keep the plantation intact. With Clytie, she gardens, learns to catch and harness a mule, and she does her part in town in a hospital for the wounded. Although she hears nothing from Bon for four years, when she receives his letter, she and Clytie begin "at once to fashion a wedding dress and veil out of rags and scraps." Mr. Compson, after brooding about this sequence of events, is forced to conclude that it bespeaks a deep love:

> Have you noticed how so often when we try to reconstruct the causes which lead up to the actions of men and women, how with a sort of astonishment we find ourselves now and then reduced to the belief, the only possible belief, that they stemmed from some of the old virtues? . . . Judith, giving implicit trust where she had given love, giving implicit love where she had derived breath and pride: that true pride . . . which can say to itself without abasement *I love, I will accept no substitute; something has happened between him and my father; if my father was right, I will never see him again, if wrong he will come or send for me; if happy I can be I will, if suffer I must I can.*

Because of what we already know of Judith, Mr. Compson's portrait here seems true, and as Oliver Billingslea has suggested, it is "borne out by her subsequent responses throughout the book."[1]

Judith seems throughout the novel to be at the very least a realistic, eminently sensible person; she does not romanticize as does Rosa, nor does she flutter like her mother. Therefore, her response to the letter, the making of a wedding dress, probably represents a well-reasoned approach to Bon's intentions. It is appropriate here, then, to examine the letter in some detail, to see what kind of man the passionate but sensible Judith intended to marry. Quentin thinks of the letter as a "dead tongue speaking after the four years and then after almost fifty more, gentle sardonic whimsical and incurably pessimistic,"[2] but the letter itself affirms that he is wrong. It begins, "without date or salutation": *"You will notice how I insult neither of us by claiming this to be a voice from the defeated even, let alone from the dead."*

This sentence does not offer apology for the long silence, but bespeaks a firm, underlying understanding between recipient and writer; it affirms that Bon is neither defeated nor dead. It is a sentence written by a proud man, but one who knows that his reader shares his pride and his love. Later in the letter he acknowledges Judith's love and patience and indirectly affirms his own: *"I do not insult you by saying that only I have waited."*

Bon goes on to note the ironic juxtaposition of the captured stove polish with which he writes on notepaper with *"the best of French watermarks dated seventy years ago, salvaged (stolen if you will) from the gutted mansion of a ruined aristocrat."* His words indicate that he is a man of taste and discernment, that he regrets the fall of *"the old South which is dead"* but considers that it was inevitable; and he exhibits a grudging respect for the *"new North which has conquered and which therefore, whether it likes it or not, will have to survive."* Bon displays, in short, a good sense of history; using the image of *"one fusillade four years ago which sounded once and then was arrested, mesmerized raised muzzle by raised muzzle, in the frozen attitude of its own aghast amazement and never repeated and it now only the loud aghast echo jarred by the dropped musket of a weary sentry or by the fall of the spent body itself,"* he asserts that the outcome of the war has never been in doubt, and predicts that the world will be very little better for four years of fighting. He is a realist.

Bon makes several observations in the letter which show him to be a man very much aware of the human suffering that he and Judith have shared with the whole South. Describing his regiment, he writes *"I wont say hungry because to a woman . . . below Mason's and Dixon's in this year of grace 1865, that word would be sheer redundancy, like saying that we were breathing. And I wont say ragged or even shoeless, since we have been both long enough to have grown accustomed to it."*

Writing just before dawn in a lonely encampment, he gives thanks that man will not be defeated: *"thank God . . . that he really does not become inured to hardship and privation."* He observes that the endlessness and sense-lessness of war drugs the soul, but that the body, the living flesh *"with a sort of dismal and incorruptible fidelity which is incredibly admirable to me, is still immersed and obliviously bemused in recollections of old peace and contentment . . . which ignores even the presence and threat of a torn arm or leg as though through some secretly incurred and infallible promise and conviction of immortality."* It is the use of just such phrases as "dismal and incorruptible fidelity" and "obliviously bemused" which strengthen Mr. Compson's contention that Bon is a world-weary aesthete, and it is understandable that Mr. Compson, with his own tired nihilism, would so interpret them. But we must remember that Bon writes at the end of a war which he now sees to be hopeless, and for four years he has lived with pain and death. That Bon finds the fidelity of his body to life "incredibly admirable" is therefore of the utmost significance; the letter is an affirmation of life, both in content and intent—to alert Judith to his return.

Though the man who writes is exhausted from sleeplessness, hunger, and privation, he devotes a good portion of the letter to describing a humor-ous event: the capture of the stove polish. His narrative shows him to be a man with a nice sense of humor, who has the ability to take the defeats of life with grace, and though he never draws attention to the fact, the tale sheds light on Bon as officer when we realize that he must have been the leader of the foraging party. He describes a group of *"homogeneous scarecrows"*— not heterogeneous, but a companionable group which fit well together. The plan of attack, *"one of those concocted plans of scarecrow desperation which not only must but do work"* was brought off *"with a great deal of elan, not to say noise."* Bon pictures the men madly struggling to open the boxes of what they hope will be ammunition only to find *"Gallons and gallons and gallons of the best stove polish . . . doubtless still trying to overtake General Sherman with some belated amended field order requiring him to polish the stove before firing the house."* The men respond to this discovery not with fury or despair, but with good humor, and Bon notes that he has learned that *"only when you are hungry or frightened do you extract some ultimate essence out of laughing."*

After the four years which have left the South destitute and her armies without even the barest essentials, food, clothing, and ammunition, the North is vigorous, able to manufacture and to afford vast quantities of a comparative luxury—stove polish. Bon sees the stove polish as an "augury," a symbol of the inevitability of the South's defeat, and he wants Judith to understand its import, too. He seems to have full confidence that she will not only understand the implications of the anecdote, but also that she will enjoy the telling. He writes to make her smile, and he uses the opportunity to reveal himself, to indicate that he has learned much about himself and about human nature from his war experiences. Further, the mere fact that he takes the time to relate the adventure, aside from its symbolic import, shows Bon to be relaxed, unhurried. His letter is not the product of a moment of passion or whim. (Indeed, his salvaging of the French paper suggests that the letter has been long planned.) Rather, Bon, a Southerner for whom the gallons of stove polish are a ridiculous superfluity, has put the spoils of his abortive foray for ammunition to positive use.

The inclusion of the anecdote, then, is far from irrelevant, and only after he has brought the incident to a close does he move directly to the point of the letter: *"We have waited long enough."* Apparently there has been a mutual agreement, or at least acquiescence, to delay the marriage. Written to the accompaniment of enemy firing, Bon's final words suggest that at least part of the reason for waiting has been a reluctance to make Judith an actual widow: *"I now believe that you and I are, strangely enough, included among those who are doomed to live."* I can find no hint in the letter of any ulterior motives, of any knowledge that he is about to commit incest or miscegenation; if Bon knew about his parentage, the letter is that of a very skillful and utterly despicable villain indeed.

To my knowledge, critics have ignored the letter, or read it through Mr. Compson's eyes, with one notable exception. Virginia Hlavsa considers it a turning point in the novel: "It is proof, after all, of a certain quality of man who existed, a man with depth, compassion and tenderness, but above all, a real man, who has experienced real hunger, fatigue, and suffering beyond the mind's comprehension of that suffering, who, because he was a breathing man of flesh deserves respect, whose death is to be regretted."[3]

Quentin's father, who takes Bon to be a fatalist, and invents him as a world-weary aesthete, postulates that he "loved Judith after his fashion" but that he also loved Henry "in a deeper sense." He imagines that Henry worshipped Bon, and used him to engage in a kind of mental incest. Quentin and Shreve fasten upon this possibility, and never return to the letter to test their hypothesis. But Mr. Compson makes one supposition that seems to be borne out by the evidence of the letter. He says: "perhaps it was even more than Judith or Henry either: perhaps the life, the existence, which they represented. Because who knows what picture of peace he might have seen in that monotonous provincial backwater; what alleviation and escape for a parched traveler who had traveled too far at too young an age, in this granite-bound and simple country spring." Bon's own reference to "recollections of old peace and contentment," and the whole gentle and sure tone of the letter, suggest that he does indeed regard Judith—if not Sutpen's Hundred in itself—as a kind of haven of sanity and peace in a world which seems more than a little mad.

If the love which the letter seems to attest did exist, then the one person who would have been most profoundly conscious of it was Sutpen's other son, Henry, and indeed the single event in the novel to which the narrators repeatedly turn is the moment in which Henry kills Bon. We have noted earlier that the reader is not told (in fact Quentin asserts that "nobody ever did know") whether Bon was aware at any time of his relationship to Sutpen. However, we know fairly certainly that Henry knew of Bon's kinship to him, first because he (or perhaps Clytie) must have told Quentin at Sutpen's Hundred and second because, in a conversation reported by General Compson, Sutpen decides that he is "forced to play my last trump card"—if not a reference to Bon's Negro blood, at least to his blood relationship—just before his war-time interview with Henry. Only in Shreve and Quentin's re-creation does Henry reveal the truth to Bon. It seems perfectly possible that Henry never told Bon. If he really loved his brother, he might well have wished to spare both him and Judith the pain of knowing; he may have murdered out of mercy for Bon as well as for Judith.

In any case, after Bon returns and dies, Judith discovers on his body the picture of the octoroon and when, several hours later, Rosa arrives, she finds Judith calm: *"if there had been grief or anguish she had put them too away . . . along with that unfinished wedding dress."* But Judith is still holding the metal case—it has obviously affected her profoundly. Mr. Compson assumes that this is a betrayal which frees Judith from grief, and Shreve guesses that Bon had intentionally substituted the picture: "if [Henry] does mean what he said, it will be the only way I will have to say to her, *I was no good; do not grieve for me."* If so, Bon's message is ignored, for Judith obviously does grieve for him: she oversees his burial and even tries to provide him with a Catholic service; she places his body in the cedar grove beside her mother and thus affirms that he is a member of her family; and most significantly, she goes a week later to Quentin's grandmother and, with a face "calm . . . absolutely serene," "comprehending . . . not even bitter," seeks to insure Bon's immortality by giving away the letter. When Mrs. Compson indicates that she fears Judith will commit suicide, Judith's reply affirms both her love for Bon and her dedication to life, "Oh. I? No, not that. Because somebody will have to take care of Clytie, and father, too, soon, who will want something to eat after he comes home. . . . Women dont do that for love. I dont even believe that men do. And not now, anyway."

Judith cries only once for Bon, but she erects a tombstone for him, otherwise going about the business of living and of sharing what she has: she gives food to passers-by and periodically takes provisions to Rosa after her return to Jefferson. Her greatest and most sustained act of compassion, though, is her reaching out to the octoroon and Bon's son. Inviting the woman and child to visit, she offers them the best that she has, apparently with no condescension or bitterness. When she learns that the boy is orphaned and Clytie leaves to bring him back to Sutpen's Hundred, Judith goes to General Compson and orders a tombstone for him to match his father's paying a hundred dollars, an immense sum for her to amass. This fact is extremely significant, and has for some reason been completely ignored: Judith commits herself *before* he arrives to the life-long care of her dead fiancé's son, knowing he is Negro. And by insuring that he, too, will have the formal recognition as a family member implicit in the gravestone, she in effect pledges to him the security and tradition which she represents. When he arrives, he sleeps on a trundle bed beside her, the customary place for a child of the time.

We cannot deny that Judith seems to fail rather spectacularly with Charles Etienne, but almost without exception, all that we are told about Judith's relationship to him is the speculation of Mr. Compson, and his contention that Judith treated the child coldly seems unlikely in view of her other responses throughout the novel. We do know that at the time Charles Etienne arrived at Sutpen's Hundred he was twelve years old—his most formative years had been spent in the isolation of an environment neither white nor Negro. His subsequent fighting and his marriage to the black woman suggest that, like Joe Christmas in *Light in August*, he would have repudiated any warmth Judith showed him. Whether she fails with Charles Etienne because, as Mr. Compson suggests, she responds to him coldly, or whether the boy had already been ruined by Bon's rejection of him as Quentin and Shreve believe, we cannot question her continued concern for him. When his fighting finally results in arrest, she rushes to General Compson, her "face emanat-[ing] a terrible urgency," for help. Her last act, that of nursing Charles Etienne, testifies to her devotion—if not to her love—even to the point of giving up her own life.

In short, rather than interpreting the octoroon's picture as an indication that she should cease to love, Judith seems to have accepted it as a message, a commission to care for Bon's quasi wife and son. Is it not possible that the picture was intended to accomplish just what it did? Bon and Judith seem to have understood one another well (witness the letter), and Bon, who himself had to grow up without a father, may have made this gesture in an effort to break the pattern, to insure that his own son could have a father to acknowledge, and a family of which to be a part.

Notes

1. Oliver La Fayette Billingslea, "The Monument and the Plain: The Art of Mythic Consciousness in William Faulkner's *Absalom, Absalom!*", Diss. University of Wisconsin, 1971, p. 232.

2. See Gerald Langford, *Faulkner's Revision of* Absalom, Absalom! (Austin, Texas, 1971), p. 146. Significantly, in the manuscript Faulkner originally ended Quentin's assessment here with the words "yet sincere," but subsequently cancelled them: the passage is in *Quentin's* mind. For him to perceive Bon's words to Judith as sincere ones would be out of keeping with his conception of Bon's complicated motivation.

3. Virginia V. Hlavsa, "The Vision of the Advocate in *Absalom, Absalom!*", *Novel*, VIII (Fall, 1974), p. 60.

The Judith-Henry-Charles Triangle: The Innermost Kernel of Faulkner's Civil War in the Heart

JUN LIU*

If *Absalom, Absalom!*[1] is William Faulkner's "Heart of Darkness," the Judith-Henry-Bon triangle is at the *very* heart. This is the case for two reasons. Regarding plot, the entanglement of the triangle is an ironic reminder of Sutpen's "innocence" just as the tragedy surrounding the triangle represents the ultimate failure of his design. Without the triangle, Sutpen's story is almost an empty shell. In this sense, the novel is not so much about Sutpen the person as about the Sutpen family. The second and more important reason is that the triangle represents a central metaphor: it not only footnotes a historical Civil War but ultimately signifies Faulkner's suprahistorical civil war in the heart. To this metaphoric center the several discourses in the novel constantly return.

This reading can be further clarified when we compare the earlier images and ideas contained in "Evangeline" with the changes Faulkner has made in detail and design in the novel. According to Elisabeth Muhlenfeld, the juxtaposition of Quentin-Shreve (replacing the Don-I framework of the short story), the Sutpen material ("Wash" and "Big Shot") and the Evangeline material "provided Faulkner with the final catalyst."[2] Muhlenfeld, based on her investigation of Faulkner's creative process, also argues that the relation between Judith and Bon is a key to the novel.[3] "Evangeline," of course, still lacks several elements necessary to the novel: there is no suggestion yet that Bon is Sutpen's son or that Bon is part negro: when the secret of the house is revealed in the end by a metal case which, instead of holding Judith's picture, contains that of Bon's first wife who is "part Negro," the meaning of "Evangeline" leans toward Bon's bigamy and lack of honor; miscegenation as a theme is not yet convincing. But "Evangeline" contains something that the other materials do not have: a composite image that would become the core of *Absalom, Absalom!*

In "Evangeline," Don tells the I-narrator a ghost story he reconstructs.

---

*This essay was written especially for this volume and is published here for the first time by permission of the author.

While the I-narrator listens, he thinks that the ghost in the house must be the emotionally wounded Judith; it is only later in the story when he enters the house that he discovers the ghost to be Henry, the living corpse. Charles Bon, from the reader's point of view, is also a ghost since his death breaks Judith's heart and haunts Henry's conscience. Thus the word "ghost" in "Evangeline" interlocks Judith, Henry, and Charles Bon; the ghostly atmosphere derives directly from their entangled love. Central to the plot of this ghost story is Don's detailed account of how Judith, waiting eagerly for her husband Charles Bon[4] on his return from the war, meets only Henry her brother. Judith infers from Henry's laconic response that Bon's body is lying in the wagon outside, but she hides her grief behind her calm and polite mask. " 'Oh,' she says. 'Yes. Yes. Of course. *There must have been a last . . . last shot, so it could end.* Yes. I had forgot.' Then she moves, quiet, deliberate. 'I am grateful to you. I thank you.' She calls then, to the niggers murmuring about the front door, peering into the hall. She calls them by name, composed, quiet: *'Bring Mr. Charles into the house'* " (my italics).[5] Charles Bon is then carried upstairs to the room which Judith had kept ready for four years. He is laid "on the fresh bed, in his boots and all, who had been killed by *the last shot of the war"* (my italics).[6]

This episode in "Evangeline" can be compared to the genesis of *The Sound and the Fury* which was, Faulkner said, "an image, a picture to me, a very moving one, which was symbolized by the muddy bottom of [Caddy's] drawers as her brothers looked up into the apple tree that she had climbed to look in the window. And the symbolism of the muddy bottom of the drawers became the lost Caddy which had caused one brother to commit suicide and the other brother had misused her money that she'd sent back to the child, the daughter."[7] What can be learned from this description is that Faulkner's incipient image is often a composite consisting of relations all tied to a central symbol. The Judith-Henry-Bon triangle that begins to emerge in "Evangeline" is also a composite image, involving entangled love relations which are tied to a central symbol: "the last shot of the war."

The triangle in "Evangeline" qualifies as genesis because it promises polysemous potentials. Its immediate *poetic* effects are grotesque, marked by a yoking of affinity and antagonism and by a copresence of the normative and the abnormal, thus representing an aesthetic condition for the kind of truths otherwise out of reach. Moreover, the triangle seems to be a new blending of themes Faulkner had used before: the mourning-as-love motif reminds us of the Emily-Homer Barron prototype;[8] the sibling incestuous possibility brings to mind the Quentin-Caddy prototype. Compared to Emily and Homer, the beloved husband-to-be in the new triangle is not a stranger in town but a brother killed by another brother. The role of the bride in the love triangle is split into that of a sister/bride versus brother/husband Bon and that of a sister/beloved versus brother/beloved Henry. Compared to Quentin and Caddy, a third person, a candidate not only for incest, but for miscegenation, is brought into the tormenting state of possible sibling incest. In this light, Judith's announcement—" 'Bring Mr. Charles into the house' "—could very well represent a moment when Faulkner, through doubling and redoubling, invented a new prototype.

As Caddy's muddy drawers are not just muddy drawers, the last shot not only alludes to the American Civil War but also to a war "civil" in other senses. The war is civil since family members are in conflict: in "Evangeline," the location where the shot was fired was probably a historical battleground since the body of Bon was brought home in a wagon. In the novel, the location is just outside the gates to Sutpen's Hundred. More significantly, there are spots in the novel which coalesce Civil War sites and the Sutpen premise into the same battleground. In Shreve's version, for instance, there is a description of how Henry was summoned by his father to his tent toward the end of the war. As Henry sat at a table facing Sutpen in a candle-lit tent, he saw "*in a second tent candle gray and all are gone and it is the holly-decked Christmas library at Sutpen Hundred four years ago and the table not a camp table suitable for the spreading of maps but the heavy carved rosewood one at home with the group photograph of his mother and sister and himself sitting upon it, his father behind the table and behind his father the window above the garden where Judith and Bon strolled in that slow rhythm where the heart matches the footsteps and the eyes only need to look at one another*" (pp. 282–83). In Henry's confusion of time and space, the garden where Judith and Bon took a leisurely walk—a love scene—is merged with the bivouac; love becomes an integral part of the war. Immediately after this narrative collage, Henry heard a command from Sutpen, his father and his army superior: "*He* [Bon] *cannot marry her, Henry*" and the reason: because Bon's "*mother was part negro*" (*Absalom*, p. 283). Since Henry's decision to kill Bon was made in the army but carried out at home, the impression that the bivouac and the family estate are the same battleground is reinforced.

In a more profound sense, the triangle is Faulkner's metaphor for his "civil war in the heart," which is not unlike Plato's "civil war in the soul." Suitable to our purpose is this definition in *The Republic*: "Hostility in the foreign sphere is called war; in the kindred sphere civil war."[9] The word "kindred," which denotes closeness in blood, nature, qualities, feeling, aptly characterizes the interlocking triangle since Judith, Henry, and Bon are kin, both lovers and kindred spirits. Ironically, much of the conflict also ensues from this closeness: their closeness in blood is actually an obstacle to their sexual closeness. And insofar as internalizing such conflict makes it a matter of heart, the heart is also the kindred sphere. The understanding that the conflict involves parties who should not be at war also creates a kindred sphere in the mind of whoever finds it senseless. Thus the narrators are implicated because of their "kindred" association. Indeed, Rosa's choice of Quentin is doubly apt because the long-standing good relations between the Sutpens and the Compsons make them near-kin too.

In fact, kindred association—involving narrators outside the Sutpen family—is a major development in the form of the novel. With Rosa, Quentin, Mr. Compson and Shreve as narrators, the design of the novel makes the triangle an inner kernel in the Conradian sense. Conrad's description of the role of Marlow in "Heart of Darkness" is worth remembering: "The yarns of seamen have a direct simplicity, the whole meaning of which lies within the shell of a cracked nut. But Marlow was not typical (if his propensity to spin yarns be excepted) and to him the meaning of an episode was not inside like a kernel but outside, enveloping the tale which brought it out only as a glow brings out a haze, in the likeness of one of these misty halos that, sometimes, are made visible by the spectral illumination of moonshine."[10] When the inside is brought out by enveloping narrations, the two are inseparably welded. Similarly, what the Henry-Judith-Bon triangle signifies as the kernel of a civil war is inaccessible to the reader except through retroactive and imaginative interpretations.

This idea of an inner kernel welded with discourses is already implied, in "Evangeline," in the metaphor of echoes. When Judith says to Henry, " 'Yes. Yes. Of course. *There must have been a last . . . last shot, so it could end,*' " her words are ironic, since the war is *not* ended by the last shot. The I-narrator, after hearing Don's story, manages to get into the house to find the dying Henry in bed, and to hear Raby, Henry's Negro half sister, reveal their secret. Seeing Henry and listening to Raby has so powerful an impact on him that he synthesizes recent happenings into the following dialogue:[11]

"And you were killed by the last shot fired in the war?"

"I was so killed. Yes."

"Who fired the last shot fired in the war?"

"Was it the last shot you fired in the war, Henry?"

"I fired a last shot in the war; yes."

"You depended on the war, and the war betrayed you too; was that it?"

"Was that it, Henry?"

"What was wrong with that woman, Henry? There was something the matter that was worse to you than the marriage. Was it the child? But Raby said the child was nine after Colonel Sutpen died in '70. So it must have been born after Charles and Judith married. Was that how Charles Bon lied to you?"

"What was it that Judith knew and Raby knew as soon as they saw her?"

"Yes."

"Yes, what?"

"Yes."

"Oh. And you have lived hidden here for forty years."

"I have lived here forty years."

"Were you at peace?"

"I was tired."

"That's the same thing, isn't it? For you and Raby too."

"Same thing. Same as me. I tired too."

"Why did you do all this for Henry Sutpen?"
"He was my brother."

The echolike effect reflects the inquisitive mind of a sympathetic outsider; it more than implies that returning to the shot produces echoes which continue to deepen the meanings of a civil war. An echo, appropriately, is a derivative metaphor of the shot. In this sense, many of the scenes and motifs in the novel are already rehearsed in this conversation. To cite only a few examples: Chapter 5 (a simulated rhapsodic monologue) begins with Rosa rushing with Wash to the house after the *shot* was fired; as Rosa is barred by Clytie from going upstairs, she realizes: *"I heard an echo, but not the shot";* this remark, interestingly enough, is found in a paragraph which begins with these words: *"That was all. Or rather, not all, since there is no all, no finish"* (*Absalom*, p. 121). In addition, the kind of echo we hear in the above exchange—" 'Yes.' 'Yes what?' 'Yes.' "—is reproduced in the novel to become Quentin's characteristic response to the narrations of Miss Rosa and Shreve. More noticeable is how this dialogue evolves into the imagined dialogue between Quentin and Henry in chapter 9 of the novel. Furthermore, either before or after the shot, there is no real "peace." The moment of peace between Henry and Bon is, ironically, that "between two young embattled spirits" who counted on the war to settle "youth's private difficulties and discontents" (*Absalom*, p. 269). The dying Henry—in both the tale and the novel—is at peace only in the sense that he is fatigued by the ongoing war inside him. As for Quentin, it is "nevermore peace" after listening to and thinking about a war for so long. Thus echoes signal the continuation of the war in the heart.

The main events involving Judith, Henry, and Bon are already summarized in the Chronology, but the novel is not a simple unfolding of these events. Instead, it is filled with echoes: Why did Bon come to Jefferson? Did he know Sutpen was his father? When did he know? How? What did Sutpen tell Henry in the library? Why did Henry renounce his birthright? Was there love between Judith and Bon? What motivated Henry to kill Bon? Without some answers to establish motives, we would feel like the I-narrator in "Evangeline" or Mr. Compson, who says: " 'Yes, Judith, Bon, Henry, Sutpen: all of them. They are there, yet something is missing' " (*Absalom*, p. 80).

Consistent with the connotations of the triangle in "Evangeline," the various discourses in the later novel also investigate conflicts in terms of love. Although Mr. Compson acknowledges the feelings of love Judith, Bon and Henry had for each other (chapter 4), he does not seem to comprehend fully the erotic power, especially in the female body. The nearest picture he can project of Bon and Judith alone together is that of " 'two shades pacing, serene and *untroubled by flesh*, in a summer garden' " (emphasis added) (*Absalom*, p. 77). When Mr. Compson suggests that Judith has the " 'true pride which can say to itself without abasement *I love, I will accept no substitute; something has happened between him and my father; if my father was right, I will never see him again, if wrong he will come or send for me; if happy I can be I will, if suffer I must I can'* " (*Absalom*, p. 96), his notion of Judith's "true pride" is more an abstracted Sutpen quality. Mr. Compson clearly suggests that if Judith had to choose between her lover and her father, her first loyalty would be to her father even if it means she must suffer. Judith is thus portrayed as " 'a Sutpen with the ruthless Sutpen code of taking what it wanted provided it were strong enough' " (*Absalom*, p. 95). In this light, Judith's love for Bon proved her more a Sutpen than a woman in love.[12]

Given his blind spot, Mr. Compson's discourse focuses on the nature of the Henry-Bon relationship or, more exactly, on how this relationship affects Henry internally. More specifically, he explains the entanglement between Henry and Bon in terms of two conflicting codes of honor: puritan and Latin. Judith is reduced to " 'just the blank space, the empty vessel in which each of them [Henry and Bon] strove to preserve . . . what each conceived the other to believe him to be' " (*Absalom*, p. 95). That Bon loved Judith " 'after his fashion' " means that he loved her with his indifference to such social customs as the marriage " 'ceremony' " which he had gone through once (*Absalom*, p. 75). Indeed, Bon seduced the brother and sister " 'without any effort or particular desire to do so' " (*Absalom*, p. 74). Judith and Henry, on the other hand, are not just the seduced. Mr. Compson also hypothesizes that Judith seduced Bon " 'with hope, even though unconscious, of making the image hers through possessions' " (note how this Sutpen takes!) while Henry *"with the knowledge, even though subconscious to the desire, of the insurmountable barrier which the similarity of gender hopelessly intervened"* (emphasis added) (*Absalom*, pp. 75–76). So Henry's feeling toward Bon has an intensity suggestive of homoeroticism. Bon, the " 'cerebral Don Juan,' " in turn " 'loved Henry the better of the two, seeing perhaps in the sister merely the shadow, the woman vessel with which to consummate the love whose actual object was the youth' " (*Absalom*, p. 86). But this hint of homosexual love between Henry and Bon is just that: a hint. Sexual desire, to Mr. Compson, is oddly incorporeal. Henry wanted " 'the pure and perfect incest' " (implying an incest " 'untroubled by flesh' "): in bringing Judith and Bon together, Henry " 'could become, metamorphose into, the lover, the husband' " and " 'could become, metamorphose into the sister, the mistress, the bride' " (*Absalom*, p. 77). Although there is a suggestion that Henry might have incestuous desire for his sister (" 'taking that virginity in the person of the brother-in-law' "), his taking seems more for the social reason that the " 'sister's virginity must be destroyed in order to have existed' "—in order to become a lady (*Absalom*, p. 77). In short, Henry's attraction to the elder man Bon is his true dilemma. Bon's urban sophistication, his sense of " 'despair' " and " 'the outlandish and almost feminine garments of his sybaritic privacy' " appeal to Henry as well as violates his puritan sense of morality.

According to this line of reasoning, Henry renounced his birthright because he refused to believe that Bon lied. For Henry, to *will* an honest Bon makes both Bon and himself *honorable*. Honor *is* love to Henry; he thought but " 'could not say to his friend [Bon], *I did that for love of you; do this for love of me*' " (*Absalom*, p. 87). Then Henry discovered Bon's octoroon " 'mistress' " and child in New Orleans. According to Mr. Compson, " 'Henry doubtless thought' " that " 'a ceremony entered into, to be sure, with a negro' " was " 'still a ceremony' " (*Absalom*, p. 87). This very thought indicates Henry's internal conflict: although he could not deny what he saw, he wanted to deny the validity of the marriage so that he could justify Bon's honor; he may also have believed that denying the marriage could be justified by the puritan values instilled in him. Henry remembered that there were, according to his upbringing, only three types of women to the Southern gentlemen—ladies, whores, and slave girls. The first two types are inaccessible to him because of the social necessity of marriage and because of money and distance. Hence only the slave girls can be taken by the slaveowner at will. Clytie, his half-sister, is a constant reminder of this reality. That is why Henry said to Bon: she, meaning the octoroon woman, is a " 'bought woman. A whore' " (*Absalom*, p. 91). Bon's reply is a complete refutation of this value system, beginning with the words " 'Not whore' " and concluding: " ' "No, not whores. Sometimes, I believe that they are the only true chaste women, not to say virgins, in America, and they remain true and faithful to that man not merely until he dies or frees them, but until they die. And where will you find whore or lady either whom you can count on to do that?" ' " (*Absalom*, pp. 91–93). Bon's point is that these Anglo-Saxon notions of sins are foolish creations, tiring to a very old God (the God for Adam and Eve?). Insofar as Bon's eloquent speech is an imagined scene, it can be assumed that it reflected Mr. Compson's own nihilist philosophy (as we know it in *The Sound and the Fury*) which, through learning and reflection, finds existing values foolish human creations. In this sense, Mr. Compson makes Bon his ghost and his echo.

As Henry insisted that Bon renounce the marriage, Bon played his trump card by pointing out that a Sutpen like Henry should not be bothered by the fact that his wife and son are both " ' "niggers" ' " (*Absalom*, p. 94). Since this theory happens to accord with Henry's upbringing, he agreed with Bon, although he still could not forgive Bon for the " 'ceremony.' " As the conflicts within Henry and between the two brothers could not be resolved, Henry locked Judith, Bon, and himself into a four-year durance. That the Civil War served as a period of temporary peace is a recurrence of the ironic motif of peace as war that we analyzed earlier.

Because of his focus, Mr. Compson leaves a key question unanswered: Did Bon *know* that Sutpen is his father and therefore Judith his sister and

Bon his brother? If he did, his courtship with Judith only betrays him as a revengeful hypocrite. If he did not, then he and Judith are more like ill-fated lovers. Shreve, in a growing communion with Quentin, fills in the gaps with another invented scenario. According to Shreve, Sutpen said to Henry in the library: " ' "They cannot marry because he is your brother." ' " And Henry replied: " ' "You lie" ' " (*Absalom*, p. 235). Thus Shreve revised Mr. Compson's scenario (which focuses on Bon's bigamy) by introducing the possibility of incest between Bon and Judith as a key factor without removing the factor of "honor." Sutpen, according to Shreve, would withhold the information of Bon's racial origin until his interview with Henry near the end of the war.

As a college student, Shreve's search for truth is steered by rationalism and, inversely, by his inexperience in life. If Henry's internal conflict is Mr. Compson's emphasis, the conflict within Charles Bon is, initially, Shreve's focus. Shreve hypothesizes that Bon knew at a very young age that his father had abandoned them, but did not know at first that Sutpen was his father and Judith his sister. Shreve also surprises us by inventing a lawyer. It was through the plotting between his mother and the lawyer that Bon came to Jefferson. Making incest possible was believed to be the lawyer's way to coerce Sutpen to pay. Even Bon's taking the octoroon wife was supposed to be the lawyer's design to keep Bon and Judith from being too romantically involved. The biggest surprise from Shreve is his speculation of whether Bon knew Sutpen was his father: when Bon accepted Henry's invitation to come to Sutpen's Hundred, he seemed to know that the man might be his father. However, this knowledge comes not from evidence but from a feeling he might have had about the lawyer's letter introducing him to Henry. Shreve's theory that *Bon is between knowing and not knowing* assigns enough innocence to Bon to acquit him of hypocrisy but keeps revenge as a possibly unconscious motive.

Shreve also speaks of love, especially Bon's love for Judith, thereby establishing the conflict within Bon to be between getting Sutpen's recognition and loving a woman who might be his sister. Unlike Mr. Compson, Shreve holds a romantic, heterosexual view of love which befits his age and character. In his account, the Bon-Henry relationship is free of homoerotic connotations: Henry looked up to Bon as an older brother; Bon lived up to that expectation—he brought the wounded Henry to safety at Shiloh (again revising Mr. Compson). About Bon and Judith, Shreve simply believes that they must have fallen in love at first sight. It is so matter-of-fact to Shreve that he speaks of a cleansing sherbert to suggest what Judith must have meant to Bon. When Quentin denies that as a good definition of love, Shreve will retort: " 'Because why not' " or " 'Jesus, some day you are bound to fall in love' " (*Absalom*, pp. 258, 259). Quentin keeps saying to Shreve: " 'But it's not love,' " thus reminding us that there is more between Bon and Judith than what Shreve acknowledges. In Shreve's mind, Bon desires getting Sutpen's recognition more than loving Judith. If Sutpen would give any sign to acknowledge him, Bon could give up anything, including his engagement with Judith. This yearning, when repeatedly frustrated by lack of any sign from Sutpen, turned to an obsession. Indeed, Bon's decision to return to Judith was an act of desperation to force Sutpen into recognizing him. At this point, the war was coming to an end. Henry had to stop Bon. In Shreve's account, therefore, it would be the possibility of miscegenation that proved fatal, not incest, since Henry had persuaded himself to accept an incestuous marriage. However, this is all still an imagined scenario. Elisabeth Muhlenfeld suggests another possibility: "Henry never told Bon. If he really loved his brother, he might well have wished to spare both him and Judith the pain of knowing: he may have murdered out of mercy for Bon as well as for Judith."[13] Muhlenfeld's suggestion is also justified by Faulkner's design which is meant to continue the echoes. Indeed, the shot is so senseless that it both demands and frustrates making any sense.

In both Mr. Compson's and Shreve's accounts of these events, Judith is peripheral. Evidence from Faulkner's creative process suggests, however, Judith Sutpen is central to the author's genesis. To Faulkner, whose great-grandfather was a colonel in the Civil War but was killed in a family feud, that the kindred sphere includes battlegrounds as well as houses and people's hearts is more than a metaphor. In "Evangeline," the house is the real location of the drama and the ghost that haunts it is at first supposed to be Judith. This element of plot which centers on Judith is collated with two stories which inspired Faulkner to write "Evangeline." Muhlenfeld informs us that the title "Evangeline" suggests that Faulkner learned from Longfellow's narrative poem about a woman's devoted waiting for her lost love. Another source is the local legend that "Judith, the beautiful daughter of 'Colonel' Robert B. Shegog who built the house [later Rowan Oak] in the 1840s, had died during the Civil War while trying to elope with a Yankee officer, and that her frail form still haunted the house."[14] These two sources embody two ideas. One is the idea of a woman enduring her loss of love. The other is the idea that the woman's lover is also her enemy. Both ideas further illustrate Faulkner's civil war in the heart.

These two ideas concerning love characterize Judith's internal conflicts, which are shown most intensely in the events involving her after the shot. With Bon dead, Judith's marital bliss is permanently deprived; Bon is thus a husband who is a not-husband and Judith a widow without having been a wife. On that body, Judith also found the metal case, now containing the picture of another woman: Is this proof of his betrayal or is it Bon's attempt, out of love, to prevent her from grieving for him? The brother she loved killed the husband she loved, and the husband turned out to be her half-brother: Which brother should she love more or, indeed, hate more? But Quentin's grandmother saw a Judith who showed the world " 'the impenetrable, the calm, the absolutely serene face' " (*Absalom*, p. 101). Her calmness is obviously a facade. In "Evangeline," Raby reports that after Judith "locked the door upon herself and her dead husband and the picture," she "heard once in the night a pounding noise from the room above and [how] when Judith came out the next morning her face looked just like it had when she locked the door upon herself." This detail is omitted in the novel, but Judith's image as seen by Rosa just as forcefully conveys the intense grief behind an ungrieving mask: *"How I ran, fled, up the stairs and found no grieving widowed bride but Judith standing before the closed door to that chamber, in the gingham dress which she had worn each time I had seen her since Ellen died, holding something in one hanging hand* [the metal case]; *and if there had been grief or anguish she had put them too away, complete or not complete I do not know, along with that unfinished wedding dress"* (*Absalom*, p. 114).

While we can infer that love is a strength in Judith, some knowledge of what Judith might have felt or thought in the aftermath of the shot is still needed. In this respect, Rosa's discourse in chapter 5 is essential. That Rosa is an "unreliable" narrator is partially true since she, in recounting those events involving Judith after the shot, tells, narcissistically, her own story, and especially her feelings toward Sutpen. But her justification of her own existence also supplies a more believable rationale for Judith's internal conflict, more believable because Rosa offers a woman's perspective and because several parallels qualify Rosa as Judith's doubling. First of all, Rosa insists on the three of them—Clytie, Judith and herself—being viewed as sisters, not an aunt with two nieces.[15] She speaks about Bon, whom she had never seen, as if Bon too was the husband she never had. She mentions how brief her courtship with Sutpen was, reminding us of Judith's brief courtship with Bon. She waited for Sutpen as Judith for Bon. More importantly, she, like Judith, also endures unfulfilled love, and her lover is also her enemy. It may be said then that Judith is Rosa's ghost.

Rosa's speech begins as a lament that this is not the time when Eve could be Adam's sister in innocence; that man and woman are no longer of one body is a painful reality for herself as well as for Judith. She speaks of the female principle and often uses Judith's experience and her own to suggest how, in a state of unfulfilled love, desire persists and increases. Rosa makes an issue of the fact that she is four years younger than Judith. Four years later she experiences *"Judith's moment which only virgins know"* (*Absalom*, p. 116). "Waiting" is what *"we call female victory which is: endure, then endure, without rhyme or reason or hope of reward—and then endure"* (*Absalom*, p. 116). Thus, insisting on roots and not on blooming means that she does not give up the dream of might-have-been; and her voice is that *"echo . . . of the lost irrevocable might-have-been which haunts all houses, all enclosed walls erected by human hands"* (*Absalom*, pp. 109–10). Because of the parallels in Rosa's and Judith's situations, we can infer that under Judith's serene appearance is the same desire with the same attendant pain, same enduring power and persistent dreams of the might-have-been.

The moment when Rosa claims to be "androgynous" is also of interest. In expressing her love for Bon whom she has never seen, Rosa becomes, in part, Judith's double and, in part, a philosophical speaker on love. Rosa says that she loves Bon *"not as women love"* (*Absalom*, p. 118). The name, she says, means: *"Charles Bon, Charles Good, Charles Husband-soon-to-be"* (*Absalom*, p. 119). Charles *Good* reminds us of Plato's concept that the possession of good is the goal for love.[16] Charles *Husband-soon-to-be* denotes a might-have-been that Judith must have felt and indicates Rosa's own desire in anticipation of Sutpen. Since Bon's name was never mentioned by the three women but Sutpen's was, their waiting for Sutpen now repeats Judith's waiting for Bon's return.

In the earlier version of "Evangeline," the reconstruction through re-membrance and imagination allows us to see, *diachronically*, a single story. But in the novel, the kernel story is tightly interwoven with the discourses to form patterns of doubling which invite *synchronic* understanding. For instance, when the Judith-Bon relation is seen through the Rosa-Sutpen relation (chapter 5), the two pairs become each other's doubles. The parallels between Shreve-Quentin and Bon-Henry, between Quentin-Father and Henry-Father, between Judith-Henry and Quentin-Caddy, between Sutpen's bigamy and Henry's bigamy, achieve the same effects. The design of the novel is such that we read it as we would read an orchestral score, not just stave after stave, but also vertically.[17] Indeed, the loom imagery Judith used when she handed Bon's letter over to Mrs. Compson is another clue to this special design (*Absalom*, p. 101).

Just as the shot is the source of echoes, Bon's letter remains the cryptic point to which various discourses repeatedly return. We cannot fail to notice how Bon's letter also expresses love in terms of a civil war. No doubt, the letter is proof of Bon's love for Judith. Bon's tone is inclusive of Judith; it is despairing but not without humor and care, befitting a lover and worthy of a beloved. Between the lines Bon expresses how love gives him extra strength to endure in a losing war. However, we get all this impression from a letter which, amazingly, never directly mentions love or directly makes a proposal of marriage. The references are to the historical war. The notepaper of *"French watermarks dated seventy years ago"* and the *"stove polish"* manufactured in the North (*Absalom*, p. 102) constitute, physically, the historical reality of the letter. Bon's train of thought is sometimes interrupted by the firing. As he concludes, he speaks of the death of the old South and of the new North with its mercantile culture as the conqueror. He says, not without irony, that the North, *"whether it likes it or not, will have to survive"* (*Absalom*, pp. 104–5), and then goes on to compare that outcome to his and Judith's fate *"you and I are, strangely enough, included among those who are doomed to live"* (*Absalom*, p. 105). This is double irony since his own life was soon ended by the last shot. Taken literally, his hope is no hope. But the love he expresses is a faith which persists. Perhaps faith, which Rosa also expresses, is what Bon leaves behind for the philosopher who could *"deduce and derive a curious and apt commentary on the times and augur of the future"* (*Absalom*, p. 102).

Notes

1. William Faulkner, *Absalom, Absalom!: The corrected text* (New York: Vintage, 1986). All subsequent page references appear in the text.

2. See Elisabeth Muhlenfeld's "Introduction" in *William Faulkner's "Absalom, Absalom!": A Critical Casebook* (New York: Garland Publishing, 1984), xxii.

3. See Elisabeth Muhlenfeld's " 'We have waited long enough': Judith Sutpen and Charles Bon" in *William Faulkner's "Absalom, Absalom!"* reprinted above, pp. 170–79.

4. Unlike in the novel, there was a wedding in "Evangeline" for Judith and Bon on the day Bon and Henry left for the war.

5. William Faulkner, "Evangeline," p. 67 above.

6. Short of naming Henry as the one who fired the shot, this whole episode is close to a direct description of the central crisis in the Sutpen family. Curiously enough, this episode is not to be found in *Absalom, Absalom!* In the novel, Rosa, the only narrator closest to being an eyewitness, rushed to the house a few hours after the shot but did not see either Henry or Charles Bon. A coffin was being made near the house, but neither Judith nor Clytie ever mentioned Charles Bon in front of Rosa. But this change suits the polyphonic design in *Absalom, Absalom!*: the image of the last shot of the war, fired by Henry, that killed Judith's man becomes more haunting when it is present only through inference; in the created vacuum echoes reverberate and perspectives abound: Why was the shot fired? What happened? Why?

7. See *Faulkner in the University*, ed. Frederick L. Gwynn and Joseph Blotner (New York: Vintage, 1959), 31–32.

8. In "Evangeline," the I-narrator is often tempted to add a rose to Don's portrayal of Judith. Don interjects this line into his telling: " '(and you can still have the rose, if you like)' " (p. 55). That could be a sign of Faulkner himself thinking aloud while searching for a new story.

9. Plato, *The Republic*, trans. Raymond Larson (Arlington Heights: AHM, 1979), 135.

10. Joseph Conrad, *Heart of Darkness* (New York: W. W. Norton, 1988), 9.

11. The dialogue seems to be between the narrator and Charles Bon (as indicated in the first two lines), Henry Sutpen (for the most part) and Raby Sutpen (as indicated in the last two lines). The following passage is on pp. 67–68.

12. That Judith is more like her father can be backed up by a scene in her childhood when she watched Sutpen wrestle with his slaves in nakedness (which made Henry nauseated). But the same scene could also suggest the awakening of her erotic desires. Mr. Compson's reasoning is not sensitive to the latter.

13. Muhlenfeld, " 'We have waited long enough,' " p. 177 above.

14. See Muhlenfeld's "Introduction" to *William Faulkner's "Absalom, Absalom!,"* p. xv. *Revolt of the Earth*, Faulkner's cinematic adaptation of the novel, also keeps this plot: Judith "runs out to a battlefield, takes a pistol from a dead soldier, and fires at a Yankee officer who 'symbolizes the murderer of her father.' She misses, and (believe it or not) they marry." See Bruce F. Kawin above, p. 77–82.

15. Indeed, this aunt was four years younger than Judith. That is perhaps why Clytie simply called her "Rosa."

16.   In Plato's *Symposium*, Diotima tells Socrates the purpose of love is to achieve good. See *Symposium*, trans. Benjamin Jowett (Indianapolis: Bobbs-Merrill Company, 1958).

17.   I am here paraphrasing what Claude Levi-Strauss said about the similarity between myth and music. See *Myth and Meaning* (New York: Schocken Books, 1955), 45.

Silence, Indirection, and Judith Sutpen

CLAIRE CRABTREE*

In *Absalom, Absalom!* William Faulkner focuses on the imagined but "interdict" relation between Judith Sutpen and Charles Bon—a mutual, abstract violation of societal taboos whose prevention by murder looms as the central incident in the novel. At the heart of Henry Sutpen's murder of his sister's fiancé, who is also his half-brother and Judith's, is a configuration of taboos upon which Southern culture may be thought to rest: taboos against incest, homosexual wishes, miscegenation, and fratricide. If Thomas Sutpen's life is about a distorted and failed patriarchal design, his children's story is about the death, by both violence and atrophy, of that dream. Speculated about, imagined, and verbally recreated by Mr. Compson, Miss Rosa, Quentin and Shreve, violence remains as central in this 1936 novel as it was in *Light in August*. By the end of the novel the story is littered with corpses: Bon, his possibly poisoned mother, Sutpen, Milly, her baby, Wash Jones, and finally Clytie and Henry Sutpen. It is Judith who perceives the underside of her father's design as a tangle wrought by "five or six people . . . each wants to weave his own pattern into the rug"[1]—a fitting emblem of the confused and contradictory motives which Quentin Compson must try to untangle.

Perhaps *Absalom, Absalom!* is most striking for its use of indirection as both a strategy and an embodiment of Faulkner's notion of the subjectivity of knowledge. Quentin tries to—or is coerced into—understanding what happened at Sutpen's Hundred half a century earlier, and why. The novel can serve as an epistemological mystery story, a quest for sexual knowledge, culminating in release and recognition when Quentin and Shreve reconstruct the actual murder. Violent acts often replace defaulted acts of sexual union in Faulkner; language in turn replaces and rehabilitates lost relations. For Quentin language is the only means of restoration, perhaps the only authentic means of human contact. But the knowledge Quentin achieves through listening to Rosa, Mr. Compson, and Shreve is a dark mixture of fact and speculation, a layering of motive and design which leaves the knower exhausted and despairing. The consummation of Judith and Bon's love is not an act of sexual union, after all, but a murder.

* This essay was written especially for this volume and is published here for the first time by permission of the author.

In the convoluted unravelling of the plot, the source of Sutpen's rejection of Charles Bon as a husband for Judith is first identified as the impediment of Bon's octoroon mistress. Later, incest emerges in the revelation that Bon is Sutpen's son, a fact which in turn leads to the revelation of miscegenation, past and predicated. With the sequential exposure of each layer of Bon's identity the system of white Southern patriarchy is exposed as more profoundly disturbed and disturbing.

Both brothers remain shadowy, with Judith hardly more vividly drawn. All are characters constructed in absence. In keeping with the geometric notion of characters as "round" and "flat," one could perhaps label the Sutpen trio hollow; presented in a series of strangely vivid but distanced tableaux, like Judith walking in the garden with Bon, the story leaves the trio's internal workings to be puzzled out by Mr. Compson, Quentin, and Shreve. The reader must incorporate information which is later doubted or denied, but whose cumulative impact constitutes, in fact, the construction of character. Faulkner's notorious self-contradictions abound: Judith, Mr. Compson avers, would kill a female rival for Bon's affections, yet she accepts with resignation Henry's murder of Bon. Faulkner delineates Judith's character in snatches, rather like the scraps of thread and fabric which become her emblem throughout the novel. The "real" Judith is not to be known—carnally, by Bon, or epistemologically, by Quentin or the reader. Thus all imputed Judiths are perhaps equally valid, an observation which is accurate for Bon and Henry as well.

Were incest not at issue, and were Sutpen's "design" for his progeny less grandiose, the marriage would still have violated the Southern code's racial taboos—perhaps more important than the incest taboo. Levi-Strauss's notion of "the exchange of daughters" is useful here, for Sutpen sees marriage as a means of economic and social control, essentially an agreement between males.[2] Ironically, to Ellen, Bon is an appropriate son-in-law. Rosa tells Quentin Bon was the shadow *"of some esoteric piece of furniture—vase or chair or desk—which Ellen wanted"* (p. 149). But Bon can't satisfy the social and economic bargain between men, since refinement and culture cannot compensate for one's "tribal," that is, racial, origin. Taboos of difference and sameness, distance and closeness, function to prohibit the union. As brother, Bon is too much the "same" as Judith; as Negro, he is too different.

Faulkner treats Ellen as an empty, but necessary, name; she hardly functions as a character. Faulkner underscores Ellen's vacuity when he describes her as unreal, a butterfly, a "substanceless shell" leaving at her death "no body to be buried: just the shape" (p. 126). Ellen is a pawn in the exchange of daughters; Judith is in her own time and her own way a casualty of a system which puts female desire and sexual agency behind economic matters and considerations of status. Yet Judith, both defiant of patriarchal interdictions and resigned to her fate, is less an Ophelia than she is an Antigone.

Indirection, then, functions not merely as technique but as both theme and entire strategy of *Absalom, Absalom!* As in the earlier *The Sound and the Fury, Sanctuary,* and *Light in August,* a central, desired sexual act fails to occur and is replaced by an act of violence, but the sexual relation at issue here is at once more distanced and more romanticized. If Judith resembles another Faulkner heroine, she is Drusilla Hawkes of "An Odor of Verbena" with her masculine strength and her borderline fanaticism. But Judith's story is even less than Drusilla's about the physicality of sex, and Judith is less a physical presence than an abstraction.

The very distance and lack of physical detail which make Judith enigmatic create a peculiar Faulknerian romanticism—an almost gothic treatment of sexuality, silence, and absence. Judith abjures language for the most part. Granted the maternal role she might have wished with Bon's child Charles Etienne, she is cold and dutiful. Nor does the narrative depict the immediacy of passion, though passion surely figures in her relations with Bon. In her ability to communicate nonverbally with Clytie, Henry, and Bon, in her imperturbability, and in her headstrong acceptance of a relation based on twin transgressions of social codes, Judith embodies Faulkner's notion of the self-contained, admirably silent woman.

If sex and death are invariably intertwined for Faulkner, the blood which he associates with women characters like Caddy Compson and Temple Drake, in earlier works, flows in *Absalom* not from the loss of virginity but from wounds to the male. Rosa imagines Bon's blood seeping onto the mattress where he lies before burial. Sutpen dies by a rusty scythe at the hands of Wash Jones. The violence is bound up with sexual transgressions. Yet where earlier works link female sexuality to liquidity, rivers, and flowers, here Faulkner uses images of barren dryness and desication, culminating in the extreme opposite of fecund liquidity—the firing of the house which Rosa imagines and Clytie effects, burning her half brother Henry and herself to death.

Even Judith, whose sexual desire for Bon is pivotal, is described in terms of dryness, a " 'scentless prairie flower' " (p. 338) next to Bon's magnolialike mistress. Only a sort of verbal hysteria in Rosa Coldfield, and on one occasion Judith, suggests the uncontrolled flow or outpouring—but here I use both terms metaphorically—associated elsewhere with women's sexuality. Ellen's tears on her wedding day resonate with the rain (p. 58) and her mad dislocation from reality is linked to hysterical laughter, while the mistress sheds copious, perhaps insincere tears at Bon's grave, as Bon's mother did in his childhood. Otherwise the women in *Absalom* are associated with ghosts, shades, age, desication, and fatigue.

Judith's silence links her to other women in the Faulkner canon: like Caddie Compson and Addie Bundren, she is more talked about, more thought about than thinking or speaking. Significantly, when Judith does speak, in Mr. Compson's reconstruction of her bringing Bon's final letter to Mrs.

Compson, she speaks in irrational, near-hysterical tones. The only extensive physical description of Judith comes here, after Bon's murder by Henry: "gaunt, the Sutpen skull showing indeed now through the worn, the Cold-field, flesh, the face which had long since forgotten how to be young and yet absolutely impenetrable, absolutely serene: no mourning, not even grief" (pp. 126–27). To Quentin's grandmother, Judith speaks in long sentences, one of over 200 words—language which by its disjointed structure suggests hysteria. Judith brings Bon's last letter, " 'because you make so little impression, you see.' " Tombstones and their "scratches," Judith insists, come to be forgotten, but a scrap of paper, even unread and unkempt, would at least "be remembered even if only from passing from one hand to another, one mind to another, and it would be at least a scratch, something, something that might make a mark on something that *was* once for the reason that it can die someday" (p. 127). Judith's incoherence is such that Mrs. Compson thinks she means to commit suicide, and to this Judith responds that her father will need her, adding that, presumably in the grave or afterlife, " 'there wouldn't be any room, now. . . . It would be full already. Glutted. Like a theater, an opera house' " (p. 128). Judith's self-effacement, born of despair rather than generosity, borders on fanaticism.

Significantly, Judith hands over a piece of writing to provide a scratch or mark on history, but the letter is male writing of which she is the object and receiver. Having created a determined and self-contained woman character, Faulkner seems to default when it comes to letting her speak. Judith's faltering and inconclusive speech contrasts with the harshly eloquent letter from Bon, the irony of which Richard Moreland examines.[3] As troubling to some readers as Faulkner's rather crude notion of hysteria in women characters may be, one could argue that Judith's language constitutes a representation of pure grief, as Benjy's incoherence documents pure loss in *The Sound and the Fury*. Her language may be viewed as hysterical and extralogical because Faulkner associates hysteria not so much with women as with grief itself.

In a novel in which indirection and vicarious experience predominate, Judith's early letters to Bon, written before Henry forbids further exchange, are dismissed as girlish scribblings. Even less direct as an exchange between people than a letter is Judith's sewing. Judith is, moreover, associated with sewing as Bon is with writing, as three incidents point up. The first is one of Faulkner's posited, then withdrawn, events: When Henry and Bon's regiment prepares for war, the soldiers carry the cut but unsewn silk of their flag from house to house for their sweethearts to contribute a few stitches. Bon and Henry are in hiding, however; none of the three takes part in this ceremonial gallantry or the farewell balls. Judith's symbolic but never-en-acted role—to stitch the flag—implies active support rather than passive waiting. Later Judith and Clytie use up all the available fabric in the house, from rugs to curtains, sewing bandages for the wounded. Finally, Judith is, at the moment of Bon's death, patching together a wedding dress. When Henry enters the house after the gunshot, brother and sister look *"at one another across the up-raised and unfinished wedding dress"* (p. 135). The detail and repetition with which the scene is described suggests the symbolic role Judith has accepted: Her role, always related to Bon, is to patch and stitch with needle on cloth, not to write with ink or even stove polish on paper. She is to be "just the blank shape, the empty vessel in which [Henry and Bon] strove to preserve . . . what each conceived the other to believe him to be" (pp. 119–20). While Bon's letter documents their having existed, makes a "mark" or "scratch," her more ephemeral task is to patch, preserve, and ultimately bury the men of the South.

Despite her allegorical role as Southern woman, Judith is in some ways androgynous, more like her father than Henry is. Mr. Compson reconstructs her years of waiting for Bon: "[H]er relations with her father had not altered one jot; to see them together, Bon might never have existed—the same calm impenetrable faces seen together in the carriage in town. . . . They did not need to talk. They were too much alike" (pp. 121–22). Judith's imputed ruthlessness surfaces in Mr. Compson's assertion " 'she would have taken Bon' " and even murdered the mistress no matter what Bon's parentage (p. 121). The affinity for violence was established in childhood, when Henry's nausea at seeing his father wrestle, with bestial violence, his Negro slaves, contrasts to Judith's fascinated interest in the same scene. Although Judith plays out the Southern woman's role of passivity, silence, and self-control, and Henry enunciates the patriarchal interdictions, Faulkner underscores the internal unsuitability of the pair to these roles.

If Judith is silent with her father, her relationships with both brother and lover are also marked by wordless communication. Henry, Judith, and Bon, paired in various configurations, are strangely united. The brothers, too, are somewhat androgynous, especially Bon, who smells like flowers, wears flowered dressing gowns, and is "almost epicene" as Ellen's potential furnishing for her house. That Henry feels an almost homosexual attraction to Bon and an incestuous one to his sister is clear: "[Henry] seduced her [to Bon] along with himself . . . as though by means of that telepathy with which as children they seemed at times to anticipate one another's actions as two birds leave a limb at the same instant" (p. 99). The enmeshment of the three may explain Judith's acceptance of Henry's act. Judith's lament to Mrs. Compson that her life seems to involve several people weaving competing patterns "on the same loom" (p. 127) resonates with the images of tangling and connection, the sewing and patching of flag, bandages, and wedding dress.

The portrait of Bon's mistress and Judith's recognition of her negritude appear as the climactic revelation in Faulkner's short first version of the Sutpen plot, the 1931 "Evangeline," which shows the author's interest in the challenge the mistress represents to Judith and Henry's Southern sensibilities. The New Orleans tradition of *placage*, or the "placing" of the light-skinned girls in formal concubinage, is imputed to be shocking to Henry, whose likely sexual experience with Memphis whores or slave women seems a simpler, less ambiguous arrangement.[4] Faulkner clearly interrogates both the simple "American" arrangement with its clear categories and the more cynical and complex "European" one. The pale skin and cultural refinement of Bon, the magnolia woman, and their son Charles Etienne profoundly threatens a social system which rests upon visible difference between whites and blacks. Significantly, it is through the lacy clothing of both mistress and son that Faulkner establishes their uneasy resemblance to the patched and tattered planter class.

In *Absalom* Faulkner underscores not only the moral ambiguity of Southern sexual arrangements but also their social consequences, represented by ambiguous and largely inarticulate characters like Clytie and Jim Bond. For Henry, who grows up with his half-sister Clytie as a slave, Bon's mistress turns " 'all morality' " upside down; " 'all of honor perished' " in the face of "[T]he apotheosis of two doomed races presided over by its own victim— a woman with a face like a tragic magnolia, the eternal female, the eternal Who-suffers" (p. 114). The *placage* woman is chosen in childhood and "raised more carefully than any white girl, any nun, than any blooded mare even," according to Mr. Compson, "through a system more formal than only that white girls are sold under since they are more valuable as commodities than white girls" (p. 117).

Thus Faulkner explicitly recognizes the exchange of daughters; the conscious irony of comparing the training of the mistress to the training of a mare counterpoints Wash Jones's rage at Sutpen's insult when Milly bears him a daughter rather than a son. And despite Henry's revulsion, his sister's virginity is a commodity or object of exchange not entirely discrete from that represented by the mistress.

As by metonymy Bon's mistress is a magnolia, redolent of scent and sexuality, so Judith, the scentless flower, becomes her virginity. Henry, Quentin argues, may have realized that his sister's virginity " 'must depend upon its loss, absence, to have existed at all. . . . the . . . perfect incest . . . brother realizing that the sister's virginity must be destroyed in order to have existed' " (p. 96). The paradox of virginity is perhaps Faulkner's favorite trope; both Quentin and Henry are obsessed with it. Henry, were it possible, would "metamorphose" into Judith's love or Bon's bride (p. 96).

Judith, Henry, and Bon form a trinity of sister, brother, and brother-outsider. Unlike Quentin, Henry has a means for mediating his relationship to his sister: he can identify both with the seducer and with the seduced sister. And unlike Rosa, who lives vicariously, Henry can in a way possess both the objects of his love—Bon through companionship and Judith through his control of her virginity. To the extent that in sibling incest the sister is a stand-in for the mother, and Bon a substitute father, Henry also achieves the triumph of slaying the father and keeping the mother figure to himself.

Near the end of *Absalom* Shreve and Quentin, two virginal college students, re-create in language the death of Bon at Henry's hands. Their dialogue takes on a rhythmic interplay as they participate in the replacement of sexual union between white and black with the murder of black by white. This almost orgasmic union in language between Quentin and Shreve, as well as the merging of Quentin with his alter ego Henry, and the outsider Shreve with the outsider Bon—"There were four of them here" (p. 336) the reader is told—consummates the allegory of the Southern racial and sexual taboos.

The central female figure is absent from this twofold struggle, the struggle of Quentin and Shreve to know, and the struggle of Henry and Bon to enact or prevent the sexual union. The absent Judith becomes both object and victim of this struggle, less a character than a symbol. Waiting for Bon, stitching the patched wedding dress while her brother negates the possibility it represents, she is left silent by Shreve and Quentin as they attempt to rehabilitate the past through the artistic, re-creative linguistic act. Even on the level of allegory, Judith, as white woman desired by her white and black brothers, is a prize to be preserved but never possessed. Despite her strength of character, her role is to serve, to be silent, and to wait.

Notes

1. William Faulkner, *Absalom, Absalom!* (New York: Random House, 1936), 127.
2. Claude Levi-Strauss, *The Elementary Structures of Kinship*, ed. Rodney Needham; trans. J. H. Bell, John von Sturmer, and Rodney Needham (London: Eyre and Spottiswoode, 1969), 12–15; 62–68.
3. Richard C. Moreland, *Faulkner and Modernism: Rereading and Rewriting* (Madison: University of Wisconsin Press, 1990), 65–71. Moreland argues that Bon takes on the role of author, in his letter to Judith. Moreland's argument is complex, including the notion that Bon "pointedly contradicts and explicitly rejects . . . [the] authorial role of cosmopolitan identification with a blank, cosmic indifference which . . . is gradually losing its persuasive force" in the novel. In Judith's speech to Mrs. Compson, Moreland finds both "blind obedience to an inscrutable cosmic irony" and "traces of still another sense *she* has not of an indifferent, cosmic design, but of other, different human designs . . . other humans' cross-purposes" (pp. 71–74).
4. Bertram Wyatt-Brown, *Southern Honor: Ethics and Behavior in the Old South* (Oxford: Oxford University Press, 1982), 308–16.

[What Clytie Knew]

LOREN F. SCHMIDTBERGER*

The narrators in *Absalom, Absalom!* think of Clytie Sutpen as somehow attuned to otherworldly forces and possessing mysterious powers. Rosa describes her as exhibiting *"a brooding awareness and acceptance of the inexplicable unseen."*[1] Quentin recalls that she approached him in the hallway of the mansion "as if she had known all the time that this hour must come and that it could not be resisted" (p. 369). Mr. Compson thinks that Sutpen selected the name Clytemnestra "to designate the presiding augur of his own disaster" (p. 62), but that he confused the name of the seer Cassandra with that of Queen Clytemnestra. Through these and other references to Clytie's strange prescience, Faulkner raises the possibility that she possessed some secret information about the Sutpen family. Exploration of Clytie's own history reveals that she probably did know some key facts, obtained, however, through normal means. In presenting this seer-like character, Faulkner does not depart from the "historical" novel's conventions of plausibility; *Absalom* contains matter-of-fact explanations of Clytie's access to secret knowledge and of her mysterious deportment and actions, however inexplicable these may appear to other characters in the novel.

There is, for example, Clytie's astounding display of competence in going to New Orleans by herself, locating Charles Bon's son Etienne there, and then bringing him back to Sutpen's Hundred. Mr. Compson sounds incredulous when telling Quentin about it: "—Clytie who had never been further from Sutpen's Hundred than Jefferson in her life, yet who made that journey alone to New Orleans and returned with the child . . . this child who could speak no English as the woman could speak no French, who had found him, hunted him down, in a French city and brought him away" (pp. 195–196).

By withholding the details of Clytie's trip to New Orleans, Faulkner invites the reader to think of her as having superhuman resources. This is the same literary effect he creates by withholding the details of the youthful Sutpen's emigration to Haiti. One gathers that both father and daughter were capable of translating themselves across the barriers of language and

*Reprinted with permission of the publisher from *Mississippi Quarterly* 35 (Summer 1982): 255–63. © 1982 by Mississippi State University. Original title: *"Absalom, Absalom!*: What Clytie Knew."

geography at will. Impressions like this remain with the reader, even after Faulkner elsewhere supplies details that suggest more ordinary explanations, as he does in this instance of Clytie's trip to New Orleans.

Clytie's mother, it will be remembered, was one of the two women in the wagonload of Haitian slaves Sutpen brought to Yoknapatawpaha County in 1833. Mr. Compson, a natural storyteller, loves to portray these people as strange, even when he knows better, as in his repeatedly calling them "wild," while yet appreciating the comical truth that their wildness occurs mostly in the imaginations of the insular Yoknapatawphans, who have never before heard anyone speak French. For storytelling purposes, Mr. Compson apparently finds it more interesting to attribute strange powers to Clytiè in explanation of her ability to find Etienne than to recall that Clytie surely retained enough of her childhood Creole to enable her to move around in the French Quarter of New Orleans. Born in 1834, within the year after her mother arrived at Sutpen's Hundred, Clytie's first language must have been French Creole, since this was still the language used by Sutpen's Negroes as late as 1838, at which time Sutpen spoke to them, according to the sometimes forgetful Mr. Compson, "in that tongue which even now a good part of the county did not know was a civilized language" (pp. 56–57).

Also mysterious, the elder Compsons thought, was Judith's and Clytie's ability to establish communications with Bon's widow to let her know that he was buried at Sutpen's Hundred. After the octoroon mistress had already come to Sutpen's Hundred from New Orleans, Clytie's going there would have been comparatively easy, especially if the woman left directions, albeit in French, for Clytie's future use. But for Judith and Clytie to get in touch with her in the first place required that one of them at least possess more information than a photograph of her and her child, and there is some evidence that Clytie knew about Bon's mistress at least as early as the summer of 1860. At that time, shortly after Bon left Sutpen's Hundred for New Orleans, Sutpen went there too. Mr. Compson, in telling Quentin this, stresses Sutpen's secrecy: "No one," he emphasizes, "but your grandfather and perhaps Clytie" (p. 70) ever knew that Sutpen made this journey. That Clytie may have known of her father's secret problems in New Orleans cannot be dismissed as an accidental implication: comparison of the manuscript of *Absalom* with the published text reveals that Faulkner twice revised the wording so as to raise the possibility that Clytie knew more than any of the other Sutpens about her father's concerns in New Orleans.[2] These careful revisions do not, of course, absolutely prove that Clytie knew something about Bon. They do show that Faulkner was scrupulously careful to leave it an open possibility that she did.

In raising the possibility that Clytie knew something about the New Orleans branch of the Sutpen family, Faulkner encourages some reflection on Clytie's own ties to Sutpen's Haitian past. It does seem natural to suppose that in early childhood she learned from her mother of Sutpen's repudiation of his first wife and son, a matter surely talked about by the Haitian Negroes, if only among themselves, since it had precipitated their relocating in this strange Mississippi wilderness. Such inside information would enable Clytie to share her father's appreciation of the coincidence in the name of Henry's friend from the university. She would understand why her father followed Bon to New Orleans, why he forbade the marriage, and why Henry finally murdered Bon. Later, as we have seen, her knowledge serves to explain how she and Judith were able to contact Bon's widow.

Clytie was the guardian of a family secret in Faulkner's earliest conception of her. In the short story "Evangeline,"[3] a skeletal version of *Absalom*, she appears under the name of Raby as Sutpen's illegitimate, part-Negro or perhaps part-Indian daughter. Like Clytie, Raby is small in size and coffee-colored in complexion. The secret she keeps for four generations is that Henry Sutpen shot Charles Bon for having married a Negro woman prior to marrying Judith. She conceals Henry (but for forty years) before both perish in the fire she sets to the mansion. Raby is rather talkative, hinting to the Shreve-like narrator that she knows a dreadful secret. In changing her name to Clytie in *Absalom*, Faulkner also made her totally uncommunicative. But he then gave readers some clues to her possession of secret information, beginning with Mr. Compson's thoughts about Sutpen's confusion in selecting her name.[4] Whereas Cassandra's knowledge was divinely derived, a gift from Apollo, Clytie obtained her information by ordinary means. But because the narrators through whom we see Clytie are either ignorant of, or inattentive to, such facts as would reasonably account for her clairvoyance and strange deportment, she appears to be responding to otherworldly forces. Rosa, for example, thought that Clytie had occult signals of her arrival at Sutpen's Hundred after the fratricide, but it is more likely that Clytie simply expected that Rosa would return with Wash Jones. Since she did not want Judith disturbed, and perhaps also wished to keep Rosa from seeing the picture of Bon's mistress and son, Clytie stationed herself so as to be able to bar Rosa's way to the stairs. Similarly, there is an ordinary explanation for Quentin's feeling that Clytie's motions in the hallway were directed by preordaining forces when he and Rosa entered the mansion. Clytie feared that the discovery of Henry was now inevitable.

In these episodes Clytie was trying to protect her family from intrusive outsiders, and her behavior typifies her fierce loyalty to her family. In "Evangeline," Raby, on being asked why she devoted forty years to the secret care of Henry, replied, "Henry Sutpen is my brother."[5] In *Absalom*, Clytie's concern for the French-speaking side of the family led her to contact Bon's widow, and the sense of family solidarity best explains why she and Judith wished to do so in the first place, and why they took on the burden of rearing Etienne.

Judith's compassion for Bon's widow, and her ultimate sacrifice of self in nursing Etienne in his final illness appear more natural if seen as examples of familial devotion. Criticism has rightly pointed to Judith's kindness to the octoroon woman and Etienne as instances wherein she transcends her father's limitations. Unless one considers her compassion as consciously familial, however—an aunt's solicitude for her nephew—Judith's actions are reduced to a melodramatic devotion to the child of an unfaithful suitor. It seems more consistent with such evidence as the text supplies that Clytie eventually explained to Judith that Charles Bon was their half-brother. Quentin, after learning that Bon was Sutpen's son, thinks Judith knew that Etienne was her nephew, imagining her as saying to him, *"Call me Aunt Judith"* (p. 208). Any guess as to when Clytie might have revealed the kinship should take into account two factors. First, when Judith gave her letter from Bon to Mrs. Compson a week after burying him, her remarks reflected utter bewilderment, an inability to make any sense at all out of this terrible turn of events.[6] Second, Bon's mistress did not visit his grave until after Sutpen's own death. These facts suggest that Clytie revealed nothing to Judith about Bon while Sutpen himself was still alive.

Sutpen's death leaves Clytie the custodian of the most closely kept secret of the family, the paternity of Charles Bon. After Etienne's arrival, her zealous watchfulness over him, so puzzling to General Compson, makes sense in terms of her desire to keep the townspeople from prying into a family scandal. In local gossip, the appearance of Etienne at Sutpen's Hundred explained why Henry shot Bon, it being assumed now that Etienne was Judith's son. Clytie headed off all attempts at questioning the boy and it was "soon well known," Mr. Compson tells Quentin, "with what grim and unflagging alertness she discovered and interrupted any attempt to speak to him" (p. 201). Discussion with Etienne might have led ultimately to disclosures even more scandalous than the town's current thoughts about Judith and Bon. Etienne may well have known that Sutpen was his grandfather. His mother could have told him, if she knew it herself, or he could have learned it from his grandmother, Sutpen's first wife, who lived in New Orleans too, presumably not too far from her son and her grandson in the French Quarter. From whose home did Clytie "fetch" Etienne, his mother's or his grandmother's? Questions like these cannot be answered, in part because Clytie prevented any delving into Etienne's past. Mr. Compson refers over and over again to her ferocity in sequestering her young charge from all components of the community, young and old, white and black. Even General Compson himself, whose special relationship to the family as Sutpen's only friend might have earned him Clytie's confidence, was nonetheless kept at a distance too. In fact, during the first year or two of Etienne's stay, the General thought that Clytie was the boy's mother, and Sutpen himself the father. He discarded that shocking possibility only after it finally dawned on him that Etienne was the child who had accompanied the octoroon woman on her visit to Bon's grave; that he was the Charles Etienne Saint-Valery Bon for whose tombstone Judith had already put down a deposit.

Along with this realization came the knowledge that the boy had some Negro blood from his mother. Left with no better explanation of Clytie's constant surveillance of Etienne, General Compson assumed that she was vexed by this trace of negritude in her young ward and wished to conceal it. He then theorized at length about the nuances of racial protocol in the sleeping and eating arrangements of this racially mixed household, imagining Clytie as scrubbing Etienne "with repressed fury as if she were trying to wash the smooth faint tinge from his skin" (p. 198). Savage reminders like this of his tainted blood, the elder Compsons thought, resulted in Etienne's violent repudiation later on of his white heritage.

It seems most unlikely, however, that Clytie subjected Etienne to such embarrassment and cruelty. We do not know how she and Judith actually treated Etienne, but we do know that both women endured extraordinary self-sacrifice on his behalf. General Compson's idea that Clytie adhered to the conventions of race in their sleeping and eating arrangements is inconsistent with Rosa's experience when she ate and slept with Judith and Clytie. Rosa is specific about there being no distinctions among the three of them *"of age or color"* (p. 155). She elaborates on how Clytie failed to observe the conventions of a caste system. Clytie twice ordered Rosa not to go upstairs, each time omitting the appellative of racial respect, and she habitually omitted it when referring to or addressing Henry and Judith (pp. 138–139, 369). General Compson himself noticed her failure to assume the posture of servility when she "looked full and steadily at his face and said nothing" (p. 204).

In spite of General Compson's speculations, all the evidence suggests that racial distinctions were not an issue in Clytie's upbringing of Etienne, or in Judith's relationship with him either. Although his several years of isolation at Sutpen's Hundred were poor preparation for entrance into the social mainstream of Yoknapatawpha County, Etienne's psychological turmoil seems to have had its origins in events that occurred before he became Judith and Clytie's ward.[7] Etienne, like Bon himself, was the child of a woman whose racial lineage disqualified her as a marriage partner, and Etienne's deepest distress may have arisen from the questionable position that he and his mother held with his father. When General Compson, having stopped the court proceedings against Etienne, told him, "You are Charles Bon's son," Etienne replied, "I dont know" (p. 203). This surliness appears to be still another example in *Absalom* of a deep sense of injury in a father-son relationship, as does Etienne's subsequent marriage, duly licensed where his father's had not been, to a black woman.

Whatever Etienne's inner thoughts, the secret Clytie hid successfully until Quentin visited Sutpen's Hundred was that Sutpen and Bon were father and son. Bon's mixed blood was a different matter, though Quentin learned of that too, of course. Because of the confusion over these separate truths in commentary on Clytie, it may be well to distinguish here between the secret filiation and Bon's negritude. Discovery of the filiation would necessarily have led to the realization that Bon was part Negro. Sutpen, in the course of his visit with General Compson during the war, gave his friend reason enough to suppose that the son he abandoned was of mixed blood (see pp. 264, 274). But he gave not even the slightest hint that Charles Bon was that son. When Quentin learned this secret, he also knew then, on Sutpen's own word as passed on through the elder Compsons, that Bon was part Negro. But the reverse does not hold. Had Quentin learned only that Bon was part Negro, he and Mr. Compson would still have had no basis for connecting Bon with Sutpen's abandoned son (though they would at last have had an explanation for the murder).[8]

Clytie may have known nothing of Bon's negritude, unless Henry told her after he returned to Sutpen's Hundred to die. There is no evidence that Sutpen himself ever told anyone of his first son's mixed blood other than General Compson, and then Henry. Although he was clearly annoyed with his wife's parents for having withheld "the one fact" (p. 264) that had required him to put his wife and son aside, his comments to General Compson imply that he did not consider either the impediment itself or the parents' concealment of it as any fault of his wife's own (see p. 240). He was most conscientious about dealing with her in what he conceived to be an honorable fashion, not wishing "to malign or traduce" her in any way (p. 272). In view of this attitude, and considering his delay in revealing Bon's negritude to Henry until forced to play his "last trump card" (p. 274), it becomes difficult to imagine that he told his wife she was a Negro. Quentin and Shreve assume that Bon did not know the nature of the impediment until he learned it through Henry. They imagine Bon as thinking until then, *"I will not even demand to know of him what it was my mother did that justified his action toward her and me"* (p. 327; see also p. 321). Bon's son surely never learned what his father himself did not know.

What Clytie knew and made every effort to conceal was the tragic truth that Judith's suitor was their half brother; that Henry was guilty of fratricide.

Notes

1. William Faulkner, *Absalom, Absalom!* (New York: Modern Library, 1951), p. 138. Hereafter cited in the text.

2. In the manuscript, Faulkner's first wording omits reference to Clytie. He then added the phrase, "or perhaps Clytie," so that the passage has Mr. Compson saying, "no one but your grandfather (*or perhaps Clytie*) ever to know" that Sutpen went to New Orleans. See Gerald Langford, *Faulkner's Revision of "Absalom, Absalom!"* (Austin: University of Texas Press, 1971), p. 97. I have added the italics to point out how this wording still effectively eliminates Clytie: in a choice between General Compson *or* Clytie, the General has to be the one who knew, since he could not have told Mr. Compson about it otherwise. In the published

text, however, the conjunction *and* replaces *or*, so that now General Compson "and perhaps Clytie" knew of Sutpen's trip.

3. Completed in 1931 but rejected for publication, "Evangeline" is now available in *Uncollected Stories of William Faulkner*, ed. Joseph Blotner (New York: Random House, 1979), pp. 583–609.

4. Because Cassandra is best remembered today simply as one whose gloomy predictions go unheeded, it may be helpful to recall that in *Agamemnon* she reminds the Chorus of the past slayings of blood relatives in the House of Atreus. The Chorus marvels at her knowledge of family history.

5. See above, p. 68.

6. For example: "You get born . . . at the same time with a lot of other people, all mixed up with them, like trying to, having to, move your arms and legs with strings only the same strings are hitched to all the other arms and legs and the others all trying and they dont know why either except that the strings are all in one another's way like five or six people all trying to make a rug on the same loom only each one wants to weave his own pattern into the rug" (p. 127).

Judith's use of the loom image, incidentally, parodies Sutpen's complaint to General Compson about the impending destruction of his own "design."

7. In her essay on Clytie as the embodiment of the tension between kinship and race, Thadious M. Davis demonstrates that racial distinctions are unmeaningful to Judith and Clytie. They become meaningful to Etienne, Davis suggests, when he discovers them in the world outside Sutpen's Hundred. See "The Yoking of 'Abstract Contradictions': Clytie's Meaning in *Absalom, Absalom!*" *SAF*, 7 (1979), 209–219.

8. Hershel Parker distinguishes carefully between these different truths about Bon. See "What Quentin Saw Out There," in the Appendix, pp. 275–78. The blurring of them continues, however. Carl E. Rollyson, Jr., after raising incisive questions about Clytie's knowledge, concludes that "it is Quentin's contact with her which seems to have generated the 'fact' of Bon's Negro blood." See "The Re-Creation of the Past in *Absalom, Absalom!*" *MissQ*, 29 (1976), 370. Similarly, John W. Hunt observes that Quentin learned "about Bon's black blood" at Sutpen's Hundred. See "Historiography in Faulkner's *Absalom, Absalom!*" *Faulkner Studies*, 1 (1980), 45. John V. Hagopian argues that Quentin's contact with Clytie produces an intuition that Bon too was black. Quentin and Shreve then realize that "it just has to be true that Bon, like Clytie, is a black Sutpen." See "Black Insight in *Absalom, Absalom!*" *Faulkner Studies*, 1 (1980), 36.

The Bon Family

◆

[The Bon Lineage]

Erskine E. Peters*

The story of the Bon lineage in *Absalom, Absalom!* which begins with the birth of Charles Bon in Haiti in 1829 and goes possibly beyond the year and the disappearance of his grandson, Jim Bond, in 1910 is illustrative of matrices so complex that often romance stands at one end and tragedy at the other. Charles Bon is the archetypal phantom, the intruder who provokes the macabre Yoknapatawpha imagination. His presence betrays the community's desires, preoccupations, and value system. It is through what Charles Bon represents in the country's imagination that the novel is able to achieve its truly gothic pitch.

The son of the young peasant-born Virginian, Thomas Sutpen and a Haitian mulatta, Bon is a product of the past who emerges to confound Thomas Sutpen's ambition to place the capstone of honor and respectability upon his life efforts. With regard to the structure of the novel, Bon's resurgence into his father's life simultaneously interrupts and advances the movement of the saga. His appearance makes it vital that Sutpen's abandoned past be retrieved and accounted for; thus, the story has to move backward. By moving backward, advancements in the plot are made in the form of revelations which only the past can provide. The overall implication, for purposes of theme as well as plot, is that Charles Bon is an agent of fate,

*Reprinted with permission of the author from *William Faulkner: The Yoknapatawpha World and Black Being* (Darby, Pennsylvania: Norwood Editions, 1983), 118–23, 130–34.

or, in a more specific sense, the agent acting in the design of his mother and her lawyer in retaliation for Sutpen's repudiation of her.

Charles Bon's whole being is bound by Yoknapatawpha myth. Miss Rosa Coldfield speaks of him with the intimacy of an acquaintance, but she never really saw him until after he had been murdered by his half-brother, Henry. Neither did Mr. Compson who is totally infatuated with the myth, and who thinks that Bon "must have appeared almost phoenix-like, fullsprung from no childhood, born of no woman and impervious to time and vanished, leaving no bones nor dust anywhere. . . ."[1] Mr. Compson is fascinated by Bon as the exemplar of the pleasurable life. Bon and the myth and the delights of octoroon existence titillate Compson's imagination into extremes of fantasy and sensual speculation. Of especial interest are the idyllic forms Mr. Compson uses in speculating how Henry Sutpen first saw his half-brother riding through a grove, crossing the campus in a French styled cloak, or even more to Mr. Compson's pleasure, Henry's formal introduction to Bon in the setting of the hedonist, reclining in delicate garments in a sunny, intimate chamber. Mr. Compson attributes to Bon such seductive powers that his passionate descriptions can be seen, rather obviously, as his own wishful thinking. Bon is the "cerebral Don Juan" whom Henry vicariously loved through his sister. Yet for all Mr. Compson's efforts to render his view of Bon into concrete form he cannot depict much more than a spectre hovering above the historical setting.

So potent is his fantasy that Mr. Compson is frustrated that he was not there to see Bon in person. The frustration leads him into making equivocal assessments about Bon, his esteemed creation. Mr. Compson never judges Sutpen for his bigamist acts, but he indicts Bon for his bigamist intentions. However, Bon is also portrayed as existing in a morally irreprehensible sphere with regard to the confusion emerging from his incursion into the Sutpen household. Even more paradoxical is the fact that Mr. Compson berates Bon for paying Judith the "dubious compliment of not even trying to ruin her."[2] In his attempt to create an image of Bon for his own satisfaction, Mr. Compson participates in the same denial and usurpation of Bon's being which he accuses Sutpen's wife Ellen of for having arranged the engagement between Bon and Judith. In addition to Mr. Compson's equivocation and paradox are his outright contradictions. If Henry was doomed to kill Bon, as Mr. Compson thinks, then also fate must have acted out a retribution upon Thomas Sutpen. On the other hand, when Mr. Compson indicts Bon's moral character, he disregards what he has already attributed to fate and insists that Bon must have been working premeditatively within a grand scheme for vengeance. Mr. Compson feels that if the hand of fate is not operating in the drama, there definitely must be some ulterior motive connected with Bon's emergence. He finds it especially unusual for this older, extremely good looking New Orleans gentleman with a cosmopolitan flair to have come to study at an unestablished, recently founded college in the backwoods of Mississippi where he meets his half-brother who will take him to their father's house as a suitor for their sister. It is Henry, Bon's murderer, nevertheless, who is the one portrayed as the innocent victim.

Ironically, Bon is expected, as his name suggests, to be good for the Sutpens. Seized upon by Ellen Sutpen as a vehicle for helping their family attain social status, Bon becomes the new life spark for Judith's heretofore stagnating existence. He would be fine clothing for daughter Judith in public. Bon is seen as a needed complement to the other furnishings of the estate. Since, in comparison to the clumsy social affectations of Henry and his father, gleaned from backwoods society and raw money, Bon's mannerisms are the exemplar of polish, he would be the perfect model for Henry's social grooming. Henry needs Bon as an image of identification beyond and in contradistinction to the harsh ruthless image provided by his father.

Bon is the ironic agent who does not act, but activates. Whereas Sutpen had been known to generate trouble, Bon brings trouble to his father, and thwarts the general course of his activity. On account of what Bon represents, we get a sense of the structure of the Yoknapatawpha psyche in its cultivation of a predisposition for what it considers moral and ethical scrupulousness and Protestant virtue. It has no qualms about the foundations of its peculiar culture having been established upon a barbarous and inhumane enterprise, which represents a flagrant travesty of true Christian virtues. Yet this is the psyche which revolts against the idea of legal marriage between the white and any other race.

The community's preoccupation with Bon's presence also brings the nature of the exploitation of both black and white women in the culture to the forefront. Both are victimized by white masculine designs and desires and are seen merely as objects. The black woman is reputed to be capable of animal sexuality, while the white woman, being used as an attendant vessel, is thought to exist ideally in a marginal void.

Henry's moment of decision to kill Bon to prevent the marriage to Judith, is the instant in which the ultimate sensibility of the culture and its truest values are exposed. It is the moment of horror in which the Southern ethos rises indomitably above Christian percept. Miscegenation is not seen at all as the mixing of the races, which the Southern fathers have carried out as a prerogative of their power over blacks, but becomes the abominable notion of introducing black blood into the white race. The double racial standard is apparent. Sex forced upon the black woman by the white man is tolerated and so is the offspring. But when occurring between a black man and a white woman it is all an abomination.

The comic irony of it all is that Bon, the man with some black blood, becomes eternally tied to the Sutpen family when Miss Rosa unwittingly enters the date of his death along with Ellen Sutpen's in the family Bible. In addition, Bon is buried next to Ellen Sutpen, who would certainly not endure her eternal rest if she knew she was spending it next to a corpse in which African blood once flowed. She could probably not endure it even though it had been her own doing to thrust Bon upon her daughter.

Bon is so entangled in the imaginations and passions of others that no one is even sure of just what Bon himself knew. No one is sure whether he knew that Sutpen was his father. The only opportunity one has for seeing Bon on his own is in a letter he wrote to Judith while he and Henry were serving in a Confederate regiment, which letter Judith gave to the grandmother of narrator Quentin Compson. One is not sure to what degree the letter reveals the total character of the man. It has a philosophic but bland prosaic opening, and is written without date, salutation, or signature. It is in no way an amorous letter. The tone is distinctly distanced and more nonchalant than contrived or pretentious. The language is generally circuitous, but amply direct when directness is intended. Bon does not speak of himself personally, nor does he speak to Judith in an involved way as one might expect in a letter from a fiancé to his betrothed when separated by war. He writes with more concern for fact than for any emotional connection. He has nothing fundamental to say about the two of them, and seems only to be performing a necessary and effortless gesture. The sense of his character comes over as easy, but as not giving, with no inclination of affection, not even through relish of style even though he uses a great deal of passionately fatalistic imagery in relating his thoughts about the war. One has the impression that he is an adept participant in the events of the war, but that he is not overwhelmed or weighted down by their implications. The ostensible absence of rhetorical flourish suggests that his intention is to debunk any notion of romance.

Charles Bon, like Cooper's Cora Munro, is the product of the marriage between a West Indian mulatta and a white father. The conditions of their lives, however, stand at great variance, mainly because one is accorded the birthright and the other is not. Racial fantasies have taken over in one world but not in the other. Owing to the reveries and daydreams of those who try to shape Bon's story, his life has been buried beneath others' notions and illusions, and the life quest of his son Charles Etienne de St. Valery Bon, who seems not to know where to search nor whom to look to for his birthright, becomes all the more inescapably tragic.

The crucial beginning of any so-called tragic mulatto is that he is a victim of someone else's imagination. St. Valery Bon's existence, like his father's, is bound up within the community's fantasies, as betrayed by Mr. Compson who harbors a tremendously romantic preoccupation with what he projects as the ceremony, splendor, and tragedy of the octoroon class. First presented in a bucolic scene in *Absalom, Absalom!*, St. Valery Bon is described as an ethereal being, and is imagined to have had an appearance which suggests that, like his father Charles Bon, he was born without human agents. He is a boy whose personal quality is more like light than human. That he looks three years younger than his actual age, when first seen, is supposed to render him an idyllic delicacy which, however, will prove more destructive than rewarding when the child becomes an orphan and has to accept the more shocking reality of life in its Yoknapatawpha form. The boy's emotional insecurity has already been made apparent in that he is portrayed as constantly clinging to the apron of his mother's duenna during their visit to his father's grave. Also, the fact that St. Valery is given a sexless face enhancing his delicacy only marks his potential vulnerability to tragedy. Although he is described as more like light than human, he is thought to be a child unused to sunlight who has grown up midst shadows and candles. Since St. Valery has had little contact with the earth, he is thought not to have breathed air but some soft radiance which emanated from his mother. Early looked upon as enigmatic and solitary he is destined for an alienated existence; for even during childhood he responds to those around him with "an aghast fatalistic terror."[3]

When he is orphaned at the age of twelve and sought out in New Orleans by the enigmatic Clytie, he is already descending from his comfortable ethereal existence. His stylish Fauntleroy clothes having gotten too small, Clytie dresses him in an oversized jumper coat, bundling his other belongings into a bandana handkerchief. Clytie's rustic mannerisms and the boy's new denim garments represent his transformation to peonage: he is now closer to the blacks who live under the imposed status as tillers of the earth.

St. Valery must adjust to the strangers, Clytie and Judith, who, on the one hand, sacrifice the pittance of food they have for him, but who, on the other hand, immerse him in water and scrub his body, not as if it were dirty, but as if there were something wrong with it, as if it were inherently stained. When he has the inclination to play with the neighboring black children he is drawn away by the coffee complexioned Clytie herself. Thus, he is cast between two categories of humanity out of which his basic life tension begins to emerge. Undoubtedly, he is being prepared for a peculiar rite of passage into what will be for him an ambiguous social domain.

St. Valery plunges into an appalling world of solitude and despair. Told that he is "negro," he soon also becomes acquainted with the meaning of "nigger," the condition of pariahship and degredation to which he is perfunctorily assigned. He comes to realize that he can accept but not control this condition, since it is enforced not simply by individuals, but by the collective community.

In time, St. Valery becomes as stoic and cynical as his surrogate mothers, accepting the denims and homemade garments and attic room without gratitude or comment. The child is left to examine the enigma of his skin color in the lonely company of a broken mirror which is later discovered hidden beneath his mattress.

That Mr. Compson is so witlessly concerned with why St. Valery needed to associate with the blacks in the community is a fundamental complicating factor in the particular victimization of blacks of this type. Mr. Compson is preoccupied with the need to justify what he perceives as the young mulatto's senseless mingling, although he must certainly be aware of the Yoknapatawpha racial mores. His ability to ignore the sinister racial design affecting St. Valery's life is astounding; yet this inability functions to illustrate the deeprootedness of the contradictions existing within the Yoknapatawpha mind. Of course, Mr. Compson probably also suspects that it is the one-sixteenth of African blood that is acting as a biological determinant for St. Valery's social desires. This perverse imagination relishes its own obsessions, yet fears what it imagines, consequently creating potentialities for great racial tension and violence. It is this imagination which Faulkner most poignantly intends to indict. This type of mind victimizes the whole of humanity and defrauds the potential of the culture to take on the greater and more humane aspects of civilization. . . .

But in his portrayal of Clytie Sutpen, Faulkner suggests that Clytie is one who endures the stigma of mixedblood status with unrelenting will. She is first mentioned in *Absalom, Absalom!* as the "negro girl" accompanying Judith stealing out to witness her father's brutal wrestling match with his slaves. That Clytie's identity as Judith's half-sister is not mentioned early on adds to the dramatic intensity when this relationship is later revealed. When she is first referred to by name the narrator attempts to characterize her in terms of her origin. She was begotten by the callous Sutpen on his "wild nigger," whom Miss Rosa Coldfield and Mr. Compson speak of with vehemence that implies a biological separation from humanity. The various storytellers in the novel are compulsive in their efforts to account for Clytie's disposition. On the basis of her name, strong disposition, and inclination to anticipate events of doom, Mr. Compson assumes that Sutpen, in ignorance, misnamed Clytie Clytemnestra when he really intended to call her Cassandra. But Clytie is more willful, like Aeschylus' Clytemnestra, than she is prophetic like the more timorous seer Cassandra. Mr. Compson is amiss in his reading of the classics as well as in his perceptions of Clytie.

Clytie's character dominates most situations. Her presence affects more than it is affected. Even during the war there is the sense that the wasted, desolate farmland is favorably affected by her disposition. Her character dominates even in those tasks which were automatically expected of her as a slave: chopping wood, keeping a kitchen garden, harnessing the mule, plowing. Therefore, we are incredulous upon hearing of Mr. Compson's speculation that Judith could not have thought seriously of committing suicide to join her dead lover because nobody would have been left to take care of Clytie. Although Clytie is a slave, she is still very independent of mind. Mr. Compson's speculation about her dependency reveals more about his own character than about Clytie's. Also, he is characterizing her according to the slavocracy's general notion that a bondwoman or man is dependent by nature.

Miss Rosa Coldfield is so astonished by Clytie's disposition that she speculates that Clytie is of another species. Both women have uncompromising personalities and are obliged only by harsh conditions to adjust to each other. One thinks of Clytie the individual rather than Clytie the slave when she learns to plow and cut wood as well or better than the man tenant farmer, Wash Jones. Even Miss Rosa, who never forgets that Clytie was slave property, finds it necessary to explain that, with the hardships the three women endured during the war, tasks were not done on the basis of age or color but according to a standard of greatest good and least expense. Miss Rosa simply cannot ignore Clytie's individuality. Furthermore, Miss Rosa is particularly careful to indicate that Clytie defies all the prejudices which the culture attributes to black being. Clytie's presence is so powerful that Miss Rosa stresses at the beginning of both her major descriptions of Clytie that the bondwoman is not witless. Yet Miss Rosa still does not see blacks as human beings. She cannot conceive of blacks as possessing a mentality from which there would emanate the will to participate in the ordering of their own lives.

That Clytie never considered herself a slave demonstrates a sense of freedom that derives from her innate disposition, not from the fact that she lived under the roof of her owner-father. The young mulatta knows for sure who she is in the eyes of her father, that strange man who, upon his return from the war, rides up to the women in the field, leans from his horse and touches only his beard to Judith's forehead as a kiss and addresses her, "Well daughter," then turns to his slave daughter with only the acknowledgement that he knows her, saying, "Ah, Clytie." Upon returning to the war, Sutpen speaks to Clytie in the language of the master to his slave, "Well, Clytie," he says, "take care of Miss Judith."[4]

In Miss Rosa's limited and unsympathetic historical perspective, Clytie represents a disquieting relic from the racial, historical past in contrast to herself and Judith who are, in her estimate, victimized Yoknapatawpha citizens. Judith supposedly has ultimate control over her half-sister, not because she has more force of character, but because she possesses the power of her social status as a white woman, granted and protected by Yoknapatawpha culture. Symbolizing a less privileged status, Clytie is the only character without a last name. Indomitable though she is, she is denied the legitimate label of her lineage.

Clytie is as integral to the atmosphere of the Sutpen household and legend as Dilsey is to the world of *The Sound and the Fury*. Her chroniclers speculate that she felt the tie to the Sutpen blood more strongly than she felt the master-slave relationship. We are meant to understand that she was acting as protectress of blood rights when, and if, she destroyed Bon's letters to Judith. Indeed she proclaims this blood bond even to Miss Rosa's face. She feels that she has participated with Judith and Henry in absolving the family of its sins. "Whatever he done," she cries out to Miss Rosa as the old spinster pushes her to the floor to enter the house, "me and Judith and him have paid it out."[5]

Clytie's refusal to let Wash Jones pass through the kitchen door while Sutpen is away serves structurally in the novel as a recapitulation of the initial impetus which set Sutpen on his ambitious road to "success" when the black servant denied him the right to enter the front door on the Pettibone Virginia plantation. Clytie is a vital participant who attends most of the novel's significant actions that occur during her lifetime. She not only assists in the physical management of the estate when Sutpen is away, but is also emotionally involved with Judith in maintaining Sutpen's room and waiting for his return. It is Clytie who probably hears with Judith the fratricidal gunshot at the gate when Henry kills their half-brother, and she helps to carry Bon's coffin down the stairs to the grave. She witnesses Sutpen's crude and imperious betrothal to Miss Rosa, makes the trip to New Orleans to find Bon's orphaned child, attends to Judith's burial, and makes the final and ultimately adamant gesture of the Sutpen line when she sets the house afire to protect family rights, thus destroying herself, Henry and all of the past within reach of the flames.

Referring to the issue of miscegenation, Faulkner explicitly acknowledges that "the American is too fired always by the emotional situation."[6] It is definitely for emotional reason that in "Delta Autumn" the septuagenarian Uncle Ike McCaslin, the last of the Yoknapatawpha patriarchs, nearly goes into shock when he realizes that a mulatta kinswoman desires to marry his nephew Roth Edmonds, for whom she has borne a son. The old man has already been overwhelmed by the encroachment of civilization upon the outer wilderness of the Yoknapatawpha world which he equates with his youth, nobility, and innocence. A sudden racial intrusion into his inner family world would be intolerable. He does finally control his emotions enough to acknowledge and offer a gift to the child who is his descendant by two blood lines, that of the McCaslin masters and that of the McCaslin slaves. Yet the notion of a white person becoming intimate with black being through the sacred Christian ceremony is too much for Isaac to endure. His racial sensibility is like that of Miss Rosa who shirks at Clytie's touch. Caught in the grips of an ultimate horror, the old man's admonition is: *"Maybe in a thousand or two thousand years in America. . . . But not now! Not now!"*[7] It is precisely this terror in the white Yoknapatawpha mind which is responsible for generations of mulattoes caught in crises.

Notes

1. *Absalom, Absalom!*, p. 74.
2. Ibid., pp. 98–99.
3. Ibid., p. 195.

4. *Absalom, Absalom!*, p. 276.

5. Ibid., p. 370.

6. William Faulkner, *Faulkner in the University: Class Conferences at the University of Virginia* 1957–58, ed. Frederick L. Gwynn and Joseph L. Blotner (Charlottesville: University of Virginia Press, 1959), p. 157.

7. William Faulkner, "Delta Autumn" in *Go Down, Moses* (New York: Modern Library, 1955), p. 361.

Eulalia Bon's Untold Story

TONYA R. FOLSOM*

> *A people without history*
> *Is not redeemed from time,*
>   *for history is a pattern*
> *Of timeless moments.*
>   *T. S. Eliot,* Four Quartets

William Faulkner's *Absalom, Absalom!* traces the systematic destruction of the Sutpen family at the hands of the family patriarch, Thomas Sutpen. The downfall of Sutpen's lineage begins with his abandonment of his first wife, Eulalia Bon, a Haitian whose ethnic heritage—once realized—threatens his ambitious goals, one of which is to gain respect and prestige within his community. Sutpen's abandonment of Eulalia sets the stage for all of his future dealings with family and friends, who are chosen and sacrificed according to their usefulness to his goals. But Sutpen's betrayal comes full circle as he and his family are ultimately torn apart when his and Eulalia's child, Charles Bon, comes to Mississippi to gain recognition as Sutpen's son. The key to the entire Sutpen legacy, then, begins with Eulalia, a character hardly developed in the text, but whose actions are the impetus for much of what unfolds in the novel.[1]

Eulalia's family history in Haiti, her happiness, her pain at abandonment, her anger at Sutpen, and her love of her son are subjects of speculation by many of the characters in the novel. What the men who knew of her regard as truth is that Eulalia was a near-psychotic woman who made it her life's work, and that of her son, Charles Bon, to ruin Thomas Sutpen. Her emigration from Haiti to New Orleans is seen through these men's eyes as yet another step in her long walk for retribution against him. Certainly it is conceivable that Eulalia is a victim of lost love. To be left without the man she loves, with a child to raise on her own, would be enough for her to make efforts to be closer to Sutpen and have her son know him. Or it is possible that Eulalia—as Shreve suggests—is motivated by a " 'fury and fierce yearning and vindictiveness and jealous rage' " to destroy the life that Sutpen made without her.[2] Beyond the

*This essay was written especially for this volume and is published here for the first time by permission of the author.

speculations of the characters, however, there might have been other possibilities for Eulalia to leave Haiti and go to New Orleans. Clearly, any conclusions are still speculations about the motivations and life of Eulalia Bon, but they can provide a more realistic view of the life of this woman who in many ways is the pivotal point in the development of this novel.

The genealogy that Faulkner added to *Absalom, Absalom!*, the only objective information about Eulalia, provides the starting point for examining the possibilities of who Eulalia Bon was: "Born in Haiti. Only child of Haitian sugar planter of French descent. Married Thomas Sutpen, 1827, divorced from him, 1831. Died in New Orleans, date unknown" (p. 307). Beyond this information, nothing can be certain about Eulalia's life. But the information provided by historians who have traced those Haitians who led lives similar to how we imagine Eulalia's can help to give us a fuller perspective on her life—what might have been her motivations for going to New Orleans and what we can construct of her personality as a result. Historians have followed the migratory patterns of wealthy sugar planters in Haiti during the early and mid-nineteenth century who after numerous slave insurrections and later continual uprisings by the newly freed blacks for political freedom, were forced to flee Haiti and relocate in an atmosphere somewhat similar to their own.[3] Because of its fertile land and a successful port that enabled Haitians to make business connections and friendships, New Orleans received most of the major migratory movements to North America from Haiti.[4] In addition, New Orleans offered a lifestyle traditionally based on slavery; thus white planters from Haiti felt a certain familiarity to the plantation life. As blacks in Haiti continued to engage in uprisings, each time coming closer to gaining political independence, increasing numbers of plantation owners fled Haiti in favor of a more stable environment. In 1809 white Haitian plantation owners, and those who were able to pass for white—like Eulalia—doubled the size of New Orleans within just three months, and Haitians continued to immigrate to New Orleans in lesser numbers until at least 1831.[5]

Slave rebellions were fought with serious consequences for planters and their families. In August 1791 thousands of slaves and mulattoes came together and began burning the plantations that lay in their path. Within just a few hours, "the finest sugar plantations of Saint Domingue were literally devoured by flames."[6] The massiveness of this uprising was never repeated, but smaller insurrections from slaves and freed blacks seeking political rights and independence lasted until 1831. The slave uprising that Sutpen describes when he tells of his first meeting with Eulalia is very similar to the actual uprisings in Haiti at about that time. General Compson relates Sutpen's story of how, while slaves were on the outside, inside the house

the five of them—the planter, the daughter, two women servants and himself—shut up in it and the air filled with the smoke and smell of burning cane and the glare and smoke of it on the sky and the air throbbing and trembling with the drums and the chanting—the little lost island beneath its down-cupped bowl of alternating day and night like a vacuum into which no help could come . . . while the two servants and the girl whose christian name he did not yet know loaded the muskets which he and the father fired at no enemy but the Haitian night itself, lancing their little vain and puny flashes into the brooding and blood-weary and throbbing darkness. (p. 204)

Sutpen married Eulalia in 1827, shortly after this incident, so we may place the slave uprising about the same time (p. 205). It is conceivable that a woman like Eulalia could have been one of these postinsurrection migrants fleeing the violence of Haiti. Faulkner does not link the insurrection at Eulalia's sugar plantation to any specific uprising in Haiti, but the description, along with the time when the uprising occurred, allows us to assume that Faulkner was well aware of the slave history of Haiti, and was able to give a realistic, if somewhat sparse, rendering of the historical, political, and social framework that surrounded Eulalia and Haitians like her. Thus for Eulalia, as a member of such a planter family that would have been the target of such revolts, flight could have been another motive for leaving. She would then not be just a driven woman seeking revenge, but part of a large group of white Haitians leaving for New Orleans to save their lives.

Another possibility for Eulalia's coming to New Orleans—and one that tells us more about her life in Haiti, as well as her relationship to Thomas Sutpen—is also revenge, not for a lost love but for the lost identity that Sutpen's departure would have caused. When Sutpen finds out that Eulalia and her father were not honest with him regarding her racial heritage, he leaves her and Haiti for a new life and new opportunities in Mississippi (p. 212). Once the secret of Eulalia's racial identity is revealed in the birth and appearance of Charles, Sutpen abandons Eulalia, thus setting in motion the destruction of his future lineage and emphasizing her inability to escape the consequences of his actions.

Faulkner traces Sutpen's journey to Mississippi and his acquisitions of wealth and family there, but leaves information concerning Eulalia's journey to the genealogy that states she died in New Orleans and to the information from the speculations of Shreve that she went to New Orleans to avenge her abandonment.

Shreve assumes that Eulalia, as a woman scorned, left Haiti for New Orleans to commence her plan to ruin Sutpen and his family. He also assumes that she is able to do this by instilling in Charles Bon a hatred for his father since childhood. Through Shreve's speculations, Eulalia becomes a psychotic avenger who has no justification to feel the way she does and who thinks no more of her son's well-being than that of Sutpen's. Revenge for lost love is certainly a possibility in Eulalia's action. She is a woman scorned. Sutpen came into her and her father's life, married her, bore a child with her, and then left her because of her racial heritage. Understandably, she would be angry. But if indeed Eulalia was mulatto passing for white, it is also conceivable that her hatred and feeling of abandonment by Sutpen could have had deeper origins. Mulattoes in Haiti were a caste above the black slaves, but they still constituted a threat to white plantation owners and planters because they conspired with the black slaves in the revolts that devastated so many of the sugar crops, and they participated in some of the massacres of white plantation families.[7] Later, mulattoes fought alongside the newly freed blacks to gain political freedom. During this turbulent period in Haiti, it was as dangerous to be a mulatto as it was to be a black slave. In fact, mulattoes taken prisoner after the Port-au-Prince massacre in 1791 were tortured, burned alive, and beheaded.[8]

Revolts with this degree of violence had subsided somewhat by the time Sutpen comes into Eulalia's life, but revolts were still going on, as the portrayal of the insurrection at the family's plantation demonstrates. For Eulalia, who was passing for white, the possibility that she might be discovered to be a mulatto would have been frightening. By marrying Sutpen, Eulalia would have reinforced the view that she was white. When Sutpen leaves her directly after the birth of their son, the community might have questioned the motive for abandonment, thus putting Eulalia's concealed identity at risk. If Eulalia were found out to be mulatto, she would surely lose the life that she had always known, her social standing, her political rights, and those of her son. Eulalia's father would also lose the life to which he had become accustomed if it were discovered that he had passed his daughter off as white and let her have privileges to which she was supposedly not entitled. She might even have been forced to give up her family ties. If this were the case, her anger would not be limited to wounded pride; rather, it would be extended to the possibility of a devastated life.

The genealogy suggests that Eulalia's life took such a turn toward devastation. Faulkner claims that Eulalia "Died in New Orleans, date unknown" (p. 307). Why is the date unknown? Is it simply because Faulkner did not want to include a date? Or is it possible that she had to break ties with her family and come to New Orleans alone, never to reestablish any connections with the rich planter family she had known? Is hers a riches-to-rags, princess-to-pauper story? This kind of social fall would have been possible for a mulatto woman passing for white like Eulalia. And such a fall, no doubt, would have been sufficient cause for her desire for retribution against Sutpen and explain to some degree her unrecorded death.

Faulkner may not have given the reader the historical details behind the Haitian uprising at Eulalia's father's plantation, but the similarity of his descriptions to the insurrections that were occurring in Haiti at the time does indicate that Faulkner was aware of Haitian history and the implications that history had on New Orleans. Moreover, Faulkner would have experienced the Haitian influence on New Orleans at firsthand because of the time he spent there with Sherwood Anderson.[9] This experience would have surely affected the creation and portrayal of Eulalia's character.

So what can we say finally about Eulalia Bon? She was a young woman and the daughter of a wealthy Haitian plantation owner who was abandoned by her husband and left with a child to raise alone. She could have spent her life brooding over a lost love and plotting to avenge her pain as Shreve suggests. It is also possible that Eulalia was the target of continued slave uprisings, jeopardizing her life and that of her son, and thus a woman who made a rational decision to leave Haiti for New Orleans. In this case, Charles Bon's meeting with Sutpen is coincidental. Finally, it is also possible that her identity may have been further at risk by Sutpen's abandonment if she was discovered to be mulatto, thereby causing her to lose her social, political, and familial position in Haiti, becoming the object of ridicule and rejection. The numerous possibilities for the stages of Eulalia's life and the motivations that caused her to make the choices she did all suggest that she is more complex and crucial to the story of *Absalom, Absalom!* than the space given her in the novel—and later devoted to her by critics.

Notes

1. Not only is Eulalia neglected in the text but she has been ignored critically. For brief mention of her, see David Paul Ragan, *William Faulkner's "Absalom, Absalom": A Critical Study* (Ann Arbor: UMI Research Press, 1987); Philip M. Weinstein, "Meditations on the Other: Faulkner's Rendering of Women" in *Faulkner and Women: Faulkner and Yoknapatawpha, 1985,* ed. Doreen Fowler and Ann J. Abadie (Jackson: University Press of Mississippi, 1986), 92–93; and Cleanth Brooks, *William Faulkner: The Yoknapatawpha Country* (New Haven: Yale University Press, 1963), 425–26, 428, 432–35.

2. William Faulkner, *Absalom, Absalom!* (New York: Vintage Books, 1990), 239. Further citations are in parentheses.

3. For additional information concerning the motivations of Haitians for traveling to New Orleans, see Carl A. Brasseaux and Glenn R. Conrad, eds., *The Road to Louisiana: The Saint-Domingue Refugees 1792–1809* (Lafayette: Center for Louisiana Studies/University of Southwestern Louisiana, 1992).

4. Brasseaux and Conrad, 1.

5. Brasseaux and Conrad, viii.

6. Carolyn E. Fick, *The Making of Haiti: The Saint-Domingue Revolution from Below* (Knoxville: University of Tennessee Press, 1990), 97.

7. For further information on the position of mulattoes, see Eugene D. Genovese, *From Rebellion to Revolution: Afro-American Slave Revolts in the Making of the Modern World* (Baton Rouge: Louisiana State University Press, 1979) and *Roll, Jordan Roll: The World the Slaves Made* (New York: Pantheon Books, 1974).

8. Fick, 132.

9. For further information about the length of time Faulkner spent with Anderson and descriptions of New Orleans at the time, see Joseph Blotner, *Faulkner: A Biography*, 2 vols. (New York: Random House, 1974).

Charles Bon: The New Orleans Myth Made Flesh

Adelaide P. McGinnis*

Of Faulkner's New Orleans characters, Charles Bon embodies most fully the qualities of the mythic New Orleanian. He is the "foreigner," the foil whom Elmo Howell finds morally inferior to Yoknapatawphans. Although Howell admits that "in some respects Charles Bon is an attractive figure," he finds him a devious and sinister contrast to simple, naive Henry Sutpen.[1] Even to his friend Henry, Bon is more of a cliché than a real person. Along with their classmates at the University, Henry is awed by " 'this man handsome elegant and even catlike' " who possesses " 'some tangible effluvium of knowledge, surfeit; of actions done and satiations plumbed and pleasures exhausted and even forgotten' " (p. 95). Henry and the other students envy Bon and despair over being able to be like him. (They view Bon as worldly but not quite damned. In the Southern version of the code of courtly love, chastity is much more required of women than of men.) Known for his " 'prowess among women' " (p. 99), Bon appears to pass from one delight to another without satiety (p. 96). A great cultural gulf separates Henry and his classmates from this foreigner, and they feel hopelessly deprived.

Howell's assumption that Charles Bon is morally inferior to Henry reflects a common misconception of Faulkner's moral stance. There is something sinister about Bon to the Yoknapatawphans, but Howell does not see that Bon represents the positive, natural side lacking in the men of Yoknapatawpha. Faulkner's treatment of New Orleanians is similar to his usual treatment of women and of Negroes, for whom the flesh is paramount. Unencumbered by a code, these characters act spontaneously, relishing life. Faulkner's mentor, Sherwood Anderson, also uses the New Orleans cliché positively in *Dark Laughter*, written in 1925. But Anderson's New Orleans Negroes, whose "dark laughter" suggests a healthy sensuality, remain stereotypes. Faulkner transcends the New Orleans stereotype in his depiction of Charles Bon, whose partial Negro ancestry is initially unknown even to

* This essay was written especially for this volume and is published here for the first time by permission of the author.

himself. Like George Washington Cable before him, Faulkner finds beneath the romantic surface of the mulatto an image of alienation by which he exposes the evil of Southern racism. Moreover, he creates in Bon a fully human character who, in his final action, becomes the most tragic character in the novel.

New Orleanian Charles Bon is consistent with Faulkner's earlier positive use of New Orleans and its French culture. Eight years before he wrote *Absalom, Absalom!*, Faulkner employed the New Orleans seductress image in the Prologue to *Mosquitoes*: "Outside the window New Orleans, the vieux carré, brooded in a faintly tarnished languor like an aging yet still beautiful courtesan in a smoke filled room, avid yet weary too of ardent ways."[3] A more extensive description of New Orleans as courtesan appears in "The Tourist," part of an early piece entitled "New Orleans," published in the *Times-Picayune* in February 1925. The city is a worldly and desirable courtesan, "not old and yet no longer young," whose conversation is "low-toned but never dull." Furthermore, "those who are not of the elect must stand forever without her portals." Not only is she intriguing, but Faulkner implies that her company is more satisfying than that of the idealized Southern virgin: "All who leave her seeking the virgin's unbrown, ungold hair . . . return to her when she smiles across her languid fan."[4]

At first, Henry Sutpen seems ready for the conversion that New Orleans offers him in *Absalom, Absalom!*. He quickly develops an obsessive, highly romantic infatuation for Bon and hopes to make him his brother-in-law. In Mr. Compson's version of the story, which omits both Bon's sibling relationship and his Negro ancestry, Henry identifies so completely with Bon that he envisions his sister's loss of virginity as " 'the pure and perfect incest:' ": "the brother realizing that the sister's virginity must be destroyed in order to have existed at all, taking that virginity in the person of the brother-in-law, the man whom he would be if he could become, metamorphose into, the lover, the husband; by whom he would be despoiled, choose for despoiler, if he could become, metamorphose into the sister, the mistress, the bride" (p. 96). Mr. Compson's complicated sentence is doubly shocking. At the semicolon, it shifts abruptly from Henry's suppressed desire for his sister Judith to his homosexual feelings for Charles Bon, " 'by whom he would be despoiled' " if it were possible. Bon's feelings for Henry likewise go beyond friendship and kinship. Referring to Bon's love for Henry and Judith, Mr. Compson says, " 'Perhaps in his fatalism he loved Henry the better of the two, seeing perhaps in the sister merely the shadow, the woman vessel with which to consummate the love whose actual object was the youth' " (p. 108). Henry's love for Bon thus rests more on an intense romantic and physical attraction than on concern for Charles Bon as a human being.

The Henry Sutpen who rides to the river with Bon on Christmas Day 1860 to take the steamboat to New Orleans has scarcely ventured beyond the immediate environs of his own home—not even to Memphis, according to Mr. Compson. (Quentin and Shreve concede, however, that he may have made "one or two trips to Memphis with his father to buy live stock or slaves" [p. 335].) Mr. Compson describes Henry's introduction to New Orleans in a characteristically packed Faulknerian sentence:

> "I can imagine him, with his puritan heritage—that heritage peculiarly Anglo-Saxon—of fierce proud mysticism and that ability to be ashamed of ignorance and inexperience, in that city foreign and paradoxical, with its atmosphere at once fatal and languorous, at once feminine and steel-hard—this grim humorless yokel out of a granite heritage where even the houses, let alone clothing and conduct, are built in the image of a jealous and sadistic Jehovah, put suddenly down in a place whose denizens had created their All-Powerful and his supporting hierarchy-chorus of beautiful saints and handsome angels in the image of their houses and personal ornaments and voluptuous lives." (pp. 108–9)

Like a religious emissary for hedonism, Bon takes the " 'innocent and negative plate of Henry's provincial soul' " and exposes it " 'by slow degrees to this esoteric milieu' " (p. 110). Because of his innocence, Henry is especially vulnerable to the romantic appeal of New Orleans. But unlike the outsider in "The Tourist" who "must stand forever without her portals," Henry is offered entrance as one of "the elect." Bon assures him that what he has seen is " ' "only just the base, the foundation. It can belong to anyone" ' " (pp. 110–11).

Then Bon dresses Henry in a new coat and escorts him to " 'a closed and curiously monastic doorway in a neighborhood a little decadent, even a little sinister' " (p. 111). The facade suggests to Henry " 'secret and curious and unimaginable delights.' " Inside, the sight of the " 'corridor of doomed and tragic flower faces' " strikes " 'straight and true to some primary blind and mindless foundation of all young male living dream and hope' " (p. 112). The "flower faces" are the octoroons, for whom New Orleanians fight duels, as the brown bloodstains on the ground bear witness. The uniformed, French-speaking attendant who admits Bon and Henry reinforces the foreignness of this little world. Henry's meeting with Bon's octoroon wife is not described in detail, nor is her name given. She is " 'a woman with a face like a tragic magnolia, the eternal female, the eternal Who-suffers,' " and the young boy " 'sleeping in silk and lace' " belongs " 'body and soul' " to his father, who can sell him like chattel if he so chooses (p. 114). When this child, Charles Etienne, leaves his sheltered world forever at age twelve, he will discover at Sutpen's Hundred that he is part Negro. Although New Orleans practices racism, Etienne has been raised in an environment where the word "nigger" does not exist, and " 'where pigmentation had no more moral value than the silk walls and the scent and the rose-colored candle shades' " (p. 199).

A comparison of the moral codes of Henry and Bon reveals a profound irony. When Henry objects to Bon's " ' "bought woman," ' " Bon reminds him that another kind of slave owner " 'could have used her with more impunity than he would dare to use an animal, heifer or mare,' " and she could have been " 'discarded or sold or even murdered when worn out or when her keep and her price no longer balanced' " (p. 116). The crime of slavery, as Bon describes it, makes Henry's scruples about sex seem trivial. Bon defends the application of " 'principles of honor, decorum, and gentleness' " to the " 'perfectly normal human instinct which you Anglo Saxons insist upon calling lust and in whose service you revert in sabbaticals to the primordial caverns.' " Bon might have added "or to the slave quarters," for Henry's world contains only three types of unmarried women: virgins, courtesans, and slave girls. Since the " 'sabbaticals to the cities' " were unavailable to young men like Henry " 'because of money and distance,' " they used the slave girls as outlets for their desires (p. 109). Henry is most likely a virgin, but if he is not, no doubt his first sexual experience was with a slave girl. When Henry objects to the morganatic marriage, also known historically as *placage*, Bon asks, " ' "Have you forgotten that this woman, this child, are niggers?" ' " Since Henry does not question the institution of slavery, Mr. Compson assumes that the morganatic marriage, rather than the relationship itself, is the final hindrance to Henry's acceptance of Bon as brother-in-law: "It would be the fact of the ceremony, regardless of what kind, that Henry would balk at: Bon knew this. It would not be the mistress or even the child, not even the negro mistress and even less the child because of that fact, since Henry and Judith had grown up with a negro half sister of their own" (p. 109).

The evolution of Quentin and Shreve's story reflects Faulkner's own evolutionary creation of the Sutpen saga, which began as the unpublished short story "Evangeline." In that story Bon is neither a Sutpen nor a Negro, and he marries Judith before the war begins. Henry kills him after learning that he has an octoroon wife and a mulatto son, born after his marriage to Judith. Thus Bon's culpability is reduced in the final version. Henry finally kills him not for something Bon has done but for the genes he was born with. However, since Mr. Compson does not know about the other impediments to Bon and Judith's engagement, he echoes the early story in attributing the murder to the morganatic marriage with a Negro woman. His extensive consideration of this supposedly interracial union sets the stage for Henry's ultimate and more profound dilemma: whether to allow Judith to marry a Negro.

As Cleanth Brooks has proposed and most critics have subsequently agreed, Quentin probably learns of the twin threats of incest and miscegenation at the same time: when he takes Miss Rosa to Sutpen's Hundred and meets Henry in the flesh.[5] Yet Quentin and Shreve introduce the fear of incest early on, saving the information about Bon's Negro ancestry for the climax, only twenty-three pages from the end of the novel. Quentin probably assumes correctly that if Henry had learned of Bon's Negro ancestry and their sibling kinship at the same time, he would not have renounced his birthright and left with Bon. Therefore, Quentin withholds the climax for the sake of both realism and narrative art. When Quentin seems ready to reveal the secret, Shreve tells him to " 'wait' " (p. 216). Like Quentin, Shreve senses that Henry's murderous act is predicated on his delayed discovery of Bon's racial identity. Moreover, Shreve's extended account of Henry's struggle with incest adds a further dimension for readers already familiar with Quentin's torment in *The Sound and the Fury*.

Accepting Quentin's story at face value, since there is little alternative, critics have wondered why Thomas Sutpen does not tell Henry about Bon's racial ancestry. Volpe blames a weakening of Sutpen's will for the omission.[6] More likely, Sutpen knows Henry will not believe that Bon is part Negro. After all, Henry has believed that Bon is his brother only after talking to Bon's mother, Eulalia, in New Orleans. He is finally convinced only when she says, " 'So she has fallen in love with him' " and sits " 'laughing harshly and steadily' " (p. 335). He struggles for the duration of the war to accept the idea of incest, telling himself that kings did it, " 'trying to reconcile what he (Henry) was going to do with all the voices of his heredity and training which said *No. No. You cannot*. You must not. You shall not' " (p. 342–43).

When, in 1865, Henry finally accepts the idea of incest, he feels a perverse relief that all the family will suffer in hell together (p. 348). Thus, Henry makes his second great sacrifice for Bon. Giving up his birthright was the first; accepting an eternity in hell is the second. Henry so identifies with Bon and Judith that he takes their sin as his own, in spirit. We should not, however, be too quick to admire Henry's sacrifice. In his Nobel Prize speech, Faulkner names several "eternal verities": "love and honor and pity and pride and compassion and sacrifice."[7] These verities form three balanced pairs—in each a human emotion is paired with an abstract quality. Implied here is the need for balance. Sacrifice, honor, and pride are empty without compassion, love, and pity.

It is the classic struggle between id and superego. Charles Bon, Henry's brother in both flesh and spirit, represents his own repressed dark nature. Paralleling Quentin's later attempt to destroy first his own shadow and then his own life in *The Sound and the Fury*, Henry sees in Bon-the-New-Orleanian and in Bon-the-Negro a natural sensuality that Henry himself fears, denies, and finally destroys. Like William Butler Yeats, who posits the antithetical self and even antithetical civilizations as a means toward achieving wholeness, Faulkner brings together opposite personalities, each of whom can fill the void in the other. Henry represents the family that Bon needs, and Bon embodies the dark, natural sensuality that is necessary for wholeness as a human being. In his archetypal role of dark seducer, Bon describes for Henry the New Orleanian concept of pleasure as "a female principle which existed, queenly and complete, in the hot equatorial groin of the world . . . a principle apt docile and instinct with strange and curious pleasures of the flesh (which is all: there is nothing else)" (p. 116). According to Bon's hedonist-existentialist credo, the " 'abstractions' " of " 'monogamy and fidelity and decorum and gentleness and affection' " are " 'as purely rooted in the flesh's offices as the digestive processes' " (p. 199). There is none of the schism between flesh and spirit that plagues Yoknapatawphans.

Charles Bon is not the villain of *Absalom, Absalom!*, as Howell and others imply. Rather, he is the would-be emancipator of Henry. If his attempt to corrupt Henry's " 'provincial soul' " in the " 'esoteric milieu' " of New Orleans had been more successful, Henry probably would not have been compelled to kill him. This is not to say the New Orleans culture would willingly accept miscegenation between a white woman and a partly Negro man, but it would tolerate it much more readily than would Yoknapatawpha. Ironically, the "moral code" of Yoknapatawpha leads to a blatant immorality: fratricide. Although Bon has probably killed men in duels in the name of honor, these men were willing participants in a contest. In killing Bon, Henry shoots an unarmed man—his own brother. The danger of honor without love, pride without pity, is nowhere more vividly depicted in Faulkner's writing.

Notes

1. Elmo Howell, "William Faulkner's New Orleans," *Louisiana History* 7 (1966), 237.
2. William Faulkner, *Absalom, Absalom!* (New York: Random House, 1936), 95; hereafter cited in the text.
3. William Faulkner, *Mosquitoes* (New York: Liveright, 1927), 10.
4. "The Tourist," in "New Orleans," *New Orleans Sketches*, 2nd ed., ed. Carvel Collins (New York: Random House, 1968), 13–14.
5. Cleanth Brooks, *William Faulkner: The Yoknapatawpha Country* (New Haven: Yale University Press, 1963), 315–17, 436–41; *Absalom, Absalom!*, 274.
6. Edmond L. Volpe, *A Reader's Guide to William Faulkner* (New York: Farrar, Straus and Giroux, 1964), 203.
7. William Faulkner, "Address upon Receiving the Nobel Prize for Literature," in *Essays, Speeches, and Public Letters*, ed. James B. Meriwether (New York: Random House, 1965), 120.

The Coldfield Family

◆

Rosa Coldfield as Daughter: Another of Faulkner's Lost Children

LINDA WAGNER-MARTIN*

The dungeon was Mother herself she and Father upward into weak light holding hands and us lost somewhat below even them without even a ray of light. . . . [1]

Throughout William Faulkner's fiction, the pattern of children uncared for—ignored, isolated, used, abandoned—is relentless. . . . In the first chapter of *Absalom, Absalom!* Faulkner presents the character of Rosa Coldfield as a diminutive child, feet dangling from her chair; and he reinforces the pathetic image of the Southern poetess by using a narrative form that reflects the chronology of her life. In the first chapter, part of her narrative occurs when she is three; part when she is four; and another segment six years later, when she is ten. In the fifth chapter, part of her story occurs when she is fourteen, and more when she is nineteen. This combination of the narrative charting of her life with the author's visualization of Rosa as childlike, or somehow stunted, forces the reader to see that Rosa was never allowed to be a child. Part of the looming tragedy of Faulkner's novel is that Rosa's

*Reprinted with permission from *Studies in American Fiction* 19:1 (Spring 1991): 1–13. © 1991 by Northeastern University.

emotional growth was both restricted and exploited through her experiences. Faulkner gives the lengthy first and fifth chapters of *Absalom, Absalom!* to this portrayal; these chapters are the reader's point of entry to the Sutpen story and to Rosa's own increasingly important narrative.[2]

What such an emphasis on Rosa's childhood means for the reader is a shift in perspective from the story of Thomas Sutpen and his surreal creation, Sutpen's Hundred, to the more generalized tale of the Southern white patriarch. For Rosa's story is only partly that of Sutpen. Much of her narrative, both in Chapters 1 and 5, is that of the Coldfield family and its acquisition of place and power as well as its denouement. Even though some of her narrative deals with her role as Sutpen's beloved, more of it charts her role within the Coldfield family as youngest daughter, beholden to and thoroughly dependent on her remaining parent, her father.[3] By casting Rosa as child, by forcing the reader to see how terrorized her life was not only by Sutpen but by her father's uncaring and naive responses to both her and to life and war, Faulkner underscores the tragedy of the misuse of parental authority. *Absalom, Absalom!* becomes the story not of the quasi-heroic Sutpen, claiming accomplishment as he wrested power from poverty, but the story of various white males who destroyed families, particularly the women and children of those families, in their rapacious pursuit of what they defined as "success." . . .

Following Faulkner's directive about Rosa's "place" in the narrative— her unquestioned role as the only living participant-narrator in the telling of the Sutpen legend—the modern reader must choose to see everything besides Rosa's narrative as further evidence of the complicit cultural support for the collusion that ensures Sutpen's "success." The way in which Mr. Compson, Quentin, and Shreve take over Rosa's story echoes the way both Sutpen and Coldfield usurped the rights that should have belonged to their wives and children, family-based rights that were instead assumed by the fathers. The way Faulkner presents this assumption in his novel is through the fathers' voices—those of Sutpen and Coldfield, as well as of Mr. Compson—as they justified their often indefensible actions. Much of that voicing is taken up with giving directives.

By following Rosa's story instead of the redactions of it, by listening and responding to the fear and pain in her primary narrative, the reader cannot fail to understand the harm done to people as Sutpen and, in his less effective way, Coldfield scramble over both traditions and human values to achieve immediate and often valueless aims. Reading *Absalom, Absalom!* as Rosa's story gives the reader a strategy to undercut the comparatively romantic appeal of the Sutpen story.[4] In the context of Southern history, Sutpen's Hundred serves no viable purpose either social or familial. Faulkner shows Thomas Sutpen to be little but animal, mating where and when he can, caring little for either his sex partners or their offspring, failing to take even perfunctory care of his family's needs. His abuse of Ellen Coldfield parallels the contempt he learned for Charles Bon's mother, for Rosa, and for Millie, whose child, if "correctly" sexed, would have earned for her at best a stable in some barn. Women having become only breeding machines, Sutpen was able to dismiss all normal human ties from his life. But first, for Sutpen to achieve his aim, he had to have as accoutrements those expected social garnishes—wife, children, social graces, religion, community.

At this point Faulkner weaves the Sutpen-Coldfield story lines together. Sutpen's most blatant affront to the community—growing out of his most audacious act—was to marry one of its upstanding, virginal women. Coldfield may have smelled financial benefit to his humble business by allowing Sutpen to court Ellen, but the fact that the eminently scrupled Methodist finds Sutpen less objectionable than does the rest of the community raises serious questions about Goodhue Coldfield's morality. Faulkner's intention as he presents the wedding scene seems to be to satirize the man's names, to paint Coldfield as thoroughly irresponsible, a characterization completed once the reader learns his reaction to the Civil War. Coldfield's mad demise suggests that he believes he can absolve himself of all responsibility for his family, his business, his community, and his region by blocking out— literally hiding from—all events of the war. Such obsessive egotism makes Coldfield much like Sutpen; they are both men who see themselves at the center of every event, who believe they can control life through sheer will. During Coldfield's last years, rather than caring for his young daughter, he treats her disdainfully, demanding sustenance and care from her. How Rosa was to secure food for him, as well as to cook and smuggle it into his nailed-shut hiding hole, was immaterial to Coldfield. For him, children were only means to ends. In this, as in all parts of *Absalom, Absalom!*, Faulkner emphasizes that Coldfield and Sutpen are both uncaring fathers. Although the ostensible plot depends on Sutpen's outrage of his role as father, Coldfield has abused the role every bit as much. Rosa's story gives the reader insight into that complicity.

Rosa's irate and sometimes hysterical lament about Sutpen's treatment of her is obviously an outcry at double injustice. In finding words for her bitterness, in belatedly choosing to tell her story, Rosa relinquishes pain and grief that has colored, and stunted, her entire life. Not only the spurned beloved, Rosa has been as well—and more consistently—the spurned daughter. Bereaved of sympathy, separated from any audience for her anguish over Ellen's madness, Rosa is driven to steal the materials to help sew Judith's trousseau. Her hatred of Coldfield is clear in that act. But so too is her great, and necessarily dependent, love for him. Her mother long dead; her sister moving further and further away from normalcy; her niece older than Rosa by four years and the product of Sutpen's tough will, a spirit very different from the Coldfield passivity; and Clytie, a strange mixture of deference and authority; Rosa had no mother, no sister, no peers. Faulkner gives the reader no evidence that Ellen ever thought about her much younger sister. So absorbed is she in maintaining her own balance, assaulted as she has been by the bestial behavior of both husband and children, Ellen gives nothing to Rosa. Faulkner's constant image of Ellen as chrysalis, of her undeveloped growth, keeps her helplessness firmly before the reader. And once she has succumbed to the horror of Henry's loss, she rouses only to ask something of Rosa. Still bereft of comfort and love, Rosa must assume the responsibility of caring for her niece Judith; that is Ellen's only legacy to her little sister.

Rosa's partially distraught monologue to Quentin Compson is both symptom and event. Her pain, so long hidden and unexpressed, breaks through the stoic shell she has assumed with some kind of primitive instinct. As her physical strength wanes, she is fired to share the one thing she has never shared, her sad emotions of loss, loss of a family who might have helped her bear what the world demanded of her, but particularly loss of the paternal love every daughter is acculturated to expect. Rosa speaks for the obverse of that Southern myth that says fathers and brothers must protect the young women of the family. In some ways, Rosa's language re-creates Caddy's less immediate, less often voiced, speech. The pain of being asked to care for everyone else, in lieu of having been cared for herself, dominates Rosa's heartbreak. . . .

Faulkner's "text" of Rosa's narrative is dominated from the first by a view of her as daughter. She meets Quentin in "what Miss Coldfield still called the office because her father had called it that" (p. 7), her habits of language and behavior formed by that father-daughter relationship. The forty-three years that have passed since she assumed her black garb might mark either the death of Goodhue Coldfield in 1864 or Sutpen's insult in 1866; those years are emphasized because Faulkner's attention falls on her long-unexpressed story, her "grim haggard amazed" voice, her "impotent yet indomitable frustration" paralleling her "impotent and static rage." The "crucified child" as she is pictured—sitting in "the chair that was so tall for her that her legs hung straight and rigid as if she had iron shinbones and ankles, clear of the floor . . . like children's feet"—has remained a child because she has never expressed that static rage directed at both father and non-husband, family and world.

The language that Rosa uses reflects that rage. Rosa says "tore violently"; Quentin writes "built." Rosa says "without gentleness begot," and Quentin omits the first two words (p. 9). Though she rages within this language, she also tries to confine her image of Sutpen to "a scene peaceful and decorous as a schoolprize water color" (p. 8). Her art attempts to transform, but it fails as Quentin heightens the romantic elements of Sutpen's life. (It is Quentin's romanticism the reader responds to, not Rosa's telling, in thinking Sutpen superior in any way.) Rosa's focus is on the family of Sutpen, himself, the two children, and "the mother, the dead sister Ellen: this Niobe without tears," the mother who sacrificed everything for the children who were slain (p. 13); but Rosa insists on her own role in the configuration: "I, a child, a child, mind you" (p. 14). Keeping Quentin's attention on her role in this macabre family romance, represented by her imaginary photo of parents and children, "the conventional family group of the period" (p. 14), from which she is absent, Rosa builds her own narrative, her accumulation of bad fortune so that at twenty, "an orphan a woman and a pauper," she had to turn for existence to her only kin, the family of her sister (p. 19). The peak of Rosa's anguish occurs in the long paragraph stressing the guilt of her father's role in giving Ellen to Sutpen, in allowing that family group to exist. Her use of refrain signals her intensity: "But that it should have been our father, mine and Ellen's father of all of them that he knew. . . . That it should have been our father" (p. 20). Her jeremiad calls the reader's attention to the repetition of "our father," the prayerful term that suggests Rosa's strained apostasy, the daughter's willed deification of the father who would do no wrong but did numerous wrongs, increasing to the final one, of abandonment through voluntary separation and death.

Rosa's paragraph serves to curse the name of Goodhue Coldfield, and after it she resumes her story, with a significant change. This time when she reaches the point of Ellen's death, rather than Ellen's asking the young Rosa to look after Judith, in this version she says "protect *them*" (p. 21). Rosa's task has broadened, and into the matriarchal line come both children, Henry as well as Judith, an interruption of male power and control that unsettles Rosa. It is as if the weight of the entire South rests on her shoulders, and she cries to Quentin "even I used to wonder what our father or his father could have done before he married our mother that Ellen and I would have to expiate and neither of us alone be sufficient; what crime committed that would leave our family cursed to be instruments not only for that man's destruction, but for our own" (p. 21). Here Faulkner establishes the "plot": the house of Sutpen, aided by the minor house of Coldfield (a house Coldfield completely usurps by co-opting its attic as his hiding place, corruption weighing heavily, and inescapably, on its top story), rising or falling depending on the community reaction to its master's outrages. Yet Rosa, who is almost alone in seeing the full range of Sutpen's criminal acts, alone, childlike, and consequently powerless to prevent his success, manages to bring about the destruction of both Sutpen's house and, for practical purposes, his line.

Quentin's empathy with Rosa at this point in the narrative, before his father begins talking with him, is clear. He is able to visualize her, "to watch resolving the figure of a little girl, in the prim skirts and pantalettes, the smooth prim decorous braids, of the dead time" (p. 21). Standing by some hypothetical fence "with that air of children born too late into their parents' lives and doomed to contemplate all human behavior through the complex and needless follies of adults . . . a child who had never been young" (p. 22), Rosa begins her countdown through vivid memories that all implicate Sutpen. At three, she remembers the mad rides to church, faces like ogres leering from the carriage, although Ellen's face is "bloodless." At four, she remembers standing outside the door to the Sutpen parlor, as her father talks with Ellen about leaving Sutpen: " 'Think of the children,' papa said" (p. 27). But Faulkner also gives the reader the necessary information that in this scene Goodhue Coldfield had not invited Ellen to bring the children and move back to his house, just as in the aftermath to the preceding church scene he had not responded positively when his sister had urged him to interfere for Ellen's sake. Rosa recounts hearing the pithy conversation: " 'Your daughter, your own daughter' my aunt said; and papa: 'Yes. She is my daughter. When she wants me to interfere she will tell me so herself' " (p. 25). Faulkner's inclusion of this scene clearly shows Coldfield absconding from the social and familial role he should play, as he pretends that his daughter Ellen could take language, could forge a voice for herself out of the malaise of Sutpen's Hundred and its completely male power, and so thereby excuse his own inaction. Coldfield was one of Faulkner's male characters who said some of the right things but never acted, and, as Rosa could so easily see, her father was never either willing or able to change things, never able to do the protecting that should have been his responsibility. Her narrative is an account of Goodhue Coldfield's failure even more than it is a story of Sutpen's success.

Faulkner's pivotal image in Chapter 1 is that of the young Rosa, only four years old, "a child standing close beside that door because I was afraid to be there but more afraid to leave it, standing motionless beside that door as though trying to make myself blend with the dark wood and become invisible, like a chameleon" (p. 27). The child afraid to be either hovering or absent, the child wishing for invisibility, is an icon of the forgotten person. The reader is convinced of the child's near, or actual, invisibility. Faulkner's locating Rosa near the door, wishing to become part of the stability that the door represented, is an ironic echo of Sutpen's compelling "door" narrative, when he is stigmatized by being sent around to the back, by a black, and refused entrance through a front door.[5] In this scene, Rosa enters no door; she is refused any entrance. She is given the role of hiding behind the door eavesdropping while she tries to figure her fate and that of the sister she loves so much. Kept away from power, hidden behind the observable actions, Rosa learns by stealth, complicity, and fear all that she needs to know for the kind of life the Southern culture will permit her to lead. In contrast, Sutpen's tactic is to wrest power from established channels, to substitute one door for another by creating his own set of doors, front and back, and with that structure a set of rules to govern it. Rosa has no house, no door, no physical location except that of her imagination and her narrative. In this scene, Faulkner makes clear Rosa's relation to the substance of male propriety.

With emphatic concision, Faulkner's narrative jumps to Rosa at age ten, speaking matter-of-factly and without self-pity: "Our aunt was gone now and I was keeping house for papa" (p. 28). She continues, "I did not have time now to play, even if I had ever had any inclination. I had never learned how and I saw no reason to try to learn now even if I had had the time." The last "story" in this first chapter of Rosa's narrative is of Judith, Clytie, and Henry illicitly watching Sutpen fight with his blacks and Ellen's horror at the corruption of her "baby girl" (p. 30). The irony of Ellen's being so horrified, when her daughter, at fourteen, is in fact the protected and privileged (if corruptible) daughter of wealth, set beside Rosa's simultaneous acceptance of her adult role as she, at ten, cares for her father and his household, shows the utter lack of concern for Rosa as younger daughter, baby sister, child.

What Rosa becomes, if her state has allowed her any time or space to "become" a female person in this inimical Southern culture, acts as a mandala to the various narratives of *Absalom, Absalom!* Her succinct realization of the cultural patterns she has been both observing and living—what happens to women's lives in the matrix of the South—is expressed in her memory of being fourteen, written as a part of her paean to the "summer of wisteria" that begins "once there was." The pithy declaration Rosa makes has little to do with fairy tales, however, as she laments "I waited not for light but for that doom which we call female victory which is: endure and then endure, without rhyme or reason or hope of reward—and then endure" (p. 144). Faulkner's telling of *Absalom, Absalom!* extends this axiom about women characters by focusing increasingly on their lives: during and after the war, the Sutpen fortunes are controlled for the most part by Judith, Clytie, and Rosa, with Sutpen's reappearance figuring only briefly. And such focus is true of the ending of the novel, which also is the ending of both the Sutpen dynasty and Sutpen's Hundred.

Rosa speaks seldom—the narrative reinforces her sense that she has little value, little power to create voice and language, as Faulkner shows Mr. Compson and the Harvard roommates re-fashioning Rosa's passionate tale—and almost never to male characters. Even in conversation with other women characters, she is laconic, hesitant. Faulkner includes a chilling scene of Sutpen's return from war, in which Judith tells him of Charles Bon's death, finally releasing her grief into the tears she has not shed during the seven months since his murder. That image suggests the analogous outpouring of Rosa's final storying, her capture of Quentin Compson so that he will not only hear her words but help her create the last of them by accompanying her in her decisive action. Her childlike insistence on her story, on telling her story to Quentin, as well as her self-protective distance from the young man's disinterest, are integral pieces of Faulkner's characterization of how a woman would speak after forty-three years of self-imposed silence. Given what the reader comes to know about these circumstances, the mania of Rosa's story as it propels her into the later stages of her narrative is plausible.

When Faulkner allows her to resume talking, in Chapter 5, she begins with Wash Jones' calling her to Sutpen's Hundred on the occasion of Charles Bon's murder. Arriving there, now nineteen, Rosa finds that the Sutpen house has become her adversary: "Rotting portico and scaling walls, it stood, not ravaged, not invaded, marked by no bullet nor soldier's iron heel but rather as though reserved for something more: some desolation more profound than ruin" (p. 136). Coupled with the indomitable, and waiting, house, Rosa finds Clytie, also a nemesis, a "force" that was destined to keep her and all who wanted to change or subvert Sutpen's Hundred away from it. When Rosa enters the house and calls out to Judith, she reverts to being powerless and fearful: "Just as a child, before the full instant of comprehended terror, calls on the parent whom it actually knows (this before the terror destroys all judgment whatever) is not even there to hear it. I was crying not to someone, something, but (trying to cry) through something, through that force . . ." (p. 137). Rosa as abandoned, and therefore disoriented, child yet perseveres. After years of private sorrow, she has learned that her abandonment gives her a kind of power; she is immune from social conventions. In this scene with Clytie, she conquers the door that Clytie would close before her; she gains access to the upper story, even though doing so means enmity with Clytie forever. The lasting insult—Clytie's calling her "Rosa" and her calling Clytie "nigger"—reifies the conflict, makes it permanent through its inscription in language. Judith, however, does not allow Rosa through the bedroom door, so she never sees Bon, never knows that his dead body is, in fact, housed in the coffin she helps to carry. Judith closes the door to Rosa as if to comment on the power of the legitimate Sutpen heirs. The closed door trope becomes Rosa's means of expressing her isolation from the life, and power, of the Sutpen family; and in a later speculation about the sound of Henry's gunshot as he killed Bon, she uses the trope once more: "No, there had been no shot. That sound was merely the sharp and final clap-to of a door between us and all that was, all that might have been . . ." (p. 158).

With the poignancy of the doom she saw in women's lives, Rosa laments that, even though she is twenty, she is "still a child, still living in that womb-like corridor where the world came not even as living echo but as dead incomprehensible shadow" (p. 162). Her fierce desire was to know life, and for a young Southern woman, "life" translated as love and romance. But again, Faulkner's pervasive trope is of closed doors, despite Rosa's readiness to open the doors of her body in accepting Sutpen's proposal. His proposal— which ominously says nothing of "love"—is delivered as if he were speaking to a child, his hand on Rosa's head, with Judith and Clytie looking on. Fatherlike in this pose, Sutpen evokes all Rosa's feelings for her biological father as well as her fantasies about patriarchal and military power: Sutpen is an important man, a brave soldier, who somehow "deserves" her virginal love. But that obeisance is mixed with Rosa's continual despair and rage at having been abandoned by Goodhue Coldfield. She, in fact, blames Coldfield for leaving her in the circumstances that made living at Sutpen's Hundred necessary (although she has earlier denied that she needed to go there to live): "She had been right in hating her father since if he had not died in that attic she would not have had to go out there to find food and protection and shelter" (p. 169). Faulkner further plays on Rosa's confusion of Sutpen and Coldfield in a subsequent scene through the use of the indefinite pronoun *him*: "And that's what she cant forgive him for: not for the insult, not even for having jilted him: but for being dead" (p. 170).

Faulkner's plot development has allowed him to bring Rosa fully into the primary narrative, to move her out of her role as observer (and her common stance, "This is what I saw" [p. 23]). Her passion, whether vengeful or erotic or both, brings her to voice as participant, and her voice—in the passage that serves to close her inscription of the story she has lived as well as told—takes on the qualities of a fully involved woman. Her voice here can be taken for that of Judith, as Faulkner juxtaposes the scenes of the women's learning of the deaths of their lovers. Rosa's recognition of Sutpen's death, " 'Dead?' I cried. 'Dead? You? You lie; you're not dead; heaven cannot, and hell dare not, have you!' " (p. 172), shows the possessiveness of the spurned woman, and her attribution of voice to him even in death suggests the heightened, raging responses she is capable of even years after her abandonment and betrayal. Faulkner opens the juxtaposed scene, in which Judith learns of Bon's death, with the image of the door, this time a door through which Henry enters Judith's room to bring her the news of Bon's murder (in contrast, Quentin cannot pass that threshold, even imaginatively):

Now you cant marry him.
Why cant I marry him?
Because he's dead.
Dead?
Yes. I killed him. (p. 172)

The immensity of Faulkner's compassion in *Absalom, Absalom!* becomes clear through his narrative structure, as he creates loss after loss after loss, and the reader is reminded of his later praise of Hemingway's *The Old Man and the Sea*: "This time he wrote about pity: about something somewhere that made them all: the old man who had to catch the fish and then lose it, the fish that had to be caught and then lost . . . made them all and loved them all and pitied them all."[6] Faulkner's *Absalom, Absalom!* is a novel about power and loss, but it is increasingly focused on the women and children (or the women as children) of the decimated South rather than on the various father-son paradigms. Drawing near the close, Faulkner leaves the reader to experience the ashes of bitter loss in both Rosa's and Judith's speeches, their lives as Southern women doomed by the deaths of men who were their means of escaping those dusty corridors of repressed sexuality.

From this point of resonant understanding, Faulkner's narrative now embroiders the already known story. For the next four chapters, control of Rosa's story is usurped by Mr. Compson, Quentin, and Shreve (who sounds more and more like the elder Compson); and even though that usurpation is partly justified at the opening of Chapter 6, with Mr. Compson's announcement of Rosa's death, the reader remains in suspense, poised to discover the end of Rosa's story. Faulkner finally concludes the novel, and the Sutpen history, with an ending that interweaves the tropes of Rosa as voiceless child, Clytie as avenger of the Sutpen dynasty, and the house as mausoleum, complete with closed doors and an identification with human lineage. The ephemeral quality of Sutpen's Hundred—as fantastic in decline as it was in inception—dominates Faulkner's late description: the house looking as if it "were of one dimension, painted on a canvas curtain in which there was a tear . . . reek[ing] in slow and protracted violence with a smell of desolation and decay as if the wood of which it was built were flesh" (p. 366).

As Quentin drives toward Sutpen's Hundred with Rosa, she does little but "whimper." As they walk into the house, her hyperventilation continues and she trots beside him, "her hand trembling on his arm . . . not talking, not saying words, yet producing a steady whimpering, almost a moaning, sound" (p. 366). Frightened by the action she has planned and provoked, Rosa becomes once more the voiceless child she was throughout most of her life except for the years when she played the role of writer, the genteel poetess of the heroic South, living in a fantasy she found possible. Her only speech at the beginning of the journey identifies Sutpen boundaries, and her own claims to inheritance: " 'Now,' she said. 'We are on the Domain. On his land, his and Ellen's and Ellen's descendants' " (p. 363). Faulkner gives Rosa such spare speech that her taut directions to Quentin, urging him to break down the front door, are particularly revealing. Convinced that the door will be nailed shut, as her father had nailed shut the attic when he abandoned her, Rosa demands revenge on both father and lover. Her act will open forever the countless doors closed against her; it will also reclaim her lost inheritances.

"Break it," she whispered. "It will be locked, nailed. You have the hatchet. Break it."

"But—" he began.

"Break it!" she hissed. "It belonged to Ellen. I am her sister, her only living heir. Break it. Hurry." (p. 367)

Three months later, Rosa returned to Sutpen's Hundred, an event that led Clytie to set the fire that destroyed the house and Henry and herself with it. Faulkner's description of Rosa as "the small furious grim implacable woman not much larger than a child," "the light thin furious creature making no sound at all now, struggling with silent and bitter fury" (p. 375), draws the reader with sympathy into the cycle of vengeance: language is sacrificed to rage, and the impassioned Rosa slips back in time, losing her human capacity to speak, to explain, to recall. Ellen Coldfield, who never learned to voice her rage, died as if turned to stone, repressing all bitter knowledge of the enormity of her life with Sutpen. Goodhue Coldfield also died without language, physically removing himself from any possibility of human community. Each adult left the child Rosa not only alone but without emotional or financial resources. And so Rosa became both the agent for vengeance and its victim.

As the Sutpen mansion burned, illustrating its "desolation more profound than ruin" (p. 136), the creation of the Sutpen legacy—with the disinherited Rosa Coldfield demanding her legacy—continued. In the immediate present of the novel, twenty-year-old Quentin, who is the same age Rosa was during the last episode she chooses to tell of her story, the episode of Sutpen's proposal and then insult, says to Shreve, "I am older at twenty than a lot of people who have died" (p. 377). The tragedy of Quentin Compson's understanding is that he sees no way to survive the pain of disinheritance; and he feels himself as abandoned by parents, community, and culture as Rosa was. As Faulkner so brilliantly charts, Rosa's aged but childlike self was the product of her abandonment by her father, her family, her lover, and her culture; yet when she finally broke through the chrysalis of self-protective fantasy, she brought down Sutpen's Hundred for all time and all memory. The concluding narrative envelope of Shreve and Quentin's dialogue, the last part of Mr. Compson's letter, and Quentin's own anguished realization subtract nothing from the poignancy and the terror of Rosa Coldfield's story. Her strangely silent discourse as the abandoned child, bereft of family and belonging, answers the elaborate rhetoric of Mr. Compson and his descendants (one linked by blood, the other by attitude) and leaves the reader wondering at the power of Rosa's largely unvoiced but ultimately assertive tale.

Note

1. William Faulkner, *The Sound and the Fury* (New York: Random House, 1929), p. 215.

2. All reference in the text are to William Faulkner's *Absalom, Absalom!* (New York: Random House, 1936). The quantity of criticism on this novel is staggering, but most of it does not give Rosa's story the prominence I do here. Recent criticism I have found most helpful includes John T. Matthews, *The Play of Faulkner's Language* (Ithaca: Cornell Univ. Press, 1982); Gail Mortimer, *Faulkner's Rhetoric of Loss* (Austin: Univ. Of Texas Press, 1983); Elizabeth Muhlenfeld's *William Faulkner's* Absalom, Absalom!: *A Critical Casebook* (New

York: Garland, 1984) and "Faulkner's Women," *Miss Q*, 26 (1973), 435–40; Stephen M. Ross, "Oratory and the Dialogical in *Absalom, Absalom!*" in *Intertextuality in Faulkner*, ed. Michel Gresset and Noel Polk (Jackson: Univ . Press of Mississippi, 1985), pp. 73–86; Olga Vickery, *The Novels of William Faulkner*, 2nd ed. (Baton Rouge: Louisiana State Univ. Press, 1964); Minrose C. Gwin, *The Feminine and Faulkner, Reading (Beyond) Sexual Difference* (Knoxville: Univ. of Tennessee Press, 1990); and Wesley Morris with Barbara Alverson Morris, *Reading Faulkner* (Madison: Univ. of Wisconsin Press, 1989). My greatest agreement is with the latter two books, though the Morrises' reading does not follow the women characters so much as their critical stance would suggest and, in fact, they continuously "read" Rosa as trying to tell the Sutpen story when she is surely more interested in telling her own, and the Coldfield family, story (pp. 180–86).

3. See Lynda Boose's introduction to *Daughters and Fathers*, ed. Lynda E. Boose and Betty S. Flowers (Baltimore: Johns Hopkins Univ. Press, 1989), pp. 19–74, and André Bleikasten, pp. 156–61. See also Philip M. Weinstein, "Meditations on the Other: Faulkner's Rendering of Women" and Ilse Dusoir Lind's "The Mutual Relevance of Faulkner Studies and Women's Studies: An Interdisciplinary Inquiry" in *Faulkner and Women*, ed. Doreen Fowler and Ann J. Abadie (Jackson: Univ. Press of Mississippi, 1986), pp. 81–99, 21–40, as well as Cleanth Brooks' chapter, "Faulkner's 'Motherless' Children" in his *On the Prejudices, Predilections, and Firm Beliefs of William Faulkner*, *Essays* (Baton Rouge: Louisiana State Univ. Press, 1987), pp. 66–79.

4. Both Gwin in her 1990 study and the Morrises persistently question whether or not Faulkner knew what he was implying in Rosa's story. To adopt the dialogic stance toward Faulkner's fiction almost mandates that the critic accept that the author's intentionality was at least partly cognizant.

5. The Morrises state that "the novel's climactic moment is in Chapter 7" (p. 189), thereby locating Sutpen's door episode as the narrative center. While such configuration may be accurate, his initial door conflict is extended countless times through Rosa's text, and life, and it surely takes on different kinds of significance in these repetitions.

6. William Faulkner, "Review of *The Old Man and the Sea*," *Shenandoah*, 3 (Autumn, 1952), 55.

The Other Coldfields:
Gender, Commerce, and the Exchange of
Bodies in *Absalom, Absalom!*

Robert Dale Parker*

For many critics of *Absalom, Absalom!*, the Sutpen family cannot finally be explained. "They are there, yet something is missing . . . ; you bring them together in the proportions called for, but nothing happens; you re-read, tedious and intent, poring, making sure that you have forgotten nothing, made no miscalculation; you bring them together again and again nothing happens: just the words, the symbols, the shapes themselves, shadowy inscrutable and serene."[1] Indeed, one standard reading sees the novel as a study in the incapacity of observations to harden into explanation, a study in the ever deferred status of explanation itself. But if the Sutpens and all that they represent remain obscure, the interior and exterior narrators who together tell the stories of *Absalom, Absalom!* set up the Coldfields as a background of secure reference points for the mystifying Sutpens. The various storytellers condense the Coldfields into received categories, nuggets of excess certainty: close-trading merchant, Puritan, embusqué, social butterfly, spinster aunt, ungrateful freed slave (the so-called "Coldfield negroes" or "negresses").

Recent critics have paid considerable and overdue attention to Rosa Coldfield, but the other Coldfields have drawn little discussion. Goodhue frequently gets a brief review, usually repeating the interpretations of him as a Puritan that already appear within the novel, and Ellen gets some general comment, especially in broader discussions of women characters. The rest of the family rarely attracts much notice. Even the novel names them only by their relation to Goodhue: his mother, father, wife, sister, and two servants. Except for Goodhue's father (referred to in passing, pp. 11, 14), all these characters are women, undeveloped in the narrative and hence little discussed in the criticism. But apart from Rosa, these "other Coldfields," Goodhue and his family and servants, are essential to understanding the anxieties about the exchange of gendered, commodified, and aestheticized bodies in *Absalom, Absalom!*[2]

---

*This essay was written especially for this volume and is published here for the first time by permission of the author.

If Americans mythologize the supposedly Protestant work ethic as a route to success, they also find a countermyth in the fast deal, the big-bucks windfall. *Absalom, Absalom!* uses Goodhue Coldfield, the close-trading, hard-working Puritan merchant with two comically Puritan names, to mock one side of the myth by showing its likely end in pettiness and disappointment, while using his sometime partner Thomas Sutpen to mock the other side by comically exaggerating its fantastic promise. When Goodhue and Sutpen somehow swing a deal that wins Sutpen his enormous wealth, they make something out of nothing, or so the improbable story goes. As Jefferson folklore, both the story and its improbability matter more than any untold, more plausible source of wealth, for we never learn what Sutpen and Goodhue did, but instead learn only that people keep telling and wondering about it, the sort of talk that fuels confidence artists and stokes the mass fantasies of market economies. Such folklore, in *Absalom*, evokes envy of the fast deal as economic possibility—indeed, many of Faulkner's own letters to his agents and publishers give sorry witness to that envy—while also parodying it as cultural myth.

When Goodhue and Sutpen trade whatever they supposedly trade—swapping, it appears, the merchant's credit for the pistol-toting upstart's bravado—they also trade Ellen Coldfield, Goodhue's daughter. While the men of Jefferson can disguise from themselves the ways that they structure their economy through the exchange of women, the women—in the narrator's nervous effort to make humor by exaggerating gender differences—are not fooled. "Probably the women had already cast about . . . for that prospective bride whose dowry might complete the shape and substance of that respectability Miss Coldfield anyway believed to be his aim. . . . The women merely said that . . . he had now come to town to find a wife exactly as he would have gone to the Memphis market to buy livestock or slaves" (p. 31). Such exchange is already Sutpen's pattern with his first wife, whom he tries to return after he decides that the goods he bought were falsely advertised, with his slaves, and with the women of Jefferson. He chooses his women slaves "with the same care and shrewdness with which he chose the other livestock—the horses and mules and cattle—which he bought later on. And he lived out there for five years before he had speaking acquaintance with any white woman in the county, just as he had no furniture in his house and for the same reason: he had at the time nothing to exchange for it them or her" (p. 48).[3] One of these slaves becomes Clytie's mother, but we hardly hear of her in that role (only vaguely on p. 48 and in the Genealogy) or any other role. Sutpen reduces her to her bodily function as receptacle of his lust and producer of slaves, including his own ambiguously enslaved daughter. As Mr. Compson puts it, linking Clytie's mother to the other women Sutpen sleeps with, Sutpen "tried to mix, blend" his slaves' "blood . . . with the same care and for the same purpose with which he blended that of the stallion and that of his own" (p. 67). (Mr. Compson does not yet know how the story of Charles Bon comes back to haunt Sutpen's care.) Certainly Sutpen does not "love" or even like Ellen; he does not even know her aside from her social and economic position, her "respectability," and her connection to his partner in the fast deal.

He repeats the process yet again when he tries to make another cold deal, this time not with the father but with the object herself, Rosa, and then again, even more abusively, with Milly Jones. Then at last the father (or this time the grandfather, Wash Jones, but still in the role of father as proprietor of the daughter) recognizes the deal as the cool exchange of women's bodies that the myth or romance disguises. When Wash sees through the ribbons and gewgaws, the petty bribes that cover the way Sutpen reduced Milly to her bodily potential for producing male offspring, he tries to obliterate the merged figurations of gender and economics by converting all parties to and products of the deal (Milly, her daughter, Sutpen, and Wash himself) into bodies at their lowest common denominator, signifieds that can seem to be without signifiers: corpses.

Like Milly or any other woman, therefore, Ellen herself is not the point for Sutpen or Goodhue. When women are the coinage of masculine economic exchange, men take women as a means of addressing other men. Goodhue, in Mr. Compson's mind, must have consented to the deal because he could not resist his curiosity about whether it would work. That is, he does it to hoodwink other men, rather than to secure wealth for Ellen. Sutpen cares so little for women that he lives in a "masculine solitude . . . whose threshold no woman had so much as seen, without any feminised softness," where he invites "parties of men" to hunt, drink, and play cards (p. 30). To men, Luce Irigaray suggests, the exchange of women is about men, not about women: "The exchanges upon which patriarchal societies are based take place exclusively among men. Women, signs, commodities, and currency always pass from one man to another. . . . This means that the *very possibility of a sociocultural order requires homosexuality* as its organizing principle."[4] As Mr. Compson says of Judith and Henry Sutpen and Charles Bon, "It was not Judith who was the object of Bon's love or of Henry's solicitude. She was just the blank shape, the empty vessel in which each of them strove to preserve . . . what each believed the other to believe him to be—the man and the youth, seducer and seduced, who had known one another, seduced and been seduced . . . before Judith came into their joint lives even by so much as a girlname" (p. 95). For Mr. Compson, the relations between Judith and Bon and between Judith and Henry each dissolve into mere currency for the relation between Henry and Bon.

But contrary to Irigaray's exaggerated notion of an economy without female agency, women in *Absalom, Absalom!*, even such conspicuous objects of masculine exchange as the Coldfield women, at the least aspire to an exchange of men and of each other. Ellen contests Sutpen for control of Judith when she substitutes her phaeton and gentle mare for the carriage and fast horses, and again when she runs in on Sutpen's "raree show" (p. 12) to find Judith. Later, Ellen wants Bon for Judith as an object of exchange among women, just as years earlier, Ellen and her aunt want a big, happy wedding to present themselves to other Jefferson women as the happy, big-spending exchangers of men. These graspings after agency are not always free of complicity with the masculine exchanges they resist (women's exchange of men, for example, hardly improves on men's exchange of women). But neither are the men's exchanges free from the feminine agencies that press men to want women in their lives (against Sutpen's prolonged effort to live away from white women) and domesticity in their homes (such as Sutpen's magnificent furnishings). Each gender partakes of the other's objectifying and also of its agency in a much more complicated pattern of economic and sexual exchange than Irigaray's model allows.

Much of this has to do with the relation between gender and class. The quantity of one's exchanges defines one's class, while the capacity to exchange marks one, in Irigaray's terms, as masculine. Yet the capacity to exchange can also mark one as feminine, as in the social mythologies that connect consumption to middle- and upper-class women. This Faulkner knew too well, for as he wrote *Absalom* he was also careening toward one of his and his wife's greatest humiliations. While *Absalom* was in press, he published a newspaper notice (which he withdrew after the familial and even national furor it provoked) disclaiming responsibility for Estelle Faulkner's purchases. Estelle had been reared to define her class position by a conspicuous consumption that Bill could never earn enough to fund. Meanwhile, Estelle's family looked down upon Bill's because the Falkners, despite their pretensions, always had to struggle over money.[5] A similar conflict shapes Goodhue's worries over the contamination of commerce and Ellen's reaction against such contamination as she spends the same profits that her father refuses (Ellen's name even suggests a faint echo of Estelle's).

When Goodhue sells Ellen to Sutpen for a profit and then refuses the profit, he acts as if to cash in would reveal his threatening likeness to his partner. Despite their differences, they each prop themselves up with the same overcalculated illusion of morality. Sutpen drinks other men's whiskey with "sparing calculation as though keeping mentally . . . a sort of balance of spiritual solvency between the amount of whiskey he accepted and the amount of running meat which he supplied to the guns" (p. 30), just as Goodhue works for and contributes to the church "for the sake of what might be called a demand balance of spiritual solvency, exactly as he would have used a cotton gin" (p. 38). Goodhue finds his "only pleasure . . . not in the money but in its representation of a balance in whatever spiritual counting-house he believed would some day pay his sight drafts on self-denial and fortitude. And doubtless what hurt him most in the whole business with Sutpen was not the loss of the money but the fact that he had had to sacrifice the hoarding, the symbol of the fortitude and abnegation, to keep intact the spiritual solvency . . . as if he had had to pay the same note twice because of some trifling oversight" (p. 66). Or at least Mr. Compson and his father describe Goodhue and Sutpen in these strikingly similar terms, which suggests that for the storytellers, that is, for General Compson, his son, Faulkner, and the cultural narratives they voice, the same moral presumptuousness contaminates the merchant's close trading and the upstart despot's seizure of economic dominion.

In the stories they tell, the Coldfields, like the declining Compsons and the rising Sutpens, worry and fuss over their class position. Such worry provokes the secret deal in the first place, especially for Goodhue (Sutpen's gambit comes, as well, from race anxiety). Rosa paints Sutpen as a social climber who marries Ellen for the imprimatur of Coldfield respectability. She exaggerates her family's distance from him, referring to "gentlefolks, our own kind" (p. 20), but she cannot sustain so transparently far off a claim, for she also describes her father as "a merchant who was not rich," *"merely . . . a small store-keeper"* (pp. 13–14, 137). With similar anxiousness, her aunt and father inflate Rosa's class position, sealing her off from the commercial, working world that defines their day-to-day life and yet seems to them contaminatingly mercantile. Thus Rosa "had never been taught to do anything practical because the aunt had raised her to believe that she was not only delicate but actually precious" (p. 65). They do not let her count, touch, or see money, not even when she shops, so that she looks *"upon fuel and meat as something appearing by its own volition in a woodbox or on a pantry shelf"* (pp. 60, 125). They train her to a delusory and abusive class role, and also to a patronized gender role, for no man, let alone one from the small merchant class, could pretend to live apart from commerce, short of nailing himself into the attic as Goodhue later does. Rosa's role, therefore, is not to trade but rather—if only the war didn't come along to upset the gender ratio—to be traded, like Ellen.

Ellen reacts to being traded with the same Coldfield anxiety over class position. Allied, at first, with her aunt, she tries to convert her own position as marriageable object into a vantage for social display. She and her aunt attempt to take control over the wedding, the metonymy of Ellen's position as object of exchange. But by the time the tale reaches us, Jefferson, Compson, and Faulknerian legend have reduced the wedding to metaphors of feminine irrelevance and weakness: the aunt's mad frenzy, unwittingly ridiculing her own social ostracism as an unmarried woman without social connections, as she wildly insists that people attend a wedding she cannot make them attend any more than she can produce a wedding for herself (or so the patronizing mythology of "spinsterhood" would suggest). Even when, later on, the aunt herself marries, she elopes, that is, she weds without a wedding. And she marries, of all people, a man whom legend reduces to the occupational tag line of a horse- and mule-trader, as if to satirize the aunt first for not submitting to the market in women and then again for submitting to it too crudely.

If legend mocks the aunt's effort to seize agency and converts it into frustrated madness and desperation, it also takes the niece's effort to define the wedding on her own terms and condenses it into her tears, which open and conclude Mr. Compson's tale of the wedding. "Ellen seems to have entered the church that night out of weeping as though out of rain, gone through the ceremony and then walked back out of the church and into the weeping again, the tears again, the same tears even, the same rain." "Yes, she was weeping again now; it did, indeed, rain on that marriage" (pp. 37, 45). As Rosa defines Judith through Judith's initial refusal and later readiness to cry over Bon's death, Mr. Compson makes Ellen's tears a metonymy of her role as feminine victim devoid of agency, a metonymy of her disappointment and her inability to do anything about that disappointment, as she cannot even walk away from the church without a masculine escort.

But after she marries, Ellen tries again to reassert agency through social display. As before she was the object of men's exchange, now she tries to convert Charles Bon into the object of women's exchange: "Ellen did not once mention love. . . . She spoke of Bon as if he were . . . one inanimate object for which she and her family would find three concordant uses: a garment which Judith might wear . . ., a piece of furniture which would complement . . . her house and position, and a mentor and example to correct Henry's provincial manners" (p. 59). Now that she is the county's most conspicuous consumer, "chatelaine to the largest, wife to the wealthiest, mother of the most fortunate" (p. 54), she would add Bon to her collection. More than she consumes purchases, however, she consumes the display of her own position, half manikin-object and half expressive subject: "She shopped . . . without even getting out of the carriage, gracious and assured and talking the most complete nonsense, voluble, speaking her bright set meaningless phrases out of the part which she had written for herself, of the duchess peripatetic with property soups and medicines among a soilless and uncompelled peasantry" (p. 54). She imagines her new position as local royalty in pointed contrast to her mercantile origins, enjoying her "carriage's weekly ritual of store to store where, without getting out, Ellen bade merchant and clerk fetch out to her the cloth and the meagre fripperies and baubles which . . . they knew even better than she that she would not buy but instead would merely finger and handle and disarrange and then reject, all in that . . . childlike imposition upon the sufferance or good manners or sheer helplessness of the men, the merchants and clerks" (pp. 57–58). In this latter rendition, she cares less to purchase, which would taint her with commerce, than to display her capacity to purchase and command and hence to reverse her earlier relation to men and merchants.

Often, as above, Mr. Compson carries Ellen's aversion to practicality and commerce so far as to describe her with terms like "nonsense," "meaningless," "unreal," and "pointless" (p. 61). That cultivation of the supposedly meaningless takes on color in the favored figure for Ellen's married maturity: Ellen as butterfly, an oft-repeated image that sets her aestheticized irrelevance in opposition to her husband's ominously weighty experience. Sutpen arrives in Jefferson looking "like a man who had been sick . . ., a man who had been through some solitary furnace experience . . . and fought through it at enormous cost" (p. 24). Ellen, by contrast, appears years later as "the foolish unreal voluble preserved woman now six years absent from the world—the woman who had quitted home and kin on a flood of tears and . . . then rose like the swamp-hatched butterfly, unimpeded by weight of stomach and all the heavy organs of suffering and experience" (pp. 54–55). The butterfly image figures Ellen's effort to escape her exchange value and replace it with aesthetic expression. Ironically, at the same time, by making her an aesthetic object it also advertises her role as object of exchange all over again. The aesthetic thus marks an aspiration to escape the supposedly masculine world of work and commerce, and yet depends on and, economically, feeds the world it would escape, making Ellen's role as butterfly a point at which a gendered economy and a marketed gender converge.

Her role as butterfly also marks an effort to repress the corporeality that Sutpen marries her for. When Sutpen buys Ellen, "bought her, outswapped his father-in-law . . . after three years to scrutinise weigh and compare" (p. 145), as Shreve puts it, he buys her for her respectable body, not for her charms or talents, but only for her social and physical capacity to produce an heir. In response, she metamorphoses into a butterfly state, a pose of bodilessness. Or at the least, the story told about her has some stake in portraying her as a pitifully ephemeral site of resistance to Sutpen's ruthless reduction of her to the exchange value, the commercial meaning, of her capacity to reproduce. Thus when Mr. Compson describes her as meaningless and without experience, he sees her as resisting a corporeality that nevertheless waits, in her very plumpness, to catch up with her: "She was in her late thirties, plump, her face unblemished still. It was as though whatever marks being in the world had left upon it . . . had been removed . . . from between the skeleton and the skin, between the sum of experience and the envelope in which it resides" (p. 54). Sutpen's corporeality attracts similar terms, but for him they turn toward rather than away from his body and experience: "The fat, the stomach . . . came upon him suddenly, . . . as though . . . the fine figure of a man had reached and held its peak after the foundation had given away and something between the shape of him that people knew and the uncompromising skeleton of what he actually was had . . . been snubbed up and restrained, balloonlike unstable and lifeless, by the envelope which it had betrayed" (pp. 63–64). When Ellen shops for clothes, therefore, she represses the exchangeable body in favor of the power to exchange its wrappings, particularly when she goes to Memphis—prematurely—for Judith's trousseau. The trousseau, and all the attention to it from Ellen and Rosa, condense Judith's wedding, her conversion into an exchangeable body, into something that Ellen and Rosa imagine they can control, as if to make up for Ellen's inability to control her own wedding. Their obsession with the trousseau covers up the female body as an object traded for sexual acts and reproduction, refiguring it as an icon of feminine agency and aesthetics.

That can work for a while, but not for long, in the patriarchal world of *Absalom, Absalom!*, where all that Ellen tries to escape by running to her feminized aestheticism comes back with a crash after "something happened" between Thomas and Henry that drives away Bon. In reaction, Ellen goes "prostrate . . . at the shock of reality," "Ellen, who would have been told nothing in the first place and would have forgot, failed to assimilate, it if she had been—Ellen the butterfly . . . with baffled incomprehension" (pp. 62–63). When they do not even tell her what happened, they produce the unreality in her that they claim to observe, whether we think of such events as straight reportage, communal legend, or Mr. Compson's careless presumption.

Mr. Compson cannot even keep straight when Goodhue's wife, Ellen and Rosa's mother, bears children and dies. Supposedly she dies bearing Rosa (p. 46), but she's absent from the description of Ellen's "courtship" and wedding, seven years earlier. At one point Mr. Compson even describes Goodhue and his wife as having "children," in the plural, when they first arrive in Jefferson long before Rosa, their second child, is born (p. 60). Like Goodhue's mother, who usually appears in the lists of family members that compose most of the references to Goodhue's wife, most of the Coldfields are mere props in the murky background of the Sutpen saga.

The only Coldfield women, besides Rosa, whom the novel releases into agency without also showing how that agency unravels are the so-called "Coldfield negroes," two women whom Goodhue buys and then frees, "putting them on a weekly wage which he held back in full against the discharge of the current market value at which he had assumed them on the debt—and in return for which they had been among the first Jefferson negroes to desert and follow the Yankee troops" (p. 66). Ostensibly he frees them from slavery, but he reenslaves them to debt, imposing on them his own submission to the market economy he despises. Still, he can move to another town (as he moves from Tennessee to Jefferson), but they, apparently, cannot. When he and Rosa visit Ellen, Goodhue "dock[s] the two negroes for the noon meal which they would not have to prepare and (so the town believed) charg[es] them for the crude one of left-overs which they would have to eat" (p. 52). Despite the terribly little that the novel tells about these two women, Goodhue's worried indebting, docking, and charging suggests more than Faulkner's stereotypical Puritan all set up for easy satire. It also suggests the two women's potential for agency, since Goodhue needs such nervous surveillance to contain them, a potential that the women act on when they run off with ("follow," Mr. Compson says) the Union troops.

Surely, no paradise of agency would await them in their newfound freedom from Goodhue and debt-slavery, although their lives would stand a better chance of improving. The novel never lets these two unnamed freed slaves become more than background characters to background characters, never follows them beyond their departure from Jefferson. All we get is Mr. Compson's tone of resentment as he reports their escape to Quentin, but that in itself suggests a fantasy of what seems to Mr. Compson an excess agency, an escape from their prescribed place in a social system that treats them as explicit objects of exchange, buying and selling them even more plainly than Goodhue sells his daughter Ellen. The white Coldfields live in fear at the constraints of gender, commerce, and the exchange of bodies, a nexus of social forces that, for less frightened, less suspicious characters, could go much farther to open possibilities for agency and expression. In material terms, that nexus confines the black Coldfields much more than it confines the white Coldfields. Yet Mr. Compson's resentment that these two barely mentioned characters escape Jefferson's surveillance elevates them implausibly into potential figures of escape from Mr. Compson's characteristic fatalism, and in some respects from Faulkner's own fatalism. That resentment turns a last irony on the white Coldfields, who provoke the agency they most desire and fear only in the figurative trace of those members of their household whom they least memorialize.

Notes

1. William Faulkner, *Absalom, Absalom!*, 1936 (New York: Random House, 1986), 80. Subsequent references to this edition will appear in the text.

2. A good number of recent critics, all writing more or less concurrently, focus on Rosa Coldfield. For examples, as well as Wagner-Martin in this collection, see Rosemary Coleman, "Family Ties: Generating Narratives in *Absalom, Absalom!*," *Mississippi Quarterly* 41, no. 3 (Summer 1988): 421–31; Deborah Garfield, "To Love as 'Fiery Ancients' Would: Eros, Narrative and Rosa Coldfield in *Absalom, Absalom!*," *Southern Literary Journal* 22:1 (1989): 61–79; Patrick O'Donnell, "Sub Rosa: Voice, Body, and History in *Absalom, Absalom!*," *College Literature* 16 (1989): 28–47; Minrose C. Gwin, *The Feminine and Faulkner: Reading (Beyond) Sexual Difference* (Knoxville: University of Tennessee Press, 1990); Richard C. Moreland, *Faulkner and Modernism: Rereading and Rewriting* (Madison: University of Wisconsin Press, 1990), which also gives considerable discussion to Rosa's father, sister, and rarely discussed aunt; and Robert Dale Parker, *"Absalom, Absalom!": The Questioning of Fictions* (Boston: Twayne, 1991). For a classic feminist discussion of "the exchange of women," see Gayle Rubin, "The Traffic in Women: Notes on 'The Political Economy of Sex' " in *Toward an Anthropology of Women*, ed. Rayna R. Reiter (New York: Monthly Review Press, 1975), 157–210.

3. There are many narrators in *Absalom, Absalom!*, including Faulkner's 1936 editors, who seem to have found this passage too frank. They cut out the equation among Sutpen's various objects of exchange—explicitly enslaved black women, implicitly enslaved white

women, and furniture—trimming "nothing to exchange for it them or her" to "nothing to exchange for them." William Faulkner, *Absalom, Absalom!* (New York: Random House, 1936), 62.

4.   Luce Irigaray, "Commodities among Themselves," *This Sex which Is Not One,* 1977, trans. Carolyn Burke (Ithaca: Cornell University Press, 1985), 192.

5.   See Joseph Blotner, *Faulkner: A Biography,* 2 vols. (New York: Random House, 1977), 2: 938–40.

APPENDIX

[The Sutpen-Bon-Coldfield Genealogy]

EDMOND L. VOLPE*

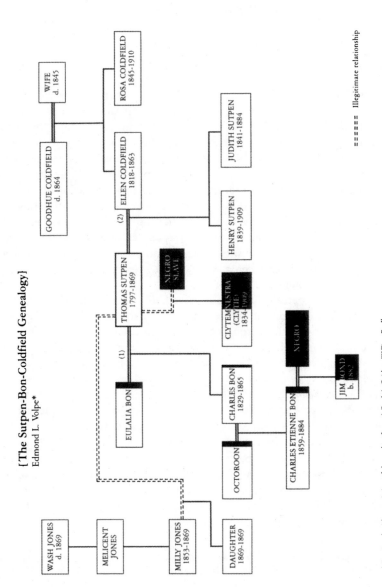

[The Sutpen-Bon-Coldfield Genealogy]
Edmond L. Volpe*

====== Illegitimate relationship

* Reprinted with permission of the author from *A Reader's Guide to William Faulkner* (New York: Farrar, Straus and Giroux, 1964), 185.

Chronology and Genealogy: The Authority of Fiction and the Fiction of Authority

ROBERT DALE PARKER*

The nature of fictional authority seems forever suspect in *Absalom, Absalom!* William Faulkner offers a series of competing explanations for a skeletal set of central facts: first Rosa Coldfield's befuddled nonexplanation, "without rhyme or reason or shadow of excuse"[1] then Mr. Compson's improbable fantasy that even he admits is "just incredible" and "just does not explain" (p. 100); then Quentin's story about fear of incest (pp. 264–65); then, finally, Quentin's and Shreve's story about fear of miscegenation (p. 355).[2] The first two explanations, Rosa's and Mr. Compson's, eventually show up as inferior histories in that they live up to the unreliability they confess to but not necessarily, therefore, as inferior stories, as inferior fictions. Thus in one sense their authority diminishes as the story expands, but in another sense their authority is both constant and also greater than readers might feel tempted to acknowledge.

Given such an extraordinary blur of what—within the confines of a fiction, that is, the confines of a novel and not a history—might be fact and what might be fiction, the chronology, genealogy, and map that Faulkner adds to the narrative of *Absalom, Absalom!* acquire an especially indeterminable status. Their relation to the novel per se exemplifies the problematic relation between any two parts of the Yoknapatawpha tales, or between the Appendix for *The Sound and the Fury* and the original version of that novel, or between *The Sound and the Fury* and *Absalom, Absalom!* itself. And yet the uncertainty in one way is more intense for the *Absalom* appendices, for they originally appeared with the body of the novel, which, as compared to the other related Yoknapatawpha pieces, makes them more inherently a part of the same text, almost like another chapter. Still, they are not another chapter; they bear no number as the chapters do but instead are set apart and appended to the end, with labels or titles, "CHRONOLOGY" and "GENEALOGY," that define them as secondary. Moreover, the chronology and genealogy

*Reprinted with permission from *Studies in American Fiction* 14, no. 2 (1986): 191–98. Original title: "The Chronology and Genealogy of *Absalom, Absalom!*: The Authority of Fiction and the Fiction of Authority." © 1986 by Northeastern University.

(pp. 379–83) are riddled with discrepancies, new and unexpected details, uncertain assertions, and outright errors. It may help to list those oddities and to speculate on the interest they hold—be it weightily critical or merely curious—for readers and critics of *Absalom, Absalom!*[3]

The chronology and genealogy both list Sutpen as born in 1807, which contradicts Shreve's guess that he was born in 1808 (p. 220). Shreve's guess would only be accurate within a year, so that readers might reasonably feel inclined to grant the chronology's and genealogy's assertion some superior authority, given that it comes directly from the author, whom people usually assume to be god of the book. Yet the same entries in the chronology and genealogy go on to say that Sutpen was born in West Virginia, which Quentin says also, but which Shreve sensibly points out, in the same breath that he guesses Sutpen was born in 1808, is impossible, because there was no West Virginia until almost sixty years later. Thus on the one hand the appended materials seem to stake claim to some superior—because autho-rial—authority, yet on the other hand they wave a comically ironic banner of fallibility, of the author's susceptibility to the same barriers of circumstance and medium that make all authority suspect in *Absalom, Absalom!*

The chronology and genealogy give other dates that conflict with the rest of the text. They say that Ellen Coldfield Sutpen was born in 1818 and died in 1862, whereas her gravestone lists 1817 and 1863 (p. 188). How readers account for such a discrepancy will bear on their interpretation of the authority of both the later and the earlier materials. Perhaps Quentin misremembers the dates on the gravestone; and yet since those dates come in an omniscient author's voice and come with more detail—month and day as well as year—than Quentin would probably remember, it hardly seems appropriate to suspect their reliability or to blame Quentin for any mistakes. Or perhaps when Faulkner wrote the chronology and genealogy he calculated dates the same way Shreve does when he calculates Sutpen's birth date and comes up with 1808 instead of 1807. Shreve subtracts Sutpen's presumed age (twenty-five) from the year he is presumed that old (1833), which leaves the possibility of one year's error, because such a method fails to consider days and months. Such small errors—if anyone wishes to call them that—matter very little. But the effort to interpret or explain them may force readers to ask whether the chronology and genealogy have an authority inferior or superior or equal to the rest of the text.

Similarly, the chronology says that Bon was born in Haiti in 1829, whereas his tombstone says he was born in New Orleans and dies in 1865 at the age of "33 years and 5 months" (p. 190). Cleanth Brooks points out that Judith orders the tombstone, which leads him to see it as a tragic sign of how little she knows about her fiance. That seems a reasonable train of thought, yet it suggests more than Brooks observes. It privileges the chronol-ogy's relatively external authority, presumably because the internal authority of Judith conflicts with the other internal authority of Sutpen's tale—a tale told to General Compson, who years later repeats it to Quentin's father, who years later repeats it to Quentin, who months later repeats it to Shreve—of begetting a son on a slave plantation in a Haiti where, in fact, there were no slaves by then (an anachronism that the book never acknowledges, as it acknowledges that there was no West Virginia), a son whom Quentin later decides or learns is Bon. All that seems logical enough but is, to say the least, awfully attenuated and seems to depend as well on some implied notion that the chronology holds superior authority because it comes directly from the author, who, the unspoken assumption implies, holds superior authority because in an appendix he speaks with the privileges of omniscience instead of the mediated and therefore tenuous authority of a character or even an author who speaks in the text proper. And yet, when the chronology differs with a character who has better cause to know than Judith does, when it differs over Ellen's birth and death dates with the tombstone erected by Ellen's sister Rosa, then Brooks discards the idea that the chronology holds superior authority, and he common-sensically labels it mistaken. That seems plausible, and yet if it can make one mistake then it can make another, suggesting that readers should be at least a little self-conscious about how readily they prefer its authority to Judith's.

Moreover, within the framework of Brooks' reasoning, Judith seems to do more than merely guess. She would not come up with such specific information, right or wrong, unless she had *some* authority, right or wrong, who gave it to her. Charles or Henry must have told her, and the details that one of them has chosen to tell carry their own significance for the story. They suggest how Charles or Henry wants Charles to be seen, as a Christ, murdered and sacrificed in the spring (May 3, 1865) at the Christological age of "33 years and 5 months" and so born at the time of Christ's birth, approximately December 25. Hence if readers privilege the chronology, they discover something new about the narrative. If they privilege the narrative, they discover that one part of the book that claims greater authority actually has less. That can be a coincidence; maybe Faulkner was careless or drunk (or both) when he wrote it (a likely enough possibility), and it does not matter.[4] Or if this ostensibly more reliable part of the book is indeed less reliable, then maybe such an irony is a deliberate or even an accidental, coincidental, but for all that still telling part of the overall implication of the book. Faulkner deliberately courted exactly such an ironic status for his appendix to *The Sound and the Fury*. Or at least he deliberately claimed and defended its discrepancies as usefully ironic once Malcolm Cowley pointed them out to him, though in that case the appendix is more fully a competing text, a full-scale piece of prose and not just a listing.[5]

In all these instances the novel gives some cause, however precarious, to rank competing authorities. Sometimes it does not. When in the chronology and genealogy Faulkner repeatedly places in 1910 incidents that the main text places clearly in 1909, something unambiguously is awry in the appended text.[6] But when the appended text says that Charles Bon's son and Judith die of smallpox and the narrative says they die of yellow fever (p. 210), it gives no means to compare the two accounts. By the same token, the narrative, the chronology, and the genealogy each give a different version of the name of Bon's son. The narrative calls him Charles Etienne Saint-Valery Bon (pp. 191, 205, and on p. 215 it confusingly abbreviates his name simply as Charles Bon). The chronology changes one vowel, drops the hyphen, and abbreviates Saint and sometimes the other middle names to make Charles Etienne St. Velery Bon; and the genealogy adds one more word to make Charles Etienne de Saint Velery Bon. Similarly, the genealogy says that Sutpen is one of several children, whereas the chronology says he is from a large family and the story Sutpen tells in the narrative, as mediated through three Compsons, vaguely describes at least six children: two older brothers, more than one older sister, Thomas Sutpen himself, and at least one younger sister (pp. 223–24, 226). The genealogy says Quentin was born in 1891, which would make him eighteen at the oldest when he talks to Miss Rosa and nineteen at the oldest when he talks to Shreve, but the omniscient narrator calls him twenty on the first occasion and he refers to himself as twenty on the second (pp. 14, 377). The omniscient narrator says directly that "Shreve was nineteen, a few months younger than Quentin" (p. 294), and yet if, as the genealogy reports, Quentin is born in 1891 and Shreve in 1890, then Shreve is older.

Occasionally, the chronology and genealogy add material never revealed in the main text: the first and last names of Bon's mother,[7] or Shreve's last name (McCannon, whereas in *The Sound and the Fury* it is MacKenzie), or that Eulalia Bon was divorced from Sutpen, which contradicts what Quentin and Shreve assume when they imagine her lawyer blackmailing Sutpen over bigamy (pp. 301, 310). But sometimes the genealogy refuses any authorially superior knowledge or perspective and simply lists matters as "unknown" (five times) or not recorded.

A writer does a peculiar thing when he or she claims not to know something about a character or event from that writer's own imagination. Such a claim, by its pretense of incomplete knowledge, calls readers to take those characters or events as exterior to the book, as nonfictional. And yet if that unsuspended part of the readers' credulity knows nevertheless that such events and characters are after all confined to the book and fictional, then those readers should see any such claim as coming from an author who, like themselves, retains a large part of his or her imagination that disbelieves the claim. The claim, in other words, is a lie, a pose, an affectation, voiced not directly by the author of a fiction but rather mediated by yet another character, imagined by the author, who claims to have composed the work not as a fiction but rather as a history. The presumed author of a fiction who claims historicity *is* a fiction and that author's author—in this case

Faulkner—who writes the fiction is himself historical. One can read a biography of him.[8]

Faulkner plays such games all the time. The typically Faulknerian use of such words as *maybe, probably, perhaps*, and so on falls strongly in the Hawthornian tradition that Faulkner proclaimed himself an adherent of in the title of his very first book, *The Marble Faun*, and in his reshaping of *The Scarlet Letter*'s plot into *As I Lay Dying. Absalom, Absalom!* marks the summit of such playful poses for Faulkner. After letting his readers learn that Henry killed Bon over some other matter than the octoroon, so that they must laboriously rethink through the whole story, Faulkner remarks with studied casualness that

> Bon *may* have, *probably* did, take Henry to call on the octoroon mistress and the child, as Mr Compson said. . . . *Perhaps* Quentin himself had not been listening when Mr Compson related it that evening at home; *perhaps* at that moment on the gallery in the hot September twilight Quentin took that in stride without even hearing it just as Shreve would have, since both he and Shreve believed—and were *probably* right in this too—that the octoroon and the child would have been to Henry only something else about Bon. (p. 336, emphasis added)

But in a fiction there is not true probability. There are only the words on the page that record what people conventionally take as certain, that is, the more than probable fact of someone in the guise of author pretending, in this case, to a historian's uncertainty.

But Faulkner is more coy even than that, for he also refers to the internal story of Bon and his mother, voiced by Quentin and Shreve from at most no more than a shred of evidence, not as probably true but instead as "probably true enough" (p. 335, twice), and says that although they get their facts wrong "there might be paradox and inconsistency but nothing fault nor false" (p. 316). That implies, as many readers have noted, that Faulkner strays from the familiar notion of facts as binary, as simply true or false, and discriminates among kinds of truth, so that Shreve and Quentin may get facts wrong but gain a higher truth by getting feelings (their subject here is explicitly love) right.[9]

Such playings with probabilities are a familiar matter to readers and critics of Faulkner and other writers in the Hawthornian mode, but something else might be happening when such matters extend beyond the novel proper and into an appendix, with its implicit claim to exterior and final authority. Perhaps for the fictional author of a history, things are thrown open when the narrator claims less than complete knowledge; but that is only a pose for that author's creator, the historical author of a fiction. Something special then happens when the ostensibly historical Faulkner steps out in his own voice to proclaim the facts of his fiction, and five times claims that those facts are unknown, and a dozen times puts them in ways that contradict the seeming authority of the fictional narrative.

Readers and critics can respond to such a curious and amusing anomaly as Brooks does with the common sense that labels discrepancies as mistakes and takes no note of the fictional pose of historicity except where it appears in the text proper. But that ostensibly simple sense causes a new set of problems. For the notion that Faulkner makes such mistakes suggests something curious, namely, that when his text assumes more authority he cares about it less, and so ends up giving it less authority, which suggests a disinterest or even disbelief in authority in the first place. In that case the position that this is all common-sensically only simple error cannot sustain a credible model or idea of such simplicity. For the proliferation of casual error in the domain of greater authority reveals the book's disinterest in the idea of facticity that lets readers identify error in the first place.

Indeed, people who see the discrepancies as simple mistakes might then wonder how they assimilate error, how they can relegate the appended material to some inferior status because of error when on the other hand they grant it superior status at other points where its information seems fuller or more plausible. Brooks implicitly does just that, with the common-sense presumption that to see the authority of a single text as variable is no more problematic than to see the authority of a character, such as Miss Rosa, as variable, because she knows some things and not others. That would thus suggest that the peculiarities of the chronology and genealogy make simply another in the long series of competing explanations for the skeleton of facts the novel keeps trying to explain. But the Faulkner who writes the chronology and genealogy at least pretends to some status superior to the inevitably fallible status of any character, pretends to that status—and fails to or at least does not reach it, which might make readers wonder if such status, such authority, is itself a fiction.

Faulkner thus refuses authority and suspends his readers in fictionality. And yet that fictionality he suspends them in, in which he can say that the fate of Wash Jones' daughter or of Jim Bond remains unknown—thus implying that such knowledge theoretically *is* known to someone other than the author—that fictionality includes a pretense to historicity, but only a pretense, so that even its historicity is fictional. Though readers might expect the chronology and genealogy to break the novel out of that circle, instead they only enlarge it, and seal it the more.

Notes

1. William Faulkner, *Absalom, Absalom!* (New York: Random House, 1936), p. 18. Subsequent references to this edition will appear in text.
2. This, of course, is the main issue and the backbone of the novel's many conflicting

explanations. For a detailed consideration of those conflicts, large and small, which does not overlap with the present discussion, see Floyd C. Watkins, "What Happens in *Absalom, Absalom!?" MFS*, 13 (1967), 79–87.

3. Cleanth Brooks, *William Faulkner: The Yoknapatawpha Country* (New Haven: Yale University Press, 1963), pp. 424–26, notes about half the discrepancies I will list, and his discussion prompted my own observation and speculation. He does not call attention to some of the other categories of peculiar material that I will mention, nor does he see any issue of problematic narrative authority. When Faulkner's chronology differs with a character who has little cause to know, then he attributes a mistake to the character. When Faulkner's chronology differs with a character who has credible cause to know, then he attributes a mistake to Faulkner in the chronology. Brooks' concern is simply to correct what he sees— with considerable common sense—as unproblematic slips.

4. Faulkner did not write the chronology and genealogy until after completing the typescript. Joseph Blotner, *Faulkner: A Biography* (New York: Random House, 1974), II, 937.

5. Malcolm Cowley, *The Faulkner-Cowley File: Letters and Memories, 1944–1962* (New York: Viking, 1966), pp. 36–47, 55–58. Once (p. 90) he explained the discrepancies to Cowley by saying that he knew better at the second writing, an explanation he turned to again to defend discrepancies in the *Snopes* trilogy. See his preface to *The Mansion* (New York: Random House, 1959). He shows a little, but only a little, more concern for discrepancies in his correspondence about *The Mansion* with his editor. See *Selected Letters of William Faulkner*, ed. Joseph Blotner (New York: Random House, 1977), pp. 422–32.

6. Everything listed in the chronology as occurring in 1910, including Quentin's September visit with Rosa, occurs in the main text (I deliberately—if perhaps fastidiously— refrain from saying "really" or as Brooks puts it "properly" occurs) in 1909, and the same holds in the genealogy for Henry's and Clytie's deaths and Jim Bond's disappearance. Brooks notes all these discrepancies. Gerald Langford, *Faulkner's Revision of "Absalom, Absalom!": A Collation of the Manuscript and the Published Book* (Austin: University of Texas Press, 1971), p. 11, notes that the manuscript (as opposed to the final text) also lists Quentin's visit with Miss Rosa as in September 1910, though in *The Sound and the Fury* Quentin kills himself in June 1910. For other discrepancies between the manuscript and the chronology and genealogy, see Langford, pp. 32–33, 38.

7. See Brooks, pp. 425–26.

8. That biography, of course, will embody its own fictions, but that does not affect the point that Faulkner's capacity to have a biography written about him distinguishes him, as an historical personage, from the fictional, narrative voice he uses in his novels and stories. Faulkner insisted to Cowley that the appendix to *The Sound and the Fury* was not written in his own voice but rather in the voice of an unnamed resident of Jefferson (like the narrator of, say, "A Rose for Emily") with a particular kind of fallible perspective. See Cowley, pp. 44–45, 57–58.

9. Faulkner endorsed the notion of *Absalom*'s commitment to multiple perceptions of truth in one of his talks at the University of Virginia. See *Faulkner in the University*, ed. Frederick L. Gwynn and Joseph L. Blotner (Charlottesville: University of Virginia Press, 1959), pp. 273–74. Similarly, when writing his editor about whether they should change discrepancies between *The Mansion* and the earlier Snopes novels, *The Hamlet* and *The Town*, he insisted that the "essential truth of these people and their doings, is the thing; the facts are not too important," and "since I believe that fact had nothing to do with truth, I wouldn't even bother to change [THE] HAMLET"; *Selected Letters of William Faulkner*, pp. 422, 430.

[The Biblical Background of *Absalom, Absalom!*]

Maxine Rose*

The title of William Faulkner's novel *Absalom, Absalom!* echoes King David's poignant lament that contains perhaps the saddest words in the Old Testament and provides the first clue to the reader that the Bible is to be a shaping influence in this novel which Faulkner once said was "the best novel yet written by an American. . . ."[1] A number of Faulkner scholars and critics have written briefly and generally of the significance of the ironic title and of some of the specific parallels between *Absalom, Absalom!* and the Bible, particularly the major David analogues.[2] However, there is more to be examined than just the David story called attention to in the title, for in a sense the whole Bible is relevant to an understanding of the work's design. Because the biblical allusions are so subtly and unobtrusively woven into a story which bristles with classical, Elizabethan, and modern allusions, a rather close analysis of the complex and many-layered biblical references is necessary in order to discover how the architectonics of the Bible provide a significant new clue to the puzzling design of *Absalom, Absalom!*

Not only does Faulkner make occasional use of biblical parallels in *Absalom, Absalom!*, but there is in this novel an overarching of structure that coincides with that of the Bible. Diction, rhythm, and syntax combine with theme, character, and image parallels to undergird the complex biblical framework. The modes of narration complete the epochal progression from Genesis to Revelation. Though these epochs overlap and the divisions are never sharply defined, the following biblical periods are echoed in *Absalom, Absalom!*: the antediluvian age, the period of the Old Law, the time of the Judges, the rise of the monarchy, the era of wisdom literature, the time of the prophets, the advent of the New Law, and the final Apocalypse.

The two major antagonists of the Bible, God-Jesus and Satan-demon-dragon, are powerful cosmic parallels for Sutpen and Bon and provide possibilities for divine and human qualities to exist in paradoxical God-Satan

---

*Reprinted with permission from *Studies in American Fiction* 8, no. 2 (Autumn 1980): 219–28. Original title: "From Genesis to Revelation: The Grand Design of William Faulkner's *Absalom, Absalom!*" © 1980 by Northeastern University.

combinations. The multiple parallels allow Faulkner the freedom he needs and give the characters and action the heroic proportions they demand. The biblical patterns reflected in *Absalom, Absalom!* contain the history of Israel from before the creation through the end of the created world. Not only do these patterns include the whole of human history, but the parallels with God-Satan extend the perspective to heaven and hell and the time to eternity.

In chapter one of *Absalom, Absalom!* Thomas Sutpen appears as a god-like character creating Sutpen's Hundred out of the soundless nothing, as God created the world in Genesis 1. Even the order of the creation is preserved in chapters one and two, the days of Genesis corresponding to years in *Absalom, Absalom!* Sutpen appears in Jefferson on a Sunday, the first day of the week; he emerges "bat-like" from primeval darkness and delimits the chaotic waters, represented by images of slimy mud, swamps, and alligators. Next, he builds gardens and plants cotton. Then the animals appear as the animals are created after the plants in the Genesis One account. Sutpen creates his estate in five years, then brings forth a son in the sixth year as God brought forth Adam on the sixth day; and Sutpen creates Clytie "in his own image" as God created Adam in his own image (Genesis 1:27).[3]

In many of the parallels with Genesis, Sutpen is also Adam as well as God and is therefore a god-man. Sutpen names all of his creation (p. 62), as Adam names all the living creatures in Genesis 2 (Genesis 2: 19–20). Sutpen and his assistants are stark naked (p. 37), as Adam was naked in the garden (Genesis 2: 19–20). When Quentin and Shreve recreate this incident, all of Shreve's body that is visible is naked like the naked earth-man Adam in the Garden of Eden, and the nakedness motif ties together the 1833 Sutpen experience with the 1909 recreation of that experience. Next, Faulkner equates Thomas Sutpen with the biblical David, even before the full implication of the Absalom theme becomes apparent. Sutpen, like David, is a hill lad of humble origin. Both boys are sent on important errands by their fathers when they are between the ages of twelve and fourteen. Both have red hair.

This early experience is crucial for David, for it is in the Vale of Elah that he encounters the taunts of the Philistine giant, accepts his challenge, kills Goliath, and, subsequent to his triumph, is anointed King of Israel. Like David, Sutpen encounters taunts (his being at the plantation door in Tidewater Virginia), is traumatically spurred on to ambitious action, subdues his own Goliath(s) in single combat, and is self-anointed to a "grand design" that establishes him as a kind of monarch.

Immediately after Sutpen is rudely ordered to the rear of the plantation home, he broods over this experience, which is presented in battle imagery that echoes the shouts, the glare of the shield, the plain setting, and the hand-to-hand combat of the David-Goliath encounter: "all of a sudden . . . it was something *shouting* . . . a bright *glare* . . . just a *limitless flat plain*. . . . He thought 'If you were fixing to *combat* them . . . you got to have land

and niggers and a fine house' " (pp. 237–38). To achieve his aim, Sutpen goes to Haiti where he defends a plantation owner and his family against nineteenth-century Goliath (slave insurrectionists) in a manner almost as mystical as David's slingshot slaying of Goliath. Significantly, Sutpen uses no weapons of war: "he put the musket down and went out and subdued them" (p. 254), as David had "put off" Saul's armor and conquered the giant with only his intelligence, cunning, and a simple slingshot. Instead of slaying his Goliaths, however, Sutpen utilizes and exploits their energies after he conquers them.

One of the real strokes of Faulkner's genius is seen in the narration of this Goliath-like encounter in Haiti. As Sutpen and General Compson sit on a log, Sutpen sees the "picture of the wild niggers and torches in front of them [their shadows]" (p. 246), and this picture "called to his mind" his Goliath encounter in Haiti, which he then relates. This whole conversation is initiated by Sutpen's discussion of the door experience and subsequent "grand design" formulation; in Sutpen's mind the Negro butler at the door, the wild "niggers' " shadows, and the "nigger" experience in Haiti are fused.

Quentin and Shreve recreate the scene in the following manner: "Then it was dark and niggers began to light pine knots. . . . The mud they wore in the swamp . . . dried hard and shiny, *glinting like glass or china* [like Goliath's shield and armor] and the shadows they cast taller than they are [they are giants]" (pp. 245–46; italics added). In the same passage, lying buried in the text are allusions to David's rejection of Saul's clothes and armor as he faced Goliath and also to the 1,000–10,000 motif used by the Israelite women who chanted antiphonally because of David's victory over the giant: "Saul hath slain his *thousands*, and David his *ten thousands*" (I Sam. 18:6–7, italics added). The 1,000–10,000 motif, used at other times during the novel, "Marrying Ellen or marrying ten-thousands Ellens" (p. 16), is repeated as Sutpen continues his story of his David-like conquest on this little island ravished by violence. Just as David's encounter with Goliath was the first real test of this courage and shrewdness, Sutpen's Haitian experience is the first real test of his courage and shrewdness, occurring as it did in a "theater for violence and injustice and bloodshed" (p. 250). The similarities between the two encounters are further underscored by the setting: both occur on a plain.

The David parallels are further enhanced in this section by the fact that the French architect whom Sutpen and Compson are chasing hides in caves, as David, the fugitive, was forced to do, and in the very subtle suggestion of the slingshot motif in the French architect's trick to elude Sutpen's posse— his use of suspenders and a sapling pole as a kind of weapon (a slingshot). Even the incident in which David cuts off a piece of Saul's robe when Saul enters the cave in which David is hiding is reflected in Sutpen's comment to Wash that he was "unable to penetrate far enough behind the Yankee lines to cut a piece of that coat tail as I promised you" (pp. 277–78). But

parallel here is ironic because it calls forth David's mercy
ntrast to Sutpen's lack of mercy throughout *Absalom, Absa-*
rd for conquering the enemy, both David and Sutpen are
David is given Saul's daughter, Michal, and Sutpen is given
a owner's daughter, Eulalia. The Michal parallel demonstrates
cal example of Faulkner's purely whimsical biblical allusions to
tory. The description of the effigy on the Haitian planter's pillow
ly recalls for the reader the effigy Michal used as a ruse to convince
ls that David was sick and to thus allow him to escape. Whereas
effigy is composed of household gods covered with goat's hair, the
a effigy is composed of "a pig's bone with a little rotten flesh still
ng to it, a few chicken feathers, a stained dirty rag with a few pebbles
up in it" (p. 252).

In some ways the French architect and the twenty wild slaves parallel
biblical Abner and his twenty lieutenants who came to Hebron to capitu-
te to David. Also similar are Sutpen's building of Sutpen's Hundred and
David's building of his house in Jerusalem after years of wandering and
struggling to establish his kingdom. After living for such a long time in
caves and tents, David regards his palace as a symbol of the permanence of
his dynasty. On a larger scale, however, Sutpen's Hundred is modeled after
the Temple in Jerusalem, which David designed and collected the materials
for, but which his son Solomon built. The measurements correspond, for
the Temple is one hundred cubits from gate to gate (Ezek. 40:19; 42:8).
And there is a striking parallel between the tablets of the Law (Deut. 10:2)
housed in the Temple and Sutpen's tombstones: both are tokens of a covenant.
Whereas Israel's tables of stone represent a covenant God made with Israel
(theocentric in nature), Sutpen's tables of stone represent a covenant Sutpen
made with himself (egocentric in nature). Just as the Ark of the Covenant
containing the Ten Commandments took on extra meaning in "their journeys
out of the wilderness of Sinai" (Num. 10:12) and in the various other places
the children of Israel, including David, dragged them, so Sutpen's marble
slabs took on extra meaning because of their difficult and dangerous journey
all the way from Italy to Jefferson, Mississippi. In the middle of the Civil
War, Sutpen "ordered [the stones] . . . from Italy, the best, the finest to
be had [and] . . . managed to get them past a [blockaded] seacoast. . . .
Then "that . . . inert carven rock . . . the next year [accompanied] . . .
the regiment . . . into Pennsylvania . . . [to] Gettysburg, moving behind
the regiment in a wagon . . . through swamp and plain and mountain pass
. . ." to Jefferson where Sutpen puts "one . . . over his wife's grave and
sets the other upright in the hall of the house . . ." (p. 190). Like the house
he built (his temple) and the sons he wanted to bear (his dynasty), though
more permanent because they are stone, the marble slabs are symbols of
Sutpen's overwhelming desire for perpetuity. They also betoken, in a tangible
way, the pledge (the covenant) of a man who said goodbye to that rejected

child back in Tidewater, Virginia. The stones convey a message: "This is me: Thomas Sutpen. I did those things I decided to do."

Significantly, the stones are cracked when Quentin sees them in the cemetery in 1909, as the biblical stones were cracked when Moses "cast [them] . . . out of his hands, and brake them" (Exod. 32:19). The crack symbolizes in both cases the breaking of a covenant. In addition to housing the mystical tables of stone signifying a covenant, Sutpen's Hundred embodies further temple motifs in the annual pilgrimages Miss Rosa and her father make there and in the fact that Charles Etienne de Saint Valery Bon comes to Sutpen's Hundred in December of 1871 at the age of twelve, as Christ came to the Temple, his father's house, at the age of twelve (Luke 2:49).

Another biblical association, the House of Saul-House of David bond, is reflected in the Sutpen-Ellen relationship, for in many ways Saul is a prototype for Coldfield. Saul's two daughters are promised to David, as Coldfield's two daughters are betrothed to Sutpen. Saul is intensely emotional and is characterized by religious paroxysms (I Sam. 10:5–6), as is Coldfield. Both men are mad. Both subject themselves to voluntary fasts. In the end, Saul commits suicide, as does Coldfield. Further, Coldfield's daughter, Miss Rosa, embodies several parallels to Saul's daughter Michal: she is the younger daughter; she loves and despises Sutpen; she is maltreated and barren. Obviously the most important David-Sutpen analogy is that incest—only threatened in Sutpen's case—is part of the evil which brings trouble on the second and third generation. In Sutpen's family, incest and miscegenation are involved. On most counts, Absalom and Henry, Amnon and Charles, and Tamar and Judith may be equated, although Faulkner's bulging parallels also allow Bon and Absalom and Henry and Amnon to be equated and the double reverberations serve to multiply the intended meanings.

Through David's willingness to accept responsibility for the tragedy in his household and to learn from it, David achieves a tragic height. His repentance makes him fit to be indirectly the Messiah's forebear. Thomas Sutpen makes no such lament; indeed his nearest approach to lamentation is his weak searching for the reason his design fails. Sutpen's sins are visited upon his successors, and ironically only Jim Bond, the heir unapparent, is left to represent the third generation. But even here the biblical pattern obtains, for the promise was for a never-ending line to the tribe of Judah, and Shreve says on the final page of the novel that the "Jim Bonds are going to conquer the western hemisphere" (p. 378).

The Davidic parallels do not end with the introduction of the Absalom theme. There is a striking parallel between the last days of David and the last days of Sutpen which is highly significant in that it shows that the Davidic parallels pervade the entire span of Sutpen's life—from his early boyhood (the errand motif) until his last years. In the final days of both David and Sutpen a young girl is exploited to serve the needs of an old man whose powers are diminishing. In neither case does the girl become the old man's wife. In the biblical story, Abishag, a young virgin, is taken into David's bed to transmit her bodily warmth to an old man bothered by poor circulation of blood. Sutpen in his old age likewise takes a young girl into his bed, but for a different reason. Since Sutpen is past sixty, he realizes that he probably has "but one more son in his loins" (p. 279). And since his only legitimate male heir, Henry, is in exile, he seduces the poor ignorant fifteen-year-old grand-daughter of Wash Jones in a last desperate attempt to sire a son who will perpetuate his dynasty. Unfortunately, the baby is a girl and the attempt fails.

The line continues through Sutpen's first born son, Charles Bon, who, as the "son of David" in the Bible, is a Christ figure and introduces a law of love.[4] Bon's obvious significance as a Christ figure comes from the following associations: he is thirty-three years old when he is murdered; his death is linked with a tree or post; while his corpse lies upstairs, Miss Rosa speaks of an "arras-veil . . . [hanging] docile . . . to the . . . rending gash" (pp. 142–43); three women—Miss Rosa, Judith, Clytie—bury Bon as three women are specifically mentioned in the gospel accounts of the burial and resurrection of Jesus.

In the absence of the ritual enactment of recognition of the son by the father, the Bon experience brings together various strands of the novel. In his first role as "the son of David," Bon is alternately Absalom and Amnon, introducing the incest-miscegenation theme and giving rise to the ironic lament which gives the novel its title. In his second role as "the son of David," he is Christ, the Savior, the expositor of love and the victim of sacrifice. In the combined roles he is god-man, as Sutpen, his father, is god-man. The Christ role allows Bon to embody the godlike qualities Faulkner so cherished: pity, compassion, love, and sacrifice. The Absalom and Amnon role allows him to retain his mortal and human qualities. But the parallels involving the "my son" or recognition formula are ironic because both David and Jehovah recognize their sons openly and proudly. David weeps and cries "O my son Absalom! my son, my son Absalom," and Jehovah gives Christ, his son, a sign—a manifestation of his approval and recognition of him as his son twice—once at his baptism and once at the transfiguration. It is this experience of recognition by his father that Bon seeks throughout Absalom, Absalom! He does not expect a verbal statement—a sign, a nod, even a certain look in the eye would have satisfied him. In this absence of recognition of Bon by his father (Sutpen-David-Jehovah) Faulkner fuses the ironic David-Jehovah referents, heightens and universalizes the parallels, and ties together various parts of the novel which seem on first reading structurally unjustified.

The modes of narration in Absalom, Absalom! complete the epochal progression from Genesis to Revelation, particularly through tone and temper, and thereby reinforce the structural unity of the novel. Peter Swiggart has pointed out that "Miss Rosa's frequent references to a divine curse upon Sutpen and upon the South provide a leitmotiv that associates her narration with Old Testament concerns."⁵ Like the Old Testament prophets, Miss Rosa brings to her narration such extraordinary personal qualities as poetic power, ecstasy, and a kind of prophetic inspiration. Her fanciful imagination and burning passion lift her out of the world of reality and into a world of dreams (pp. 141, 147, 180). She creates this world, as the Old Testament prophets did, not according to logic or reason, but through a rushing flow of words, often obscure in meaning, but always powerful and evocative. Like Jeremiah, she echoes a sense of despair, of loss, of defeat. She regards the fall of Sutpen the demon and of the South as results of a curse, as God's punishment for evil doing. Though the parallels for Miss Rosa's language and allusion are most numerous in Genesis, Jeremiah and the Song of Solomon, she also echoes in her narration many of the New Testament books.

Mr. Compson's narrative stance is very different from Miss Rosa's. There is no note of high sacrifice and surrender in the sections he narrates. And there are no confessions. Also absent are the shrill, hysterical, illogical dream-like utterances. Instead, Mr. Compson tries to be rational, detached, uninvolved personally. Sometimes there is a mask (p. 62), always a lesson; therefore, his trademark is ironic didacticism. His attitude toward the Sutpen legend bears a striking resemblance to the attitude of the preacher in Ecclesiastes, whose outlook is likewise pessimistic, questioning, and somewhat agnostic. Mr. Compson is a fatalist, believing that all events are predetermined by fate and unalterable by man (p. 68). To him, Sutpen is merely a victim of fate. Similarly, the writer of Ecclesiastes believes that the order and time of all events are predetermined by God and are incomprehensible to man. God is a blind fate. Man's suffering is not caused by his actions. There is no justice, merely chance. And, since "time and chance happeneth to them all" (Ecclesiastes 9:11), since man cannot alter his destiny, a hedonistic approach to life is best. Live as joyfully as possible, the preacher in Ecclesiastes suggests, as does the Epicurean Mr. Compson.

Although General Compson is only an indirect narrator, he reflects in his role the Old Testament Judges—Samuel, in particular, who supposedly wrote the first book of Samuel, Judges, and Ruth. General Compson is not blind to Sutpen's faults, and he paints as realistic and lifelike a portrait of Sutpen as Samuel did for David.

In the final four chapters of the novel, Quentin and Shreve, aided by the voice of an omniscient author here and there, attempt to go back to the origin of things, back to Sutpen's life before he came to Mississippi, back further than Miss Rosa or Mr. Compson have been able to penetrate. In this respect, their narrative technique follows that of the Bible, for in Revelation, the last book of the Bible, the writer goes back beyond the creation, back to the fall of the devil from heaven, and eventually back to the war between Michael and Satan. It becomes increasingly clearer as the novel progresses that Quentin corresponds in numerous ways to St. John on Patmos, the author of the book of Revelation. St. John is told "What thou seest, write in a book" and he "turned to see the voice" (Rev. 1:11–12). Quentin, also, is told that he can "write this" (p. 10), and he hears a "voice" (pp. 7–8). The apocalyptic book of Revelation presents the end of an era ruled by Satan (or the "demon") and the beginning of another era ruled by Christ. So in *Absalom, Absalom!* the novel begins near the end and presents the fall of a demon (Sutpen) and the rise of a new generation sired by Bon, a Christ figure.

Like St. John on Patmos, the seer Quentin receives a revelation. With the aid of Shreve, who functions as a priest and reflector, Quentin is finally able to explain Sutpen's fall. In addition to their moral roles, it is evident, then, that the narrators function aesthetically, also, as purveyors of the Sutpen myth by reflecting the various spokesmen of the Bible—prophets, judges, priests, wise men, apostles. Their rhetoric, therefore, and their temper complete the synthesis of biblical analogues initiated in theme and character. Thus, the architectonic structure of the Bible provides a clue to the major patterns in *Absalom, Absalom!* The two major antagonists of the Bible, God-Jesus and Satan-demon-dragon, offer powerful cosmic parallels for Sutpen and Bon. The major two-part division of the Bible—the Old Testament and the New Testament—is reflected in the creeds of Sutpen and Bon, who represent respectively the Old Law, a rigid and inflexible code, and the New Law, based on love and grace, which abolishes all caste, color, social distinctions (no Jew or Gentile, no bond or free). The New Testament Apocalypse is ironically inverted in the final chapter of *Absalom, Absalom!*, where Quentin, like St. John, finds new ways of looking at time and space. Where St. John looks two ways, backward to the war in heaven and the fall of the devil and forward to a new Jerusalem of peace and joy, Quentin looks to a past filled with violence and suffering and forward to a "nevermore of peace" in a future filled with moronic Jim Bonds.

The Bible, which provides the skeletal framework for *Absalom, Absalom!*, spans the history of Israel from the time before the creation through the end of the created world. Not only does it include the whole of human history, but its scope extends to Heaven and Hell and its time to eternity. To see the significant influence of the architectonics of the Bible on the design of *Absalom, Absalom!* is to perceive the mythic significance, structural integrity, timelessness, and universality of the greatest of Faulkner's novels. Thus, *Absalom, Absalom!* becomes Faulkner's own Bible, reshaped and recreated from Genesis to Revelation.

Notes

1. Joseph Blotner, *Faulkner: A Biography* (New York: Random House, 1974), p. 927.
2. See Lawrance Thompson, *William Faulkner: An Introduction and Interpretation*, 2nd ed. (New York: Barnes and Noble, 1964), pp. 64–65; Lennart Björk, "Ancient Myths and

the Moral Framework of Faulkner's *Absalom, Absalom!*," *AL*, 35 (1963), 196–204; Irving Malin, *William Faulkner: An Interpretation* (Stanford: Stanford Univ. Press, 1957), p. 76. One study broadens the scope of the biblical framework of *Absalom, Absalom!* by exploring the various ways in which Sutpen's failure to establish a dynasty parallels the futile attempts of Old Testament rulers to establish permanent dynasties. See Ralph Behrens, "Collapse of Dynasty: The Thematic Center of *Absalom, Absalom!*" *PMLA*, 89 (1974), 24–33. In another study, Jessie Alma Coffee, "Faulkner's Un-Christlike Christians: Biblical Allusions in the Novels," Diss. Nevada 1971, pp. 91–213, catalogs twenty-five specific biblical allusions in *Absalom, Absalom!* as a part of a larger study showing five basic thematic patterns in Faulkner's novels: patriarchs, sons and siblings, patrimony, sacrifice, and salvation. However, no attempt has heretofore been made to show how the biblical parallels in the novel have been expanded to such a degree as to become the skeleton on which the whole novel is built in much the same way that the *Odyssey* functions in Joyce's *Ulysses*.

3. William Faulkner, *Absalom, Absalom!* (New York: Modern Library, 1964), p. 136. All subsequent references in parentheses will be to this facsimile of the first edition (1936).

4. The Christ figure as a compelling metaphor for suffering, sacrifice, and hope has been a favorite literary tool for centuries. Among the most significant characters who have been identified and discussed by twentieth-century critics as Christ figures are Don Quixote, Prince Myshkin, Billy Budd, Jim Conklin, and Joe Christmas.

5. Peter Swiggart, *The Art of Faulkner's Novels* (Austin: Univ. of Texas Press, 1962), p. 154.

What We Know about Thomas Sutpen and His Children

Cleanth Brooks*

All the information the reader has comes through Quentin directly or through Quentin's conversations with his father, Mr. Compson, and with Miss Rosa Coldfield. The information from General Compson comes to Quentin presumably through Mr. Compson, for though the General did not die until Quentin was ten years old, there is no indication in *Absalom, Absalom!* that the General discussed the matter with his grandson, nor is it likely that he would have done so.

Fact or Event	*Ultimate Authority*	*Page*
Sutpen's life in Jefferson from 1833 until 1860.	Gen. Compson and Miss Rosa	p. 8 and passim
Sutpen in 1834 tells Gen. Compson about his early life; stops with his engagement; then waits 30 years to go on with it.	Gen. Compson	pp. 219–58
Bon's friendship with Henry and Judith.	Gen. Compson and Miss Rosa	p. 67 and passim
Charles Bon visits Henry (Christmas, 1859, and summer, 1860).	Gen. Compson	p. 70
Sutpen visits New Orleans summer (or late spring), 1860.	Gen. Compson	p. 70
Henry brings Bon home (Christmas, 1860), quarrels with his father, and leaves home with Bon.	The Negro servants at Sutpen's Hundred (as reported by Gen. Compson).	pp. 78–79
Charles Bon and Henry enlist. Bon is soon made a lieutenant.	Gen. Compson	pp. 122–24
Henry and his father meet and talk in Carolina, 1865.	Gen. Compson	p. 276

*Reprinted with permission from *William Faulkner: The Yoknapatawpha Country* (New Haven: Yale University Press, 1963), 429–36. © by Yale University Press. Reprinted by permission of the author.

Bon's letter to Judith in 1865, telling her that he is coming back to marry her.	The letter was preserved by Gen. Compson	pp. 129–32
Judith makes her wedding gown.	Gen. Compson	p. 132
Judith finds on Bon's dead body the picture of the octoroon woman and her child.	Gen. Compson, who presumably learned this from Judith (Miss Rosa probably went to her grave believing that the picture was of Judith).	pp. 90, 95 p. 142
Sutpen returns (autumn, 1864) with the gravestones and tells Gen. Compson about his first marriage and his "design."	Gen. Compson	pp. 188, 270
Sutpen's return from the war (Jan. 1866) and his subsequent life at Sutpen's Hundred.	Miss Rosa and Gen. Compson	p. 158 and passim
Sutpen refuses to join the Ku Klux Klan.	Miss Rosa	p. 161
Sutpen makes his proposal to Miss Rosa.	Miss Rosa	pp. 164–68
Sutpen sets up his little store.	Gen. Compson	p. 180 and passim
Gen. Compson overhears Sutpen and Wash talking about Milly.	Gen. Compson	pp. 283–84
Wash kills Sutpen.	The Negro midwife	pp. 185, 285–88
Wash kills his daughter and is killed.	Gen. Compson	pp. 291–92
Judith buries her father.	Gen. Compson	pp. 185–86
Bon's octoroon mistress visits his grave (summer, 1870).	Gen. Compson	pp. 192–95
Etienne Bon is brought to Sutpen's Hundred (Dec. 1871).	Gen. Compson	p. 195
The piece of mirror is found under Etienne Bon's bed.	Gen. Compson (from information presumably communicated by Judith).	p. 199
Etienne Bon's indictment.	Gen. Compson	p. 203
Etienne Bon marries.	Gen. Compson	p. 205
Judith nurses Etienne Bon.	Gen. Compson	p. 210
Judith and Etienne die (1884).	Gen. Compson	p. 210
Henry returns to Sutpen's Hundred (1905).	Quentin	p. 373

Quentin learned something on his visit to Sutpen's Hundred (Sept. 1909) which altered his notion of the Sutpen story.	Quentin	p. 373
Clytie sets fire to Sutpen's Hundred; she and Henry die (Dec. 1909).	Mr. Compson	pp. 374–76

What Miss Rosa and General Compson Did Not Know

Miss Rosa did not know that the picture that Judith found on Bon's body was that of his octoroon mistress.	p. 142
Gen Compson did not know that Bon was Henry's part-Negro half brother.	p. 274
Neither did Miss Rosa know this, unless she learned it at the same time that Quentin did, in Sept. 1909.	p. 18

The More Important Conjectures Made about Thomas Sutpen and His Family

Conjecture	Made by	Page
Sutpen named all his children including Charles Bon.	Gen. Compson	p. 61
	Mr. Compson	pp. 265–66
Miss Rosa hated her father.	Mr. Compson	p. 83
During the war Judith knew where Henry and Bon were.	Mr. Compson	p. 87
Bon must have learned of Sutpen's visit to New Orleans when he himself returned to New Orleans in the summer of 1860.	Mr. Compson	p. 92
Sutpen told Henry of Bon's "marriage" to the octoroon woman.	Mr. Compson	p. 90
Bon brought Henry to see the octoroon woman in New Orleans.	Mr. Compson	pp. 108–18
Henry's objection to the marriage of Bon and Judith was the fact that Bon had gone through	Mr. Compson	pp. 118–19

the ceremony with the octoroon woman.

Henry and Bon hoped that the war would settle the dispute by removing one of them.	Mr. Compson	p. 120
Judith did not ask her father what his objection was to Bon.	Mr. Compson	p. 120
Henry and Bon returned to Oxford only long enough to enroll in the company being formed at the university.	Mr. Compson	p. 122
Bon was wounded at Shiloh and carried back to safety by Henry.	Mr. Compson (Or does Mr. Compson *know* this? Shreve questions it on p. 344.)	p. 124
Sutpen's first wife was in New Orleans and Sutpen journeyed there in 1860 to buy her off.	Mr. Compson conjectures this after Quentin had seen Henry. The "Genealogy" printed at the back of the Modern Library edition states that "Eulalia Bon died in New Orleans," and thus provides auctorial sanction for this conjecture. Mr. Compson's first conjecture had been that Sutpen went to New Orleans to check on Bon's octoroon mistress.	pp. 268–69
The conversation between Judith and her father when he returned in 1864.	Quentin	p. 271
At Christmas Sutpen told Henry that Bon was his brother and that Bon knew this; but Bon did not know it.	Shreve (On p. 303 it is said that Shreve was speaking though "it might have been either of them and was in a sense both." But it is clearly Shreve who is speaking from p. 303 to p. 333, from p. 336 to p. 345, from p. 350 to p. 351, and from p. 358 to p. 359. Moreover, save for a dozen or so words, nothing in section 7 is *specifically* assigned to Quentin.)	pp. 293–96
There was a lawyer in New Orleans counseling Sutpen's first wife.	Shreve	p. 304

Perhaps Bon's mother discovered that he had an octoroon mistress and child.	Shreve	p. 307
Bon's mother had made the lawyer promise not to tell Bon who his father was.	Shreve	p. 309
The lawyer discovered where Sutpen lived and that Henry attended the University of Mississippi.	Shreve	pp. 309–10
The lawyer wrote to Henry; Henry showed the letter to Bon; and Bon suspected that Henry might be his brother.	Shreve	p. 313
Bon accepted Henry's invitation to visit him, thinking that he might see his father.	Shreve	p. 319
Bon did not know "whatever it was in mother's [blood that Sutpen] could not brook."	Shreve	p. 321
Bon wanted only a hint of recognition from his father; he would not even demand to know "what it was my mother did that justified his action toward her and me." (Shreve evidently assumes at this point that Bon knew nothing of his possession of Negro blood.)	Shreve	p. 327
Bon believed that Sutpen had gone to New Orleans to make sure that Bon was truly his son.	Shreve	p. 329
Bon having returned to New Orleans did not learn whether Sutpen had seen his mother, but continued to believe that he had.	Shreve	p. 331
Sutpen told Henry on the second Christmas visit that Bon was his brother.	Shreve	p. 334
Henry and Bon visited Bon's mother and heard her say "So [Judith] has fallen in love with [Charles]," and Henry "knows" that Bon is indeed his brother.	Shreve ("that drawing room of baroque and fusty magnificence which Shreve had invented and which was probably true enough" and "this slight dowdy woman . . . whom	pp. 335–36

	Shreve and Quentin had likewise invented and which was [a construction] likewise probably true enough")	
The lawyer congratulates Bon and Bon forces an apology.	Shreve	pp. 338–39
In 1862, when Bon was recovering from his wound, he received his octoroon mistress' picture and an appeal for money: she wrote that the lawyer had fled and that she could not find Bon's mother.	Shreve	p. 339
Henry wrestled with his horror of incest and asked Bon: "must you marry [our sister]?"	Shreve	p. 341
Bon did not know what he meant to do though he pretended he did. Henry knew what he meant to do, but had to say that he did not know.	Shreve	p. 341
Henry allowed Bon to write one letter to Judith.	Shreve	p. 342
It was Henry, not Bon, who was wounded at Shiloh.	Shreve	p. 344
In 1864 Bon asked Henry whether he had his permission to marry Judith, and Henry told him to write to Judith.	Shreve or Quentin?	p. 349
In 1864 Sutpen met Henry and told him that he had seen Charles Bon. (But p. 352 seems to contradict this. Compare also with the conjecture that Bon would have abandoned his courtship of Judith if he had had only a nod of recognition from his father, p. 327.)	Shreve or Quentin?	p. 353
Sutpen also told Henry that Bon's mother was part Negro.	Shreve or Quentin?	pp. 354–55
Bon said to Henry: "So it's the miscegenation, not the incest, which you can't bear." Does this conjecture imply that Henry proceeded to tell Bon what his	Shreve or Quentin?	p. 356

father had just told him (pp. 354–55)? (As late as p. 327, Quentin and Shreve take for granted that Bon did not know that he had Negro blood.)

Bon told Henry that mere recognition could have stopped him, but now "I am thinking of myself."	Shreve or Quentin?	p. 357
Bon offered his pistol to Henry, but Henry hurled the pistol away.	Shreve or Quentin?	p. 358
Bon's motive in substituting the picture of his octoroon mistress and child for that of Judith was to say to Judith—if Henry did kill him—"I was no good; do not grieve for me."	Shreve	pp. 358–59

What Quentin Saw "Out There"

HERSHEL PARKER*

CRITICS OF *Absalom, Absalom!* have resolved the question of what Quentin learned at the Sutpen house in September 1909. As Cleanth Brooks says, "if one will look at pages 181 [1986:147–48] and 266–74, [214–20] he will find that Quentin must have learned the secret of Bon's birth on his night visit to Sutpen's Hundred with Miss Rosa, that he did tell his father about it, and that this knowledge altered his father's view of the meaning of the story."[1] However, it is not so clear *how* Quentin gained this knowledge. Brooks thinks that Miss Rosa might possibly have told him on their way home, but that more likely the information came directly from Henry: "Quentin probably had ten minutes to talk with Henry—although their conversation *may* have been much longer. The fragment of it that keeps running through Quentin's head does not pretend to give more than the awesome confrontation. There is no warrant for concluding that it represents all that was said"[2] The timing hardly allows for so long an interview: Miss Rosa and Jim Bond have left the house before Quentin enters Henry's room, but when he leaves the house himself he is soon within earshot of their voices, though it is too dark to go fast. Also, there is reason for thinking that the italicized twelve lines on page 298 are indeed meant to represent the whole of the conversation between Quentin and Henry. The symmetry of the sets of questions and answers is hard to account for unless one takes it as marking Quentin's physical and psychological approach toward the man who is in a state of living death, then his retreat away from him. The formality of the patterning may even imply a choreography in which Quentin physically advances through the first half of the conversation and retreats in the second, repeating the same questions at the same spots where he had first asked them. At the least, the symmetry of the speeches argues for their completeness, for their being a closed unit, not a fragment.

In any case, Quentin knows what he knows even before he sees Henry. In the section after Miss Rosa's encounter with Clytie (p. 296), the manuscript read this way: "He [Quentin] remembered how he heard Miss Cold-

*Reprinted by permission of the publisher from *Mississippi Quarterly* 27, no. 3 (1974): 323–26. © 1974 by Mississippi State University with minor changes and emended notes by the author written especially for this volume and published here for the first time.

field's. feet and saw the light of the torch approaching along the upper hall. . . ." Later Faulkner (perhaps deliberately clarifying how Quentin learned about Bon) inserted another "remembered how" clause in the margin; after tinkering with the construction, Faulkner left it reading "how he thot *It's Jim Bond. It's the heir to the house.*"[3] The past tense is unequivocal: in Faulkner's revised manuscript, Quentin "remembered how" (at the time, before he had seen Henry) he had identified Bond as *"the heir to the house."* In the published text, Quentin "remembered how he thought, 'The scion, the heir, the apparent (though not obvious).' " While the wordplay complicates the statement somewhat, the timing is clear: at this moment, not later, Quentin thought of Bond as the scion—which can hardly mean anything but the scion of Sutpen.[4] Quentin cannot have learned this from Miss Rosa, who does not know it herself (later she ignorantly, not ironically, says to Bond, "You aint any Sutpen!"), and he does not learn it from Clytie (who has not mentioned Bond to Quentin and who may well not know the secret of Bon's birth herself). Since Quentin knows it before he sees Henry, he must have learned it without being told. The answer to the question "Who told Quentin?" is "No one."[5]

Instead, Quentin seems to have learned it by himself, from seeing rather than hearing. What he saw was Bond, and whether or not he realized all the complex implications at once, what he saw must have been Sutpen features on the "slack-mouthed idiot face." Quentin already knew that there was a distinctive Sutpen face. Only that afternoon he had heard Rosa's horrific account of her sister's seeing "two Sutpen faces" (Judith's and Clytie's) in the loft (p. 22), and only that afternoon he had heard Rosa tell of the time she herself mistook Clytie's "Sutpen face" for Henry's "Sutpen face" (p. 109). He even knew what that face looked like, having scrutinized Clytie's face, body, and clothing during an escapade in his childhood (pp. 173–74) and having just seen her again and spoken to her (p. 296). On that earlier occasion he had also seen Bond, but apparently without making any significant deductions; Shreve says that Quentin "hadn't even thought that he must have a name" (p. 174). Presumably if Quentin had noticed a resemblance between Clytie and the boy he had not concerned himself with it—what more natural than that two part-Negroes living together should resemble each other? A child himself, Quentin would hardly have worried about which ancestors, black or white, the pair had in common. Now, with the story filling his mind all afternoon, Quentin is prepared not only to see the Sutpen face on Clytie but in short order to realize the significance of Bond's also having one. Some time between the moment when Quentin looks down the stairs at Clytie and Bond together in the lamp-lit hall and recognizes Bond as the "scion" and the next day when he corrects his father's elaborate, contradictory suppositions (p. 214), Quentin makes all the connections, realizing that to have a Sutpen face Bond must have gotten it through Charles Bon, who therefore must have been Sutpen's son.

Like Brooks's explanation, this one is not wholly satisfying. No contemporary witness cites Bon himself as having, much less transmitting, a Sutpen face. If he had one, the question is why someone at the university or at Sutpen's Hundred had not realized it, especially if Henry was aping Bon's dress. (One answer is that such a recognition would blast the plot apart.) Yet the book turns on the fact of there being a "Sutpen face." The white Sutpen children have it, as Clytie does, though hers is a "Sutpen coffee-colored face" (p. 109); Bon ought to bear it, however disguised, and transmit it. Quentin twice reveals that he thinks Bon had a Sutpen face. On 214, interrupted by Shreve, he repeats his father's recreation of the afternoon when Henry arrived with Charles Bon at the Sutpen house and Thomas Sutpen "saw the face" of Bon and felt his design crash down. Then, recreating Bon's mental processes at the war's end, Quentin imagines Bon putting himself in Thomas Sutpen's way and looking "at the expressionless and rocklike face, at the pale boring eyes in which there was no flicker, nothing, the face in which he saw his own features" (p. 278). Shreve in creating the past out of clues from Quentin's stories (p. 254) envisions Bon as having the Sutpen features. In Shreve's version, Bon looks at Henry and does *not* think this: "*there but for the intervening leaven of that blood which we do not have in common is my skull, my brow, sockets, shape and angle of jaw and chin and some of my thinking behind it, and which he could see in my face in his turn if he but knew to look as I know.*" The reason Bon (according to Shreve) does not think these thoughts is not that he and his half brother do not look alike; rather, Bon would not have been interested in his own similarity to his half-brother but in what he might discover of his father in Henry's face. This is what Shreve thinks Bon really thought: "*there, just behind a little, obscured a little by that alien blood whose admixing was necessary in order that he exist is the face of the man who shaped us both out of that blind chancy darkness which we call the future.*" Although invented, Shreve's version has some value as testimony because it fits with the full revelation. Shreve is silencing him whenever he attempts to interrupt, but Quentin is free to correct Shreve later if in fact Bon's grandson does not resemble him. Shreve's use of "scion" (p. 255) may even be indebted to an earlier use by Quentin himself in telling of that night in September; Quentin uses it again at Harvard as he imagines "Jim Bond, the scion, the last of his race," howling during the conflagration (p. 300).[6]

It seems safe, then, to accept Faulkner's own language, which stresses not what Quentin heard at Sutpen's but "what he had seen out there" (p. 297). He had seen three faces, one coffee-colored (p. 295), one saddle-colored (p. 296), one wasted and yellow (p. 298), but all "Sutpen faces."

Notes

1. Cleanth Brooks, *William Faulkner: The Yoknapatawpha Country* (New Haven, 1963), pp. 436–437. [1995 note: In this reprinting from the Summer 1974 *Mississippi Quarterly* I change my page numbers from the 1936 text to the Random House corrected text edited by Noel Polk (1986), which restores passages deleted from the 1936 text by the house editor. At two or three points I bolster my argument by the citation of additional passages in the novel. Otherwise I leave the text of the little piece alone, proud that in typescript it caused no less a Faulknerian than Cleanth Brooks to reread *Absalom, Absalom!*, then later to mull my arguments over in his *William Faulkner: Toward Yoknapatawpha and Beyond* (New Haven: Yale University Press, 1978), pp. 324–325. A would-be Faulknerian, I had enough sense to stop while I was ahead.]

2. Brooks (1963), p. 441.

3. Gerald Langford, *Faulkner's Revision of ABSALOM, ABSALOM!* (Austin, 1971), p. 356. Langford points out (p. 40) that the most significant revision of Chapter 9 after the initial manuscript inscription "is the added emphasis given to Jim Bond in the closing pages of the book"—a fact that lends some support to my arguments advanced below. Users of Langford's book should be aware of Noel Polk's stringent warnings in "The Manuscript of *Absalom, Absalom!*" *Mississippi Quarterly*, 25 (Summer 1972), 359–367; Langford does not mention Faulkner's typescript setting copy of the novel, but Polk kindly checked relevant passages for me in a photocopy of that document, which is essential to any true study of Faulkner's revisions of *Absalom, Absalom!*

[1995 note: The holograph manuscript of *Absalom, Absalom!* and the galleys are both at the Humanities Research Center at the University of Texas in Austin. Having spent two weeks in Austin with Noel Polk studying the manuscript in 1975, I warn still more strenuously against relying on Langford's book. Faulkner scholarship on the novel, if not criticism on it, has been transformed in the last two decades. Besides the 1986 Random House corrected text of *Absalom, Absalom!*, Noel Polk edited for Garland Publishing, Inc., the typescript setting copy of *Absalom, Absalom!* as No. 13 in the series *William Faulkner Manuscripts*. In 1989 Polk and John D. Hart edited a two-volume concordance to *Absalom, Absalom!* for UMI Research Press, based upon the corrected 1986 text. As Polk assured me in 1973, the passages omitted from the typescript in 1936 and restored in the published text in 1986 do not happen to contain anything relevant to my arguments about what Quentin saw "out there."]

[1995 note: 4. The reader comes to this passage with the word "scion" in mind, Shreve having imagined Bon as wondering how he might behave "if conditions were reversed and Henry was the stranger and he (Bon) the scion" (p. 255).]

5. Perhaps I should comment on a related problem—that of when and how Quentin realizes that Bon is part Negro. General Compson had ample clues that Sutpen had put aside his first wife because she had Negro blood, though he had no reason for associating the Haitian child with Charles Bon (see pp. 220 and 222 especially). Presumably Quentin's revelation the day after going to the Sutpen house prompts Mr. Compson to tell him (perhaps not for the first time) the full story of Sutpen as General Compson had known it; together they make the final discovery of Bon's Negro blood (pp. 214 and 220).

[1995 note: 6. Mr. Compson at one point (p. 158) still thinks that Charles Etienne Saint-Valery Bon is only one-sixteenth black. In relaying his father's description of the olive-faced C. E. St-V. Bon in the courtroom, Mr. Compson emphasizes that "the justice and the others present did not recognise him"—presumably did not recognize him as the son of the octoroon (p. 164). In Mr. Compson's account, General Compson (p. 165) identifies the olive-faced youth as Charles Bon's son, but nothing in the passage recalls that there is such a thing as a Sutpen face.]

Index

♦

Only substantial references are indexed. Works and characters appear under the author's name except in the case of Faulkner where they are listed separately *in italics*. Only significant notes or significant bibliographical references in notes are included. Material in the Appendix is also incorporated.

ISBN-13:978-0-8161-7314-3
ISBN-10:0-8161-7314-1

90000